Them That Believe

Them That Believe

The Power and Meaning of the
Christian Serpent-Handling Tradition

Ralph W. Hood Jr.
W. Paul Williamson

UNIVERSITY OF CALIFORNIA PRESS
Berkeley · Los Angeles · London

University of California Press, one of the most distinguished university presses in the United States, enriches lives around the world by advancing scholarship in the humanities, social sciences, and natural sciences. Its activities are supported by the UC Press Foundation and by philanthropic contributions from individuals and institutions. For more information, visit www.ucpress.edu.

For acknowledgments of permissions, please see page 285.

University of California Press
Berkeley and Los Angeles, California

University of California Press, Ltd.
London, England

© 2008 by The Regents of the University of California

Library of Congress Cataloging-in-Publication Data

Hood, Ralph W.
    Them that believe : the power and meaning of the Christian serpent-handling tradition / Ralph W. Hood Jr. and W. Paul Williamson.
        p.   cm.
    Includes bibliographical references and index.
    ISBN 978-0-520-23147-4 (cloth : alk. paper)
    ISBN 978-0-520-25587-6 (pbk. : alk. paper)
    1. Snake cults (Holiness churches).   2. Serpents—Religious aspects—Christianity. I. Williamson, W. Paul (William Paul). II. Title.

BX7990.H6H66   2008
289.9—dc22   2008010509

Manufactured in the United States of America

17 16 15 14 13 12 11 10 09 08
10 9 8 7 6 5 4 3 2 1

This book is printed on Natures Book, which contains 50% post-consumer waste and meets the minimum requirements of ANSI/NISO Z39.48-1992 (R 1997) (*Permanence of Paper*).

We dedicate this book to John Brown Sr. and his family, who strive to live out their faith, as did "Punkin" and Melinda, to the fullest measure.

Contents

Illustrations

Tables

Preface

Perhaps one of the most interesting forms of American religion involves Christians who, in response to a perceived mandate in the Bible, include among their worship practices the handling of poisonous serpents. What appears to the casual observer as a dangerous and bizarre activity is a simple act of obedience that holds great significance and meaning for believers who subscribe to a literal interpretation of a passage in the Book of Mark. For the past fifteen years we have spent time with these believers as participant-observers in their church services (although neither of us has ever handled serpents), as guests in their homes, and as friends who keep in touch by telephone and email. Through all of this, we have attempted to come to a better understanding of this tradition and its practice of taking up serpents. This book presents what we have discovered in our study and discusses the worldview and cultural context of these believers, which we hope will allow others to gain an appreciation of their religious practices.

This book has been delayed years beyond our original intended completion date. A major reason for this delay was our desire to make available a comprehensive database on the serpent-handling churches of Appalachia. That database, the Hood-Williamson Research Archives for the Holiness Serpent Handling Sects of Appalachia, housed in the Lupton Library of the University of Tennessee at Chattanooga, is now established.[1] It currently consists of 184 DVDs and extensive interviews with contemporary handlers focusing on what is like to handle serpents, as well as with those who have had near-death experiences after being bitten. Included in this collection are DVDs of lethal bites during services and rare VHS footage (converted to DVD) of services in private homes. Funerals, both with and without the handling of serpents, are documented. Perhaps most important is the unedited footage of entire services of some of the major serpent-handling churches, including the Church of the Lord Jesus in Jolo, West Virginia, probably the most photographed but now struggling to survive; and the Old Rock House Holiness Church in Macedonia, Alabama, a vibrant and thriving congregation that continues a tradition many thought was incapable of surviving into the twenty-first century. Other DVDs trace the history of the rise and fall of other churches, for example, the Church of the Lord Jesus Christ in Kingston, Georgia, which, once powerful, has faltered and is now but a shadow of its former self. Much of our footage covers churches for more than a decade, allowing longitudinal documentation of handlers, their faith, and the congregations in which they participate. All of our documentation is "unedited" in the sense that, except for the focus of the camera, which necessarily excludes what is not in the field of view, every effort was made to simply document the services, though in some cases we have emphasized the variety of activities that endow serpent-handling services with such intensity and passion. Something rarely documented are entire sermons and testimonies of believers.

It is this database from which we have developed our own understanding of a tradition that has been more maligned and ridiculed than understood and that we have come to appreciate for its depth of faith and sincerity of belief—a tradition that is now being practiced by a fourth generation of believers.

We begin in chapter 1 by providing a basic introduction to the tradition. To establish the context for the eventual emergence of serpent-handling churches, in chapter 2 we render a general history of Holiness-Pentecostalism and the rise of the Church of God (and Church of God of Prophecy) as a common sectarian Holiness group that came to embrace the charismatic signs of Pentecostalism in the first decade of the twentieth century—largely through the influence of its transformed leader, A. J. Tomlinson. George Went Hensley, the man generally credited with the emergence of religious serpent handling, is the topic of chapter 3. We follow Hensley's conversion, his revelation of serpent handling, his ministry as an itinerant preacher, his influence on the development and spread of serpent handling, and his eventual death from a practice that he loved so dearly. In chapter 4 we chronicle the acceptance of both Hensley and his serpent-handling practice into the Church of God at a time when the church's primary concern was to convert the lost and to proselytize wayward Christians in search of convincing demonstrations of God's power. As the Church of God (and the Church of God of Prophecy) transitioned toward denominationalism, it marginalized the practice of serpent handling and eventually divorced it from its history, leaving the faithful to continue as independent churches.

Turning our attention to more contemporary concerns related to the serpent-handling tradition, in chapter 5 we address the topic of snakes, including the biology of the species handled by believers, as well as snake symbolism. In chapter 6 we focus on the sociopsychological dynamics of trance states that have been long associated with the practice of various Pentecostal signs—including glossolalia and serpent handling. Chapters 7 through 10 are based on the phenomenologically oriented research we conducted over the past several years centering on the meanings of extemporaneous sermons on serpent handling (chapter 7); the actual experience of handling serpents (chapter 8); the experience of the anointing (chapter 9); and the experience of receiving a near-fatal bite from a serpent and the anticipation of death (chapter 10). Music is a crucial part of worship in the serpent-handling tradition, and in chapter 11 we present research on the types and meanings of songs that are popular among the serpent-handling churches we frequented. Chapter 12 presents the history of the laws that have targeted serpent-handling Christians; in the view of public officials, this religious practice is a danger both to those who engage in it and to those who simply gather to observe it. Our experimental research illustrates that prejudice against serpent handlers—rather than rational reasoning—was and is the most likely motivation for the persistence and enforcement of these laws. In chapter 13 we bring this study to a close by looking at the state of contemporary serpent-handling churches and their promise for the future. The appendixes provide data on individuals who have died from serpent bites in the practice of handling (eighty-nine to date), individuals who have died from drinking the "deadly thing," and the methodology used in chapters 7 through 10.

As is true of any work of this nature, there are many people who are responsible for making important contributions along the way; their number is greater than we have space to list. However, we must say that we are deeply indebted to our editor at the University of California Press, Reed Malcolm, who first saw the potential for developing this book after reading an early article on our work (Williamson & Pollio,

1999). His keen interest, unwavering support, and patience have played a crucial role in bringing this book to fruition. We would be greatly remiss if we did not express our deep appreciation to the hundreds of Christian serpent handlers who have influenced what we have presented on these pages and helped to make this book possible. We have gone to church with them, fellowshipped with them, dined with them, celebrated with them, and even mourned with them. We have spent untold hours in both formal and informal interviews and in group and personal conversations learning about this rich religious tradition and its spirituality. We have striven to present a complete and balanced portrait of a tradition that continues to outlive its obituary. We trust that it will lead general readers as well as scholars to pay more attention to and come to a greater appreciation of what is arguably America's most intriguing form of religious expression.

CHAPTER 1

"They Shall Take up Serpents"

The contemporary serpent-handling churches of Appalachia remain fiercely independent. They have been referred to as the renegade churches of God. The phrase is apt, for these churches identify with the great Pentecostal movement at the turn of the twentieth century and two of the major denominations that emerged from it, the Church of God and the Church of God of Prophecy.[1] However, in what is widely recognized as the official history of the Church of God, Charles Conn (1996) only reluctantly admits to the role of serpent handling, for this Pentecostal denomination no longer endorses that practice or the practice of drinking deadly poisons. In the first edition of his history, published in 1955, Conn relegated serpent handling to a single footnote. In the third and "definitive" edition, published in 1996, Conn reluctantly devotes a bit more space to the role of serpent handling in the church but still minimizes its influence and effect. We discuss the initial endorsement and progressive abandonment of serpent handling by the Church of God in chapter 2 (see Hood, 1998; Hood, Hill, & Williamson, 2005, chap. 5; Williamson & Hood, 2004b). For now we want to note that the renegade churches scattered throughout Appalachia continue to believe and practice what many in the Church of God and the Church of God of Prophecy once perceived as normative.

In the beginning, both denominations endorsed the plain meaning of Mark 16:17–18. The plain meaning was not simply preached; it was believed and put into practice (Hood, 1998, 2003a). This passage, which has become a foundational text for serpent-handling churches, has been associated with many Pentecostals who never endorsed serpent handling, at least since the historic 1906 Azusa Street revival, as we discuss in chapter 2 (Hollenweger, 1972; Church of God, 1910). In the King James Bible it reads as follows:

> And these signs shall follow them that believe; In my name shall they cast out devils; they shall speak with new tongues; They shall take up serpents; and if they drink any deadly thing, it shall not hurt them; they shall lay hands on the sick, and they shall recover. (Mark 16:17–18)[2]

Adherents of contemporary serpent-handling churches accept these words of the resurrected Jesus as imperatives for true believers and view the practice of four of these signs as unconditional mandates; the practice of drinking deadly substances is considered conditional because of the prefaced word *if*. Serpent-handling churches that practice all five signs do so simply to obey what they believe is the command of Christ. In this sense serpent-handling churches are similar to the Catholic Church and mainstream Protestant denominations that take communion in response to Christ's imperative to do so. Believing Appalachian serpent handlers can no more conceive of Pentecostalism without this practice than Catholic believers could conceive of Catholicism without the Eucharist. The irony is that many of the early Pentecostals focused on Mark 16, and contemporary Pentecostals still do, while ignoring the more dangerous practices of serpent handling and drinking poison. For instance, Poloma (2006, p. 61) has documented the revival of healing rooms, a throwback to John Dowie's "healing homes," which used prayer, rather than medicine, to cure the sick. While no longer practiced in opposition to medicine, the use of *pray-ers* is officially justified by a selective use of Mark 16:17–18. Poloma (2006, pp. 65–66) notes that the official website for the International Association for Healing Rooms states, "Our commission is based on Mark 16:17–18: 'And these signs shall follow those that believe[;] . . . they shall lay hands on the sick, and they shall recover.'" Serpent handlers are quick to note this selective use and refuse to omit what others—for obvious reasons—find difficult to practice.

Technically, serpent-handling churches are sects; that is, they stand in tension with the larger culture (Spilka, Hood, Hunsberger, & Gorsuch, 2003, chap. 12). With the exception of West Virginia, at one time or another the Appalachian states, where serpent handling has been practiced, passed laws against this ritual. The courts have ruled that states may regulate religious behaviors, as opposed to beliefs, if they have an overriding interest. Protecting believers from being bitten, maimed, or killed seems a sufficient overriding interest for many states. However, laws against serpent handling have seldom been effective. For instance, Kimbrough and Hood (1995) have documented the persistence of serpent handling in Carson Springs, Tennessee, despite the outlawing of the practice by the state. Even though the Tennessee State Supreme Court upheld the law on appeal, serpent handling continues in the Carson Springs area today, with active churches in Morristown and Del Rio.

While practicing a religious ritual that has been ruled illegal is sufficient to identify a religious group as sectarian, we do not refer to serpent-handling *sects* except when discussing their struggles with the local and larger societies. Serpent handlers identify themselves as members of a church. Thus when we discuss serpent handling from the perspective of the believers' understanding, we refer to serpent-handling *churches*. Our aim is to understand serpent handling both from within and from without. As such we walk a difficult line. As with Wacker's (2003) treatment of the history of the first quarter century of Pentecostalism, we wish to respect the understanding serpent handlers have of their own tradition, as well as reflect on it from a variety of perspectives. We make no claim of objectivity but rather admit to an empathic understanding derived from our many years of participant observation. While neither of us handles serpents (less from fear than a refusal to mock the faith of those who believe), we have witnessed believers being bit and maimed, even dying. Our overall view is that serpent-handling believers have not been fairly treated by academics, scholars, or the media. While neither of us identifies with the religious beliefs of serpent handlers, we have a deep appreciation and understanding of their faith. We wish to avoid stereotyping these people, a trap even social scientists fall into, especially when they are confident of their own objectivity (Hood et al., 2005). Social scientists have not proven more reliable than the media when they study traditions far removed from their own (Birckhead, 1993, 1997; Hood, 1998, 2003a; Hood et al., 2005).

Some sense of what this book is about can be achieved by a description of a typical serpenthandling service. Unlike many mainstream Pentecostal denominations, serpent-handling church worship has not been "routinized" (Poloma, 1998, p. 101) or "regularized" (Wacker, 2003, p. 107). However, below we suggest a template for serpent-handling worship by which deviations can be easily recognized.

TEMPLATE FOR SERPENT-HANDLING WORSHIP

Serpent-handling churches typically meet at least once weekly (and often more) to worship God and experience manifestations of the spirit. As they gather for the service, members greet each other and any visitors present with warm handshakes and exchanges of conversation; in some churches bodily embraces are reserved for the faithful and those of the same sex. At the opening of worship it is standard practice for the pastor or another designated person to cordially welcome everyone and encourage all to obey God as he moves in the service.

From the front, the leader, usually the pastor, announces the presence of serpents that have been brought to church in specially crafted boxes placed beside the pulpit. These boxes typically bear engraved biblical references or a simple phrase of deep meaning to handlers, such as "Wait on God." Handlers take great pride in the boxes they have made. All contain latches with small padlocks for protection and safekeeping of the serpents until the service begins. It is usually men who bring the serpents to church. Only when they place their serpent boxes near the altar do they unlock them. In some churches a jar of a poisonous solution sits near the altar. In the past the poison was red lye or carbolic acid; in recent years, it is usually strychnine. In fewer churches there will be a blowtorch or a bottle with a kerosene wick. Fire may be handled but less frequently than serpents. The preacher acknowledges to visitors what all believers recognize as an ever present fact: "There is death in these boxes." He is referring to the rattlesnakes, water moccasins, and/or copperheads in the boxes. Also, he says that there is "death in this jar," referring to what is typically a mason jar clearly labeled "Poison." No church is without a small bottle of off-the-shelf olive oil used to anoint believers for prayer.

After an initial prayer spoken by all congregants in unison, someone begins a song, which is followed by the strumming of guitars, beating of drums, clashing of cymbals, and shaking of tambourines, as others clap their hands and join in with expressions of praise to God. With the onset of music, what seems at first to be a cacophonous exhibition soon gives rise to a synchrony of living worship in which believers move freely about and celebrate what is felt to be the presence of God. Suddenly, and without announcement, someone moves toward one of the special wooden boxes, unlatches the lid, and calmly extracts a venomous serpent. As others gather around the activity, participation in worship increases with a more compelling sense of God's presence and direction, and other serpents are taken out and passed among the obedient. Amid these manifestations, a believer passes by the others, almost unnoticed, to take the mason jar from the pulpit, remove its lid, and swallow a portion of its toxic contents. The jar is resecured and quietly returned to its place as the believer takes a moment to worship God in solitude and reverence. When the atmosphere of worship is sensed to have shifted, the serpents are returned to their boxes, at which time the sick, oppressed, and spiritually needy are offered ministry through prayer and the laying on of hands. At such times the focus becomes helping others receive what they need from God by personal surrender and obedience to the spirit. These activities are then followed by songs sung by individuals, personal testimonies of praise, and extemporaneous sermons that are meant to exhort the righteous, admonish the backsliders, and persuade the unbelieving. As the two- to three-hour service draws to a close, believers fellowship once more, then leave one by one.

Although this pattern may vary in order and duration, most services include these basic components that were common, except for serpents and poisonous solutions, in early Pentecostalism. It is Pentecostalism's rejection of serpent handling and poison drinking that needs an explanation as much as the renegade churches' continuation of these practices. If there is a parallel renegade tradition, it is the practice of polygamy in defiance of the law and the Church of Latter-day Saints (Williamson & Hood, 2004b). However, while the Mormon tradition allows for continual revelations, the Pentecostal tradition and serpent-handling churches accept only the revelations contained in their sacred text. Hence much of the debate in Pentecostalism is over the textual justification for serpent handling.

THE PARADOX OF TEXTUAL JUSTIFICATION

It is well established that the major Pentecostal denominations sought to justify textually a particular expression of emotionality, glossolalia or "tongues speaking" (Conn, 1955; Frodsham, 1946; Hollenweger, 1972; Synan, 1971). The justification came from concerns about the wide range of emotionally expressed behaviors emerging in Pentecostalism. A psychiatrist who visited a contemporary serpent-handling service describes what historians have documented as characteristic of Pentecostal services before the routinization or regularization of worship as Pentecostal groups advanced to mainstream denominational status: "Their exaltation superficially resembles mania. At these times, they shout, scream, cry, sing, jerk, jump, twitch, hoot, gesture, sway, swoon, tremble, strut, goose-step, stamp, and incoherently 'speak in new tongues'" (Schwarz, 1960, p. 408).

To Schwarz's list, historians of early Pentecostalism added such curious practices as crawling on hands and knees and barking like dogs to "tree the devil," as Synan (1971) reported occurred at the 1801 Cane-Ridge revival. What is at issue here is the apparently limitless expression of spontaneous emotion under perceived possession by the Holy Ghost. As Wacker (2003) rightly notes, if Pentecostals sought a sense of empowerment by the Holy Ghost they balanced this with a pragmatic concern with worldly success. Pressure emerged for Pentecostalism to have a more decorous style of worship.

Emotionally spontaneous behaviors have always been a concern to the Pentecostal movement, especially among leaders who sought worldly success. Pentecostals began to search their Bibles for criteria that would indicate legitimate possession by the Holy Ghost. Clearly one factor in seeking textual justification for possession was to limit as much as justify emotional expression in worship (Creech, 1996; Synan, 1971). This has been the case especially in those segments of the Pentecostal movement whose appeal has been to the white middle class and who tried to distance themselves from aspects of rural lower-class white and African American spirituality. Creech (1996) notes that Charles Parham, leader of the Apostolic Faith Movement (which eventually joined with others to form the Assemblies of God) made his African American student, William J. Seymour, of later Azusa Street fame, sit outside his classroom. Parham also demanded restraint in worship, excluding from the legitimate expression of the Holy Ghost "all the chattering and jabbering, windsucking, and holy-dancing-rollerism" (Creech, 1996, p. 412).

Yet where there is justification for speaking in tongues there can be justification for handling serpents. The texts used to justify tongues speaking are crucial to the theological rift that emerged within Pentecostalism itself, eventually serving to separate out serpent-handling churches as renegade churches, usually with reference to their origins in the Church of God as it gradually moved toward rejecting the practice of serpent handling (but not tongues speaking, despite the linkage of both practices in Mark 16:17–18).

As Pentecostalism moved from Azusa Street in Los Angeles to the South and to the mountains of Appalachia, it found soil too fertile to restrict the imaginations of those fated to split from what would become the more mainstream Pentecostal denominations. Tongues speaking came to be generally accepted as evidence of baptism of the Holy Ghost by most Pentecostal groups (as it is by serpent-handling churches today) in part because of its clear textual justification and also because it can be easily scripted and controlled in worship services. But it had already been practiced in the South as one of many unscripted and spontaneous indicators of Holy Ghost possession. Tongues speaking was not endorsed by all Pentecostal groups, and those groups that endorsed it did not demand that all believers experience it (see Wacker, 2003, chap. 2). However, members of Pentecostal groups that endorsed tongues speaking had significant social pressure to evidence their possession by the Holy Ghost in this way, even though as many as 50 percent of such Pentecostal churches did not then, and do not now, speak in tongues (see Poloma, 1989, 1998; Wacker, 2003, chap. 2). Similar social pressures exist in contemporary serpent-handling churches.

Parham's demand for scriptural justification of indicators of possession by the Holy Ghost was a two-edged sword. Scripture does not always justify tongues speaking in isolation. In Appalachia and the South generally, the totality of Scripture was recognized as authoritative and was well known to even the illiterate from a rich oral tradition. As noted above, in what was to become the foundational text for serpent handling churches, Mark 16:17–18, tongues speaking is but one of the five signs. Two others of the five, casting out devils and laying hands on the sick, were widely practiced and remain common in mainstream Pentecostal denominations and in serpent-handling churches today. However, taking up serpents, once endorsed by the Church of God and its sister church, the Church of God of Prophecy, is today the outsider's definitional criterion by which serpent-handling churches are perceived to be unique. It is the imperative command associated with taking up serpents and not the conditional one associated with drinking poison that has led the media to identify these obedient as *serpent-handling* churches. We have never heard or seen them identified as *poison-drinking* churches. However, in both academic and popular media accounts of serpent-handling churches, the handling of serpents is treated as a bizarre practice initiated by a deviant sectarian group within the Church of God, and it is abnormal enough to require an explanation for why it persists in Appalachia. The claims that serpent handling played only an insignificant role in the history of Pentecostalism and that serpent-handling churches cannot continue to survive ignore the long struggle within Pentecostalism over the issue of practices for which apparent textual justification is so troublesome to modernity (Frodsham, 1946).

Pentecostalism came into its own around the turn of the twentieth century (Synan, 1997). Holt (1940) has suggested that this brand of ecstatic religion achieved success in the first half of that century, particularly in the South, as a manifestation of nature's power to bring healing to those who had experienced psychological isolation and insecurity from the process of urbanization. As the farm population migrated to urban areas to find work, displacement from rural values, strict social controls, and a particular mode of existence—coupled with low income and social discrimination by the more established urban population—often led to psychological tension, cultural shock, and maladjustment. The rise of Holiness and Pentecostal churches was said to help migrants strike a psychological balance as they confronted the urban trends toward permissive social values combined with mainline religious tendencies toward liberalism, both of which conflicted with their more conservative values. Hence these new churches became both a successful buffer for the estranged and a manifest protest against modernist social and religious developments of the time (Synan, 1997).

During this period, the most successful Holiness and Pentecostal churches dominated the attention of social scientists, and the need to explore their less organized factions went largely unnoticed (Holt, 1940). Such investigations, Holt said, might reveal how the religious experience among these groups serves to provide meaning and a sense of hope in their confrontation with hostile environments. Yet he noted the difficulty of studying these less organized denominations:

> It should be recognized that not all Holiness and Pentecostal religion is organized. Of all formalized types of denominational religion, it is closest to the unorganized waves of summer revivals which sweep the South when crops are "laid by," leaving no permanent traces because the poor are too poor to build a church or meeting house. Research concerning unorganized Pentecostal and Holiness religion should be done as soon as possible. (Holt, 1940, p. 740)

Cobb (1965), twenty-five years later, and Hood (1998), almost five decades later, have observed that social scientists' neglect of fringe groups, such as serpent-handling churches, persists as the norm, thus leading to the notion that these groups are pathological (La Barre, 1962/ 1974, 1972) and to media reports that refer to their practices as a "bizarre" expression of faith (Birckhead, 1993, 1997). Even McCauley's (1995) wonderfully apologetic defense of Appalachian Mountain religion makes but the briefest mention of serpent-handling churches, not wanting to stereotype it, as the media have done.

Wacker's (2003) justly praised history of the Pentecostal movement in America from 1900 to 1925 makes one mention of serpent handling (and in one sentence, on p. 74). This is despite Wacker's interest in this period when serpent handling was gaining in strength and popularity, not only in Appalachia, but also as far away as Texas and some midwestern states, and was supported and practiced by the Church of God (and the Church of God of Prophecy) as indicative of the power of the Holy Ghost operating in and through believers. Handling serpents was clearly a legitimate sign for "them that believe" (Mark 16). It was never intended to be a test of faith or required for salvation (Hood, 1998). However, as controversy arose over the practice, A. J. Tomlinson (1922), the first General Overseer of the Church of God, plainly said, "I would hate to be in the shoes of some who are so bitter against taking up serpents" (p. 12).

As mainstream Pentecostalism moved into the middle class, however, studies that first pathologized these denominations (Cutten, 1927; La Barre, 1962/1974; Laffal, 1965; Stagg, Hinson, & Oates, 1967) soon gave way to studies that normalized and legitimized them (Coulson & Johnson, 1977; Hine, 1969; Kildahl, 1972; Malony & Lovekin, 1985; Poloma, 1989, 2003; Richardson, 1973; Samarin, 1972c; Smith & Fleck, 1981; Spanos & Hewitt, 1979). This transformation can be seen as stemming from two factors: the tendency of modern Pentecostal groups to distance themselves from intense emotional experiences at odds with the larger society (Holt, 1940; Hood, 1998; Poloma, 1989; Wacker, 2003); and the willingness of social scientists to take the religious experiences of these groups as a legitimate focus of study (Malony & Lovekin, 1985). With respect to the emotion issue, Poloma (1989, p. 247) has documented the "routinization of charisma" within the Assemblies of God, a Pentecostal group that has never endorsed serpent handling. Wacker (2003, p. 167) notes the "pressure for regularization" across all Pentecostal groups, including those that initially endorsed serpent handling. For both Poloma and Wacker, routinization and regularization often centered on debates over tongues speaking, a phenomenon well studied by both psychologists and anthropologists (Malony & Lovekin, 1985; Goodman, 1972a, 1972b). However, one practice that cannot be easily routinized or regularized is serpent handling. How and when serpents are handled can be regulated; whether they will strike, bite, maim, or kill cannot. It is for this reason that Pentecostal groups that moved toward greater worldly success abandoned a practice that others, the contemporary serpent handlers of Appalachia, maintained.

Maguire (1981, p. 179), concerned with the legitimacy of Pentecostal experiences, has called for research into serpent-handling churches that uses descriptive methodologies that move beyond the sensationalized reports of earlier investigations. Birckhead (1997), an anthropologist, and Hood, Williamson, and Morris (2000), psychologists, have demonstrated not only that attitudes toward serpent-handling churches are rooted in prejudice, based on assumptions that religious rituals ought to be "safe," but also that stereotypes held by most of society regarding serpent-handling churches are media supported. Even the research presented in this book continues the notion that Pentecostal experience—especially that associated with serpent handling—is worthy of scientific inquiry.

The template for serpent-handling worship described above is likely familiar to many Pentecostals. Serpent-handling services have their origins in the practices that were especially common in the first quarter century of Pentecostalism and that can still be detected in the routinized and regularized major Pentecostal denominations of today (Poloma, 1998; Wacker, 2003). What makes serpent-handling churches most identifiable is not simply that they handle serpents and drink poison, but that these practices were the first to be eliminated in Pentecostal groups that once endorsed them. As what were to become the major Pentecostal denominations routinized and regularized their worship, so too did they back away from rituals that could maim and kill. While it is far from the case that most Pentecostal groups handled serpents, those that did soon recognized that denominational success required the regulation of extreme emotional displays and the elimination of practices that jeopardize health and well-being. If modern Pentecostal groups no longer avoid medical care, serpent handlers must decide whether to seek medical care if bitten during a service. In other respects, serpent handlers are less unusual than one might imagine. Like Pentecostals across America, serpent-handling Pentecostals mirror their local culture. As Wacker (2003, chap. 12) notes of early Pentecostals, if they were distant from their Congregationalist and Episcopalian counterparts in affairs that define education, wealth, and class, they stood above the Southern Methodists and Baptists in their direct and immediate experience of God. So it is with serpent handlers. Some are fourth-generation handlers. Some are uneducated, while others have college or advanced degrees. Some are poor, while others have wealth to which few can realistically aspire. Then and now, they are less distant in belief, wealth, education, or other criteria by which we locate groups within the larger culture than the stereotype of the rural, uneducated Pentecostal suggests. One ought not confuse a chosen style of worship, typical to Pentecostals in general and serpent handlers in particular, as necessarily indicative of much more than that. The lack of a scripted order for the service, the dress of congregants, and the freestyle manner of participant worship contrast not only with other religious groups but also with much of what mainstream Pentecostalism has become today (Poloma, 1989). However, as we note in a variety of ways throughout this book, it is with serpents and with those who believe in taking them up that routinization and regularization perhaps reached an unexpected limit, so that in many respects contemporary serpent-handling churches still mirror Pentecostalism in the first quarter of the twentieth century. To document the history of serpent handling, we must take seriously Holt's (1940) concern that the unorganized Pentecostal groups have yet to be studied and, we want to add, to have a fair hearing. However, a literature on serpent handling is emerging in which the voices of handlers can be heard. While throughout this text we cite all relevant literature on serpent handling, we want to pause here to note the few texts that try to understand rather than explain away this remarkable tradition.

Under the pressure of postmodern criticism, social scientists are looking at the voices that have been omitted from their discourse (Cahoone, 2003; Rosenau, 1992).With respect to Pentecostalism, otherwise excellent histories such as Wacker's (2003) will no longer be able to ignore voices that must be heard. Among the available texts is the oral history of Jimmy Morrow, pastor of a serpent-handling church in Del Rio, Tennessee, whose family has a long tradition in Appalachia (Hood, 2005). In addition, three major serpent-handling clans (a term that these families probably would not use but one that represents the firm family basis of serpent-handling churches) have had their personal histories told (Brown & McDonald, 2000). A good descriptive history and participant observation study of eastern Kentucky serpent handling, especially of the Saylor clan, has recently been reissued (Kimbrough, 2002). Schwartz (1999) has published a series of photographs of the Kentucky handlers, emphasizing the range of their humanity, not simply their practice of handling serpents. Finally, the widely publicized trial of Glenn Summerford, who was convicted of trying to kill his wife by forcing her to be bitten by a serpent, has been brilliantly illuminated by Burton (2004); the story of Summerford's conviction and ninety-nine-year sentence (due to a "three strike" rule in Alabama) is told from the perspectives of believers within the serpent-handling community. Burton is also to be credited with one of the first serious works on serpent handling to be fair and balanced in an effort to present this tradition to the outsider (Burton,

1993).[3] As one pastor of a serpent handling church in Georgia said, "If you do not believe in serpent handling, pray for those who do."

We place the history of serpent handling where it belongs, as a vital part of the Pentecostal struggle to be successful *in* the world, yet not fully *of* the world. Wacker (2003) has suggested a useful way to conceptualize this dynamic by contrasting Pentecostalism's pragmatism with its *primitiveness*. If the meaning of pragmatism is obvious to the reader, primitiveness is less likely to be. According to Wacker (2003, p. 12), *primitiveness* suggests that the believer's longing is to be guided solely by God's spirit, and it further denotes a return to foundational things—that is, it reflects a desire to return to first, or original, things. This desire creates what Hood (1995) identifies as foundational beliefs, which have been shown by Hood, Hill, and Williamson (2005) to characterize not only the Church of God and the Church of God Prophecy but also their bastard children who persist as the renegade Churches of God. We now turn to an exploration of this twisted history. It is a prologue to a more correct understanding of the serpent-handling churches and their more legitimate brothers who now do little more than scorn them as they deny their common ancestry.

CHAPTER 2

The History of Pentecostalism Absent the Serpent

Pentecostalism has become a major movement in contemporary Protestant Christianity (Synan, 1997; Cox, 1995). In little more than a century, it grew from meager beginnings at Azusa Street in Los Angeles to nearly half a billion followers (including neo-Pentecostals) around the world. Once thought attractive only to the poor, disenfranchised, and disconnected (Holt, 1940), the modern movement has spread across class and ethnic lines and includes the educated of the world (Cox, 1995; Synan, 1997; Wacker, 2003). Given its success, few would dare speculate that this institution shares a common descent with those who practice the handling of venomous serpents in their worship. However, a perceived direct encounter with God was what made early Pentecostalism appealing to many observers, and such an encounter involved manifestations that were believed to be supernatural signs—all of which persist today as important markers in the serpent handling tradition. To better appreciate these contemporary "signs" believers, we present in this chapter a brief history of the emergence of Pentecostalism and its crucial acceptance by a certain Holiness sect, the Church of God, that would come to embrace and further the sign of serpent handling as a compelling manifestation of the Holy Ghost.

THE LARGER HOLINESS-PENTECOSTAL CONTEXT

Some contemporary writers (Cox, 1995; MacRobert, 1988) place the origin of Pentecostalism at the renowned 1906 Azusa Street revival, but the movement can be traced to an earlier period (Creech, 1996; Synan, 1997; Wacker, 2003). Synan (1997) has argued that Pentecostalism can be traced to the Wesleyan Holiness tradition that took root in the Great Awakening of the eighteenth century and eventually spread throughout the American colonies by means of enthusiastic revival campaigns. The doctrine conceived by John Wesley was a reaction to the Calvinist doctrine of predestination that dominated the period. Where Calvinism taught that only the elect could be saved, Methodism argued that eternal salvation was open to all who desired it; and while the Calvinist could not know of God's personal election for certain, the Methodist was persuaded of salvation because of a crisis conversion that was "heartfelt."

Fundamentally, Wesley's thesis taught that there are two defining experiences for the Christian (Synan, 1997). The first is salvation, a crisis experience in which confession of personal sin brings about forgiveness and justification before God. Though the person is justified, however, his sinful nature is retained and continues to influence spiritual life—thus the need for a "second cure." In a second crisis experience, the person can be purged from this "Adamic" nature through sanctification and, thereby, become filled with perfect love toward God and others. For Wesley, this second blessing was not a deliverance from temptations and human failures but an instant transformation of inner motives—a change in personal desire from pleasing the flesh to pleasing God. Once consecrated by this experience, self-examination and discipline would become the predominant avenues of life. With its implications for the psychology of experience, this new life-changing doctrine was effective in meeting the spiritual needs of the period and was successfully transplanted to America by the last quarter of the eighteenth century.

As revivals spread in America, the firm grasp of Calvinism eventually gave way to this fervent new kind of gospel, especially in areas where debauchery was reportedly rampant. In Brunswick County, Virginia, for example, Robert Williams led Methodist meetings that were punctuated by religious fervor and change. While pleading God's pardon for inbred sin, "some would be seized with a trembling, and in a few moments drop on the floor as if they were dead; while others were embracing each other with streaming eyes, and all were lost in wonder, love and praise" (Synan, 1997, p. 9). By 1776 half of all Americans in Virginia—a region reportedly known at the time for its moral corruption and decay—were Methodists (Synan, 1997). For the most part, this emerging religious fever was not linked to historically identified individuals. In many respects, as has often been said, Pentecostalism was a movement without a man. That is to say, it was linked to unknown individuals whose passion fueled a movement but left little in the way of personal identification or documentation that fit neatly with the historian's demand for fact.

Another important issue of this period was the concern of early settlers to loosen the power of the Anglican Church in the colonies (Pitts, 1993). This "European" institution was perceived as lacking in sufficient personal religious experience and moral conviction for the day—hence the depraved conditions. To bolster revival meetings and dislodge the influence of the Anglican Church, black slaves often were invited to revival campaigns and encouraged to take an active part. Pitts (1993) has suggested that two elements made participation especially appealing to slaves. First, the meetings condemned many of the activities of rich plantation owners as sinful and excessive; second, the high level of emotionality experienced in the worship was familiar to black slaves from the traditions of their African homelands. Intrigued by such an opportunity, slaves became major participants in the emotionally charged revivals and gained some degree of acceptance among the white participants, though only for a short time. Joyner (1994, p. 37) has cautioned that slaves did not indiscriminately embrace the Christian God, or related beliefs, but simply "reinterpreted the elements of Christianity in terms of deep-rooted African religious concerns." Thus the first major conversion of African slaves to Christianity came on the tide of revivalism during the Great Awakening, and this had a significant influence on the later emergence of Pentecostalism.

Pitts (1993) saw revivalism of the mid-eighteenth century as important for three reasons. First, it provided whites with a religious outlet for the economic frustration they experienced at the hands of wealthy plantation owners. Second, revivals of the period to some extent bridged the gap between races: the whites who attended were employed as slave patrollers, yet they invited slaves under their overseership to meetings where all participated equally in worship. Third, blacks and whites were converted together to a new type of Christianity that emphasized emotionality—a type that involved being overwhelmed by the spirit and one that foreshadowed the Pentecostal experience to come. Not only did revivalism offer spirituality to its participants; it also was somewhat significant in lowering racial barriers at the time—a claim later made by Cox (1995) for Azusa Street Pentecostalism at Los Angeles.

It has been observed that the emotional religious experience characterizing early Methodism was in stark contrast to the mechanical and depersonalized experience found in institutional religion (Synan, 1997). In this sense the extensive debate in the modern psychology of religion over religion versus spirituality echoes a tale old and told often (Hood, 2003b; Zinnbauer & Pargament, 2005). This "heart religion" not only had a strong attraction for the "poor and disinherited" (Synan, 1997, p. 10) of colonial and frontier America but also for Americans less commonly seen as succumbing to its broad appeal (Wacker, 2003). As circuit riders of the late eighteenth century carried their message throughout the South, they found willing listeners (Synan, 1997). The early pioneers had need of a rugged, emotional religion to suit the challenges of a rugged, emotional life in the wilderness. The most famous Pentecostal-like revival occurred in 1801 at Cane-Ridge, Bourbon County, Kentucky. Led initially by a group of Presbyterian ministers, later joined by Methodist clergy, the revival continued for more than a year and was characterized by intense emotionality not usually seen in American Protestantism. The interest and excitement of this event escalated to the level of a large-scale camp meeting, giving birth to what would become known in modern times as the American camp meeting revival. The vigorous disposition required for successful wilderness life was complemented by the religious fervor experienced by worshipers:

> Accustomed to "braining bears and battling Indians," they received their religion with great color and excitement. Their "godly hysteria" included such phenomena as falling, jerking, barking like dogs, falling into trances, the "holy laugh," and "such wild dances as David performed before the Ark of the Lord." . . . After "praying through some would crawl on all fours and bark like dogs, thus "treeing the devil." Others would fall into trances for hours. . . . In some services entire congregations would be seized by the "holy laugh," an ecstasy which could hardly be controlled. (Synan, 1997, p. 12)

The meeting climaxed in August 1801, with attendance reaching twenty-five thousand. Because such religious experiences were found to have personal value for everyday life, the majority of Christian Kentuckians were persuaded to this type of early Methodism by 1805. It was from eastern Kentucky that the Holiness tradition was to spread throughout the southeastern Appalachian regions of Tennessee, North and South Carolina, western Virginia, and Georgia. Everywhere revivals took place the same kind of religious phenomena were said to have occurred—including that of speaking "in unknown tongues" in an 1801 meeting at the University of Georgia (Synan, 1997).

By this time, many of those who attended camp meetings had entered the middle class, some owning slaves themselves (Pitts, 1993). Having thrown off the hand of the Anglican Church, American churches began to effect changes in the way revivals were conducted. Though slaves were permitted to attend and participate in services, there was markedly less social cohesion in the events—and more resistance to their presence. By the mid-1820s the revival era ended, leaving a few slaves with opportunities to organize their own churches. A number of slave rebellions brought these churches under intense scrutiny, and they were either dissolved or forced to meet in secret in "brush harbors" (Pitts, 1993, p. 50).

The Holiness movement continued to spread as the century progressed, although institutionalization and concerns about the doctrinal issue of sanctification had the effect of less "frenzied" worship experiences (Synan, 1997). As perfectionism became the dominant religious and social theme, revivals and their periodic "awakenings" became more cyclical in occurrence and less intense. The period also saw a proliferation in various periodicals devoted to the furtherance of Holiness teachings. In the 1860s, for example, the first paper dedicated exclusively to the publication of Holiness doctrine, *The Guide to Holiness,* reached a circulation of some thirty thousand. As a Christian alternative to the Emersonianism of the period, this "evangelical transcendentalism" (Synan 1997, p. 30) and its emphasis on perfectionism continued to spread until the Civil War. Given the wide distribution of print material associated with the Holiness movement, it is well to be reminded that Americans from all walks of life were succumbing to the broad appeal of Holiness and what was to become Pentecostalism (Wacker, 2003).

Although "sanctified" Christians considered slavery a blot on society and greatly desired its end, this attitude was not shared by southern Methodists (Synan, 1997). In fact, this rent in the fabric of the church was destined to bring about its division, with the northern faction condemning slavery and the southern remnant supporting it. The great awakening revival of 1858 was influential in the North, whereas the South, striving to sustain the institution of slavery, failed to experience the movement altogether. From 1830 on, the quest for holiness was abandoned by Methodists in the South, resulting in the Methodist Episcopal Church, South, and all but removing Wesleyan holiness and perfectionism from its literature and sermons by 1858. With the evils of slavery and the onset of war, the era of the early Holiness movement in the United States came to a close.

After the Civil War, moral depression and "battlefield ethics" found
their way into the affairs of government and business, and there was
renewed emphasis on Wesleyan principles and sanctification (Synan,
1997). In 1867 a modern Holiness crusade was begun in a Vineland,
New Jersey, camp meeting in an attempt to unite and restore all Christians to holiness. This National Camp Meeting for the Promotion of
Holiness, which met with unqualified success, was an interdenomina-
tional call to all Christians initiated by Methodist ministers that would
eventually be responsible for the emergence of more than one hundred
denominations throughout the world and would have an indirect
impact on the birth of Pentecostalism.

With the return of "fanaticisms," "sinless perfection," "fire," and
divine healing, however, came a rift within the Methodist church—the
more traditional faction substituting the second definite work of sanctification with one more progressive and gradual (Synan, 1997). In 1894,
the denouncement of the Holiness movement by the General Confer-
ence of the Methodist Episcopal Church, South, sparked the formation
of scores of new Holiness denominations composed of "come-outers"
who protested against such issues as the doctrinal compromise on sanctification, escalating modernism in the church, and higher (academic)
criticism of the Bible. Among the most successful churches of the
Holiness Associations that organized were four denominations in the
Southeast: the Fire-Baptized Holiness Church, South Carolina (1895);
the Pentecostal Holiness Church, North Carolina (1900); the Church
of God in Christ, Memphis, Tennessee (1897); and what later became
known as the Church of God, Cleveland, Tennessee (1896). These
major denominations were destined to play a significant role in the
spread of Pentecostalism in the South.

For historians who seek to link a movement to a man (Creech, 1996;
Cox, 1995; MacRobert, 1988; Synan, 1988, 1997), Pentecostalism can
be traced to Charles Parham, a white Holiness preacher from Topeka,
Kansas, who was trained as a Methodist. Although glossolalia—speaking
in tongues—had already been experienced in various Holiness churches
and even in other cultures (Goodman, 1972b; Malony & Lovekin, 1985;
Wacker, 2003, chap. 1),[1] it had never been articulated as the exclusive
doctrinal evidence of spirit baptism until Parham made the argument
based on Acts 2:4 in December 1900.[2] At his Bible school, in an all-night
service, one of Parham's students, Agnes N. Ozman, received the baptism
of the Holy Ghost and spoke in tongues just after midnight, January 1,
1901, thus becoming the first person ever to receive such an experience

according to this new theology. What was significant about tongues speaking in Topeka in 1900 is that it was now framed as evidence of Holy Ghost baptism, or possession, in accordance with a specific textual justification. Other individuals present at the Topeka meeting also received the experience and were said to have spoken in various foreign languages (Creech, 1996; Synan, 1997).

In 1901 Parham launched a series of revival meetings throughout the country, preaching the doctrine of spirit baptism by tongues (Creech, 1996; Synan, 1997). (He later turned to an emphasis on faith healing because of little recorded success [MacRobert, 1988]). By 1905 he had relocated his headquarters to Houston, Texas, where he opened yet another training institution, the Bible Training School. It is at this point that William Joseph Seymour, the preacher-son of emancipated Louisiana slaves, crossed paths with Parham and became a student of the new Pentecostal doctrine of tongues. Because of Parham's prejudice, however, the future Azusa Street apostle was required to sit outside the classroom with the door ajar, a condition he evidently accepted without complaint. Seymour soon received an invitation to assume the pastorate of a new Holiness mission in Los Angeles that had been established after its members were expelled from a Baptist church because of their embracement of sanctification.

Armed with a new Pentecostal doctrine he had yet to experience for himself, Seymour encountered glaring opposition when preaching the subject to his new flock and was literally locked out of the building by dissenting members after the first service (Cox, 1995; MacRobert, 1988; Synan, 1997). His message was an affront to the fledgling group that had only recently sacrificed its former denominational ties for the acceptance of sanctification, a second blessing beyond conversion; now this neophyte pastor was asserting the need for a third blessing—Holy Ghost baptism and speaking in tongues.

Refusing to be discouraged, Seymour conducted prayer meetings at the house where he was living. At one such gathering in particular, on April 9, 1906, at least seven members of the all-black group fell to the floor in ecstasy and spoke in tongues—Seymour himself receiving the experience a few days later. As news of the happenings at this meeting traveled, curiosity seekers arrived at the house in increasing numbers, eventually requiring Seymour to preach from the front porch to congregants on the street. Seymour located an old, vacated Methodist church at 312 Azusa Street that had been converted first to a warehouse and then to a stable, and he and his followers moved into the crudely furnished structure.

Pentecostal revival services at Azusa Street were marked by highly
emotional demonstrations of worship, which in some ways were reminiscent of the Cane-Ridge revival in Kentucky nearly a century earlier:

> A visitor to Azusa Street during the three and a half years the revival con-
> tinued would have met scenes that beggared description. Men and women
> would shout, weep, dance, fall into trances, speak and sing in tongues, and
> interpret their messages to English. In true Quaker fashion, anyone who
> felt "moved by the Spirit" would preach or sing. There was no robed choir,
> no hymnals, no order of services, but there was an abundance of religious
> enthusiasm. (Synan, 1997, p. 98)

Because of Los Angeles media coverage of the events, news of the phenomena was soon circulated throughout the United States and Europe.
Consequently, thousands converged on the meager building to experience its lively worship three times a day, seven days a week, over the
course of the next three years. Both Synan (1997) and Cox (1995) have
observed that the revival was truly egalitarian in structure and interra-
cial in its makeup, for worship involved spontaneous, interpersonal
ministry among men, women, blacks, whites, Chinese, Japanese, and
Mexicans—an interactive ministry that flowed indiscriminately from
one person to another. Religious leaders from all regions of the United
States and from other countries traveled to the "New Jerusalem" to
experience the Holy Ghost baptism with tongues. MacRobert (1988)
stated that within two years more than fifty nations had been directly
affected by the events at Azusa Street.

As events intensified, Parham was summoned to the revival by Seymour, who was at a loss for direction in controlling the ecstatic demonstrations of worshipers. Parham was "shocked by the 'holy roller' aspects
of the services and made efforts to correct the 'extremes and fanaticism'
which he felt had gone 'beyond the bounds of common sense and reason'" (Synan, 1997, p. 102). He attempted to impose order on the meetings but was met with forceful opposition by key laypersons who asked
him to leave—which he did, in disgust, all the while denouncing the
revival as a "prostitution" of spiritual power at the hands of "holy
rollers" and spiritualists. The fervent revival continued without pause.

The increasing interest in the revival coincided with a number of
interrelated factors, two of which, based on a fundamentalist logic of
the text, seem of particular concern (Ammerman, 1991; Kirkpatrick,
Hood, & Hartz, 1991; Hood et al., 2005). The fundamentalist Holiness
movement, which was instrumental to Azusa Street, held fast to a pre-
millennial doctrine that expected the literal return of Jesus, who was to

rapture his church just prior to a tribulation period of God's judgment on earth. After this period of wrath, it was believed that Jesus would return to earth with his church and set up a kingdom to rule in peace for one thousand years. Thus one concern of the religious in 1906 was the fact that the new century ushered in an expection of the imminent return of Jesus (Creech, 1996). With the perceived evils of modernism, Darwinism, and higher criticism directed toward the "inerrancy" of the Bible, believers became sensitive to the eschatological "signs" of the time and gave frequent warnings to the "lost" concerning the rapture and judgment of God to come.

Given this dynamic, perhaps one of the most fortuitous events serving to intensify the Los Angeles revival was the great earthquake that shook San Francisco and the entire West Coast on April 19, 1906, less than two weeks after the meeting had begun (Synan, 1997). What was most compelling about this incident was that the previous day the *Los Angeles Times* had published its first news release about the Azusa Street revival, which included a description of the "frenzy and religious zeal" of participants, along with a prophecy given by a revival supporter based on a revelation received in church: "In his vision, he saw the people of Los Angeles 'flocking in a mighty stream to perdition.' He then prophesied 'awful destruction to this city unless its citizens are brought to a belief in the tenets of the new faith'" (cited in Synan, 1997, p. 97). On the very next day, the *Times* intimated that the "awful destruction" had indeed come; its description of the earthquake's devastating impact on San Francisco was headlined, "Heart Is Torn from Great City" (p. 98). Perceived as divine providence, the event made clear to the religious that occurrences at Azusa Street were a divine preparation for final things to come—a "last days" pouring out of spirit baptism that would effect world evangelism before the imminent return of Jesus.

A second factor affecting the magnitude of the revival was the influence of a similar meeting in Wales that had begun in 1904 (Creech, 1996; Synan, 1997). News concerning the uncommon phenomena of the Welsh revival reached Southern California, where it inspired certain leaders, among them Frank Bartleman, to anticipate a modern replication of Holy Ghost visitation to an "American" Jerusalem as on the Day of Pentecost (Acts 2)—this time, for the restoration of the New Testament church before the return of Jesus. Hence the British revival became an initial frame of reference that awoke within key American figures a spiritual longing for a "second" Pentecost that would occur at Los Angeles.

In his comments on the events of Azusa Street, Hollenweger raises a
noteworthy point that eludes most Pentecostal historians and their critics, for reasons that are implicit:

> The Pentecostal experience of Los Angeles was neither the leading astray of
> the Church by demons (as the German Evangelical movement claimed), nor
> the eschatological pouring out of the Holy Spirit (as the Pentecostal move-
> ment itself claims) but an outburst of enthusiastic religion of a kind well-
> known and frequent in the history of Negro churches in America which
> derived its specifically Pentecostal features from Parham's theory that
> speaking with tongues is a necessary concomitant of the baptism of the
> Spirit. (Hollenweger, 1972, pp. 23–24)

More important than the notion of Azusa Street as the "second" Pentecost is the recognition of its emotional, spiritual character as related to
a particular people of the Southeast—slaves—and, we would venture,
of Holiness whites of the Appalachian region who at times had wor-
shiped with them (Pitts, 1993). The "fixing" of glossolalia as the single
evidence of spirit baptism at Los Angeles can be seen as a phenomenon
that (1) articulated a cogent Pentecostal doctrine (Creech, 1996), (2) de-
limited the range of emotionality expressed in the experience as a form
of social control (Hood, 1998), and (3) ironically began the "pressure
for regularization" (Wacker, 2003, p. 167) that is one of the dilemmas
of institutionalization. Even Pentecostal believers trained in the social
sciences who study their faith tradition have identified this pressure,
though by other names. For example, Poloma (1989, p. 247) writes of
the "routinization of Charisma" with specific reference to the Assemblies of God, but as both Wacker and Poloma assert, pressures to rou-
tinize are keenly and ironically present in the type of religion that, as
many a serpent handler has said, "is better felt than told."

As Creech (1996) has noted, Pentecostalism bifurcated into subcultures: a more conservative one in the Midwest and Southwest, which
distanced itself from Azusa Street; and a less conservative one in the
Southeast, which acknowledged its ties to Azusa Street. The phenomenon of Azusa Street was characterized by egalitarianism and ethical
restoration; discrimination in regard to education, race, social status,
and gender was erased in a worship context given to spontaneity and
ecstasy. According to Creech, the western, more conservative arm of the
movement, led initially by Parham, was primarily concerned with forging the order of a new Pentecostal denomination that would eventually
resurrect the pre–Azusa Street issues of education, race, and social sta-

tus—all of which would seemingly lead to the loss of much of the spontaneity and ecstasy in worship. In fact, Poloma (1989) has documented the downward spiral of emotionality experienced among the Assemblies of God in relation to its concerns for institutional development. In the southeastern segment, however, the Pentecostal doctrine spread to institutions that predated the Azusa Street revival—most of which had already associated spontaneity and ecstasy in their worship with what was believed to be the direct experience of God, particularly in the Appalachian regions. Certainly, most of these institutions already had issues regarding race and gender, yet the Pentecostal doctrine from the West more clearly defined their worship experiences and was easily embraced.

Among the many important religious leaders attending the Azusa Street revival was C. H. Mason, leader of the black Church of God in Christ located in Tennessee (Cox, 1995; Synan, 1997). With his conversion to the doctrine of tongues, Mason led his Memphis-based church to eventually become the largest black Pentecostal denomination in the United States (Synan, 1997, p. 70). C. B. Cashwell, associated with the Pentecostal Holiness Church of North Carolina, heard of the revival through news reports and traveled to Los Angeles, where he himself received the Holy Ghost with tongues. On his return home, Cashwell became instrumental in taking the tongues doctrine to the three remaining major Holiness denominations of the South: the Pentecostal Holiness Church of North Carolina, the Fire-Baptized Holiness Church of South Carolina, and the Church of God, which by this time had relocated to Cleveland, Tennessee. Through these four major denominations, the Pentecostal message with tongues was assured in the South and became synonymous with Holiness. Another important figure was the Baptist minister W. H. Durham of Chicago. It was he, after his Pentecostal conversion, who would become instrumental in formulating the "finished work" doctrine of salvation—a central tenet adopted by the Assemblies of God denomination when it organized in 1914.

It is from this point that Cox (1995) and others (Creech, 1996; MacRobert, 1988; Synan, 1997) center on the later expansion of the Pentecostal movement, its return to racial segregation, and its success in adapting to various worldwide cultures. As recipients of Holy Ghost baptism left Azusa Street, they carried a doctrine of tongues as "biblical" proof for their experience and spread it across the United States and throughout the world.

THE CHURCH OF GOD BECOMES PENTECOSTAL

The brief historical account of Pentecostalism is important in two ways: it provides a foundation for Pentecostal experience, and it provides a broader context for the emergence of the Church of God (Cleveland, Tennessee) and its transition to Pentecostalism. It was the Church of God that, for a time, would practice the handling of venomous serpents as one of its most convincing evangelistic signs.

At the turn of the twentieth century, the Church of God (Cleveland, Tennessee) was in the process of becoming (Synan, 1997). Charles Conn (1996), the denomination's celebrated historian, has pointed to 1886 as the church's origin. At that time R. G. Spurling Sr., a Baptist minister, became discontented with creedalism in his own denomination and organized, with seven others, the Christian Union Church in Monroe County, Tennessee. Willing to abandon denominational creeds, which were held to be unscriptural and divisive, this small group committed itself to the task of restoring pristine biblical Christianity and unity among all believers. Despite this worthy attempt at reformation—and the appointment of Spurling's younger son to leadership—the Christian Union dissolved shortly thereafter "for lack of interest" (Synan, 1997, p. 73) as charter members, including the elder Spurling, returned to their former churches. Inspired by his father and his own theology, however, Richard G. Spurling Jr. continued his itinerant ministry in the mountains of Appalachia, establishing a few small "independent" congregations wherever he briefly settled—as has remained the typical practice of the region's Holiness preachers to the present day (McCauley, 1995). Given that these small groups were independent, it seems unlikely that most survived the elder Spurling's departure. Without doubt, though, the major impetus for the Church of God came about through a significant Holiness revival that took place at Camp Creek, North Carolina, in 1896 (Synan, 1997).

From the frontier revivals of the early 1800s, the unique religion of Appalachia was, and remains, a blend spun together from various cultural traditions that adapted to the landscape, from a personal "awareness" of such traditions, and from the very nature of the mountainous terrain itself (McCauley, 1995). Mainly of Celtic, Scottish-Irish, English, and Germanic descent, settlers of the area came to depend on a mysticism-oriented religion, rooted in heartfelt conversion, that equipped them for the emotional demands of challenging mountain life (Photiadis, 1978). The important perception of a direct encounter with

God provided a powerful personal experience, giving religion both depth and rich meaning. For these individuals, God was experienced as a participant in the daily affairs of personal living, and it was such people who gathered at Shearer Schoolhouse, at Camp Creek, North Carolina, to experience a noted Holiness revival.

From the ministry of B. H. Irwin and his Fire-Baptized Holiness Association, revivals with Pentecostal-type activities had already spread to much of the Southeast by 1896 (Synan, 1997). Followers of the movement were accustomed to emotionally charged meetings in which participants would experience a third blessing beyond that of sanctification, often referred to as baptism with "fire." According to Irwin's theology, three experiences were available to seekers: salvation, which provided forgiveness of sins; sanctification, which eradicated the sinful nature and made possible a holiness life; and baptism with fire. Recipients of this third experience would reportedly "shout, scream, speak in other tongues, fall into trances, receive the holy dance and holy laugh, and even get the 'jerks'" (Synan, 1997, p. 52).

Having had contact with this movement, three evangelists—William Martin, a Methodist; Joe Tipton, a Baptist; and Milton McNabb, also a Baptist—began the series of meetings in 1896 in the Shearer Schoolhouse at Camp Creek that were to affect the community profoundly. Moved by enthusiastic, fire-baptized preaching, scores of converts were said to have fallen into the altars seeking sanctification and the "fire," which, when encountered, were characterized by various ecstatic demonstrations, including tongues speaking. The following description illustrates the kinds of experiences they encountered:

> The people earnestly sought God, and the interest increased until unexpectedly, like a cloud from a clear sky, the Holy Ghost began to fall on the honest, humble, sincere seekers after God. While the meetings were in progress, one after another fell under the power of God and soon quite a number were speaking in tongues as the Spirit gave them utterance. . . . The power of healing was soon realized, and a number of miraculous cases of healings were wrought by the power of God. The people knew but little about the Bible, but they prayed, and shouted and exhorted until hundreds of hard sinners were converted. (*Book of minutes*, 1922, p. 11)

News of these events attracted the interest of people in the region, prompting many to come and investigate the source of the spiritual fervor (*Book of minutes*, 1922). Reactions were mixed, however, with some being persuaded and others being critical and hostile. After the revival closed, meetings were moved first to a log church, which antagonists soon dismantled and destroyed, and then to private homes (Davidson, 1973). As might be expected, rejection of this type of religious emotionality by the community, especially by established churches, became intense, even to the extent of home burnings. However, the leadership of W. F. Bryant, a local Baptist lay minister, helped to guide the group through these persecutions. Because it failed to organize as a church, however, the group lacked consistent government and teaching to safeguard against persecution and sedition and thus dwindled to no more than twenty members by 1902 (Stone, 1977).

Through the influence of Irwin's movement, Richard G. Spurling Jr. had also come to embrace the Holiness doctrine of entire sanctification and holy living and to reject the evils of society (Synan, 1997), though he protested the "fanaticism" usually associated with such Holiness meetings (Conn, 1996). In frequent visits with Bryant's group, the itinerant preacher had encouraged his fellow believers to organize for the sake of surviving persecution and false doctrines; but it was not until May 15, 1902, that the group finally organized as the Holiness Church at Camp Creek, with twenty charter members and Spurling as pastor (*Book of minutes*, 1922). Over the next year, the new Holiness church continued its struggle to survive and exist according to Spurling's concept of the New Testament church.

A. J. Tomlinson, an Indiana-born salesman for the American Bible Society, often visited the home of W. F. Bryant on his treks through the Appalachian Mountains (Conn, 1996; Stone, 1977; Robins, 2004). It was there he grew in fellowship with the Holiness Church at Camp Creek, preached to its small membership, and encountered Spurling's teaching concerning the restoration of the New Testament church. Invited to the group's Saturday Bible study, Tomlinson arrived at Bryant's home the previous evening (Evans, 1943). The next morning, he fellowshipped with the family at breakfast and then climbed to the top of nearby Burger Mountain, where he spent time in prayer over whether to join the small congregation. Feeling resolved, he descended the mountain and was moved to join the church by covenant "with the understanding that it IS the Church of God [of the Bible]—not going to be, but IS the Church of God" (Evans, 1943, p. 12).

Because of his notable leadership abilities, Tomlinson was selected to be pastor of the Holiness Church at Camp Creek the same day he joined—June, 13, 1903 (Synan, 1997). Within two years, the church expanded to three additional congregations, located in Luskville and Union Grove, both in Tennessee, and in Jones, Georgia. Toward the end of 1904, Tomlinson transplanted the home base of the church from the heart of the mountainous Appalachian region to the nearby valley town of Cleveland, Tennessee, whose central location and easy access to commerce would further the church's growth (Stone, 1977; McCauley, 1995). Although the church left the mountains, it did not leave behind its religious tradition centering on a perceived direct experience with God, characterized by emotion that found meaning in everyday life.

Throughout 1907 the small Holiness church experienced notable growth, establishing a few new congregations in North Carolina, Tennessee, and Georgia (Stone, 1977). By this time, all congregations of the group had met twice in annual General Assemblies—both moderated by Tomlinson—to discuss and settle important points of doctrine and practice (O'Neal, 1992). It was at the 1907 General Assembly that the group officially adopted the name Church of God to distinguish itself from scores of other independent Holiness congregations using variations of the same name. Because accurate records were not kept during this period, it is impossible to measure precisely the extent of church growth, though there is some evidence of notable growth in the General Assembly minutes. Because of concurrent events in Los Angeles, California, however, a new chapter of history soon would begin for the Church of God the following year.

Through various religious periodicals of the time, it is probable that Tomlinson received news of the much-publicized Azusa Street revival, which began in April 1906, sometime during that same year. In fact, he preached on the subject, "The Baptism of the Holy Ghost and Fire," at the following General Assembly, January 23, 1907 (O'Neal, 1992). As Synan (1997) has observed, although some of its members had experienced glossolalia earlier, at the 1896 Shearer Schoolhouse revival the church had yet to embrace that manifestation as the doctrinal sign of Holy Ghost baptism or possession. That the Church of God did not link spirit baptism exclusively with tongues until *after* the 1906 Azusa Street revival is further suggested by evidence in its own historical documents—such as Tomlinson's personal diary *(Journal of happenings)*, the General Assembly minutes, and early articles found in the church's official publication—written concurrently with the events they describe.

A careful reading of Tomlinson's personal journal reveals that, before June 14, 1907, he referred to the ministry of the "Holy Ghost" no less than eight times, and in two of these instances he stated, "Some received [or got] the Holy Ghost" (Tomlinson, *Journal of happenings*, Aug. 4, 1904; Aug. 17, 1904). However, "speaking in tongues" was not mentioned until June 14, 1907, more than a year after the Azusa Street revival began. It is of further interest that in June 1907 Tomlinson had personal exposure for the first time to the Pentecostal doctrine of tongues, in Birmingham, Alabama, through M. M. Pinson, a Methodist minister who had experienced the phenomenon during a revival tour of C. B. Cashwell, who had just returned from Azusa Street with the Pentecostal experience (Synan, 1997). After the June 14 entry, the phrase "speaking in tongues" began to occur quite frequently in Tomlinson's journal entries.

Tomlinson did not receive the Holy Ghost baptism with tongues for himself until January 1908 (*Journal of happenings,* Jan. 13, 1908; Synan, 1997; Robins, 2004). At the invitation of Tomlinson, Cashwell came to the Cleveland church and preached on the Pentecostal doctrine. During the discourse, Tomlinson, who was seated behind Cashwell, slipped off his chair to the floor and moments later experienced his own Holy Ghost baptism and spoke with tongues. After this life-changing encounter—described in detail in his diary (*Journal of happenings,* Jan. 13, 1908)—Holy Ghost baptism, uniquely evidenced by glossolalia, became widely preached in the Church of God. Historical records reveal that significant revivals were conducted in the following years during which hundreds—and eventually thousands—were reported to be converted, sanctified, filled with the Pentecostal blessing, and joined to the church (Stone, 1977; Tomlinson, *Journal of happenings;* O'Neal, 1992).

For example, later in 1908 Tomlinson began a Pentecostal tent revival in Chattanooga that continued for several weeks and ended with the establishment of a new church with forty-nine members. At the revival's conclusion, he stated:

> I preached last Sunday under the power of the Spirit to about 1000 people, and God wonderfully confirmed the word with signs following. Glory! What followed is almost indescribable. Shouts, speaking in tongues, a sister played organ controlled by the Spirit. I was enveloped in a kind of sheet of power and controlled, and they said my hair stood up on my head. Glory! It was wonderful. Since our meeting commenced there the first of May until the close last night there have been about seventy-five who received the baptism of the Holy Ghost and spoke in tongues, which is the Bible evidence. . . . I preached to about 5,000 people on a lake shore where we were baptizing. (*Journal of happenings,* Aug. 4, 1908)

The addition of this Pentecostal doctrine, and its sign of tongue-speaking, not only inspired results in Chattanooga; it was significant in a revival begun one week later in Tomlinson's own town, Cleveland. According to his journal entries, thousands attended the ten-week event, at which various demonstrations of the Holy Ghost were said to commonly occur—"tongues," "manifestations and miracles," "visions," "[faintings] under the power," "blue vapor," "[a] streak of fire," and so on. These Holy Ghost signs were convincing to such a degree that scores of seekers reportedly "piled" into the altar most evenings—as many as one hundred on one occasion—and received salvation, sanctification, and Holy Ghost baptism with tongues. On the last night of the revival, Tomlinson wrote, "Closed out tonight after a 10 weeks successful battle *[sic]*. 105 profession and 163 received the baptism of the Holy Ghost. 78 baptized in water. 106 accessions to the Church. Quite a number healed. We had a glorious meeting tonight. About 75 in the altar" (*Journal of happenings*, Oct. 14, 1908). Such meetings were not atypical for the Church of God in the years following Tomlinson's spirit baptism but rather the norm—as evidenced in revival reports in the *Evangel*, the denomination's official publication since 1910.[3] As the church became more Pentecostal in nature, ministers as well as members saw themselves as sufficiently empowered to evangelize their communities and beyond with the gospel (Stone, 1977).

Although the "Holy Ghost" and "Holy Ghost baptisms" had been acknowledged in proceedings of the early General Assemblies—the first of which convened in 1906—it is of interest that the Church of God did not officially adopt the baptism "with tongues" until the sixth assembly, in 1911 (O'Neal, 1992, pp. 87, 89). The church had first published the teaching only a few months earlier, in the *Evangel* (The Church of God: Teaching, 1910), though it was not until the following assembly that the doctrine was actually accepted with other Bible teachings referenced in the same article. At least three other articles published in the *Evangel* that same year gave direct credit to the 1906 Los Angeles revival as the fount of the recent Pentecostal movement (Tomlinson, 1910; Whidden, 1910; Pentecostal Testimony, 1910). Given these facts and the accounts in Tomlinson's personal journal, it seems likely that the early self-understanding of the church was more one of Holiness than Pentecostal in terms of doctrine and practice—at least through 1907, the year preceding Tomlinson's baptism experience.

Though this observation mitigates the 1896 claim of the Church of God as being Pentecostal (Conn, 1996; Bowdle, 1999), it does not diminish the prominence of Holy Ghost experiences and manifestations reported at the Shearer Schoolhouse revival. It simply attempts to place them in proper historical context by clarifying how they were understood by those who experienced them at that time rather than glossing them as reinterpretations of those events decades later (Conn, 1996; Bowdle, 1999; Stone, 1977; Davidson, 1973; *Book of minutes,* 1922). The evidence is clear, however, that after Tomlinson's 1908 experience the Church of God became more markedly Pentecostal in nature and, from that time, widely preached and defended the Pentecostal doctrine of Holy Ghost baptism signified solely by glossolalia. The importance of this observation is not trivial to the present study insofar as the Church of God's acceptance of the sign of spirit baptism—tongues speaking—occurred just before its acceptance of yet another sign of Pentecostal empowerment—the taking up of venomous serpents. From records of its history, it appears that these two signs, along with others in Mark 16, became instrumental in the early success of the young church.

SIGNS WITHIN A PENTECOSTAL CHURCH

Once it became Pentecostal, the Church of God was afforded a religious context of experience within which certain manifestations of the Holy Ghost could emerge as persuasive signs for evangelism. As for the tongues-speaking experience, the same passage in the sacred text that provided it with justification also provided justification for other manifestations or signs involving possession by the spirit. As noted in the very first publication of its teachings (The Church of God, 1910), a biblical text found popular among Church of God members included the words of Jesus just prior to his ascension: "But ye shall receive power, after that the Holy Ghost is come upon you: and ye shall be witnesses unto me both in Jerusalem, and in all Judea, and in Samaria, and unto the uttermost part of the earth" (Acts 1:8). Another prominent text for Pentecostals that follows this passage observes Peter giving an explanation to the multitude who had gathered to investigate the curious manifestations on the day of Pentecost:

> For these are not drunken, as ye suppose, seeing it is but the third hour of the day. But this is that which was spoken by the prophet Joel; And it shall come to pass in the last days, saith God, I will pour out of my Spirit upon all flesh: and your sons and your daughters shall prophesy, and your young men shall see visions, and your old men shall dream dreams: And on my servants and on my handmaidens I will pour out in those days of my Spirit; and they shall prophesy: And I will show wonders in heaven above, and signs in the earth beneath; blood, and fire, and vapour of smoke: The sun shall be turned into darkness, and the moon into blood, before that great and notable day of the Lord come: And it shall come to pass, that whosoever shall call on the name of the Lord shall be saved. . . . Then Peter said

unto them, Repent, and be baptized every one of you in the name of Jesus Christ for the remission of sins, and ye shall receive the gift of the Holy Ghost. For the promise is unto you, and to your children, and to all that are afar off, even as many as the Lord our God shall call. (Acts 2:15–21, 38–39)

A Pentecostal belief held early in the Church of God was that infusion by the Holy Ghost—evidenced by speaking in tongues—empowers the believer to be an effective witness for Jesus, which may thus convince potential converts of the need for salvation (He hath shed forth this, 1910). It is not necessarily tongues speaking itself that convinces unbelievers but any demonstrations of the spirit within the believer that may manifest at the will of God in various ways for convincing the unsaved. In Pentecostal theology, spirit baptism also equips the believer for the exercise of a variety of supposed supernatural gifts that are designed to edify believers as well as convince unbelievers (Horton, 1934/1975).

This theology is based on a literal interpretation of the text—a fundamentalist tendency—that, according to Hollenweger (1972), functions as a "ritual" for preserving a specific worldview. In contrast with Cox's (1995) claim that Pentecostalism is not fundamentalist in nature, Hollenweger (1972) and Synan (1997) have both observed that American Pentecostalism emerged from the late-nineteenth-century Holiness movement, which rejected, as did other conservative Protestant groups, the rising tide of evolutionary theory and biblical higher criticism. According to Hollenweger (1972), the poetic beauty and elegance of the King James Version Bible is such that fundamentalists esteem it as perfect and beyond scholarly criticism—that is, it is perceived factually as the expressed word of God. For them, he said, the "ritual" of literal biblical interpretation becomes a phenomenon, very sensitive to contextual cues, that harmonizes a poetic and aesthetic expression of the "Truth" with a perspective of the world that provides understanding and meaning—a process preselective according to context. It is through its faithful devotion, moreover, that this ritual guarantees salvation, protection, and order to its adherents. Higher criticism of the Bible, especially that concerned with the potential errancy of Scripture, is not tolerated, else the ritual is challenged and leads to the collapse of the worldview. Although rational arguments can be levied against the ritual of literal interpretation from outside, adamant resistance by fundamentalists to enter such debates sustains its practice, which in turn stabilizes their structured and contextualized view of the world. The power of Fundamentalism to maintain a system of meaning lived out with ritual support is what

Hood and colleagues (2005) have referred to as intratextuality. Non-fundamentalists' search for meaning from several sources—intertextuality—lacks the clear boundaries found in a single authoritative text. Hence Pentecostals early in this century held to an intratextual understanding of Scripture in which the Holy Ghost was felt to be directly experienced and necessary for empowerment in a spiritually discerned world. As a bumper sticker once popular in the South expressed it, "The Bible said it. I believe it. That settles it."

It is important to note that a literal reading of the Bible is not the defining criterion of either Pentecostalism or Fundamentalism. We have argued elsewhere that Fundamentalism is best understood as taking an intratextual stance toward the Bible (Hood et al., 2005). This means that the text itself guides interpretation, including what is to be taken literally and what is to be understood in other than literal terms. Under this view, both the Church of God and the Church of God of Prophecy are fundamentalist groups, as are the serpent-handling churches (Hood et al., 2005, chaps. 4, 5).

That spiritual empowerment became a predominant theology in the early Church of God is clearly reflected in an *Evangel* article, "All Need the Holy Ghost" (1910)—presumably written by Tomlinson, or at the very least endorsed by him—that stressed the need of Holy Ghost baptism with tongues. Encouraging people to seek the Pentecostal blessing, the article stated:

> Nothing can take the place of the Holy Ghost in the life of the believer. A man can be learned and eloquent and orthodox, as well, but he is as much in need of the Spirit as any one else. One may be able to draw good crowds and to entertain them with beautiful discourses, and even preach much truth, deep truth at that; but unless it is backed up by the power of the Holy Ghost, it will bear little fruit, and perhaps none to perfection. . . . Christ said, "Tarry till ye are endued with power from on high," but to-day men are saying, "Tarry till you graduate." After Pentecost, the Church was full of men who were full of the Holy Ghost and power, faith and wisdom, but their power was from God, and their faith was in God, and their wisdom was from God. There were men who were unlettered and ignorant, so far as worldly wisdom is concerned, but the wisest men among the Jews were unable to resist the wisdom with which they spoke. . . . The signs and wonders in great measure are following the preaching of the Word in many places. . . . The people are speaking in other tongues. The sick are being healed; and some are prophesying. . . . Some have come to our meetings, and have tarried till they were baptized in the Holy Ghost, and spoken in tongues, and gone forth to labor for the Lord. (All need the Holy Ghost, 1910, p. 2)

As the direct experience of the Holy Ghost was for those of the Bible, the Church of God fully expected the same measure of empowerment for the modern believer based on a literal understanding of Scripture. Their primary dependence on this Pentecostal theology for evangelization was in fact guided by an unrelenting faith that often rejected the contemporary "wisdom" of the larger religious world.

Indeed, Pentecostal doctrine and practice became a mobilizing force in the early success of the Church of God. The most reliable record for the earliest years, 1886–1904, reports church membership to have begun with 8 persons in 1886; to have increased to 130 the same year as the 1886 Shearer Schoolhouse revival; to have declined to 20 by 1902; and to have increased again to 39 members in 1904 (Conn, 1996, p. 580). No official membership reports exist, however, for the years 1905–8. One possibility for this lapse is that no procedure had yet been developed by the church for reporting its membership until the General Assembly of January 1909, when action was taken to make printed report forms available to the local churches (O'Neal, 1992).

Among oral accounts given in that 1909 Assembly—for the church work in 1908—M. S. Lemons reported a membership of 60 in Chattanooga, with 75 Holy Ghost baptisms, and W. F. Bryant reported some 30 professions at Red Knobs. The only other minister at this time to report specific numbers was Tomlinson, who stated that the Cleveland church had increased Sunday School enrollment from 60 to 230, experienced 300 professions, and witnessed 250 receive the Holy Ghost (O'Neal, 1992, pp. 57, 59). It should be noted that Tomlinson's "fruitful" report to the General Assembly was in review of his first year of ministry *after* his Holy Ghost baptism with tongues.

Due to a new reporting system that was in place by this time, Tomlinson—now General Moderator/Overseer of the overall church—was able to give a detailed report to the 1911 General Assembly that revealed the notable growth of the church achieved during the years 1909 and 1910 (*Minutes of the sixth annual Assembly,* 1911, p. 3). The number of churches reported to the 1910 Assembly, for the year 1909, was 31. The number of new churches gained in 1910 was 27, which increased the total number of congregations to 58. The number of members reported at the 1910 Assembly, for the church's work in 1909, was 1,005. Concerning membership gains in 1910, there were 310 new members added to the "old churches," whereas 540 members were added through the establishment of new congregations. The net gain of 850 new members in 1910 almost equaled the entire membership reported for the previous year's work (1909), bringing the official membership to 1,855. Thus the evangelistic efforts of the Church of God, for the work in 1910, resulted in almost twice the number of churches and members reported for 1909. This growth pattern was continually seen in membership reports during years that followed: 1915, 6,503 members; 1920, 15,051 members; 1925, 25,231 members; 1930, 27,149 members; 1935, 52,913 members; and 1940, 83,552 members (Conn, 1996, p. 581).

It is not difficult to associate the Church of God's acceptance of Pentecostal doctrine with its notable growth. It seems clear that during this period a cornerstone teaching that became prominent in the church's theology, and vital at least in part to its early evangelistic success, was the Pentecostal notion that "supernatural signs" would accompany the true New Testament church in its mission. In fact, an article published in the August 15, 1910, issue of the *Evangel* begins, "The Church of God: Stands for the whole Bible rightly divided. The New Testament as the only rule for government and discipline. Below is given some of the teaching that is made prominent" (The Church of God, 1910, p. 3). Following this was a list of twenty-five specific teachings with scriptural references—among them, number 12, which states, "Signs following believers: Mark 16:17–20, Rom. 15:18–19, Heb. 2:4" (p. 3).

The linkage of the signs with the church's Pentecostal theology and evangelistic mission is evidenced in a vision the General Overseer experienced during his own Holy Ghost baptism. The following is an excerpt from the much longer account of the event.

> Also the 16th chapter of Mark came up [before him], these signs shall follow, dwelling on casting out devils, speaking in tongues and taking up serpents. I seemed to try to get to the healing of the sick, but could not quite get to that. Numbers of people came before me whom I could see coming. Among them were my wife and children. I seemed to see us all on a missionary journey. Glory to God! I must not fail to tell about the song I sang in unknown tongues. Oh, it was glorious!
>
> This was really the baptism of the Holy Ghost as they received Him on the day of Pentecost, for they all spake with tongues. With all I have written it is not yet told, but judging from the countries I visited [in this vision] I spoke in ten different languages. It seemed that the Spirit was showing me these countries with a view to taking me there. In each place I saw lots of people coming to the light and baptism. I could see multitudes coming to Jesus. I don't know if God wants me to go to these places or not, but I am willing to go as He leads. (Tomlinson, *Journal of happenings*, Jan. 13, 1908)

And go Tomlinson did, inspired by a Pentecostal theology with signs that helped gain for the Church of God significant growth, including some of its earliest members outside the United States (Tomlinson, *Journal of happenings,* Apr. 11, 1911). The signs following passages of the Gospel of Mark had a significant role in the growth of the Church of God. However, it is worth noting here that critics who argue that contemporary serpent handlers overemphasize a few passages from the Bible fail to appreciate that it is precisely because they are constantly challenged to defend this practice that they continue to use Mark 16:17–18 to legitimize a ritual that is consistent with the totality of Scripture—not simply based on a fixation with a few biblical passages. In this sense, contemporary handlers' insistence on the entire Gospel of Mark has, and continues to play, a significant role in Pentecostal theology and history (Thomas & Alexander, 2003; Kelhoffer, 2000; Wall, 2003).

Early revival reports and personal testimonials, published in the *Evangel,* almost always gave witness to manifestations of the Holy Ghost—especially the Pentecostal sign of speaking in tongues—that were persuasive in Church of God meetings and personal life. For example, T. L. McLain wrote of his 1908 conversion to Pentecostalism when unusual manifestations at Tomlinson's tent revival drew interest from reportedly thousands in Cleveland, Tennessee (McLain, 1910). On hearing of these demonstrations, he and his friends attended a service to see for themselves the ecstatic worship taking place. Though apprehensive at first and somewhat embarrassed about being present at such a meeting, McLain soon experienced "conviction" in his heart when witnessing a female participant manifest the sign of tongues speaking in a song. He wrote, "The moment she began singing [in tongues] the power of God struck me in both hands, and ran to my elbows. I was convinced of it being the word of God" (McLain, 1910, p. 5). So convincing was this sign that McLain returned for service the following Sunday and fell into the altar with others to seek and receive this Pentecostal experience, after which time he grew to a position of prominence in the expanding church (Conn, 1996; Davidson, 1973).

Still others were drawn to the Church of God because the signs of divine healing and casting out of devils were compelling. As one of many examples, such was the case reported in a 1910 Church of God revival at Coalburg, Alabama:

> The Holy Ghost had full control through the entire meeting, and the Lord was present in mighty power, and confirmed the Word with signs following. . . . Large crowds attended the meeting, and the people knew very little about salvation, but conviction prevailed among them, and numbers were at the altar seeking the Lord. Those who at first stood back and

mocked were struck with conviction as the Holy Ghost manifested His
mighty power and presence. . . . Devils were cast out and the sick were
healed by the power of God. A child which was possessed with an unclean
spirit from its birth, and would roll its head from side to side continually
and throw its hands and arms, and be in a continual move, until its mother
could scarcely hold it in her lap, was delivered. The mighty power of God
fell, the devil was rebuked and the child looked at us and smiled and went
to sleep. . . . We closed the meeting with about twenty-five professions. . . .
A number were sanctified and some baptized with the Holy Ghost. (Cotton,
1910, p. 7)

Such reported manifestations of the Holy Ghost as these—speaking in
tongues, healing the sick, casting out of devils—were important for
much of the success enjoyed by the Church of God in the early twentieth century (Crews, 1990). However, when one begins to link speaking
in tongues, laying hands on the sick, and casting out devils, it is not far
from the foundational passage most linked to the justification of serpent
handling. From Parham and Pentecostalism, the Church of God had
Acts 2:4 as a sacred canopy under which that Holy Ghost baptism was
justified; however, there would emerge another man and a movement
that looked to Mark 16:17–18 for as much. That man was George Went
Hensley, and the movement is the subject of the rest of this book, the
contemporary Christian serpent handlers of Appalachia.

CHAPTER 3

The Media and the Man

George Went Hensley

Those who have traced the history of serpent handling have generally credited one man with originating this ritual practice. It is unlikely, however, that serpent handling has a single origin. Many emerging Pentecostal groups considered that the biblical justification for tongues speaking, Mark 16:17–18, also encompassed serpent handling. While some Pentecostal groups such as the Assemblies of God and the Pentecostal Holiness Church rejected serpent handling as a legitimate religious ritual (Crews, 1990), they did interpret Mark 16:17–18 to mean that if believers accidentally handled serpents they would not be harmed. This interpretation alludes to the story of Paul in Acts 28:3–6. While laying sticks he had gathered upon a fire, a viper came out and fastened onto Paul's hand. Onlookers are said to have believed that Paul was a murderer whom "vengeance suffereth not to live" (Acts 28: 4). Paul shook the viper off and "felt no harm" (Acts 28:5). The onlookers anticipated swelling or sudden death; seeing neither, they changed their minds about Paul and "said that he was a god" (Acts 28:7).

Pentecostal groups that affirm that Mark 16:17–18 refers to protection from accidental bites salvaged a meaning too distant from the text. The plain meaning of the text was interpreted by other Pentecostal groups as an imperative "they *shall.*" The conditional meaning applies only to poisons ("*if* they drink") and would more appropriately allow for the accidental interpretation that the Assemblies of God and the Pentecostal Holiness Church tried to apply to serpent handling. Interestingly, the same imperative applied to tongues speaking in Mark 16:17 is also applied to serpent handling in Mark 16:18. Thus the early Church of God and Church of God of Prophecy endorsed the more consistent position as reflected in the stand taken by their first General Overseer, A. J. Tomlinson: "The Church stands for the whole Bible rightly divided, and it is wrong dividing to cut out the tongues and serpents" (Tomlinson, 1930, p. 1).

The concern with serpent handling and various interpretations of Mark 16:17–18 among different Pentecostal groups suggests that individuals may have been handling serpents as a religious ritual even in the early Pentecostal groups that came to explicitly reject the practice. Furthermore, for more than the first quarter of the twentieth century, a period that Wacker (2003) argues is foundational for Pentecostalism, the Church of God and later its schism sister denomination, the Church of God of Prophecy, endorsed the practice. Thus discussions and witnessing of handling occurred across the Appalachians and Ozarks, areas where serpents were plentiful and where serpent handling was part of folk practice long before the emergence of Pentecostalism (Anderson, 1979, pp. 92–93). Although the Church of God never required serpent handling as necessary for salvation, some individual ministers did. One such minister left the mother Church of God and eventually formed the Church of God with Signs Following (Anderson, 1979, p. 263) and became responsible for spreading the full gospel of all five signs in many places throughout the Southeast. His name was George Went Hensley, and for many historians and scholars, he is the Saint Paul of serpent handling.

While we accept Hensley's influence in spreading serpent handling among numerous churches, it is unlikely that he had the degree of influence that often is attributed to him. One reason is the simple fact that serpent handling was more readily accepted in areas where it was an established part of time-honored folkways (Anderson, 1979, pp. 92–93). If Hensley is to be credited with influencing the practice within the Church of God, it was most likely through his linking of serpent handling and tongues speaking in Mark 16:17–18, thus giving biblical justification for both as legitimate *religious* rituals. However, Hensley was not alone in the linking of tongues speaking with serpent handling. Further, serpent handling spread rapidly in the foothills of the Ozarks and in the Appalachian Mountains, even in places where Hensley did not visit (Anderson, 1979, pp. 92–93). Even in the Appalachian Mountains it is likely that serpent handling had several independent origins (Vance, 1975). As with tongues speaking, the issue was one of denominational endorsement or rejection of the practice, not whether it existed in various subcultures as an established folk practice. The major difficulty is that most historians and scholars have relied on media documentation of serpent handling, and this has largely followed from reporting on charismatic preachers such as George Hensley or, as the practice became more common, on bites and death.

What is needed to complement archival studies of serpent handling is collection of its oral history, which few have bothered to do. One exception is Hood's (2005) editing of Pastor Jimmy Morrow's narrative history of serpent handling. Morrow carefully documented, in thousands of laboriously written and typed pages, the oral histories of his Appalachian neighbors, including generations of serpent-handling families for whom the Appalachian Mountains have been both home and burial ground. His oral history of handling helps to demythologize the notion that George Hensley was the sole originator of the serpent-handling tradition.

Jimmy Morrow came across a July 3, 1944, issue of *Life* magazine in which several people are pictured handling serpents, including two women, one pregnant (p. 59) and one elderly (p. 60).[1] Later Morrow was told by an aged preacher that his son said that a sister had a picture for Morrow. This turned out to be a picture of the elderly woman he had seen in *Life*. Morrow traced the picture to the Kleiniecks of Appalachia and found that the heretofore unknown woman shown handling in *Life* was Nancy Younger Kleinieck, a prophetess in the Jesus' Name tradition, to which Morrow also belongs. Morrow's oral history of Kleinieck identifies her as handling serpents, which a young George Went Hensley witnessed (Hood, 2005, chaps. 1, 2). It documents tales of serpent handling in coal mining camps in Wise County, Virginia, as early as 1890, nearly two decades before Hensley is said to have begun the practice (Hood, 2005, chap. 1). Morrow notes that the Hensley family moved to Stone Gap, Virginia, in the 1890s, and that is where George Hensley witnessed Kleinieck and others handling serpents at coal camp revivals (Hood, 2005, pp. 1–2).

The value of Morrow's oral history of serpent handling is that it both supplements and provides alternatives to histories written from archival sources, largely based on media reports (contemporary newspaper reports, church bulletins and minutes, and, later, television coverage) that have left much of the folk practice of serpent handling invisible. Our book draws on archives and oral histories to provide a more detailed and balanced treatment of a practice that likely came into more public visibility when time-honored folk practices in many rural mountain regions met the increasing vocal demands of Pentecostals—that is, the need for evidence of Holy Ghost possession and for the "signs and wonders" that follow. It was this convergence of folk practice and emerging Pentecostal groups that would eventually move the handling of serpents from brush arbor meetings into the churches and raise the issue of its legitimacy as a denominationally sanctioned religious ritual.

It was amid a climate of Pentecostal signs that George Went Hensley first made his appearance in the Church of God, which was spreading from Bradley County to neighboring regions in Tennessee. There is no clear agreement among scholars (Burton, 1993; Kimbrough, 1995/2002; Kane, 1979; Vance, 1975; La Barre, 1962/1974) about the precise date Hensley first handled a serpent. Most scholars admit that even if Hensley was not the sole originator of serpent handling, he was at least indirectly responsible for the spread of the movement in the South. However, Vance (1975) has argued that serpent handling sprang up as an independent movement in various regions unrelated to Hensley. For example, according to Vance, the tradition began in Alabama and, later, in Georgia, through Jim Miller, who is said to have begun serpent handling in northern Dekalb County, Alabama, as early as 1912, without previous knowledge of the practice or Hensley. Miller's contact with Church of God minister J. B. Ellis in those early years, however, casts doubt on this argument. Ellis, who had received the Holy Ghost baptism in 1910, was well aware of serpent handling in the Church of God, as indicated in an *Evangel* article (Ellis, 1914), and was likely to have at least mentioned the newly emerged Pentecostal sign to Miller on an earlier occasion. However, this does not mitigate the claim that one of the reasons serpent handling so easily entered the Church of God was that the practice had widespread support from folk practices, as did fire handling, which also entered some churches, especially in the Kentucky region of Appalachia (Kane, 1979).

Vance (1975) has argued that by 1934 one Albert Teester of Sylva, North Carolina, also began handling serpents as an independent phenomenon without any prior knowledge of the practice or of Hensley. Again, his thesis is called into doubt by the fact that by 1930 there already had been eleven reports of serpent handling published in the *Evangel* from at least nine different locations in North Carolina, ranging from Hayesville in the western part of the state to Washington in the eastern part. Serpents had been handled in Hayesville, fifty miles west of

Sylva, as early as 1917 (Martin, 1917), while the practice had taken place at Leicester, fifty miles east of Teester's home, by at least 1919 (Hopkins, 1919). Given the wide circulation of the practice in North Carolina before 1930, the claim to have identified the "first serpent handler" seems no more likely and makes no more sense than that of having identified the "first tongues speaker" amid the cross-cultural existence of tongues speaking. It may be true that neither Miller nor Teester had ever heard of Hensley, but news of the practice was certainly available to both of them, from printed sources as well as folkways common to their Appalachian region.

However, given the discussion in various Pentecostal groups in coming to grips with Mark 16:17–18, there were likely many reports of serpent handling to be found. Not all need to be linked directly to Hensley. The spread of religious serpent handling in the South was surely indirectly influenced by Hensley as he traveled and preached the signs. However, he sometimes preached to the choir, already convinced by folk practice, and others, influenced by the rise of Pentecostal groups, that what for some was a folk practice ought to become a religious ritual. Oral histories suggest a genealogy of serpent handling as a folk practice, often linked to religion but not with the clarity and fervor practiced when serpents, tongues, and faith converged in the emerging Pentecostal groups. While oral histories contain their own mythical claims, they are consistent with the general claim of Pentecostals. Even though critical histories suggest that tongues speaking was not practiced after the fourth century (Anderson, 1979; Wacker, 2003), some Pentecostals claim it was continually practiced after the day of Pentecost but was driven underground and maintained only as part of the oral history of the church. Those who handle serpents make the same claim. There always has been serpent handling.

We are not claiming that the early Christians handled serpents. We have sought evidence in official histories and can find none. However, we have sympathy for Appalachian folk wisdom and its reliance on a rich tradition of oral histories. For the Appalachian handlers, the only book to be trusted is the King James Bible. They do not look to other books for truths. They rely on stories and narratives, told by those who they believe know. However, until additional oral histories of serpent handling emerge, we are left primarily with tracing Hensley's influence from archival material and occasional supporting oral testimonies.

Various scholars (Burton, 1993; Hood, 2005; Kane, 1979; Kimbrough, 1995/2002; La Barre, 1962/1974) have reconstructed Hensley's personal history and situated his first known contact with the Church of God at Owl Hollow, just outside of Cleveland, Tennessee. It should be noted, however, that these sources rely heavily on an account rendered by Homer A. Tomlinson (1968), A. J. Tomlinson's eldest son, whose accuracy in reporting various historical events, both religious and secular, has met with well-deserved criticism (Burton, 1993; Hunter, 1988b). Nevertheless, Burton (1993) has carefully analyzed and related various other sources that also suggest that details of Hensley's emergence, as rendered by Tomlinson, may generally be accepted. Kimbrough (1995/2002) and Kane (1979) also reached similar conclusions based on personal interviews with relatives of Hensley.

As the tradition goes, in 1908 the community of Owl Hollow had readily accepted the Holiness-Pentecostal revival begun by the Church of God and had constructed a small church for its worship (Tomlinson, 1968). For its dedication, the group had invited A. J. Tomlinson to be the keynote speaker; however, the minister's busy travel schedule precluded his appearance, which resulted in the sending of Homer, his sixteen-year-old son, in his stead. Having preached only one other sermon in his life, the youth struggled through his discourse in the morning service and was later horrified to discover that he was expected to speak yet again in the afternoon service following a fellowship dinner. While standing in the pulpit in the afternoon, he found himself reading the story of Nicodemus in John 3 and—feeling encouraged—decided to extend an invitation to those desiring to be saved, sanctified, or baptized with the Holy Ghost to come forward. To his amazement, five young men responded, knelt in the altar, and "prayed through." One of those five was George Went Hensley.

Within Appalachian culture, the predominant practice of transmitting history through oral tradition gives rise to various discrepancies and versions of "truth" that account for a certain past event (McCauley, 1995); the particular version one takes as truth depends largely on which of the primary sources are consulted. This is no less true for Hensley's role in introducing the Pentecostal sign of serpent handling into the Church of God and the precise time at which it actually occurred. From what is known, however, Hensley's experience at Owl Hollow was such that he willingly forsook tobacco, moonshining, and "worldly" friendships and fully embraced the Holiness-Pentecostal doctrine and the zealous way of godly life it stressed (Kane, 1979; Kimbrough, 1995/2002; Burton, 1993). Being a man of devout and sincere faith, he became deeply concerned sometime during this period about

Mark 16:17–18, which was commonly preached among Holiness-Pentecostals as a textual justification for their unique worship practices as well as for evidence that they were believers and practitioners of the whole Bible. The preaching of these Pentecostal signs troubled him greatly, especially given the fact that only three of the signs were being manifested by believers. The speaking of tongues was widely practiced in the Pentecostal meetings he attended, as were the casting out of devils and the healing of the sick, but what of the taking up of serpents? It was reported that this discrimination among the signs caused him considerable spiritual unrest (Collins, 1947). If Jimmy Morrow's oral history is correct (Hood, 2005, chap. 2), it also is likely that at least some of Hensley's unrest was due to childhood memories of observing Nancy Kleinieck handle serpents.

Hensley was said to have climbed atop nearby White Oak Mountain to seek God in prayer and ultimately decide this spiritual struggle (Collins, 1947).[2] Resolving that manifestations of the signs in Mark 16 were in fact commands that believers must obey, he felt his eternal security rested on obedience to these mandates—and specifically, at the present moment for him, the taking up of serpents. Collins reported:

> His decision was to risk his life in order to have rest from his spiritual burden. Thus it was that he set out on probably the first religious snake hunt in modern civilized history.
> In a great rocky gap in the mountainside he found what he sought, a large rattlesnake. He approached the reptile, and, disreguarding [sic] its buzzing, blood-chilling warning, knelt a few feet away from it and prayed loudly into the sky for God to remove his fear and to anoint him with "the power." Then suddenly with a shout he leaped forward and grasped the reptile and held it in trembling hands. (1947, pp. 1–2)

It was from this life-changing experience that an inspired Hensley descended the mountain, with rattlesnake in hand, and launched only a few days later his first evangelistic effort in his own community of Grasshopper Valley, with a challenge that believers should practice *all* that Jesus had commanded—including taking up serpents (Collins, 1947).

As noted earlier, the precise time of this event is difficult to ascertain. In his classic work on serpent handling, La Barre (1962/1974) placed this event in 1909, probably relying on Collins (1947). Kane (1979) initially situated the event about two years after Hensley's 1908 salvation experience at Owl Hollow, approximately 1910, the same year that Kimbrough (1995/2002) regards as more certain. It should be noted, however, that Kane (1984, 1987, 1989) later claimed that Hensley began the practice around 1913, though no evidence is given for this date. Rather than pinpoint a specific time, Burton (1993) presented several possibilities, ranging from 1908 (H. A. Tomlinson's claim) to 1914 (the first documented reports of serpent handling in the *Evangel* and local newspapers). In summary, Burton (1993, p. 39) said, "As rewarding as it would be to know exactly where and when George Hensley first took up a serpent—or whether in fact he initiated the practice—the solution to the mystery remains elusive." In the final analysis, the exact date is secondary to the issue of the emergence of serpent handling itself as a legitimate Pentecostal sign and its effect on evangelism. Drawing from role theory, Hood and Kimbrough (1995/2002) have observed that the critical issue is the appearance of a charismatic figure that acts out a role for others based on the narrative of a sacred text.

From a psychological perspective, Hensley's serpent-handling experience can be seen as the result of being troubled by believers practicing only selected signs among those explicitly stated in a text of Scripture already embraced by his religious tradition. When atop White Oak Mountain and confronted with a rattlesnake in the context of prayerful meditation, he took on the role of a true believer as constructed from the text, and also the role of God that led to his feeling of being divinely directed in the activity.[3] God was felt to be directly encountered as a present divine reality who sanctioned Hensley's obedience as a true believer in observing Jesus' expressed command. Never to be the same again, Hensley descended the mountain to launch by example a religious practice that would hold tremendous meaning for those who would fully believe and obey. He also practiced with full biblical justification what he likely remembered from his youth when he witnessed Nancy Kleinieck handle serpents.

If Hensley's serpent handling did begin in 1909, or even 1910, evidence seems to indicate that it produced only marginal results in Grasshopper Valley for the first few years (Collins, 1947). He continued to preach in community churches, brush arbors, and homes, expounding on the third of the Pentecostal signs of Mark 16 (Kane, 1979; Kimbrough, 1995/2002). At such meetings scoffers and those hoping to make a public spectacle brought venomous serpents to Hensley and his followers, challenging them to fulfill their claims as obedient believers of the Scripture—and they did, with impunity and often with persuasive results. On one such occasion, Homer Tomlinson (1968, pp. 41–42) claims a result of "this amazing miracle [was that] a revival broke out that brought thousands from everywhere, walking, and by every means of transportation." Kane (1979, p. 36) quotes Tomlinson and relies on his account to conclude that Hensley's meetings were "noteworthy events," although the local newspaper in Cleveland did not mention serpent-handling activities until 1914 (Snakes in demand, 1914, September 17; Religion and snakes, 1914, October 1). Nevertheless, Hensley continued his ministry with Pentecostal signs and joined the Church of God in 1912 (Conn, 1996).

It was sometime between 1912 and 1914 that Hensley's ministry of serpent handling gained the attention of the community and Church of God leaders. In September 1914 Hensley and Bishop M. S. Haynes conducted a revival meeting in the South Cleveland Church of God tabernacle with results that drew wide attention from the religiously interested, as well as from the *Cleveland Herald* (Snakes in demand, 1914, September 17). During the revival, Hensley had preached on the signs of Mark 16, and skeptics were sparked to challenge his claims. General Overseer A. J. Tomlinson summarized the events that followed:

> On Friday night it was there. Some body had brought in a fierce "Rattlesnake Pilot." None of the saints had made any plans or said what they would do about the matter and even went to the meeting with little or no expectation of such a thing. The power of God was demonstrated successfully, however, and several handled it and no one was injured by it. Some were bitten, but with no damage to them.
>
> The sensation was so great that outsiders got enthused and wanted to test the matter further. So on Sunday night Sept. sixth they took in a "Copperhead." This was handled with as much success as the first, and many were made believers on account of the demonstration of God's power. The meeting went on after that with seekers in the altar and good results until Thursday night Sept. 10th. (Tomlinson, 1914b, pp. 2–3)

So impressive was the man and his message that Tomlinson allowed space during the next General Assembly of the Church of God for Hensley and Tennessee State Overseer G. T. Brouayer to conduct services in a revival tent outside the main auditorium at the same time that another evangelistic service was held inside by H. B. Simmons and J. A. Davis (*Minutes*, 1915, p. 13). Given the large attendance at the Assembly, simultaneous services were commonly conducted at different locations to accommodate the evening crowds. By the time of this event, the practice of serpent handling already had been mentioned in at least twenty *Evangel* articles—five of which specifically named Hensley (Williamson, 1995; Williamson & Hood, 2004b). Later that same year, Hensley—then thirty-seven—was licensed as a Church of God minister

(Index to the roster of ministers, n.d.). Interestingly, his credentials were issued on Christmas Day, 1915, and signed by A. J. Tomlinson and F. J. Lee, pastor of the main Cleveland church.

During his association with the Church of God, there is mention of Hensley and his ministry at least nine times in the *Evangel,* though other sources (Burton, 1993; Collins, 1947; Kane, 1979; Kimbrough, 1995/2002) have suggested that his ministry was much more active at this time. The first mention of his name was by his wife, Amanda (also known as Manda) Hensley (1914), who wrote of her own healing and her husband's success at revivals in Evansville and Dayton, Tennessee—ten saved, eight sanctified, four baptized with the Holy Ghost, and several healings. In 1914 Hensley was named in three articles: two were accounts of the same South Cleveland revival that seems to have launched serpent handling in the Church of God (Bro. George Hensley is conducting a revival, 1914; Tomlinson, 1914b); the third reported on revival work with M. S. Haynes at Ooltewah, Tennessee, where rattlesnakes were taken up and fire was handled (We had the pleasure, 1914).

In August 1915 Hensley and Pastor N. P. Mulkey (1915) conducted a successful revival at an unspecified location "out on the mountain"—most likely near Chattanooga—where a rattlesnake was handled, fifteen were converted, several received the Holy Ghost, sixteen were baptized in water, and twelve became members of the church. The article went on to state that both ministers were currently conducting a revival at Soddy, Tennessee, with converts being saved and receiving the Holy Ghost.

In September Hensley and Mulkey were again in revival at the Church of God at Dividing Ridge, Tennessee, where "in one of the services every sign was seen following but one [drinking poison, most likely]" (Miller, 1915, p. 4); four people received the Holy Ghost during the meeting at this eighty-three-member church. Tomlinson (1916) later wrote that "thirty or more" had received the Holy Ghost through Hensley's ministry at Harrison, Tennessee. An article expressing thanks for his preaching of Holiness doctrine and the Church of God message was penned from Birchwood, Tennessee (Headrick, 1918).

The last article found Hensley, in late 1921, in Fostoria, Ohio, where he conducted a revival with his sister, Bertha Weaver, of Walbridge, Ohio, who was also a licensed Church of God minister (Burkhart, 1922; *Minutes,* 1920). Although no serpents were said to have been handled, a vision of fire was described flickering against the church walls, along with other various Holy Ghost manifestations. Results of the meeting were reported as 6 conversions, eight sanctifications, seven Holy Ghost baptisms, and eight new church enrollments. Hensley, who was then of East Chattanooga, and his sister were highly recommended by J. B. Burkhart to *Evangel* readers for revival services.

There seems to be little doubt, as evidenced in *Evangel* articles, that Hensley's serpent-handling practice influenced and inspired unknown numbers in the Church of God, as well as others in independent groups, to follow his lead. For instance, Collins (1947) documented the activity of a serpent-handling church in Grasshopper, Tennessee, which appears to have been unrelated to the Church of God. It may well have been a group that Hensley was associated with before he joined the Church of God in 1912. This congregation, which met in brush arbors and homes, gained recognition as the foremost group practicing serpent handling on a consistent basis. When one of its key members, Garland Defriese, received a near-fatal snakebite in 1919, however, the church dissolved, marking the end of the practice as a customary observance by any known Tennessee congregation for several years. However, serpents were handled at Church of God revivals in Tennessee on at least two occasions after that date (Dalley, 1921; Beard, 1924).

Hensley's time with the Church of God ended in 1922, ten years after becoming a member; he resigned his ministerial credentials because of unstated family problems and relapsed into a lifestyle that predated his serpent-handling days (Burton, 1993; Conn, 1996). He became increasingly estranged from his wife, Amanda, and their seven children, and by the end of March 1923 he was arrested on charges of moonshining, which resulted in a sentence to a county workhouse near Chattanooga (Burton, 1993). While sent on a errand as a trustee, he fled and escaped custody, eventually arriving at his sister's residence in Ohio. Shortly thereafter, he reclaimed salvation and resumed his practice of "preaching, holding revivals, and faith healing" (Burton, 1993, p. 44). Divorced from Amanda by late 1926, he took a second wife, Irene Klunzinger, only a few months later and spent the next several years in various cities in northeastern Ohio. Never being consistent at work, Hensley failed to provide sufficiently for his new wife and the two children who were born, yet preached all the while wherever possible.

By 1932 Hensley moved his family back to the Appalachian region, this time to Pineville, in eastern Kentucky, where he began the East Pineville Church of God and served as pastor (Kane, 1979). It was from this vantage point that he made evangelistic tours through eastern Kentucky, southwestern Virginia, and other Appalachian states and as far south as Florida, introducing serpent handling and "proselytizing" converts to the practice from among miners and farmers—most with Holiness-Pentecostal backgrounds—with significant success. On one occasion in Norton, Virginia, more than five hundred "followers" were reported to have been present, many of whom participated with Hensley in the taking up of serpents (Burton, 1993). While preaching in 1936 from a tent in Bartow, Florida, he drew a crowd of more than seven hundred, not only from among the religiously interested but also from various press and camera reporters who were intrigued by his practice of serpent handling (Kane, 1979).

Burton (1993) stated that in preaching of the Mark 16 sign to prospects, Hensley would assert that it demonstrated a modern-day example of God's deliverance for his children. According to Hensley, serpent handling was "a modern manifestation of Old Testament deliverance by the Lord, such as Daniel from the lion's den, the three Hebrew children from the fiery furnace, and Jonah from the belly of the whale: 'But you don't know that,' he said. 'That was before your time. I'll show you something in your time. I'll show you how to handle a rattlesnake, and you all know the result of rattlesnakes'" (Burton, 1993, pp. 45–46). For many people who were daily challenged by the difficulty of mountain life, such preaching with live demonstration was certainly convincing—especially when combined with the fact of Hensley's small frame, quiet disposition, and personal friendliness with the crowds.

In the midst of such enthusiasm, there were always some present who would join with Hensley in the handling, and inevitably some were bitten—and even died. Such was the case of twenty-seven-year-old Alfred Weaver, who attended the Bartow, Florida, meeting:

> When the power fell . . . Weaver . . . reached into one of the two snake boxes and came out with a rattler hanging from his hand, its fangs deeply embedded in his flesh. He flung it to the ground and again attempted to pick it up. The snake struck him on the wrist. In a few moments, Weaver lost consciousness and fell into the arms of two men behind him. Devotees carried the stricken man out of the tent. Revived by the night air, Weaver started to walk about and shout praises of the Lord, saying God would not let him die. (Kane, 1979, p. 62)

Taking the young man to a fellow worshiper's home, Hensley, along with other believers, prayed for his healing. Explaining that handlers bitten far worse had recovered, Hensley assured the concerned that Weaver, who had refused medical aid, would live. Despite this encouragement and the victim's professed faith, the young convert died the following day. Hensley later gave testimony before a coroner's jury, which deliberated only minutes before declaring Weaver's death a result of his "personal carelessness." This event, however, touched off concern in Bartow and resulted in the adoption of a city ordinance prohibiting such demonstrations of religious faith. As a result, Hensley closed the meeting and left town. This local action in Florida was an omen of legal problems for serpent handlers yet to come (see Kane, 1979; Kimbrough, 1995/2002).

After the move to Kentucky in the early 1930s, two more children were born into the Hensley family, a complication that brought further difficulties to a man who had not fared well in domestic responsibilities (Burton, 1993). As in his previous marriage, such tendencies were a point of contention with his second wife and were fueled by his frequent absences on evangelistic excursions throughout the Southeast. After briefly relocating first to Duff, Tennessee, in late 1941 and then to Evansville, Indiana, he and Irene separated. They reconciled a short time later and then returned to Pineville, Kentucky, in 1942. After only a year, however, the family disintegrated, resulting in Hensley's return to Birchwood, Tennessee, near Grasshopper, and the family's move to Chattanooga. It was here, in 1944, that Irene died, leaving the children distributed, ironically, among family members from Hensley's first marriage—a situation that seems to have worked out surprisingly well. Hensley paid his final respects to Irene as she lay in state but then returned to evangelism, having no further contact with his family.

The practice of serpent handling in the Grasshopper area had abated with Defriese's near-fatal experience in 1919 (Collins, 1947). Several attempts to revive it had been initiated through the years, though none were successful for any sustained period, most likely because of rejection by the community and the more mainstream Pentecostal churches of the area (Burton, 1993). Hensley, now blemished among Holiness believers by a suspicious family history, attempted with little success to revive the work. In late spring 1943, however, Raymond Hayes, a staunch convert of Hensley's from Kentucky, arrived in Grasshopper—Bible and serpents in hand—with the same kind of fervor that had kindled Hensley himself some thirty-four years earlier (Collins, 1947). Preaching the sign as a requirement for heaven, he and Hensley saw backsliders of yesteryears repent and new converts enlist to reestablish the practice in the community under the name the Dolly Pond Church of God with Signs Following. Weekend services in the roughly constructed building were filled to capacity with the faithful, the gainsayers, and the religiously curious—all eager to witness demonstrations of the third sign of Mark 16.

After the rebirth of the church in Grasshopper, leadership responsibilities were given over to young Tom Harden, whose father had been among the first area converts of Hensley's decades earlier (Collins, 1947). For the next two years, the group generated notable interest from outside the community through Lewis F. Ford, a young truck driver who through his public witness was indirectly responsible for drawing media attention to Dolly Pond. In short order, photographs and reports of serpent handling were published over the wires of the Associated Press, giving the small community outside of Chattanooga national visibility. In fall 1945, however, local opposition to the church emerged with Ford's own death by snakebite when attending a brush arbor service in Daisy, Tennessee, and then escalated with the snakebite death of Clint Jackson near Daisy only a few months later—the consequences of which factored into legal action by the state against serpent handling. Despite the law, the faithful continued to practice their religious beliefs.

Hensley continued his evangelistic work in the Tennessee region, often having skirmishes with the law over his religious practices (Burton, 1993). By 1946 he had a third marriage with the widow Inez Riggs Hutcheson, a union that lasted only six months because—according to her son—"George was not the kind of person Inez thought he was" (Burton, 1993, p. 55). Nevertheless, generally known as a "good, gentle, [and] sincere man" (p. 58), he enthusiastically continued his preaching and serpent handling in an itinerant fashion. By 1951 he had married a fourth and final time to Sally Moore Norman in Chattanooga; Sally joined him on his evangelistic campaigns throughout the Southeast.

After moving to Albany, Georgia, Hensley held meetings on both sides of the Georgia/Florida state line (Burton, 1993). It was at a gathering in Altha, Florida, that he would meet his death. For three weeks no serpents had been handled until a large five-foot rattlesnake was brought in on Sunday afternoon. After handling the serpent for several minutes, Hensley was struck on the wrist with a bite that proved fatal after several hours of intense agony. At the end of his suffering, he was reported to have said, "The snake would not have struck—if fear had not come over someone here" (Burton, 1993, p.57). With that, the man who possibly had more influence on the serpent-handling tradition than any other single individual let out his last breath at age seventy-five—the date, July 24, 1955. In his lifetime, Hensley claimed to have been bitten as many as 446 times; his death, brought about by this last bite, was ruled a suicide by the Calhoun County sheriff (Burton, 1993, p. 57).

According to his grandson, the last twenty-five years of Hensley's life were spent at home in eastern Kentucky, though he traveled constantly over several other states of the Appalachian region—Virginia, North Carolina, West Virginia, Tennessee, Georgia, and Florida (Burton, 1993). For most of his ministry, he remained transient, preaching the doctrine of serpent handling and inspiring followers almost everywhere he went.

We have purposely included Hensley's domestic difficulties in this historical review of what has been described as his "checkered career" (Conn, 1996, p. 168). A faith tradition that persists by pointing to its legitimacy in a sacred text, however, cannot be dismissed based on exceptions taken to its major leaders. If this were indeed the case, a closer look at some key figures in the rise of Pentecostalism itself— B. H. Irwin, Charles F. Parham, Agnes N. Ozman, C. B. Cashwell, Aimee Semple McPherson—would cast doubt on the legitimacy of the larger movement (see Synan, 1997; MacRobert, 1988). In fact, most members of contemporary serpent-handling churches we have interviewed possess no personal knowledge of Hensley or his role in the history of the tradition. More to the point, though, it is sufficient to note that despite social rejection and dismal forecasts by early researchers (La Barre, 1962/1974; Nichol, 1966), serpent-handling churches have indeed emerged and survived, and may continue to do so as long as people take as literal the reading of a text that models for them an experience of God that gives purpose and meaning to life.

Hensley became a minister in the Church of God at a fortuitous time in its historical development and wielded a major influence in the practice and spread of serpent handling. It will be our task, from this point, to use a wider lens in placing George Went Hensley within a tradition that not only denied his credentials but also came to deny the endorsement of the religious ritual so much associated with his name.

CHAPTER 4

Serpent Handling Endorsed by the Church of God

The contemporary serpent handlers of Appalachia trace their roots, as most Pentecostals do, to the Holiness tradition and to what became one of the major Pentecostal denominations, the Church of God. Indeed, while serpent-handling churches have different names, most of their names begin with or include the phrase "Church of God." For instance, Jimmy Morrow's church is the Edwina Church of God in Jesus Christ's Name, and the church once located at Carson Springs was the Holiness Church of God in Jesus' Name, a name shared by churches at Sand Hill and Big Stone Gap, Virginia, and elsewhere in Appalachia.[1] That the mainstream denomination, the Church of God, currently minimizes and even denies its earlier endorsement of serpent handling is something that serpent handlers are keenly aware of and resent. They insist that they are the true followers of the Gospel, including, of course, Mark 16:17–18. To make sense of the serpent-handling history, we make use of what sociologists refer to as church-sect theory. But first we need to make a clarification concerning the Church of God and its sister church, the Church of God of Prophecy, both of which practiced serpent handling with significant frequency in the first half of the twentieth century.

THE CHURCH OF GOD AND THE CHURCH OF GOD OF PROPHECY

As mentioned previously, the Church of God and the Church of God of Prophecy share a common ancestry. The Church of God emerged as a small Holiness sect toward the end of the nineteenth century but made no significant progress in terms of sustained growth until the arrival of A. J. Tomlinson in 1903 (Conn, 1996; Stone, 1977). The fledgling group soon made notable gains in membership through Tomlinson's hands-on leadership and the Pentecostal-charismatic evangelism he inspired. However, dissention arose over his direct approach to church governance and escalated in summer 1923 with his impeachment and dismissal as General Overseer by the governing board of appointed Church Elders at a special meeting (Williamson, 1999). Not surprisingly, this development led to a division within the church involving the majority who supported the Elders and less than a third of the membership and clergy who supported Tomlinson. The fifty-eight-year-old Tomlinson continued as General Overseer with the small faction that followed him after his departure from the Church of God, and the group later became known as the Church of God of Prophecy.

As we shall soon see, a preponderance of evidence exists that serpent handling was embraced for a time by the Church of God; however, we also have found evidence that Tomlinson's Church of God of Prophecy also practiced the handling of serpents through the 1920s and on into the 1930s in its official periodical, the *White Wing Messenger* (see Williams, 1923; Anderson, 1924, 1925; Stover & Keffer, 1925; Gaddy, 1926; Shults, 1933; Ballard, 1933; Chavies, 1937; Priest, 1938; Sullivan, 1938). Although no specific accounts of serpent handling were discovered in the *White Wing Messenger* after 1938, the leadership of the Church of God of Prophecy continued to strongly defend and encourage the practice.

For example, in 1945, then–General Overseer M. A. Tomlinson, the youngest son of A. J. Tomlinson, was editor of the *White Wing Messenger* and most likely wrote the lead article, "Signs Following Believers." The opening paragraph boldly states:

> The Church of God [of Prophecy] stands for the whole Bible rightly divided. We accept it all just as it reads. We don't leave out anything in the blessed Book. Then we take the New Testament as our only rule of faith and practice, government and discipline. In the New Testament are the signs that follow believers. They are one of our teachings made prominent and I believe they are an important part. Of course all the Bible is important, but when we think what the signs meant to the early Church, then I feel they are of vast importance in these last days. (Tomlinson, 1945, p. 1)

In continuing, Tomlinson called attention to the fact that *all* the five signs were important, had been practiced by the disciples of Jesus, and were to follow those who believed in Christ in the present day. In stressing the validity and effects of serpent handling in particular, he went on to say:

Some people will accept the new tongues, casting out devils and . . . laying hands on the sick, but they want to make the clause that refers to the
serpent read like the one about the deadly thing, but the Scripture still
reads "they shall take up serpents." It doesn't say if we pick up a serpent
accidentally, it won't hurt us. God has been glorified and people blessed
more times than one in these last days by the handling of serpents. When
the enemy has been raging against us and snakes have been brought to our
services, God has manifested His power through His children and the serpents were taken up and many times they were as gentle as any pet. Even
when they have injected their venom into the flesh of God's children, no ill
effects were suffered. We do not make a show of taking up serpents, but if
they are brought to us and God's power is present to manifest this sign that
follows believers, then we give God the glory for it. (Pp. 2, 4)

Thus it appears that the leadership of the Church of God of Prophecy
strongly endorsed and defended the handling of serpents as a legitimate
sign among its members well into the 1940s and even beyond.

On at least two later occasions, M. A. Tomlinson acknowledged serpent handling as an important sign that followed believers. For
instance, a decade later he wrote an article that emphasized the need for
demonstrations of God's power in the Church of God of Prophecy as
evidence of divine sanction when declaring the *true* interpretation of the
Bible to others (Tomlinson, 1956). As examples of the commonality of
these events, he recalled, "Some times the power would fall upon only a
few so they would dance, leap, shout, talk in tongues, handle serpents
and fire, and other times it would fall upon scores and even hundreds in
large congregations" (p. 2). Three years later, Tomlinson (1959) began
an article with a quotation from Mark 16:15–20, after which he
emphasized that "signs following believers" was among the prominent
teachings of the Bible as set forth by the Church of God of Prophecy. In
their defense, he proclaimed, "That these signs shall follow believers
and the preaching of the Word is clearly set forth in the Scriptures. If
one is to eliminate this point of doctrine, he might as well eliminate the
Scriptures which teach justification, regeneration, sanctification, divine
healing or any of the others" (Tomlinson, 1959, p. 2). With regard to
the lack of biblical accounts concerning some signs, he admitted:

Paul's experience with the serpent is the only such incident recorded in the
New Testament, and there is no direct reference to anyone drinking any
deadly thing and failing to suffer harm from it. However, this cannot be
taken as an indication that these signs were not also prevalent along with
the ministry of the apostles in the early Church. The Scripture definitely
states that after the ascension of Jesus the disciples went everywhere—

throughout the known world—preaching the Word and the Lord worked with them confirming the Word with signs following believers. Since this record follows so closely in the Scripture the words of Jesus with regard to the signs that would follow, it leaves little doubt that *all of the signs* mentioned were in evidence in the early Church. (P. 14; emphasis added)

Although Tomlinson argued that the confirmation of the Word with signs following was as important for modern believers as for the apostles in biblical times, he firmly declared that it is God who is to confirm the signs and not the believer. Just as there was no need for a minister to carry around "invalids and people who need healing" for the sign of healing to be verified, there was no need for one "to carry serpents and deadly poisons with him in order to prove to the world that he is a believer" (p. 14). Rather, said Tomlinson, it was Jesus who was to confirm the Word with signs—not believers themselves.

Although it is clear that the Church of God of Prophecy endorsed serpent handling past the mid-twentieth century, there is little documentation to support that it was practiced widely. We found only eight articles in the *White Wing Messenger* that reported specific events of serpent handling (Williams, 1923; Stover & Keffer, 1925; Gaddy, 1926; Shults, 1933; Ballard, 1933; Chavies, 1937; Priest, 1938; Sullivan, 1938). There are at least three reasons that serpent handling may not have been as widely practiced—or at least as widely reported—in the Church of God of Prophecy, although there is good reason to suspect that it may have occurred in some quarters as late as the early 1960s. First, the church was considerably smaller after the dissension of 1923; some estimates claim that less than one-third of the Church of God membership followed A. J. Tomlinson after his dismissal as General Overseer (Stone, 1977; George, 1987; Williamson, 1999). A significant reduction in troops might mean that there were simply fewer people who handled serpents among the ranks.

The second reason, which may be more telling, is that, based on *White Wing Messenger* articles at large, A. J. Tomlinson shifted the focus of his ministry toward establishing a strong centralized government to solidify his base and, as a result, became strangely quiet on the topic of serpent handling after 1923. With his sudden expulsion from the Church of God, there no doubt came widespread confusion among its members, who did not fully understand the events surrounding the departure of their influential leader of two decades. Thus proselytizing and rebuilding a church membership, which sometimes involved legal disputes over both general and local assets, became major occupations for Tomlinson and his small band of followers in the decades following 1923 (Williamson, 1999). All this may have left little time for concern with serpent handling. Twenty years after his ouster, Tomlinson led what eventually became known as the Church of God of Prophecy to a worldwide membership greater than that of the Church of God itself at the time of the 1923 dissension, which was a consuming occupation of time for the leader.

The third reason for the scarcity of serpent handling is the fact that the Church of God of Prophecy eventually came to have the same concern as its sister church, the Church of God—achieving denominational status. Although M. A. Tomlinson defended serpent handling as late as 1959, after 1938 actual reports of serpent handling events were not found in the *White Wing Messenger*. Pages in the periodical became increasingly filled with progress reports on church membership gains, announcements concerning acquisitions of more modern church facilities and new properties, and strides made in international evangelism. The Church of God of Prophecy saw itself as an exclusive institution with a divine mandate to attract members throughout the world—something that would be unlikely to occur if the dangerous practice of serpent handling were to continue. For these reasons, the analysis in the remainder of this chapter is based on serpent handling that took place only in the Church of God, as reported in the more numerous accounts in the *Evangel*. However, the same dynamics that led to the eventual rejection and demise of serpent handling in the Church of God also surely apply to the Church of God of Prophecy. It is simply that the *Evangel* gives us much more data.

However, before we focus on the history of serpent handling in the Church of God, we want to note that recent critical studies of the longer ending of Mark support the thesis that while it is most likely that Mark 16:9–20 was added in the second century, this "longer Mark" was accepted as canonical by the Catholic Church and was never excluded from any Protestant Bible (Kelhoffer, 2000; Thomas & Alexander, 2003). Furthermore, as Kelhoffer (2000, pp. 346–88) has carefully documented, it was precisely because non-Christian religious movements were gaining status by handling serpents in the context of numerous references to serpents in Greco-Roman culture that the unknown author of the "longer Mark" included the handling of serpents as one of the signs that believers in Christ also could accomplish. Pentecostal theologians are beginning to urge the Pentecostal tradition to restore Mark 16:17–18. Thomas and Alexander (2003, p. 147), who rely heavily on Kelhoffer's (2000) masterful study, urge "those within the Pentecostal tradition to reappropriate this most significant passage [Mark 16:9–20] in the articulation of contemporary Pentecostal theologies." Likewise, Kelhoffer (2000, p. 416) notes that while it is not conclusive that early Christians actually handled serpents, the twentieth-century praxis of handling serpents received its legitimate justification from the longer Mark. Thus as the Church of God struggled to follow all signs specified in Mark 16:17–18, they were following in the footsteps of the early Christians who believed in and witnessed what for them were miraculous signs and wonders. To more fully appreciate the serpent-handling history in the Church of God and the path it followed, we must now introduce church-sect theory.

THE BACKDROP OF A MODIFIED CHURCH-SECT THEORY

Despite criticism, empirical researchers continue to find church-sect theory useful for explaining a counterintuitive fact: It is precisely the religious organizations that social scientists predicted would decline that have grown and have experienced continued vitality. These "conservative" churches, with their strict demands, doctrinal specificity, and high-cost participation, continue to flourish, whereas the more "liberal," doctrinally open, scientifically compatible, and low-cost participation churches continue to decline. Although the history of this generalization is well known, the precise parameters of this debate are not the concern of this chapter (see Hood, Spilka, Hunsberger, & Gorsuch, 1996, pp. 300–337). We only wish to summarize here, at the start, a few empirical generalizations of church-sect theory to provide a matrix within which we shall explore our larger concern: the abandonment of serpent handling by the Church of God and the practice's subsequent continuation by small churches in Appalachia—that is, the differential maintenance and growth of religious organizations relative to their acceptance and rejection of high-cost behaviors. As we shall see, the emergence of bites that maimed and killed believers is an obvious high-cost behavior Pentecostal denominations could ill afford to continue to support as they entered the mainstream.

We focus first on four generalizations well supported in church-sect literature. First, we shall ignore the considerable effort to refine church-sect theory based purely on conceptual terms. Despite the value of such approaches, Welch (1977, p. 127) has noted, "Few existing sect classification schemes—both unidimensional and multidimensional varieties—are able to offer true discriminatory power when put to the empirical test." Second, at the empirical level, we accept the strategic wisdom of operationally defining "sects" in terms of their degree of tension with the larger culture. This operationalization started with Johnson's (1963, p. 542) claim that churches (denominations) have much less tension with the larger culture than do sects. Stark and Bainbridge (1979, 1985) continued to refine the operationalization of "tension" in terms of the degree of difference from, antagonism with, and separation from the larger culture. In this sense, serpent-handling churches (as they identify themselves) are best defined within church-sect theory as sects. Hence, where appropriate, we refer to them in this chapter as sects without any disrespect but simply for theoretical clarification.

Third, scholars most recently have used the operationalization of "tension" to link church-sect theory with rational choice theory and a free religious market economy. This assumes that religious organizations compete for "market share" and must appeal to individuals who make rational choices as to which organization they will join. For instance, Finke and Stark (2001, p. 177) have observed that participation in religious organizations follows a bell-shaped curve. Organizations at either end of the curve can gain membership only by moving toward the center. Thus *increasing* tension can facilitate growth in religious organizations in extremely low tension with the larger culture, whereas *decreasing* tension can facilitate growth in organizations in extremely high tension with the larger culture. To this, we add that those organizations seeking to sustain their status (e.g., not grow) can do so by maintaining their distinctive tension, or lack thereof, with the larger culture. It is the maintenance of religious sects over time that often is ignored by social scientists in view of their concern with churches that appear more successful, insofar as success is measured by growth. However, it also is important to recognize that as some sects grow by abandoning high-cost behaviors, a residual group that maintains these behaviors survives—although it may be seen as less successful when emphasis is on growth rather than survival. The contemporary serpent-handling churches of Appalachia maintain the high-cost behavior of handling serpents that assures their survival as small sectarian groups, as it prohibits their likelihood of ever achieving major denominational status. These sects remain of interest precisely because they do not abandon the practice whose high cost, in terms of both physical maiming and death, assures their persistence even in the face of laws that make the practice illegal. A good example is the controversy surrounding two deaths at the Carson Springs, Tennessee, church and the persistence of serpent handling despite legal and other pressures to abandon the practice (Kimbrough & Hood, 1995). Indeed, the existence of laws against serpent handling simply add to the high cost of membership with its limited but intense appeal to a small share of the religious market (Finke & Stark 2001, p. 177). Serpent-handling sects persist not despite the laws against them but precisely because of these laws (Kimbrough & Hood, 1995).[2]

Finally, as Dittes (1971) has noted in a too often ignored article, both church-sect theory and intrinsic-extrinsic theory have had long histories of mixing evaluative and empirical claims. The notion is that just as intrinsic religion is more "mature" than extrinsic religion, sects are more "pure" than churches. By focusing on operational criteria of various tensions between religious organizations and the cultures in which they exist, the evaluative issues are minimized. For instance, we do not equate "sect" with more "conservative" or denomination with more "liberal" classifications. Niches of activist liberal groups that are vital can exist and thrive, as both Ammerman (1977) and Wellman (2002) have argued. Likewise, there can exist niches of traditional religious organizations whose "conservative" nature is simply to maintain powerful beliefs and practices that lead not to growth but to maintenance of a meaningful form of life, even if in opposition to the larger culture (Hood, 2003a; Hood et al., 2005). It is this that sustains the renegade Churches of God in modern Appalachia. They are not an arrested form of religion; neither are they to be meaningfully explained by various forms of deprivation (Kimbrough, 1995/2002; McCauley, 1995) any more than mainstream Pentecostalism is explained by various forms of deprivation (Wacker, 2003). Serpent-handling sects share with the more growth-oriented organization that spawned them the same fashion and fervor of belief. They speak in tongues, lay hands on the sick, cast out devils, and accept speaking in tongues as the one sure sign of Holy Ghost baptism and possession. But they continue to do all this while being maimed and sometimes killed by the serpents they handle, a consequence that proved too costly for their parent sect, the growth-oriented Church of God (Hood, 1998; Synan, 1997; Williamson, 1995, 1999).

These renegade Churches of God are similar to renegade Mormon sects still scattered in the western United States who continue to defend or practice plural marriage, a custom abandoned in 1890 by the hugely successful mainstream Church of Latter-day Saints (Quinn 1993). The persistence of these renegade Mormon and Church of God sects is as important to understand as the successful growth of their parent organizations. Today, as with most renegade Mormon sects, the renegade

Church of God sects have a majority of members who never belonged to the mainstream parent organization. These renegade churches have a legitimate place in the history of the Pentecostal movement that is only beginning to be appreciated—as is their persistence as a legitimate, even if highly controversial, expression of modern Pentecostalism.

Because of its association with maiming and death, we take it as relatively nonproblematic that serpent handling is unlikely to ever be accepted as a normative practice within a major denomination as defined by numbers of believers (e.g., market economy models of "religious market share"). To engage in a religious ritual that maims and kills is simply unacceptable to the larger American culture. However, its appeal in the rural, mountainous regions of Appalachia is less problematic (Hood 1998, 2003a). Serpent handling was no small part of the initial appeal of Pentecostalism in this region, in other mountainous regions such as the foothills of the Ozarks, and even in lowland regions where serpents were plentiful, particularly where folk practices supported serpent handling and prepared the way for it to become a religious ritual. The abandonment of serpent handling by a church from which it once received support is less an obituary than a story of survival. Many fiercely independent serpent-handling sects, scattered throughout Appalachia, still identify themselves as the true Churches of God, as we noted above, in defiance of denominations that bear the legal right to that name.

SERPENT HANDLING AND THE CHURCH OF GOD

In chapter 2 we discussed how what were to become the great Pentecostal denominations struggled with textual (biblical) justifications to allow the expression of and at the same time constrain the possible range of emotional manifestations considered as signs of Holy Ghost possession. Eventually, as most historians assert, tongues speaking became the most typically accepted expression and sign of Holy Ghost baptism and possession. Yet the focus on tongues speaking was part of a hard-won victory in which more extreme textual justifications were first solicited and then gradually rejected. Within the Church of God, the various biblical passages used to justify tongues speaking also appeared to legitimate other practices likely to elicit intense emotion (Hood & Williamson, 1998). One of the more controversial of these was (and still is) the taking up of serpents, as stated in Mark 16:17–18: "And these signs shall follow them that believe; In my name shall they cast out devils; they shall speak with new tongues; They shall take up serpents; and if they drink any deadly thing, it shall not hurt them; they shall lay hands on the sick, and they shall recover." The acceptance and then rejection of this sign by a sect that would be a church are interesting, though sometimes debated, facts of historical significance that have yet to be documented. It is to these issues and this concern that we now turn.

The Church of God Acceptance of Serpent Handling

It was at Owl Hollow, Tennessee, which had readily accepted the Holiness-Pentecostal revival begun by the Church of God around 1908, that George Went Hensley was converted to the Pentecostal tradition. And it was at nearby White Oak Mountain, during his spiritual struggle, that he encountered a deadly rattlesnake that he handled through the anointing without harm. On his descent, he began preaching and practicing with strong conviction what he believed all true believers should want to do in obedience to the explicit command of their Lord—manifest all five signs described in Mark 16.

Although we have found no historical records that account for Hensley's precise activities from 1908 to 1914, we can assume that he continued to preach and practice the Pentecostal signs of Mark 16. We do know, however, that by 1914 he had attracted the attention of leaders in the Church of God. The sect itself was growing notably in membership at this time—137 churches and 4,339 members by November 1914 (O'Neal, 1992, p. 313)—through evangelistic efforts characterized primarily by the Pentecostal signs of tongues speaking, divine healing, and the casting out of devils. As discussed in chapter 3, the event that gave Hensley first notice was his handling of serpents in a revival conducted with M. S. Haynes, a reputable Church of God minister, at the South Cleveland Church of God tabernacle (Tomlinson, 1914b). The event caused considerable interest among the members as well as the community at large, such that it was published in the local newspaper (Snakes in demand, 1914).[3]

On returning to Cleveland from church travels, General Overseer A. J. Tomlinson (1914b) learned of the events and wrote detailed descriptions of the revival in the next issue of the *Evangel*. One of his motivations for doing so, however, was that he had recently received a letter from an unnamed "uninformed personality" who had charged that the Church of God was lagging far behind other Pentecostal groups with respect to supernatural manifestations and success in evangelism. Responding to this criticism with pen in hand, he suggested that, in addition to reports

that "multitudes" were being healed, the "dead" were being raised, and
fire was being handled, readers also should consider other evidence that
had surfaced at the most recent South Cleveland revival where the signs of
Mark 16 had been preached. As a response to this preaching, a rattlesnake
and a copperhead had been brought to the services by scoffers. Through
demonstrations of "successful handling" by several members, unbelievers
were said to have come forward with conviction to seek salvation. Noting
that many of the unbelieving had been converted to the faith through this
sign, Tomlinson closed the article with the claim, "All these signs are
being demonstrated by those who are members of the Church of God"
(Tomlinson, 1914b, p. 3). He also warned, however, that believers should
carefully discern proper anointing for the sign and the appropriate context for its manifestation, lest extremism should bring reproach on "the
worthy cause we love so well" (p. 3). It seems clear that Tomlinson's concern was that serpent handling be considered as one of the legitimate Pentecostal signs but not emphasized above others or practiced to extreme.

Through convincing demonstrations at the South Cleveland revival
and the evangelism it generated, the Church of God and its leadership
must have become increasingly persuaded that the literal taking up of
venomous serpents in Mark 16 was as legitimate a Pentecostal sign as
speaking in tongues, casting out devils, and healing the sick. Clearly, if
three of the signs—tongues speaking, the casting out of devils, and healing—were understood as literal practices for Church of God believers,
it made for good theology that other signs outlined in the same text
were equally justified in practice (Hood 1998).[4]

That such was the case is demonstrated by Tomlinson's use of the
Markan imperatives as support for another theological argument—that
biblical doctrine will in fact be revealed to the faithful and should be
received:

> My doctrine shall drop as the rain. His doctrine is good doctrine. (Prov. 4:2)
>   For I give you good doctrine. Nourished up in the words of faith and of
> good doctrine. (1 Tim. 4:6)
>   The word shall in this lesson is the same as the shall of Mark 16:17, 18.
>   They SHALL speak with new tongues; they SHALL take up serpents;
> they SHALL lay hands on the sick, and they SHALL recover. There's no use
> talking against it the doctrine just has to drop down, and if we do not get
> it, it is because we are in the house of some selfish opinion. This is the time
> when the doctrine has to fall. (Tomlinson, 1914e, p. 2; original emphasis)

The way in which Tomlinson used the Mark 16 reference strongly suggests its theological acceptance in the Church of God as a literal imper-

ative for the signs mentioned—including serpent handling. It is of further interest that Tomlinson also gave support to the third sign in two other articles in the *Church of God Evangel* before the end of 1914 endorsing the practice and claiming it as a unique Church of God manifestation (Tomlinson 1914c, 1914d).

That the church embraced serpent handling as a sign is supported by four other observations. First, at the November 1914 General Assembly, Tomlinson stated in his highly regarded annual address:

> The souls that have been saved and the backsliders reclaimed would probably number up into the thousands, judging from the many reports that have come in from every direction. Churches have multiplied, and the dear old doctrine, heralded by the faithful messengers as they ran to and froe *[sic]*, is becoming sweeter and more glorious. Under the illumination of God's love and mighty power many signs and wonders have been wrought in the name of the Holy child Jesus. Many miraculous cases of healing have been witnessed. *Wild poison serpents have been taken up and handled and fondled over almost like babies with no harm to the saints.* In several instances fire has been handled with bare hands without being burned. Glory to our God! Have seen no reports of anybody outside the Church of God performing this miracles *[sic]*. We are beginning to surpass all others in miraculous signs and wonders. The magicians of Egypt could do some things like Moses and Aaron, but there came a time when Moses and Aaron far surpassed them. God is preparing us for the "greater things." We are on the run. Let us continue to humble ourselves and increase our speed until God's church will shine out with so much more brilliancy than anything else in the world that all men will, like Jannes and Jambres, acknowledge it is the "Finger of God." (Tomlinson, 1914a, p. 15; emphasis added)

By endorsing serpent handling as a legitimate "miracle" in the church's Pentecostal theology, Tomlinson gave license to its acceptance and practice in Church of God evangelistic endeavors.

Second, Hensley, along with George T. Brouayer, conducted evangelistic services at the 1915 General Assembly outside the main auditorium while other evangelistic services were held inside the building (Tomlinson, 1915, p. 13). That Hensley, the most renowned serpent-handling preacher of the time, was given a platform at the General Assembly, the church's most important annual meeting, lends further support to the hypothesis that serpent handling was coming to be seen as a legitimate Church of God practice. By this time, at least twenty articles on serpent handling in the Church of God already had appeared in the widely circulated *Evangel* (Williamson, 1995; Williamson & Hood, 2004).[5] In eighteen of them—five naming Hensley—serpent handling was regarded positively as a Pentecostal sign with significant advantages for Church of God evangelism.

Third, the licensure of Hensley himself as a Church of God minister in December 1915 (Index to the roster of ministers, n.d.) attests his endorsement by the church and its leadership. This event was some fifteen months after the South Cleveland revival, by which time the evangelist and his serpent handling must have been well known and accepted within the church through both the *Evangel* and his appearance on the program at the General Assembly.

Fourth, there is compelling evidence in the *Evangel* itself that suggests this manifestation was adopted theologically for a time by a significant base of the Church of God membership. In further analyzing the data collected by Williamson (1995), we document (1) the frequency of serpent handling reported in the *Evangel;* (2) the locations at which it occurred and the number of persons who practiced the sign; (3) the identities of ministers involved at such meetings; and (4) the contribution of serpent handling to early evangelism by the young sect. The following is a brief summary of these findings.

Frequency of Handling Reports   Articles on serpent handling appeared in the *Evangel* with notable frequency (table 1). Eighty-nine articles that only reported handling in Church of God services were published from 1914 to 1935.[6] Of this number, 53 were published from 1914 to 1920, with most (13 reports) appearing in the *Evangel* during 1915; 35 different instances of serpent handling were published from 1921 to 1930, and most (13 reports) for this period occurred in 1921; only one additional incident of serpent handling was reported in the following decades, in 1935. Most of the practice of serpent handling on record took place in the Church of God during the late 1910s and early 1920s, although an article supporting the practice as a legitimate Pentecostal sign was published as late as 1943 (Whitehead, 1943). Although it is difficult to assess the percentage of these serpent handling reports in relation to other revival-type reports in the *Evangel,* it is clear that their frequency indicates a notable degree of approval of the practice in the Church of God.

Locations and Number of Handlers   As shown in table 2, the reports were distributed among fourteen states, with most events occurring in Tennessee and Alabama, 18 and 12, respectively.[7] Serpent handling occurred in eighty-two different towns and communities located mostly

TABLE I. FREQUENCIES OF SERPENT-HANDLING REPORTS IN THE CHURCH OF GOD NORTH AMERICAN MEMBERSHIP

Year	Reports	Membership[a]	Membership Gains[b]	Membership Gains by Decade[b]
1914	3	4,339		
1915	13	6,159		
1916	10	7,690	39	
1917	10	10,076	94[c]	
1918	1	N/A		
1919	7	12,341	68	
1920	9	14,606	17	218
1921	13	18,564	190	
1922	6	21,076	13	
1923	2	22,394		
1924	5	23,560	5	
1925	1	24,871	6	
1926		25,000		
1927	2	25,340	3	
1928	2	24,332	6	
1929	2	24,891		
1930	2	25,901	42	265
1931		29,354		
1932		41,680		
1933		46,735		
1934		46,923		
1935	1	49,644		
1936		57,417		
1937		63,229		
1938		55,424		
1939		58,823		
1940		63,216		0
1945		72,096		
Reports: $N = 89$		Membership Gains: $N = 483$		

SOURCE: Adapted from Williamson and Hood (2004, p. 157). © 2004 Religious Research Association, Inc. All rights reserved. Reprinted by permission.

[a] Membership data were derived from Conn (1977, pp. 430–31).

[b] Membership gains associated with reports of serpent handling. These data were extracted from *Evangel* reports.

[c] This number includes an estimate of three members from one report (Henson, 1917), since the number of new members reported was given in the following phrase: "and *some* were added to the church" (Henson, 1917, p. 3; emphasis added).

TABLE 2. FREQUENCY DISTRIBUTION
OF SERPENT HANDLING REPORTED IN THE
CHURCH OF GOD BY STATES, 1914–1935

	States	Number of Locations	Reports[a]
	Alabama	12	12
	Arizona	1	1
	Arkansas	6	6
	Georgia	8	8
	Illinois	2	2
	Kentucky	9	9
	Louisiana	1	1
	Mississippi	8	9
	Missouri	1	1
	North Carolina	9	11
	South Carolina	1	2
	Tennessee	18	21
	Texas	5	5
	West Virginia	1	1
Totals	14	82	89

SOURCE: Adapted from Williamson and Hood (2004, p. 158). © 2004 Religious Research Association, Inc. All rights reserved. Reprinted by permission.
[a] Some reports were of the same serpent-handling events.

in Appalachia, the primary region in which the practice persists. Clearly, this represents a notable distribution of the practice in the sect involving many different individuals. From the eighty-nine reports, it was found that 105 different persons were specifically mentioned by name and were described as participating in meetings in at least one of three ways: by handling serpents, by moderating or preaching in services at which the sign was manifested (it is very possible that some of these persons also may have handled serpents at these times, although such was not stated in the articles), or by simply being present at such meetings. An analysis of the data, based on these three categories, found that 41 different and named individuals definitely handled serpents; 45 others were identified as either moderating or preaching in services at which serpent handling took place; and 19 others were named who at least witnessed the handling of serpents in services. It should be noted that those named as handling at some services sometimes appeared in other reports as only moderating or preaching or as being present during handling at other services. For the purpose of the present analysis, however, such persons were assigned membership to only one of the three categories. In addition to these identified persons, reports often stated that "several," "many," "a number," or "most of the saints" handled at these meetings, an indication that scores of "unnamed" others also took up serpents at these events. These anonymous handlers were not included in this analysis.

Identities and Credentials of Participants   What is as compelling as the number of Church of God members handling serpents is the *status* of those who handled them or at least attended services at which handling took place. Among the 105 different persons named in the articles, at least 58 were either licensed Church of God ministers at the time of the reports or persons who would become licensed within the next few years (Index to the roster of ministers, n.d.; also see Conn, 1977, table 44). Among these 58, 22 either were serving as Church of God State Overseers at the time of reports or would be serving in that capacity at some time thereafter—the most notable of these being J. C. Jernigan, who became General Overseer of the Church of God in 1944 (table 3).[8]

At least seven of these present or future State Overseers were reported to have taken up serpents: W. A. Capshaw (1917, 1922; Muncy, 1923), W. S. Gentry (Tomlinson, 1914e), M. S. Haynes (Tomlinson, 1914e), T. L. McLain (Tomlinson, 1914e), J. A. Muncy (1925), L. G. Rouse (Dalley, 1921), and G. G. Williams (Walker, 1927). Although none of the *Evangel* reports specifically stated that an eighth State Overseer, G. T. Brouayer, personally handled serpents, one report that appeared years later (Stover & Keffer, 1925), in the *White Wing Messenger,* after Brouayer followed Tomlinson's exodus from the Church of God, stated that he had handled a serpent and was bitten but without being harmed. Thus he likely was active in handling serpents during the Church of God meetings in earlier *Evangel* reports that mentioned his name. The Pentecostal sign of serpent handling certainly seemed a common feature at Brouayer's own revival meetings (Patterson, 1915; Hagwood, 1916; Brouayer, 1915, 1917a), and even his married daughter, also a preacher, was reported to have been bitten when handling on one occasion (Brouayer, 1917b).

Evangelistic Appeal   The Church of God's acceptance of serpent handling as a Pentecostal sign is further evidenced by the influence the manifestation had on its evangelistic endeavors, particularly in the early years. For example, some young scoffers had heard the pastor of a local church in Odum, Georgia, preach on the signs of Mark 16 (Roberson, 1935). Eager to harass the minister and create a public spectacle, they brought a wooden box containing a large rattlesnake to a later service

TABLE 3. SERPENT HANDLING
AND THE CHURCH OF GOD STATE OVERSEERS

State Overseers Who Handled Serpents at Services/Revivals[a]

Capshaw, W. A.	State Overseer, LA, 1914–15; NC, 1916–18
Gentry, W. S.	State Overseer, AL, 1914–16
Haynes, M. S.	State Overseer, MS, 1915–16; LA, 1916–21; Exec. Council, 1917–24
McLain, T. L.	State Overseer, TN, 1912–13, 1925–27; VA, 1913; 1916–18; NC, 1923–24; AL, 1924–25, 1928–29; WV, 1927–28; GA, 1929–30; Exec. Comm., 1926–29; Exec. Council, 1917–29
Muncy, J. A.	State Overseer, NJ, 1932–34; 1937–38; ME, 1937
Rouse, L. G.	State Overseer, AR, 1933–34
Williams, G. G.	State Overseer, MS, 1931–32

State Overseers Who Moderated/Preached at Services/Revivals[a]

Beard, S. F.	State Overseer, AR, 1930
Coats, C.	State Overseer, IN, 1924–25; MO, 1924–25; LA, 1925–27; AR, 1929; TX, 1932–33
Cotnam, R. L.	State Overseer, OK, 1916–17, 1918–19; MS, 1917–19
Cross, W. H.	State Overseer, SC, 1917–21
Danehower, J.	State Overseer, AR, 1926–29
Fore, G. A.	State Overseer, KY, 1923–27, 1928–29; IL, 1924–25; Exec. Comm., 1926–29; Exec. Council, 1924–29
Gammon, F. W.	State Overseer, VA, 1919–20; KY, 1920–21; IN, 1921–22
Haynes, E.	State Overseer, OH, 1916–21, 1924–36; MI, 1921–24; MS, 1923; Exec. Comm., 1926–32; Exec. Council, 1924–35
Jernigan, J. C.	State Overseer, VA, 1926–28; KY, 1930–36; FL, 1936–39, 1941–44; SD, 1939–40; TN, 1940–41; Exec. Comm., 1944–48, 1952–54; Exec. Council, 1935–54; General Overseer, 1944–48; Lee College Pres., 1951–52; Asst. Gen. Overseer, 1952–54
Letsinger, M. W.	State Overseer, TN, 1920–24; IL, 1925–28; Exec. Comm., 1927–29, 1930–31; Exec. Council, 1927–29, 1930–31
Trim, H. L.	State Overseer, VA, 1914–16
Walker, W. A.	State Overseer, SC, 1916–17

State Overseers Present at Services/Revivals Where Serpents Were Handled[a]

Brouayer, G. T.	State Overseer, GA, 1912–13; NC, 1913; AL, 1913–14; TN, 1914–16; TX, 1916–18, 1920–21; KY, 1918–19; NC, 1921–22; Exec. Council, 1917–23
Bryans, A. H.	State Overseer, NC, 1913–14
Scoggins, H. N.	State Overseer, TX, 1918–20, 1921–24; WV, 1924–27, 1932–35; TN, 1927–30, 1937–40; IL, 1930–32; MS, 1936–37; Exec. Comm., 1930–32; Exec. Council, 1930–35

[a] Information on overseership and administrative service was derived from Conn (1977, 1996).

that was filled to overflowing with both members and skeptics. As one of the young men placed the screened box on the altar, an observer reported:

> God took charge of the rest of the service. The power fell, and personally speaking, I have been in services almost regularly for the past nine years, but I've never felt such great power. It seemed that angels were in and around the altar. . . . Brother Sanders pulled the screen back. The snake was still standing on his rattles, and as he walked back and to with His [sic] Bible in his right hand and prayed, the boy who brought the snake went to him and told him not to put his hand in that box, as the snake's fangs had not been removed. Brother Sanders prayed on. As he came back by the snake, he had ceased his rattling. He put his left hand in, took him out, stood on the altar and rubbed him like a little kitten, placed him about his neck, held him for a few minutes, placed him back in the box and felt no harm. Sinners screamed, cried and stood on benches. Hard-hearted men who had fought holiness for years said, "I'll never doubt it any more." (Roberson, 1935, p. 15)

This descriptive scene of witnessing what was perceived as an awesome display of Holy Ghost power over dangerous serpents was no doubt replicated in many Church of God services reported in the *Evangel* and must have contributed at least in part to the church's marked growth, especially in the late teens and the early 1920s. We might add from our own field research that however one might want to explain the success of contemporary believers in handling serpents, it remains a fascinating event to observe.

Articles describing meetings in which serpent handling occurred often included other information concerning religious experiences received at the services—whether individuals were saved (converted), sanctified, baptized with the Holy Ghost (as evidenced by glossolalia), or baptized in water (tables 1, 4). We found that while some descriptions of these experiences were in general terms—"God is saving people"; "several were sanctified"; "a number received the Holy Ghost"—many gave the precise numbers of these experiences. A summary of these specific numbers finds that 256 were saved, 202 were sanctified, 340 received the Holy Ghost, and 310 were baptized in water.

Furthermore, some of these same articles also reported church and membership gains (see table 4). The revivals and services resulted in the organizing of twelve new Church of God congregations with a combined membership of 287; an additional 196 new members joined existing Church of God congregations. The number of new members gained overall from meetings at which the sign of serpent handling was seen

TABLE 4. EVANGELISTIC RESULTS
AND NEW CHURCHES/MEMBERS RELATED
TO SERPENT HANDLING

Evangelistic Results Related to Services/Revivals Where Serpents
Were Handled[a]

Converted	256	
Sanctified	202	
Holy Ghost	340	
Baptized in Water	310	

New Churches Organized with New Members from Meetings in Which Serpents
Were Handled[a]

Location	New Members	Date	Organizing Minister(s)
Walling, TN	24	1916	J. F. Dover, I. D. Bain, G. Sprinkler
Ladonia, TX	27	1917	G. T. Brouayer
Sevierville, TN	20	1917	H. L. Trim
Point, TX	22	1917	G. T. Brouayer
Natural Bridge, AL	19	1919	J. F. Dover
Lubbock, TX	15	1920	minister unnamed
Nauvoo, AL	78	1921	A. Edmonds
Denmark, AR	11	1921	C. Coats
Pangburn, AR	16	1921	C. Coats, F. Duncan, W. Ledford
Bude, MS	16	1921	G. G. Williams
Maryville, TN	27	1921	H. N. Scoggins
Jefferson Co., KY	12	1922	J. K. Horton
N = 12	N = 287		

Summary

Total of new churches	12	
Total of new members received overall (see table 1)	483	
Total of new members received into new churches	287	
Total of new members received into established churches	196	(N = 483 − 287)

SOURCE: Adapted from Williamson and Hood (2004, p. 162). © 2004 Religious Research Association, Inc. All rights reserved. Reprinted by permission.

[a] These data were abstracted from articles that appeared in the *Church of God Evangel* and are based on actual numbers reported.

totaled 483. To claim that these increases can be attributed directly to the practice of serpent handling would be an overstatement; several factors often contributed to the success of revival meetings: the perceived presence of God; the interest of congregants; the quality of preaching, worship, and prayer; the manifestation of spiritual gifts; and the practice of other Mark 16 signs. On the other hand, to minimize the taking up of serpents among the Pentecostal signs, as manifested in the early Church of God, and to marginalize its significance at that time is to ignore clear evidence to the contrary.

Despite the present Church of God claim that serpent handling was marginal among its ranks, practiced only by a few misguided, fanatical, and extreme members, it seems evident—even if only *Evangel* articles are considered—that this was not the case.[9] Born in the heart of Appalachia and transplanted to the valley town of Cleveland, Tennessee, the Church of God's inherent predisposition to heartfelt religious experience soon discovered a meaningful redefinition in terms of a Pentecostal theology based on the Scripture texts Acts 2 and Mark 16. The church's readiness to accept serpent handling as a biblical sign predated Hensley in its embracing of what were already perceived as direct experiences of various manifestations of God—tongues, healing, the casting out of devils, and demonstrative worship. The Church of God welcomed Hensley's serpent handling into its evangelistic arsenal and persisted in its practice several years beyond his 1922 departure. Hensley was simply a fortuitous instrument, appearing at a critical time in history, who modeled the role of a believer from a biblical text already held central in the theology of this emerging Pentecostal church. Once noted in the text, and observed from Hensley himself, a significant number of Church of God members and its leadership were convinced and followed his example, holding firmly for a time to the practice of serpent handling as a legitimate Pentecostal sign. This adherence provided the believer with a direct encounter with God that had great personal significance—in terms of experiencing the Holy Ghost and demonstrating the power of God to unbelievers in a convincing way.

The Church of God's Rejection of Serpent Handling

Gradually, from the late 1920s on, the Church of God moved toward rejecting serpent handling in its services, forcing those who continued the practice to the periphery of its fellowship and eventually to form independent sects (Hood, 1998; Williamson, 2000). Undoubtedly, the fact that maiming and death are largely a function of frequency of handling became a concern. Thus, as the practice continued, "victory over the serpent was less assured" (Hood, 2003a): members began to experience severe bites, maiming, and death. There is no clear evidence that other major Pentecostal denominations (other than the Church of God of Prophecy) ever practiced the sign. In fact, the Pentecostal Holiness

Church and the Assemblies of God both rejected it as a religious ritual
from the beginning (Kane, 1979; Crews, 1990, p. 91). However, as noted
in chapter 2, they did interpret the accidental handling of serpents as in
accord with the story of Paul. Hence as the Church of God began to join
ranks with mainstream Pentecostals, it discouraged serpent handling (as
a high-cost behavior). As has been documented elsewhere (Williamson,
1995; Hood, 1998), the church never officially repudiated the practice in
its 1928 General Assembly, despite early claims to the contrary by Conn
(1955, 1977) and Crews (1990). *Evangel* articles criticizing the sign did
appear with increased frequency and virulence. The first such article was
penned by S. J. Heath in 1928. His diatribe read in part:

> There is not very much stress upon casting out devils, speaking in tongues,
> and laying hands on the sick for their recovery. But many have gone into
> rank fanaticism, and false teaching, bringing reproach on the Church, and
> disgust to intelligent people over the handling of serpents. . . . I believe
> every gift, and every sign is in the body and God can use men that will
> properly submit to Him, and will do it, but when it comes to using the
> Church of God as a medium to advertise snake shows it is absurd and
> ridiculous. I have seen a few of these displays undertaken in the spirit of
> boasting men, and when bitten by the poisonous reptiles, severe sickness
> and sometimes death has resulted. And again it has caused much suffering
> to the victims, and many times has taken much prayer to save life, then we
> are made a laughing stock to the world and a reproach for the cause.
> (Heath, 1928, p. 3)

From a social-psychological and church-sect perspective, it seems likely
that serpent-bite issues of "severe sickness," "death," and "reproach"
were high-cost factors incongruent with a sect seeking denominational
success. Criticism had been unleashed and opened the door to yet more
critical reviews of serpent handling (Clark, 1934, 1942; Harris, 1949;
Simmons, 1939, 1940).[10]

It was during this period that the Church of God's membership and
social acceptance began growing by even greater margins (Bowdle,
1999; Conn, 1996; Williamson, 1995, 2000). Between 1927 and 1936
alone, membership more than doubled, from 25,340 to 57,417, as
greater emphasis was placed on more mainstream social values such as
education, modern worship facilities, affluence, and ecumenical concerns (Williamson, 1995). As a result of this shifting of focus, values
and behaviors once held sacred by the church—the taking up of venomous serpents, the casting out of devils, the more ecstatic forms of
worship—were now found unappealing and too costly when consider-

ing denominational prospects. Consequently, they were gradually targeted, marginalized, and finally rejected by the church in its transition from sect to denominational status. Serpent handling, a once-significant part of its Pentecostal theology, was eliminated from Church of God practice as early as the mid-1940s and then denied its role in history by the sect that would be a church (see Conn, 1955, 1977, 1996).[11]

For obvious reasons—and as church-sect theory would predict—a sect hoping to become a denomination cannot retain practices that threaten the safety of its membership and hold out potential for injury and even death. While adhering to its propensity for emotional worship, the Church of God abandoned the more extreme practices of serpent handling, poison drinking, and (to some extent) casting out of devils, as other signs in less tension with society and more easily constrained gained prominence, that is, the laying on of hands for healing and glossolalia. Even in a modern society, prayer for physical healing is not problematic so long as medicine also is taken and so long as medical intervention is given immediate priority in the face of life-threatening situations—a curious intermingling of the sacred and secular among contemporary Pentecostals. Neither are glossolalia and other spiritual gifts problematic if restricted to certain contexts and guidelines: "Let all things be done decently and in order" (1 Cor. 14:40 [KJV]). In this case, the mitigating factor would seem to be the degree to which larger social values influence what is considered decent and orderly. For instance, the sudden outburst of tongues speaking in a department store likely would be judged inappropriate by most modern Pentecostals. Thus the safer, less conflictive, and more manageable signs of laying on hands and tongues speaking became the emphasis of practice in the Church of God.

However, what were rejected as the more extreme and costlier signs by the Church of God, in its quest for denominational status, were retained and embraced by independent sects who remain persistent as such to the present day. Holding to these disputed practices, these sects constitute a religious tradition that lays claim to a basis in biblical text that provides them with a meaningful, though controversial, existence as a Christian subculture of "true believers" who continue to live in opposition to and in tension with what is perceived as a compromising, modernist world. Given their unwillingness to relinquish *any* of the perceived mandates of Mark 16, it is not surprising that their numbers remain typically few—from ten to twenty believers per congregation on average. However, the high cost of their beliefs and practices in terms of social acceptance affords them what is believed to be a privileged and meaningful description of character given by Jesus himself as "them that believe."

Our analysis of *Evangel* serpent-handling reports has supported precisely what church-sect theory would predict—that, as an ambitious sect holding values and practices in high tension with the larger culture, the Church of God would come to exchange such high-cost beliefs and behaviors for the enjoyment of success in its search for denominational status and growth. However, what is too often ignored in church-sect theory, especially in its operationalization, is that extreme tension with the larger culture means not only that growth can occur by moving toward less tension (as did the "official" churches) but also that a faith can be strictly maintained and passionately defended by a minority of believers (as do the renegade Churches of God) in contemporary Appalachia. If these churches are indeed "renegade," it is because from the Bible they find so much that guides their life, gives it meaning, and establishes a ritual that survives maiming and death. Truly the signs follow "them that believe." Not only do they believe, but over the years the renegade Churches of God have developed their own theology, something seldom appreciated by those scholars who have studied serpent handlers. This is the first attempt to present that theology in its broad outlines.

ON THE THEOLOGY OF SERPENT HANDLING

A significant justification for the theology of practicing signs lies in the literal interpretation of a text long familiar to Pentecostals—Mark 16:17–18 (Hollenweger, 1972).[12] Referring specifically to this passage, Jackson (1936, p. 3) admitted, "Surely there is not a verse in the Bible that we Church of God folks quote more than this one. We like to tell them that if these signs don't follow them they are not altogether on the Bible plan." From an interpretive stance, perhaps the most resounding case for handling serpents made from this text was by General Overseer A. J. Tomlinson in a new publication of the Church of God, the *Faithful Standard*. In it he wrote:

> And you say that the disciples did not handle serpents? You cannot read of it anywhere in the Bible? I wonder what kind of a reader you are! Doesn't the Book say that these signs shall follow them that believe, and isn't taking up serpents one of these signs? Were the disciples believers, or were they a set of unbelievers like a good many in these days? . . . Jesus plainly said, They shall take up serpents. Who? Believers. Who? Disciples, because they were wholehearted believers, and no one dare deny it. Then they took up

serpents, did they not? "And they went forth, and preached everywhere, the Lord working with them, and confirming the word by the signs that followed." Who went forth? The disciples. Who preached? The disciples. Who did the Lord work with? The disciples. In what way was the Word confirmed? By the Signs that followed. What signs? Those mentioned above, of course. Who took up serpents? The disciples. And who dares to wrest the Scriptures to their own destruction (2 Peter 3:16) and offer a denial? In the face of this plain analogy I would certainly hate to be in the shoes of some who are so bitter against taking up serpents. (Tomlinson, 1922, p. 12)

Clearly a literal interpretation of the text itself was taken into account and thought sufficient for justification of the practice. Four observations of Tomlinson's theological argument are readily apparent: (1) it is based entirely on the Bible as written; (2) it makes a claim for literal compliance with the mandate by the disciples; (3) it recognizes the sign as being a visible confirmation of God's Word brought about by obedient, "wholehearted" believers; and (4) it expresses grave concern for anyone so bold as to distort the "plain" understanding of the sign as revealed in the text—an odious ploy deserving of God's judgment.

This last observation was shared by F. J. Lee (1925), Tomlinson's successor as General Overseer. In addressing the third sign as literally understood from the text, he argued, "I didn't put this in the Bible and I am sure I am not going to take it away for I know what the curse is to those who take from or add to" (p. 2). Even as leader of the Church of God, his statement seemed to indicate that taking up serpents was justified in a literal interpretation of the text. Perhaps the theological argument for the sign can be no more persuasively stated than by Pastor Liston Pack: "Regardless of how people read it, the Bible is still the Bible, and we should leave it just like Jesus left it. I believe the Bible says what it means and means what it says" (quoted in Pelton & Carden, 1974, p. 21).

In denouncing the practice of the sign, Pentecostal historians (Conn, 1996; Nichol, 1966; Synan, 1997) have commonly asserted that serpent handling is a "proof" or "test" of personal faith in God. In fact, Conn (1996) has judged the "morbid spectacle" (p. 170) to be an act of "tempting" God, which, he suggests, warrants condemnation by Jesus (Luke 4:9–12). This view, however, ignores the fact that modern-day sects practice serpent handling only as a response to the perceived command of Jesus—as a simple act of obedience (Hood, 1998). Pelton and Carden (1974, p. 15) state, based on personal interviews with serpent handlers, that the practice "*is not* proof of their godliness. Its one and only purpose *is* 'to confirm the Word'" (original emphasis). Hence obedience—not proof of faith—is the central tenet of the theology of serpent handling.

In a more recent *Evangel* article, Church of God evangelist G. B. Horton (1989) rejected serpent handling on the basis of an exegesis of Mark 16:18. Calling attention to the fact that "they shall take up" is translated from the Greek word *airo,* he noted its use 102 times in the New Testament, as well as its various translations: "take up, remove, take away, destroy, put away, do away with, kill" (Horton, 1989, p. 20). He concluded, "There is no *command* in the passage that the full-gospel believer must take up serpents or drink poisons. It does not state that the believer is to purposely take hold of snakes to show that he is a believer" (p. 20; original emphasis).

However, a close look at other Scriptures in which *airo* is translated reveals that it can in fact be taken as a command (Strong, n.d.). For instance, Jesus spoke an imperative to a paralyzed man: "Arise, *take up* thy bed, and go unto thine house" (Matt. 9:6). To the weary, Jesus instructed, "*Take* my yoke upon you, and learn of me; for I am meek and lowly in heart: and ye shall find rest unto your souls" (Matt. 11:29). To his followers, Jesus made clear that discipleship was a condition of purposive action: "If any man will come after me, let him deny himself, and *take up* his cross, and follow me" (Matt. 16:24) (Bullinger, 1975; Bullinger's emphasis). Furthermore, Bullinger (1975) refers to the fact that the rendering of *airo* in Mark 16:18 is affected by the reading of the entire clause; that is, its structure actually requires insertion of the phrase "also, in their hands" between "take up" and "serpents." Hence a more accurate and explicit translation of the clause might be, "They shall take up also, in their hands, serpents." Even in an exegetical analysis of the text, there seems room for serpent handlers to stake out a theological claim in Mark 16 for practicing the third sign.

If an appeal is made to higher criticism of the Bible, there seem to be additional difficulties for those who would outright dismiss the theology of serpent handling as illegitimate (Hood & Williamson, 1998). Should the latter portion of Mark 16 be considered only an addition to the original manuscript—as suggested by some biblical scholars (Bruce, 1979; Ehrman, 2005; Wuest, 1973)—still the question can be posed as to why a passage that included a reference to taking up *serpents* was incorporated into the text (Hood & Williamson, 1998). Despite the notions of some (Daugherty, 1978; Hunter, 1988a), serpent-handling sects are not unaware of this criticism but sincerely believe that whatever is currently contained in the King James Bible is due to divine providence and must be accepted entirely on those terms as the expressed Word of God (Carden & Pelton, 1976). Even if the debated text is excluded, Burton (1993) has listed various other biblical passages that serpent-handling sects use to support their theology: Exodus 4:3–4; Job 26:13; Ecclesiastes 10:8; Luke 10:19; John 20:30–31; Acts 2:43, 5:12, 28:3–5; and 1 Corinthians 10:9.

Concerning another criticism—that signs were for only the apostolic era—serpent handler Richard Williams made an observation with which most of his fellow believers would agree:

> Jesus told the apostles, "Go ye into all the world and preach the Gospel to every creature." All He did there was tell them to preach. "He that believeth and is baptized shall be saved." Believeth what? Believeth the Gospel those boys preached! "These signs shall follow . . ." Who, the apostles? It didn't say that. . . . [It said] "them that believe." Believe what? Believe the Gospel! The five signs were made for *everyone* who believes the Gospel. (quoted in Carden & Pelton, 1976, p. 161; original emphasis)

What is key in this response is its rationale based on an understanding of a sacred text that stems from a fairly complex and consistent local theology (Hood, 1998; see also Schreiter, 1985). It is one that has emerged from a certain religious tradition through the struggle of its adherents in the process of making sense of their spiritual experiences and one that has been passed on orally with modifications that reflect nuances of personal experience that have emerged to demand theological explanation—for example, the theology of the just suffering a serpent bite or dying from a serpent bite.

What is of far greater consequence for Pentecostals in general—and others who might follow their lead—is that those who would make use of extratextual factors to refute certain signs of Mark 16 must do so from outside their own tradition (Hood & Williamson, 1998). By taking such a stance, however, they themselves become vulnerable to the same types of criticisms in regard to doctrines they too hold sacred—for example, the Virgin birth, resurrection of Jesus, and miracles (see Sheehan, 1989; Grant, 1977; Ehrman, 2005). On the other hand, should the disputed text of Mark be allowed to stand within a tradition, the question of selectivity among the signs again becomes an issue and the matter of a local theology (Schreiter, 1985), one that demands a fair hearing.

In conclusion, historical opposition, persecution, and circumstance have forced serpent handlers to develop a theological understanding of their faith. They would not use the term *theological* but simply refer to a *biblical* understanding. From a sociological perspective, there are other positive functions that opposition to the host culture's wholesale rejection of serpent handling serves its adherents. It seems probable that these marginalizing dynamics have circumscribed boundaries of group identity, promoted membership cohesion, and even cultivated a sense of chosenness by God (see Williamson & Pollio, 1999)—all of which have added to the historical context of the tradition and have served to affect religious experience at some level. In this sense, serpent-handling sects have parallels with the Amish (Hood et al., 2005, chaps. 5, 6). All aspects of cultural history, when taken together, contribute to a certain "throwness" (Heidegger, 1927/1962) into the world of existence. Isolated religious groups seem to feel this most. While people can certainly agree to disagree on the meaningfulness of serpent handling, they cannot deny the serpent handlers' struggle with their Bible to understand what it is God demands of them. As we have tried to demonstrate in this excursion into their theology, serpent handlers have their reasons and justification for what it is their heart desires. Hood (1998) has noted parallels between Pentecostals and Otto's *Idea of the Holy* (1917/1928), in which the numinous both repels and attracts the believer in ways far beyond rationality. While this may be seen an effort to possess the Holy Spirit, our view is that the serpent, as we shall see in chapter 5, is both a sign and a symbol of this effort to be possessed and to be directed by the Holy Spirit. If eighteenth-century "rattlesnake gazing" was as common in North America as one authority on popular religion asserts, it was likely due to the folk understanding of the biblical story of Eve and the attribution of supernatural powers to the serpent (Lippy, 1994, p. 79). In this respect, it makes us wonder how much more powerful an appreciation for the supernatural powers of the serpent is likely to be—especially for those who handle the serpent with a likely mixture of fear and fascination that Otto notes is the nonrational response to the holy. Who is to say that the serpent handlers have not found in Mark 16:17–18 what others seek to find in response to God?

CHAPTER 5

The Serpent

Sign and Symbol

In a tradition with a ritual that poses the potential for injury and even death, it is only natural that outside observers will be curious about it and its sometimes adverse consequences. As we argued in chapter 4, it was the gradual recognition of the dangers of serpent handlingthat led the Church of God and the Church of God of Prophecy to abandon the practice and now to deny that it ever played a significant role in their history. States began to outlaw religious serpent handling precisely in response to the resulting deaths. As the Tennessee State Supreme Court stated in upholding a law against religious serpent handling, "a religious practice may be limited or curtailed or restrained to the point of outright prohibition where it involves a clear and present danger to society" (*Chattanooga Times,* 1975, p. 29). "Danger to society" is often cited as the motivation for legislation against religious serpent handling, even among consenting adults, beginning in the 1940s (Burton, 1993).[1] Whether consenting adults who handle serpents are a danger to society is an issue we confront in chapter 11.The pejorative stereotype of the Appalachian serpent-handling Christian owes much to the infrequent TV news program or newspaper article reporting in detail the recent death of a believer who died practicing the faith. The concern about this aspect of serpent handling has led to the ritual being excised from its context of understanding, sensationalized, and misconstrued (Birckhead, 1993). The notoriety compels persistent interest from outsiders, in particular, with respect to the rare bites and the even more rare maiming and death. For many, it is difficult to understand that such a religious ritual can be genuine participation with the holy.

Serpent bites are of concern to serpent-handling believers themselves. In over fifteen years of continuing field research and attendance at hundreds of services, we have witnessed no more than twenty-five snakebites.[2] In each of these cases, those who were bitten always received special concern from other believers in terms of immediate prayers and support, as well as continued personal contact in the days that followed. This concern also is evidenced in casual conversations, especially with the genuinely curious observer. It is common for handlers to freely discuss details of their personal experiences with bites, especially the more serious ones, and to answer sincere questions. They also talk about others who have experienced bites, again, especially the most serious ones. There are few churches in which one does not notice a missing finger or a paralyzed limb among the believers who have been maimed in the practice of their faith. Contrary to what some might suppose, those with a history of serpent bites are commonly (though unintentionally) ascribed some degree of stature or honor within the tradition as believers who are willing not only to live but also to die for what they believe. Whenever a serious bite occurs, news of it travels quickly through the strong network of communication that links these autonomous churches. Such news becomes a conversation of interest among believers and has a significant role not only in keeping them apprised of the person's condition but also in the reinforcement of what makes the tradition unique and the maintenance of its beliefs.

It is difficult to verify precisely how many believers have been maimed or killed by serpent bites. Jimmy Morrow states, "In a hundred years of serpent handling I know only about thirty deaths in the signs" (Hood, 2005, p. 78). This number is certainly too low, perhaps because Morrow will only confirm the deaths of those he knows personally. Several scholars have tried to compile a complete list of deaths. We have benefited from unpublished lists initially by begun by Kane (1979) and supplemented by Kimbrough (1995/2002). Burton also compiled an unpublished list of deaths. We have used these lists and the results of our own search of various newspaper archives to identify what is likely the most accurate list of deaths available. The list contains eighty-nine individuals (see Appendix 1), all of whose deaths are documented by at least eyewitness reports or newspaper accounts. If anything, it underrepresents the actual number of deaths as it is likely that those that occurred in the earliest years of handling went unrecorded. The earliest documented death by serpent bite is Jim W. Reece, bitten sometime in 1922 (Griffin, 1922). By 1922 handling had been practiced for more than a decade, using the most conservative estimate, and it is unlikely that no person was bitten before Reece. We have verified only nine deaths from poison drinking (see Appendix 2), two of which occurred in a single service in Carson Springs; Jimmy Ray Williams and Buford Pack died after drinking strychnine. Obviously, from a purely scientific perspective, persons who drink poisons and do not die have simply consumed a sublethal dosage. However, serpent bites vary in terms of amount and type of venom, and hence there is uncertainty about whether death will occur from any single bite. In the history of serpent handling, deaths of fathers and sons from the same family as well as husbands and wives have occurred but on different occasions. Melinda Brown died from a bite she received in 1995 at Middlesboro, Kentucky. Three years later, her husband, John "Punkin" Brown Jr., died while preaching a revival in Sand Mountain, Alabama, at the Old Rock House Holiness Church.[3] The facticity of maiming and death is an important aspect of the religious serpent-handling tradition, and its meaning is linked, at least in part, with an understanding of the serpent as both sign and symbol.

THE SERPENT AS SIGN

Serpent handlers are not naive about the dangers inherent in their practice. They understand full well, and will be first to point out, that the passage in Mark 16 provides no guarantee that serpents will not bite— only that believers of Jesus will take them up. Although it is rare, the fact remains that believers sometimes get bitten; they sometimes get maimed; and they sometimes die as a result of handling venomous serpents. Thus the fear of serpents is basic insofar as they are a natural sign of immediate danger. Of course, not all snakes are poisonous. However, natural selection likely favored a generalized fear of snakes, assuring that poisonous snakes, often hard to distinguish from nonpoisonous snakes, will be avoided.

To more fully appreciate the ritual of serpent handling and its possible outcome, we discuss various types and characteristics of the snakes most often handled and chronicle, in Appendix 1, the names of believers who were not successful, from the outsider perspective, in handling them. However, it is important to note that from within the tradition, death from serpent bite does not deny that, in the words of handlers, "the Word is still the Word." Some snakes do maim and kill, which is the natural sign value attributed to all snakes. Of course, the sign value is maximized when the serpents are venomous and have neither been defanged nor milked. And it is only these serpents that are handled in churches.

Serpents Handled in Churches

Based on our field research and interviews with serpent handlers, the most common types of venomous snakes used in serpent handling are pit vipers of the southeastern region of the United States—primarily rattlesnakes and copperheads and occasionally cottonmouths. Although some snakes are purchased from animal dealers, most are supplied by serpent handlers themselves from snake-hunting expeditions or by friends of the churches who happen upon them near their homes or on highways.

The timber rattler *(Crotalus horridus horridus)* and the canebrake *(C. horridus atricaudatus)* are the most common subspecies of rattlesnakes used by serpent handlers. The eastern diamondback *(C. adamanteus)* and the western diamondback *(C. atrox)* are less often handled, since they are from outside the region; they are especially valued among serpent handlers, however, for their more aggressive behaviors and are used in worship if available. The cottonmouth *(Agkistrodon piscivorus)* is thought by serpent handlers to be somewhat more aggressive than the related copperhead *(A. contortrix)* but is handled far less frequently, largely because two subspecies of the copperhead—the northern (*A. contortrix mokasen*) and the southern (*A. contortrix contortrix*)—are more readily obtained in the region. On a few occasions we have observed the handling of cobras. We also have been informed by participants that other nonregional venomous snakes, for example, coral snakes, have been handled on rare occasions. Puff adders and bamboo vipers have also been handled. What follows below is a discussion of the various aspects of the serpents that believers handle in church, documenting their sign value as markers of potential harm or death.

Characteristics of Snakes. The characteristics of each of the species and subspecies of the live-bearing pit vipers mentioned above have been carefully documented (Ernest, 1992). The copperheads are the most docile of those commonly handled. They can reach a maximum length of 135 centimeters. The amount of venom usually stored by this reptile averages from 40 to 70 milligrams—25 to 75 percent of which would be expected to be discharged in a single bite.[4] Since the lethal dosage for an adult human is estimated to be at least 100 milligrams, it is no surprise that only one death has been recorded due to a copperhead bite—that of a fourteen-year-old male, who was not a serpent handler, in an accident (Ernest, 1992, p. 61).

The temperament of the cottonmouth varies according to the individual snake (Ernest, 1992). If unable to escape from a captor or predator, it usually coils and strikes repeatedly. This reptile may eventually reach a length of 189 centimeters, depending on the subspecies. An average yield of venom for the cottonmouth ranges from 100 to 150 milligrams—the same amount estimated to be the lethal dose for an adult human. It also is estimated that at least 50 percent of bites delivered by cottonmouths result in maimed appendages (Allen & Swindell, 1948).[5] The closely related subspecies, the timber rattler and the canebrake, retreat from danger if possible but will strike if provoked (Ernest, 1992). A timber rattlesnake has been documented to reach a length of 189.2 centimeters, though three-year-old adults may grow as long as 80 to 90 centimeters. A typical *Crotalus horridus* stores from 100 to 200 milligrams of venom; the estimated lethal dosage for a human adult is 75 to 100 milligrams. There has been at least one known case in which human death resulted from a wound inflicted by the decapitated head of a canebrake rattlesnake (Ernest, 1992, p. 116).

Although most eastern diamondback rattlesnakes range from 100 to 150 centimeters cm in length, fully mature adults have been known to measure 244 centimeters (Ernest, 1992). Its behavior, when discovered in the wild, is typically to first lie still but then coil and strike when provoked. The venom content of an average adult eastern diamondback has been found to range from 492 to 666 milligrams, based on different studies.[6] It has been speculated that the lethal dose for humans is about 100 milligrams. Victims of a bite from this snake, if they escape death, will usually suffer maiming of some degree to the affected limbs and appendages.

The western diamondback rattlesnake is perhaps the most aggressive rattler that serpent handlers use in their ritual (Ernest, 1992). Once provoked, this snake will coil, raising its head to a striking position as high as 50 centimeters, and often advance toward its captor or predator—presumably for the purpose of improving its striking range. Its length has been known to reach over 210 centimeters. While the storage of venom for a typical adult may average from 200 to 300 milligrams, one snake, measuring 165.5 centimeters, was found to contain 1,145 milligrams of venom—underscoring the fact that the volume of venom increases with size of the reptile. It is estimated that the delivery of 100 milligrams would be necessary to cause death in an adult human. The complex chemistry of the western diamondback's venom renders it more dangerous than most other rattlers, making it more likely responsible for the majority of human deaths by snakebite in the United States.

Striking Tendencies. Two striking tendencies have been observed among rattlesnakes: one for prey and another for defense (Rubio, 1998). When attacking prey, the strike is downward with a twisting motion that deeply embeds the fangs, whereas the defense maneuver is typically initiated in an upward direction—resulting in the shallow penetration of fangs. During a strike, the snake controls through a contraction the amount of venom injected through each fang according to the size of the prey. No single bite depletes the entire venom reserve, and even less venom is usually injected in bites for defense. This may account for the number of "dry" bites received by humans, as well as the improper position of the jaw and fangs in an upwardly angled strike for defense. It should be noted, however, that as practitioners handle serpents, they are often in a position to strike in a downward fashion, as if at prey.

A small number of snakebites at serpent-handling churches have been observed by several researchers (Kane, 1979; Minton & Minton, 1980; Rubio, 1998; Schwarz, 1960; Tripp, 1975)—which seems surprising to many, given the frequency of handling. The actual base rate of snakebite per handlings is unknown, as serpent-handling churches produce the only data of this nature. As we shall see, serpent handlers have offered explanations from their tradition as to why snakebites are infrequent, although from a purely secular perspective there are two interesting studies on this subject.

Concerned with the mechanisms of psychiatric syndromes, Svorad (1957) studied the effects of motion on various animals while measuring EEG responses (only for rabbits). In his investigation he included samples of cats, rats, rabbits, roosters, and lizards *(Lacertaviridis)* and in a special apparatus rotated each subject about its vertebral axis from the zero position of Magnus to 180 degrees. Only the lizards, roosters, and rabbits exhibited a sudden "paroxysmal inhibition" (p. 536), as characterized by a loss of posture and a hypnotic state (based on rabbit EEGs), for significant periods—an average of over eighteen minutes for the lizards. Only the roosters were more susceptible to this phenomenon than the lizards. It is tempting to relate the motion treatment of the lizard and its immobilizing effects to the sometimes vigorous handling of serpent handlers who seldom suffer bites. Before such a comparison, however, it should be noted that though believers sometimes handle their snakes in an excited manner, no observations have been made from our field experience in which believers rotated them in the fashion described in Svorad's experiment. Only on extremely rare occasions—three or four times at most—have we seen serpents held in other than an upright position, and then only for brief moments.

On the other hand, findings from at least one other experiment suggest that snakes that are handled might be more prone to bite. Herzog (1990) studied three groups of juvenile eastern garter snakes *(Thamnophis sirtalis)* to determine how they might react defensively to different types of handling. The treatments were as follows: one group was picked up and briefly shaken by a model predator (harassed group); a second group was taken up and gently handled by the experimenter (handled group); and a third group served as a control, receiving no treatment in handling at all. After three weeks of treatment, a defense test that measured the striking tendencies of the snakes found that the harassed group struck significantly more often than did the control group, whereas the handled group was found at midpoint of the range established by the other two groups. A second part of the study, which reversed treatment conditions for the harassed and the control groups, found the following effects after three additional weeks: (1) the newly harassed control group significantly increased its striking tendencies; (2) the previously harassed but now unmolested group continued its high rate of strikes; and (3) the handled group, which was continued in the same treatment as received earlier, increased its moderate striking tendencies. While various species of snakes clearly differ in behaviors and temperaments, such findings offer interesting considerations in addressing the low frequency of snakebites among serpent-handling churches. Despite suggestions that frequent handling of serpents has taming or calming effects (see Kane, 1979), Herzog (1990) has shown that under controlled experimental conditions aggressive and even mild handling in fact increases the tendency of snakes to strike over time. It is most interesting to note that after the three additional weeks of no treatment at all, aggressively treated snakes continued to strike more frequently—an observation possibly suggesting that all snakes kept by serpent handlers, even those handled periodically, pose an increased risk for snakebite. Again, however, we point out the obvious: garter snakes differ from venomous snakes in various ways, and comparisons between them should be made with care. However, the comparison of venomous and nonvenomous snakes is relevant given that the general sign value of all serpents is the same, even when the erroneous attribution of the possibility of death to nonvenomous snakes is made.

However, Herzog's findings would seem to indicate that the frequent handling of venomous serpents by believers would increase their striking tendencies, not reduce them. Added to this is the fact that those specializing in the study of venomous reptiles (Minton & Minton, 1980; Rubio, 1998) have visited serpent-handling churches to witness their practices and found no satisfactory explanations for why handlers are not bitten more often. Such observations about snakes' striking tendencies among these religious sects are both intriguing and perplexing and add to the study of serpent handling.

The Severity of Snakebite.   It has been noted that three variables determine the seriousness of a snakebite (Kane, 1979). First is the age, size, sex, and health of the victim as well as individual allergic reactions and susceptibility to protein poisoning. The emotional state of the person and even the layers of clothing worn at the time of the bite are factors. Second, the snake itself is a factor in terms of its species type, size, and excitement when inflicting the bite. The condition of its venom sacs and their volume are important, including the recentness of feeding. The severity of the bite is affected by the condition of the snake's fangs and the level of microorganisms present in its mouth. Third is the bite itself, which influences the nature of the wound. The location of the bite is important—a bite on the face, for example, would be far more serious than one delivered to the hand. Whether one or both fangs were embedded, the depth of penetration, and the volume of venom injected are important determinants in the severity of a bite, as is the length of time a snake holds on by its jaws to the area of attack. To these observations, Rubio (1998) added age and health of the snake, climate, time of day, and season of the year. All these factors determine the severity of a snakebite.

Snake Venom.   The chemistry of snake venom is of two types: hemotoxic, which prevents blood clotting and destroys blood vessels; and neurotoxic, which acts on the nervous system, paralyzing muscles involved in the cardiovascular and respiratory work of the body (Rubio, 1998). Rather than think of hemotoxin and neurotoxin as distinct types of venom, however, they are best understood as two basic properties found in all snake venoms in varying degrees, according to species and subspecies. Environmental factors, as well as preferred types of prey, play a significant role in the chemistry of venom. The toxin is composed of complex proteins, enzymes, and polypeptides—all of which contribute to the process of breaking down body tissue in the prey. Pinney has described the common components of venom:

> Among the components found in most or all venoms are: hyaluronidase, which destroys the matrix of connective tissues; ribonuclease, which destroys RNA, the cell's protein-making genetic material; deoxyribonuclease, which destroys DNA, the genetic material of all animal cells; phosphodiesterase, which breaks the molecular bonds of many important cell components; and ATPase, which destroys the cell's major energy-carrying molecule, ATP. (1981, pp. 141–43)

Because the snake can only swallow its prey, the venom's biological effect at the bite, and its subsequent dissolution of tissue, seems to aid in the digestion of prey while leaving permanent deformities and atrophied limbs with those who, like many serpent handlers, survive.

At the site of the wound, swelling and intense pain result from the breakdown of cell membranes and the flooding of histamines and bradykinin (polypeptide hormones that dilate blood vessels of injured tissue) that are produced by the victim's immune system (Rubio, 1998). The disintegration of lymphatic vessels and cellular membranes results in the collection of fluids at the site of the wound, along with blood and plasma that are released by dissolved capillaries—all of which lead to swelling of enormous size and excruciating pain. Acute necrosis may develop in the surrounding tissue and eventually require surgical removal. Uncommonly, pulmonary complications may spread to vital organs, including the lungs, kidneys, and alimentary tract, at which sites hemorrhaging occurs. Depending on the degree of envenomation, an immediate drop in blood pressure may result, causing further difficulties.

Venoms with higher levels of hemotoxin produce symptoms of severe headache, nausea, and abdominal cramping—which are precursors of cardiac and circulatory failure—whereas venoms more concentrated with neurotoxin tend to manifest impaired locomotion, visual and auditory perception, and gastrointestinal functions. Symptoms, in the latter case, are also abnormalities in cognition, speech, and bodily sensations as well as severe headaches.

Although thousands of snakebites are experienced yearly in the United States, it is estimated that only about a dozen on average prove fatal (Ernest, 1992; Rubio, 1998). In one study (Parrish, 1980), deaths caused by venomous animals in the United States were found due to the following: 40 percent by insects; 33 percent by snakes; and 18 percent by spiders and scorpions. In 1959 it was reported that 14 of 6,680 persons who were treated for snakebite died—a statistic that predicted that one in 10 million Americans would die of snakebite each year. The lapse of time between the bite and treatment is crucial; the survival rate is 99 percent for those receiving antivenin within two hours of the inflicted bite (Rubio, 1998). Those bites that prove fatal usually claim their victims between six and forty-eight hours after envenomation.

Snakebite Immunity. Some researchers (Minton & Minton, 1980) have looked at the question of immunity to snakebites. In one study, a total of fourteen interviews were conducted with snake handlers, herpetologists, biologists, and animal dealers who had been bitten from two to twelve times each by venomous snakes—mostly by North American pit vipers. As a result of the bites, individuals experienced various symptoms, ranging from mild to near-fatal. Many of the interviewees experienced severer symptoms from the same species of snakes in later bites—thus no evidence for the development of immunity was found from repeated bites. Two explanations are given for this finding: first, time intervals between bites were too variable for the systematic development of immunity; second, the amount of venom injected with each bite was unknown.

There is other evidence, however, that immunity from snakebite does develop but only with respect to a specific venom that is injected systematically over time (Minton & Minton, 1980). If periodic injections are discontinued, the level of antitoxin in the blood diminishes, leaving the person increasingly vulnerable to the venom. On the basis of this study and the observance of low rates of bites among serpent handlers, it seems unlikely that the vast majority of handlers—if any at all—would develop significant immunity to snakebite. The evidence of maimed appendages and atrophied limbs—not to mention death itself—tends to support this hypothesis. For example, a thirty-four-year-old who had agreed to participate in one of our studies died within several minutes of a serpent bite only five days before the scheduled interview; it was reported that he had been bitten on at least twenty-three occasions prior to the fatal bite. Thus receiving multiple snakebites is no guarantee of immunity from death.

With respect to a handler receiving a snakebite, Hood (2003) has proposed a parsimonious explanation based on archival footage. Simply put, the probability of a bite is a function of the frequency of handling. That is, on any given occasion the likelihood of a bite is low. Most serpents can be successfully handled. However, as one handles more, the probability of a bite increases. Likewise, among individuals who are frequent handlers, there are few who have not been bitten. Such frequency of handling assures a continual and wise understanding of the power of the serpent to elicit a conditioned fear even among those not bitten. There is an evolutionary basis to the natural sign quality of serpents: the elicitation of fear in recognition of a clear and present danger.

The Natural Sign Value of Snakes

Fear is an intense emotion with which serpent-handling sects contend (Hood, 1998; Williamson & Pollio, 1999; Williamson, Pollio, & Hood, 2000), yet fear of these reptiles is a universal human response that has been generalized even to nonvenomous snakes (Mundkur, 1983). Based on cross-cultural studies, Mundkur (1983) has maintained that the reaction of fear to the snake is rooted in a sensitivity to its form and sinuous movement—a genetic adaptation in the human psyche that manifests in particular social behaviors and religious beliefs whenever the snake is involved. Mundkur denies the possibility of an unconscious to nonhuman primates but acknowledges that they, like humans, display a fear of snakes. Based on this observation, he argues against a universal theory of an unconscious to explain snake veneration and symbolism and suggests instead an evolutionary hypothesis to account for the fear of snakes common to all cultures. Emotion is said to be a physiological state of arousal stimulated by a cognitive framework and intensified by the release of epinephrine in the bloodstream. Cultural myths—including those related to animals such as snakes—contribute to such mental frameworks, thus affecting related emotions that may range on a continuum from clinical ophidiophobia to fascination and awe. What facilitates this process is thought to be a complex visual-motor affect mechanism cued to features that come into the field of perception—in the case of the serpent, its limbless shape and sinuous locomotion. Other characteristics of the serpent's mystique that contribute to the cultural cognitive framework are its occasional abnormalities (two heads or tails on a single body), the ability of its body to continue movement after severance from the head, and a generalized potential for danger.

According to Mundkur's (1983) theory, veneration of the serpent resulted from the migration of precivilized humans who eventually developed agricultural skills to survive. The advancement of horticulture necessitated the clearing of land that brought about the flooding of altered landscapes by rain and the subsequent invasion of snakes seeking higher altitudes and drier habitations—often in human dwellings.

Eventually the simultaneous appearance of snakes and certain climato-
logical conditions became linked, which then led to the introduction of
these reptiles into religious rites devised to influence the sun and rain for
agricultural purposes. With an increase of grains came an increase in
rodent populations, which in turn led to an increase in the presence of
snakes, along with a heightened awareness of their unique qualities,
leading to their veneration by humans—that is, their shape, sinuous
movement, and potential danger, all of which persisted in the evolution
of cultures that later emerged. Even to the present day, "the serpent's
power to fascinate certain primates is dependent on the reaction of the
latter's autonomic nervous system to the mere sight of reptilian sinuous
movement—a type of response that may have been reinforced by memories of venomous attacks during anthropogenesis and differentiation
of human societies" (Mundkur, 1983, p. 6). For Mundkur, modern
recognition of such serpentine attributes continues to stimulate cultural
responses that are rooted in a common primordial fear of snakes.

Studies on the Sign Value of Snakes

Laboratory studies have focused on the possibility of a genetic predisposition to the fear of snakes in primates. Joslin, Fletcher, and Emlen
(1964), for example, compared the fear reactions of rhesus monkeys
reared in a laboratory with others reared in the wild when confronted
with a bullsnake and a range of snakelike objects: snake models, ropes,
and tubes. As expected, wild monkeys took significantly more time than
laboratory animals to reach for food when presented with a live snake
and snakelike stimuli and demonstrated significantly more emotional
disturbance. The researchers suggested three possible explanations for
these differences: (1) an aberration of an innate response in lab monkeys due to impoverished environmental conditions; (2) a tendency in
lab monkeys to habituate to originally aversive stimuli; and (3) a lack of
learning experience among lab monkeys that would otherwise result in
avoidance responses to live snakes and generalize to other similar stimuli. Because of the design of the experiment, however, it was not possible for Joslin and colleagues to make final judgments concerning these
possibilities.

   Building on these themes, Mineka, Davidson, Cook, and Keir (1984)
conducted two experiments focused on primate fear of snakes, the first
of which was a near-replication of the Joslin et al. (1964) study but used
wild-reared Rhesus monkeys and their lab-reared offspring as subjects.

The Wisconsin General Test Apparatus (WGTA), which was used in the earlier study, was employed here to present each monkey with a live snake, various snakelike stimuli, and neutral objects in random order. As in the earlier study, Mineka and colleagues (1984) found the wild-reared monkeys took significantly longer than their lab-reared offspring to reach for food when presented with the snake and snakelike stimuli and displayed more behavioral disturbances related to this fear. Another testing apparatus, the Sackett Self-Selection Circus, independently confirmed the findings. The Sackett Self-Selection Circus was a specially designed apparatus composed of a common center cage of hexagonal shape with an entrance into other cages extending from each of its six walls. Five of these six cages extending from the center cage were used in the experiment. One of the cages was used as an entrance chamber for monkeys to access the common center cage. The other four were used as stimuli chambers in which access was gained on entrance for viewing one of the following stimuli: a real snake, a model snake, a toy snake, or a neutral unpainted wood object. Monkeys were free to enter and leave chambers as they chose. Time spent in each chamber was recorded and used for comparisons. To test observational learning theory—that monkeys learn to fear snakes by observing such fear exhibited by other monkeys—a subset of monkeys from the first experiment paired lab-reared offspring as observers with their wild-reared parents as models in a second experiment (Mineka et al., 1984). The first experiment's procedures were repeated in the second experiment for the parents but this time with their offspring in close proximity to observe their fear reactions during the presentation of each stimulus. After a designated number of trials, the lab-reared offspring were then tested and found to exhibit the same types of avoidance and disturbance behaviors as their wild-reared parents. After a three-month period, follow-up testing by both apparatuses found that the fear of snakes learned by lab-raised monkeys from observations of their wild-raised parents had indeed been retained, thus supporting the theory of observational conditioning in regard to fear of snakes for primates.

With respect to these findings, several observations of Mineka and colleagues are worth noting. First, that the learning of fear was acquired so rapidly is striking as direct contact with snakes for the offspring was rare; even their wild-reared parents, who demonstrated high levels of disturbance, had not had contact with snakes during the past twelve years of captivity. Hence such rapid acquisition of fear seems congruent with an "adaptive/evolutionary" perspective, which predicts that although direct contact with such a predator by a monkey would not be a common phenomenon in the wild, mistakes in fast learning could prove fatal. This dynamic also might account for the widespread fear of snakes in humans, who have little contact with snakes, yet acquire a strong fear reaction easily from little exposure and experience. On the basis of this study, it was suggested that various phobias in both primates and humans are the consequence of "prepared" observational conditioning, which seems to be a biological predisposition that can be initialized by observing reactions of high-level disturbance in others (see Mundkur, 1983).

The evolutionary and laboratory studies relative to the sign quality of serpents can be extrapolated to the significant fact that although successful handling is common in worship services, our field research has found there is virtually no longtime believer who has not witnessed a serpent bite, along with its sometimes damaging consequences. In fact, almost all experienced serpent handlers of our acquaintance bear the physical marks of long-term obedience to the practice of their faith, whether in the form of scars, gnarled or missing appendages, or atrophied limbs. Furthermore, virtually all have either witnessed or known of an acquaintance (or relative) whose death was related to a serpent bite sustained while practicing the faith. The powerful serpent-handling families that have handled serpents for three or four generations have deaths from bites. The list in Appendix 1 indicates individual deaths in such influential families as the Browns, the Elkinses, the Pelfreys, and the Williamses, whose last names are heralded across the Appalachians. Just as nonhuman primates are easily conditioned through observation to fear snakes, serpent-handling believers likely have been conditioned to fear serpents. It is the fear of serpents that is the norm among handlers, and the obvious sign value is understood: serpents can maim and kill. Handlers know this, yet they take up serpents, a fact that is not unrelated to the more controversial claim regarding the symbolic value of serpents.

THE SERPENT AS SYMBOL

Mundkur (1983) has noted that the snake has symbolic signification in almost every culture of the world. Since psychoanalytic theory has been used as a basis for studying serpent handlers (Hood & Kimbrough, 1995; Kane, 1979; La Barre, 1962/1974), it is helpful to consider the idea of symbolism first from a psychoanalytic perspective. In a chapter dedicated solely to this topic, Jones (1961) viewed the symbol as an indirect substitute for a primitive idea that had been repressed from conscious awareness by affective inhibition. Symbols are distinguished from metaphors and other poetic figures in that their meanings are invariably unconscious and have failed, insofar as their symbols are concerned, to be sublimated into modifications found more acceptable in society. According to Jones, universal cultural symbols number fewer than one hundred, the vast majority of these concerning the phallus, with the serpent its most constant symbol. Christianity, Jones finds, is rooted in an unconscious concern for a real phallus. With the repression of such affective tendencies, the resulting intrapsychic conflict shifts toward the fusing of related unconscious and conscious elements into a compromise-formation that eventually comes to stand as a symbol for the primitive notions—a sufficient substitute infused with unconscious meaning. Hence the serpent as a persistent cultural symbol is an unwitting equal to the phallus. All other meanings of sexuality related to the serpent are derived primarily from this fundamental concept. That this association gained wide acceptance in psychoanalytic theory is demonstrated by various studies (e.g., Fortune, 1924; Hassall, 1919; Reed, 1922).

Perhaps the most detailed account of snake symbolism related to religious serpent handling was given by La Barre (1962/1974), a Freudian-oriented anthropologist. La Barre traced the origin of snake cults to Egypt and observed that the common role of snakes emerged within diverse cultural mythologies that generally centered on themes of creation, death, and immortality—a blended motif undeniably linked with sexuality. For example, dual phallic functions were ascribed to snakes in their mythological roles as water gods who produce rain and hence life on the earth—a phenomenon paralleled in the rod of Moses that produced water from a rock and sustained the Hebrews in the wilderness. Other phallic qualities, variously abstracted from myths, included the snake's hairiness (particularly in American myths), its tumescent and detumescent capabilities, and its relationships to ancestry, husbandry, and masculinity. For La Barre, the ubiquity of these cross-cultural observations was so convincing as to ask, "Where is the snake *not* a phallic symbol?" (p. 74).

La Barre (1962/1974) pointed to various associations in the Bible of the serpent with life and death that ranged over time from the symbolism of a high god to that of an archdemon. Beginning at the Garden of Eden, the serpent was viewed as the procreator, the teacher, and the punisher, as well as the incarnation of immortality, the phallus, and evil. On the one hand, it was seen as the giver of earthly life and even eternal life and, on the other, as God's instrument of destruction and death.

Despite this plethora of related meanings, claimed La Barre, the real serpent is none of these but rather a symbol of the psychological source from which they all flow—the human father, specifically, the father's phallus. For La Barre, then, the serpent was unequivocally equal to the phallus, as held in classic psychoanalytic theory.

From another psychoanalytic perspective, Eigen (1981) rejected a strict interpretation of the serpent as a phallic symbol for one that is relative to a given context. The structural limitations of the serpent as phallus were viewed as apparent in that, for example, the penis cannot curl like a snake, and neither is a serpent fully extended except when dead and held up by the tail. According to Eigen, the symbolic meanings of the serpent, both conscious and unconscious, are based on the specific field of perception in which it occurs and the particular serpentine qualities most featured.

Relying largely on Freudian theory, Rousselle (1984) compared the serpent handling of Hellenistic Greece with that practiced among serpent-handling sects of contemporary America. A brief survey of early Greek literature found links between the snake and the phallus, as well as heroes who had gained semidivine status after death. At least two Greek cults, those of Sabazius and Dionysus, were observed to have practiced ecstatic serpent handling. While the activities of the first cult are obscure, the handling rites of the second are more well known and center on women who danced ecstatically while in trance states for days with large nonvenomous serpents in hand—an act interpreted as female hostility aimed at castrating male dominance, which met with limited success. Shifting focus to modern times, Rousselle drew parallels with certain religious sects of the American South that were said to take up serpents unwittingly as an ecstatic expression of repressed sexuality. In this context, female aggression observed among the Greeks was thought to be manifested once again in the patriarchal South as women handled serpents until they were "limp as a necktie" (p. 483), another Freudian phallic symbol, whereas the injection of venom through snakebite, and its aura of death, was equated to coitus and the depletion of the life-force. Though the serpent also was afforded symbolism of the Christian devil, immortality, and wisdom, these associations were eclipsed by its link with sexuality.

Other investigations not given to psychoanalytic theory have attempted to describe the symbolic meaning of the serpent. In tracing the origins of snake worship, Howey (1926) suggested that the predominant symbolism of the serpent was that of deity as portrayed in Egyptian hierographs of the "Encircled Serpent." When representing the cosmos in such depictions, the Egyptians would

> delineate a serpent bespeckled with variegated scales, devouring its own tail, the scales intimating the stars in the Universe. The animal is extremely heavy, as is the earth, and extremely slippery, like the water, moreover, it every year puts off its old age with its skin, as in the Universe the annual period effects a corresponding change and becomes renovated, and the making use of its own body for food implies that all things whatever, which are generated by Divine providence in the world, undergo a corruption into them again. (Howey, 1926, p. 17)

Variations of this theme, said Howey, evolved over time with the dispersion and diversification of cultures, though all, including that of the phallus, are rooted in the symbol's foundational meaning of life—in particular, everlasting life. Hence any phallic connotation cannot be taken as an end in itself but only as a certain marker in a greater context of meaning that points toward the essence of life and its regeneration.

Taking careful account of the serpent cross-culturally, Mundkur (1983) observed a wide variety of symbolic meanings, other than sexual, that are expressed through cultural myths and artifacts, including deity, evil, protection, ancestry, and prosperity. At the same time he noted various animals, other than the serpent, that take on sexual significance as cultural symbols—for example, the hippopotamus of Egypt, the fish of Spain, and the mating dragons of China. In some cultures—the Maya, for example—no evidence was found for sexual symbolism of any kind. Hence Mundkur found the classic psychoanalytic view of serpent symbolism far too restrictive. Our analysis of the serpent as exclusively phallic agrees with Mundker's concern that this is too restrictive. Pruyser (1963), in his review of La Barre's (1962/1974) work, went so far as to say that the serpent might symbolize Christ, as well as immortality and the Devil.

Kelhoffer (2000, pp. 346–88) offers an extensive discussion of the Greco-Roman depiction of snakes that includes the common image of a serpentine staff that predates the classical period by a millennium (p. 365). Common examples in the classical period are Asclepius, who often was depicted holding a serpent above his head, and Hermes, messenger of the gods, who carried a serpentine staff. In these cases the serpent is a positive symbol. Asclepius was a healer, and in some interpretations the serpent itself had the power to heal (p. 370). What is significant in Kelhoffer's discussion of snakes in the Greco-Roman period is that there is some historical justification for the linkage of the Asclepian cult and Mark 16, in which both serpents and healing are among the signs that follow "them that believe."

Nonphallic interpretations of serpent symbolism are emphasized by Pedrini and Pedrini (1966) in their critique of poetry from the Romantic period. They deliberately avoided sexuality as a category in an effort to highlight the range of other symbolic possibilities of the serpent. They observed a tendency among the most noted idealist poets who emerged from the restraints of the eighteenth century to employ the serpent in representing a wide range of concerns best understood by five categories of symbols: idealism, the Fall of Man, materialism, man against man (tyranny and injustice), and institutions against man.

Nonphallic interpretations of the serpent are integral to avoiding a purely reductionist interpretation of religious symbols. Perhaps Jung's (1964) definition of a symbol is most useful here. He identifies something as symbolic "when it implies more than its obvious and immediate meaning" (p. 20). This is an important insight, and it is our clue to extend the phallic symbolism of the serpent into domains that directly concern symbols of the tradition within which serpent handling is a religious ritual. We accept Mundkur's (1983) criticism that to make the serpent exclusively a symbol of the phallus is too restrictive. However, a broader use of even classic psychoanalytic symbol theory such as proposed by Hood and Kimbrough (1995) provides a basis for linking the sign and the symbolic nature of the serpent in ways that are nonreductive.

Discussions of snake symbolism rely heavily on analyses of cult sects, folktales, and mythologies (Henderson & Oakes 1963; La Barre, 1962/1974, pp. 65–87; Minton & Minton, 1969, pp. 143–75). Within various psychoanalytic schools of thought, symbols are assumed to contain projections of the body. This holds for private fantasy (inherently symbolic) and for culture conceived as a system of intersubjectively shared symbols. Shared symbols are integral to myth, legend, folktales, and religion. These shared symbols derive from two sources: cultural transmission and the continual possibility for independent creation of symbols, based on the commonality or universality of the human body. These are not mutually exclusive processes since to some extent every myth has objective meanings and private or idiosyncratic meanings, each symbolically linked to origins in largely unconscious body symbolism. It is unlikely that any tradition exists that fails to link the serpent with the penis, even when cultural transmission has been ruled out (Henderson & Oakes, 1963; La Barre, 1962/1974; Minton & Minton, 1969). However, this is not problematic within psychodynamic assumptions. Phallic symbolism can be expected to be as universal as the human male body itself, or in psychodynamic terms, as universal as "Oedipal Homo Sapiens" (LaBarre, 1962/1974, p. 186).

While we accept the possible phallic symbolism of the serpent, we do not accept it in a reductionist fashion. One does not have to accept the total corpus of psychodynamic psychology to employ aspects of its powerful theory of the role of the human body in symbol formation. Only two points need be emphasized: first, body symbolism can activate fantasies involving the total body, including a wide variety of infantile fantasies associated with various developmental stages (Jones, 1948); and second, overt cultural transmission of symbols in legends, myths, and religions can be read as supported in part by the repression of bodily desires that find release in these symbols (La Barre, 1962/1974, 1972; Chasseguet-Smirgel, 1986). A psychoanalytic theory of symbols assumes that once the serpent has been engaged as an unconscious body symbol, it can express every modality of the body (Jones, 1948; La Barre, 1962/1974, p. 94). Given these caveats, we can focus on the least controversial (at least among those who are influenced by psychodyamics) associations with snake symbolism: the penis, the vagina, and death. We then link our discussion of serpent symbolism to our concern with the serpent as sign.

Penis Symbolism

Recognizing the serpent as a phallic symbol helps to explain many of the associated myths. For instance, there are a wide variety of myths associating serpents with water. The use of defanged rattlesnakes in the Hopi snake dance is a sacred means of bringing rain (Minton & Minton, 1969). Furthermore, the linkage we observed between serpents and the ability of Moses' rod to bring forth water (Num. 20: 7–11) is easily conceived as phallic, as is the explicit connection made in the earlier passage of Exodus 4:1–5 of the Hebrew Bible (La Barre, 1962/1974). We also pointed out that other phallic qualities of the serpent are found in cultural myths. For example, the "feathered snake" of the American Zuni, among other things, suggests a postpubescent male penis, as does the claim of "hairy" or "bearded" snakes common in some African cults (La Barre, 1962/1974, pp. 53–64; Minton & Minton, 1969. pp. 173–175). Thus the linkage of penis and serpent is not simply ad hoc if we assume the relevance of body symbolization. The serpent *may* symbolically represent the penis and vice versa.

Vagina Symbolism

That the serpent can symbolize the vagina may be puzzling, but in psychodynamic theories of symbols, opposites are often evoked in body symbolism. Thus it is not surprising that in many traditions the serpent is linked to the vagina as well as to the penis. Perhaps the most common example is that many cultures have variations on the folk belief that menses is caused by a serpent bite that produces a magic wound that periodically bleeds but is never healed (Henderson & Oates, 1963; Minton & Minton, 1969, pp. 188–197).

The symbolic linking of the vagina and the serpent is evident in folktales of various cultures. The Yuki Indians of California believe that the dangerous agent in rattlesnake venom is menstrual blood. Other native Americans, including the Zuni and Hopi, believe that menstrual blood attracts serpents, and the Makusi of Guiana believe that menstruating women attract serpents (Minton & Minton, 1969, p. 191). The Tsimshian and Kwakiutl of the Northwest Pacific specifically identify the vagina with a rattlesnake's mouth (Minton & Minton, 1969, p. 191). Of course, the classic case is the Hindu goddess Kali, the phallic snake mother whose *vagina dentate* (fanged vagina) devours the male penis (Newman, 1955, p. 149). Thus, in terms of psychodynamic views of body symbolization, the dual nature of serpents as both phallic and vaginal is neither problematic nor unnoticed in folktales and myths. The serpent *may* symbolize the vagina and vice versa.

Death Symbolism

Earlier we touched on the symbolic link between the serpent and death. That serpents can be both a sign and a symbol of death has not been properly emphasized. The symbolic link is obvious in two senses. First, sexual fantasies rooted in body symbolism elicit the inevitable link between eroticism and death (Bataille, 1986; Freud, 1961). Frazer (1892/1955, pp. 475–575) considers the biblical snake scene in the Garden of Eden a fragment of an earlier myth in which the immortality intended for humanity is stolen by the serpent. This echoes numerous folktales around the world in which snakes are immortal, as evidenced by the shedding of their skin. Some scholars have linked the origin of male circumcision to imitating this shedding of "snake skin" to achieve immortality (La Barre, 1962/1974, pp. 78–84).

Here we come closer to the central symbol of Christianity, the resurrected Christ and the hope for eternal life. Campbell (1974) documents
the existence of a medieval coin designed by Hieronymous on which the
crucified Christ appears on one side and a serpent-entwined cross on the
other. Jaffé (1964, p. 239) provides a photograph of both sides of this
coin and asserts that the crucified Christ is shown as both man and serpent. For both Campbell and Jaffé, death and resurrection are linked
with the serpent perhaps in reference to John 3:14–15: "And as Moses
lifted up the serpent in the wilderness even so must the Son of man be
lifted up: That whoever believeth in him should not perish, but have
eternal life." Thus the serpent has been connected with intercourse,
birth, death, and resurrection.

THE CONVERGENCE OF SIGN AND SYMBOL IN THE SERPENT

Given that the serpent is both a sign and a symbol of death, it is worth
noting Daugherty's (1978, p. 104) observation that serpent-handling
sects celebrate sacraments such as the Lord's Supper infrequently if at
all. The reason is that their central ritual of serpent handling serves as
the central function of the sacraments of the Christian faith, especially
the Eucharist (Catholic) or the Lord's Supper (Protestants). They do
this, we contend, because of the convergence of the meaning of sign and
symbol in the handling of serpents in obedience to the Gospel of Mark
16. We can move easily between the sign and the symbol by noting two
curious facts.

First, many folk traditions and most primitive cultures believe that *all*
snakes are poisonous. This, as we noted above, makes sense from an evolutionary perspective: the safest survival mechanism is to avoid all snakes,
whether poisonous or nonpoisonous. However, at the symbolic level, the
linkage is easy as death is symbolized by all serpents, not simply venomous ones. All snakes are equally "phallic" (and hence "vaginal,"
"erotic") and symbolic of death. Likewise, persons who fear snakes, even
at the phobic level, tend to fear all snakes, not simply poisonous ones.
Thus normal cultural myths and individual snake phobias, even when
they differentiate serpents at the sign level (poisonous vs. nonpoisonous),
combine them into one category at the symbolic level ("snakes").

Second, as noted above, churches handle only poisonous serpents,
and the serpents are never milked, tamed, or defanged. Thus the serpent-
handling churches acknowledge overtly (as a sign) what is unconsciously

affirmed (as a symbol): to handle serpents is to confront death. The serpent-handling believer enacts in his or her handling a "return of the repressed" (Badcock, 1980; Marcuse, 1955): a willingness to come closer and closer to that primal fear that is released and overcome in the powerful affective expression not of denying the body but of affirming its eternal life (we have more to say about this in the chapters on the content of sermons and phenomenology of handling and being anointed). Serpent handlers, who can be viewed from a classical psychoanalytic perspective as acting out repressed sexuality, need not thereby be denied that this acting out has profound significance for a central theme within the Christian tradition: the resurrection. This symbolic interpretation converges with the sign value of the handlers' choice of vipers—serpents that can maim and kill. Handlers literally overcome and transcend death each time they are successfully obedient to the imperative of Mark 16. Bromley (2007) has recently suggested that "spiritual edgework," a phrase from Hunter S. Thompson that describes persons who use extreme situations, especially those involving the risk of death, to heighten their sense of life, may be applied to serpent handlers. We think that this concept not only is useful at a descriptive level but also is enriched at the explanatory level when the symbol and sign value of the serpent are seen as convergent.

If handlers are rightly accused of emphasizing the sign value of serpents over any symbolic interpretation, they are seldom granted respect for understanding Christ's imperative as they do. To acknowledge that there is danger in a ritual that nevertheless is in God's Word is not to refute what nevertheless must be done for them that believe. This overcoming of death is often approached by those whose focus is purely on the symbolic. While we accept the symbolism of the serpent in terms of death and resurrection, merely as symbol it loses much of its power. It is ironic that those who are most committed to purely symbolic interpretations miss obvious sign values. Perhaps the most telling example is La Barre's (1962/1974) stereotyping of handlers at Dolly Pond, which also rivals Covington's (1995) stereotyping of the handlers on Sand Mountain, Alabama. La Barre (1962/1974) describes the men of the Dolly Pond Church of God with Signs Following as wearing open-neck shirts with the parenthetical remark "(for no Bible text can be discovered which says Jesus or the Apostles wear neckties)" (p. 16). Such descriptions are not only demeaning to those seeking biblical sanction for behavior and dress but also obviously false. In the ten photographs of handlers (obviously not from Dolly Pond) in La Barre's book, all men are wearing suits—and most are wearing neckties! It must be emphasized that sign-following believers follow the signs. Symbolic interpretations of serpents are legitimate scholarly attempts that fail if they deny the obvious sign value. The sign value returns the symbol to its bodily source.

McGuire (1990) has appealed to social scientists to take seriously that humans are embodied and to overcome the refusal to bring their embodiment into an understanding of religious ritual. Serpent handlers affirm embodiment as they both handle and tread on serpents. This powerful ritual, involving flesh and viper, surely accounts for Daugherty's (1978, p. 104) comment noted above. Serpent-handling churches minimize the Lord's Supper in favor of an even more powerful ritual that is a literal confrontation with and overcoming of death. Handlers hold death and life in their hands—a real and a resurrected body. If the serpent does not kill, death has been denied; if the serpent does kill, death has been overcome. There is wisdom in this tradition precisely embodied in the edgework that is integral to those who take up serpents in obedience to their understanding of the Word of God.

CHAPTER 6

Trance States

Tongues Speaking and the Anointing

In the previous chapters we placed the serpent-handling churches in the context of what became the major Pentecostal denominations. The gradual recognition of tongues speaking as a biblically justified sign of Holy Ghost baptism or possession has led social scientists to attempt to explain this phenomenon in other than biblical terms. We address the issue in this chapter in two senses: first, whether trance states are necessary to engage in tongues speaking; and second, with respect to serpent handling, whether trance states are necessary for those who handle either by "faith" or by "anointing." The major efforts to explain trance states have, of course, been physiological. Thus here we focus on possible physiological correlates of both glossolalia and the handling of serpents. Let us first confront the issue of tongues speaking.

TONGUES SPEAKING AND TRANCE

Although studies focusing on trance states among serpent-handling churches have been limited, there is an abundance of research on Pentecostal groups that link trance with tongues speaking (Malony & Lovekin, 1985; Wacker, 2003, chap. 2). The two terms most often used by investigators to describe mental states thought related to glossolalia are *trance* and *possession*. Though various definitions have been offered for each of the phenomena (see Swanson 1978 for an interesting theory), a basic distinction involves perspective: "Trance is the phenomenon observed from the outside, whereas possession is the experience reported from the inside" (Malony & Lovekin, 1985, p. 98). Trance is inferred by the researcher, based on observation and measurement, whereas possession is judged by the individual undergoing the experience and by the tradition according to cultural expectations. Among those who speak in tongues, the culture of Pentecostal theology and experience claims that Jesus continues his presence on earth through the agency of the Holy Ghost, who is received as an indwelling presence and believed at times to possess the individual for the purpose of fulfilling the will of God. Hence possession by the Holy Ghost may not always involve trance, or loss of self-awareness. Since the once-suspected link of pathology with glossolalia now seems no longer a concern (Alland, 1962; Coulson & Johnson, 1977; Gerlach & Hine, 1968; Hine, 1969; Kildahl, 1972; Lovekin & Malony, 1977; Richardson, 1973; Spanos & Hewitt, 1979; Wood, 1965), the major focus of research has shifted to the debate over whether glossolalia requires a trance, or altered state, for its occurrence.

Though several investigators (Cutten, 1927; Lapsley & Simpson, 1964; Sargant, 1949) have linked glossolalia with dissociation, perhaps the most ardent proponent of this theory is Goodman (1969, 1972a, 1972b, 1988), who has concluded that speaking in tongues is an "artifact" of trance states. On the basis of cross-cultural research, she has argued for a genetic predisposition through which the practice of a religious ritual induces an alternate state of consciousness. For her, this religious trance "is the vehicle that does not just transfer the participants to another plane of emotion, but rather propels them to an altogether different aspect of reality, or, as others see it, to an alternate one. A careful look at rituals reveals that *without exception* they contain a signal to the participants indicating that this is the point where they should make the switch to this different mode of perception" (Goodman, 1988, p. 34; emphasis added).

Pointing to the widespread frequency of religious trance—experienced by some 92 percent of small societies in one survey—Goodman suggested it is a normal and often an unconscious event in Western cultures, especially when institutionalized as a ritualized action, conditioned and controlled by ritual cues. Despite its frequent occurrence, Western religions have been much less aware of trance in their rituals than Eastern religions, largely because of the West's cultural notion that such states are psychologically deviant and pathological. In contrast, Eastern traditions have highly valued such states of consciousness and easily recognize their manifestations.

According to Goodman (1972b, 1988), religious trance occurs as the person removes himself or herself from the ordinary perception of reality, an event marked by various stages. If examined in a religious context, "the start" is induced by participation in an established ritual that may include singing of songs, clapping of hands, reciting of prayers, and moving of the body. These specific aspects of the ritual do not themselves produce the trance but rather are thought to stimulate a necessary expectation required for the phenomenon to occur—hence the wide range of trance stimuli across cultures and contexts. Within this ritual of activity, concentration is continually focused and eventually leads to a notable shift in perception—an experience often described as "getting past a barrier."

In this second stage, called "sojourn," the body continues to move rapidly and manifests a range of observable phenomena: "The observer notes pallor to perspiration, trembling, twitching, extremely rapid motion, sometimes even what looks like a swoon, a catatonia-like rigidity. The latter is actually the sign of tremendous excitation, so intense that movement is no longer possible" (Goodman, 1988, p. 38). According to Goodman, these manifestations of ecstatic experience are common across cultures but context-dependent for interpretation and nuanced for meaning by the specific tradition in which they occur. Hence the common process of religious trance admits various cultures to different realities. Although most participants return to an ordinary state of consciousness at this point, others may experience a mystical encounter.

The third phase of religious trance, "dissolution," is an awakening to ordinary consciousness, which may be signaled by a ritual cue or by the ending of the ritual itself. Goodman (1988) has observed that while in religious trance novices tend to be less responsive to such cues than experienced participants but soon, with practice, also become conditioned to the appropriate time for ending the experience. The final stage of religious trance, "aftereffects," is marked by an overwhelming sense of joy and intense euphoria. These qualities are experienced for longer durations among neophytes than experienced participants since they become less pronounced over time. Whether the content of ecstasy in religious trance is later recalled depends on the expectations of the religious community; any amnesia regarding the event, according to Goodman, is related to suggestibility by the tradition during trance.

Goodman bases her theory on cross-cultural studies of Pentecostal groups (Goodman, 1969, 1972b) and controlled laboratory experiments (cited in Goodman, 1988). In the latter studies, religious trance was induced among participants while physiological measures were taken. Trance states were found to involve an increased heart rate (with a concomitant drop in blood pressure); lowered levels of adrenaline, noradrenaline, and cortisol; and higher levels of beta endorphins that persisted even after the trance experience ended. EEG patterns revealed electrical brain activity in the theta range, whereas direct current measurements found negative charges of 1,000 to 2,000 microvolts in some participants, the values of which are sizable in comparison to the usual 250 microvolts that accompany the experience of learning. The paradox of slow theta waves (6–7 cps) combined with the significant magnitude of negative electrical charges, said Goodman, is a puzzling aspect in the experience of trance and deserving of further laboratory study. The wider EEG patterns obtained by Goodman (1988) resembled those measured by Persinger (1984) in another glossolalic study but differed from beta patterns recorded from a serpent-handling preacher during an experience of the anointing (Burton, 1993)—an inferred trance state.

The variability found in EEG studies of meditation has been noted by Hood and colleagues (1996) and Wulff (1991). While Zen masters tend to manifest synchronized patterns in the theta and delta range, expert Yogis produce dysynchronized beta patterns in deep meditative states. It can be inferred from Wulff's (1991) observations that this distinction may be due in part to differences between the two systems of thought: Zen focuses on awareness of the world, whereas Yoga concentrates on withdrawal from the world. In terms of EEG protocols, it is curious that the anointing encountered by one experienced serpent handler (Burton, 1993) correlated more with the meditative states of expert Yogis than with those of Zen masters, the latter of whom have meditative states that resembled those of entranced glossolalics (Goodman, 1988; Persinger, 1984). At another level, however, these confounding results only demonstrate the complexities of determining the meaning of altered states assessed by physiological measures.

The difference between the findings of Goodman (1988) and Burton (1993) may be understood at two levels. First, Goodman (1988) used a standard trance induction technique to achieve the experience of glossolalia among her participants, whereas Burton's (1993) serpent handler improvised from his own tradition a method for experiencing the anointing in the laboratory. Second, these studies involved Pentecostal participants who were from differing subcultures of the religious tradition and hence from nuanced realities of religious experience. The variable findings indicate that while physiological measurements and laboratory procedures reveal some degree of insight into Pentecostal anointing and/or trance states, they are insufficient in themselves to yield the depth of understanding required from a religious point of view. It is indeed the variability of the experience itself that merits attention.

In earlier research, Goodman (1972b) made claims that trance states were necessary for glossolalia. Although observed stages of trance may become less pronounced over time, she argued for their presence on the basis of data deriving from seven different cultures and four different languages, which, when analyzed and compared, produced a consistent configuration of linguistic patterns from glossolalic utterances. On this basis, Goodman (1972b, pp. 123–24) concluded, "Such agreement of patterns despite linguistic and cultural differences, to my mind, can be explained only if we assume that glossolalia is not simply uttered while in dissociation but is an artifact of the mental state, or rather of its neurophysiological processes."

In a review of Goodman's (1969, 1972b) research, Samarin (1972a, 1974) took a strong opposing stance. From his perspective, glossolalia mostly occurred independent of trance states, though it also could be manifest at such times (Samarin, 1972b). Samarin (1972a) criticized Goodman's (1969) "artifact" hypothesis based on three observations. First, he argued that glossolalia is a sociolinguistic phenomenon developed within a religious tradition that exerts social influence. In fact, said Samarin (1973), it is a learned behavior that emerges from a context that (1) requires it for community membership, (2) sanctions—through frequency of practice—certain features of utterance over others, and (3) demonstrates the borrowing of glossolalic syllables and sequences among speakers. Second, Samarin (1972a) charged that Goodman's (1969) samples were not cross-cultural but simply subcultures of a larger Pentecostal tradition that already shared a common glossolalic tradition. In his view, they were not truly independent cultures, hence no universal claim could be legitimate. The third exception to Goodman's (1969) thesis was the analysis of common intonational features in glossolalia, spoken among samples, that were mistaken for what is more correctly understood as a "style of discourse"—a phenomenon commonly found in any particular religious subculture. Among Pentecostals, for example, the same pattern of intonational emphasis found in glossolalia is consistent with that observed in the group's prayers and sermons. Hence Samarin (1972a, 1973) concluded that glossolalia is not the result of a universal trance state but rather is a learned behavior, extremely sensitive to contextual cues.

In response to these criticisms, Goodman (1972a) argued that her technique of analysis was indeed justifiable from a methodological perspective and that her subsequent observations warranted a causal explanation, one she believed is rooted in an altered state of consciousness. In defense of her cross-cultural claims, she called attention to the fact that one group's history had no connection with American Pentecostalism and that an additional culture was later studied and found to support her position. Since variations exist even among specific languages of a particular language family, Goodman argued, the mythical "style of discourse" loses value in accounting for cross-cultural similarities in glossolalia that can be explained only on the basis of an altered mental state.

Malony and Lovekin (1985) have discussed various controlled experimental studies designed to test the validity of Goodman's (1969, 1972b, 1988) thesis of trance state glossolalia, although none have been convincing in finding support. In fact, there were no differences found between glossolalic and nonglossolalic conditions in the assessment of heart rate, breathing, and brain wave patterns (Pavelsky, Hart, & Malony, 1975); photographed energy fields of participants (Strom & Malony, 1979); or memory recall of words and matching tasks (Spanos & Hewitt, 1979). Despite these findings, Malony and Lovekin (1985) agreed more with Goodman than with Samarin for two reasons: the self-report of glossolalics that they are under the control of God is itself an indication of some degree of change in consciousness, and consciousness might be more appropriately thought of as a continuum rather than a juxtaposition of states in which so-called altered ones are simply contrasted with others considered more "normal." Nevertheless, the debate surrounding trance and glossolalia is still largely open—depending primarily on how both trance and glossolalia are operationally defined in empirical research. Perhaps one of the best summaries of whether glossolalia requires a trance is given by a Christian historian, G. Wacker (2003, p. x), whose "head" requires that he now identify himself as an evangelical Christian but whose "heart" remains attached to his Pentecostal background. After careful review of competing theories of glossolalia, identified as cultural and dissociative (trance), he concludes that Pentecostals sought and mastered dissociative or trance states but that they also learned precisely how to enter and exit such states. Rather than an either/or choice among alternatives, Wacker suggests, as we have, a "both/and" solution. Physiologically dissociative or trance states have been subtly mastered by Pentecostals so that cultural clues allow them to enter, control the depth of, and exit from them. This explanation helps to illuminate and integrate the existing social scientific literature. Wacker quotes an "unnamed first generation pundit" who describes what it is like to speak in tongues: "To receive Holy Spirit baptism . . . we must fully surrender the tongue to [the Holy Spirit's] control. It takes time for most people to learn how to do this" (Wacker, 2003, p. 56). Wacker believes the unnamed pundit is A. J. Tomlinson, who not only endorsed tongues speaking but the handling of serpents as well. The combination of contextual cues and physiological dissociation that likely interact to explain tongues speaking is also as likely to interact to explain handling, especially insofar as handlers identify an "anointing" that is the cue to approach the serpent—for those who do not handle by faith alone.

SERPENT HANDLING AND TRANCE

Although trance states have not been linked directly to the anointing, Hood and colleagues (1996) have suggested they more closely parallel the experience of handling serpents by "the anointing" than by "faith." It is more likely that the anointing is more fully or deeply a trance state than handling by faith as handlers themselves can identify an "anointed" state. We explore the phenomenology of this anointed state in chapter 9. However, for now, we want to discuss the physiological correlates that have been identified with anointing. In general terms, a psychophysiological theory assumes a link between neural and psychological processes (Lundin, 1991). Insofar as one postulates a trance state it is imperative that some identifiable physiological differences between "trance" and "nontrance" states be identified. Given that handlers themselves distinguish between handling by faith (no sense of anointing) and by anointing (a self-identified state), the possibility exists that trance and anointing are similar if not identical states from a purely physiological perspective.

Anointing among Serpent-Handling Sects

Kane's (1974b, 1978, 1982) field research among serpent-handling sects addressed the nature of "the anointing" that was reported by believers to make possible the successful practice of handling fire. He described the concept of anointing as essentially "the belief that the Holy Ghost moves upon the believer and takes possession of his faculties, imparting to him supernatural gifts, which qualify him for service to the Lord" (Kane,

1974b, p. 296). Based on his observations, he further suggested that practitioners, who believe themselves possessed by the Holy Ghost, experience an altered state of consciousness, or trance state, which was defined as "a complete or partial dissociation, characterized by (apparent) loss of voluntary control over motor functions, body-image changes, perceptual distortions, diminution of inhibitions, sudden and unexpected outbursts of emotion, and impairment of reality testing to various degrees" (Kane, 1974b, p. 296). Kane then related various aspects of sect behavior—emotional fervor, intensity of experience, invincibility to fire, rhythmic response to music—with possession trance and suggested that such an experience among believers was a complex phenomenon woven together of various biochemical factors, psychological variables, and contextual cues. He concluded, however, that those who experience the anointing cannot be viewed as psychopathological but rather as participants in an institution whose socially sanctioned beliefs, rituals, and symbols contribute to the effective social and cultural functioning of its members in the larger community. This is not inconsistent with our summary of the literature on trance and glossolalia in that handlers may learn to enter into, control, and exit from the anointing. This in no way denies the claim to possession by the Holy Ghost that handlers affirm. Rather it suggests that the possession is both culturally cued and entered into, yet as a trance state identifiable as other than one's normal state. It is interesting to note here that Jung (1964, p. 35) used photographs of serpent handlers from Dolly Pond, Tennessee, to illustrate the handling of serpents, which he attributed to hysteria "induced by music, singing, and handclapping." Obviously, whether "hysteria" or "trance," the state is induced by social cues and practices that permit entering into, controlling the depth of, and exiting the state, as is the case with trance states associated with tongues speaking.

It is noteworthy that Kane (1978, 1982) attempted to relate anointed states of religious fire handlers to hypnotic states of subjects in controlled experimental studies. On the basis of hypnotic suggestion, subjects were observed to experience no tissue damage from noxious stimuli and yet to develop tissue damage in the absence of these materials. Based on these findings, Kane suggested that the success of "entranced" fire handlers was due to the activation of protective neurological mechanisms (unspecified) that were mobilized by belief to produce immunity to the flames of their torches.

In a unique study, Burton (1993) was successful in obtaining EEG readings from the serpent-handling preacher Liston Pack who agreed to seek the anointing in a laboratory setting in an electrically shielded room. After being properly connected to a six-channel electroencephalograph, the Reverend Pack prayed with eyes closed until he felt the anointing. The technician who performed the study drew four conclusions based on the EEG recording: (1) there was no evidence of abnormality in the frequency patterns that might indicate seizure activity; (2) preparation for the anointing involved an EEG state similar to that of mediation; (3) with report of the anointing came a sudden conversion from alpha to beta frequencies—an aroused state within normal parameters; and (4) the patterns of frequencies recorded during the session were similar to what might be expected from individuals who are good candidates for hypnosis—that is, persons who reflect in their EEG patterns whatever state is suggested. Given this interpretation, the technician hypothesized that a key to understanding the physiological and neurological functioning of those who experience the anointing may lie in the literature on hypnosis rather than meditation, although such a proposition was not thought to devalue the religious experience of the anointing. This is especially the case when hypnosis is viewed as a form of focused concentration that allows one to enter into a hypnotic trance (Hood, 1973).

Schwartz (1999) reported a study in which blood samples were drawn from an anointed serpent and fire handler and analyzed for adrenaline, beta-endorphin, and cortisol levels. When believers experienced the anointing, Schwartz had hypothesized that the euphoria and altered perceptions of stressful stimuli were due to increases in these neurological chemicals produced by the body. The investigators drew three blood samples, of ten milliliters each, from a volunteer handler (1) approximately two hours before serpent- and fire-handling experiences; (2) moments after both practices had been completed (the participant continued to speak in tongues as blood was being drawn); and (3) two hours after the events had taken place. Analyses of the blood samples obtained during the handling indicated that the participant experienced a 61 percent increase in adrenaline, a 28 percent increase in beta-endorphins, and a 525 percent increase in cortisol; two hours later there remained only a slight elevation in beta-endorphins when compared to the preanointed stage. Schwartz concluded that the handler's energetic behavior during the anointing was suggestive of an adrenaline "high" and that his fearlessness could be understood in terms of an elevated beta-endorphin level. The lack of pain experienced in the fire handling was attributed to the endorphin-related euphoria combined with a psychological expectation for success in the practice—a suspected combination that both lowered anxiety and inhibited pain perception. In conclusion, Schwartz suggested that the endorphin-related euphoria and the adrenaline high experienced in the anointing may be linked to a "psychic reward system" that reinforces an addiction to such a religious experience.

The language of addiction is not denigrating. Handlers often use comparison to drug and alcohol states to emphasize how different in intensity the anointing is. Thus not only are there likely physiological indicators of hypnotic-like trance states experienced with the anointing but also other physiological indicators of arousal and euphoria that are not unanticipated. Qualitative differences in anointing and trance states are best illuminated by the use of phenomenological methods. In chapters 8, 9, and 10, we discuss the phenomenology of successful serpent handling, the anointing, and near-death experiences from serpent bites, respectively.

Anointing and Dissociative Trance States

In the studies reviewed above, success in manifesting the various signs among serpent-handling sects was attributed to the anointing, a phenomenon described by practitioners as a direct experience of feeling God and observed by researchers as a type of trance or dissociative state (Burton, 1993; Hood et al., 1996; Kane, 1974b, 1978; Moore, 1986; Sargant, 1949; Schwarz, 1960). In describing such states, for example, Schwarz observed:

> The members appear as if they were intoxicated, and their facies are very similar to those seen with reactions induced by mescaline and LSD 25. They describe the depersonalization phenomena as: "I feel high in the spirits" . . . "happiness in the bones" . . . "a shield has come down over me" . . . "I've got conviction" . . . " lose sight of the whole world" . . . " I can't tell if my head and face are all together" and "I can't stand under the power of God." (1960, pp. 408–9)

Schwarz (1960) further noted that at the climax of this ecstatic experience members would engage the "ordeals" without apparent harm. These observations, described by believers as God moving on them, were hypothesized to be trance states with neurological and physiological implications that were viewed by Schwarz as the only possible explanations for success in the practices—especially those involving fire handling and ingestion of poison. Although we do not deny the likelihood that trance states are involved in the anointing, one must be cautious in attributing too much explanatory power to the state itself. For instance, given the rarity of deaths by poison drinking and the fact that there are wide individual differences in tolerance for strychnine and carbolic acid (common poisons drunk by handlers), it is more likely that churches simply have what by definition are sublethal doses of poison on their altars. This is not to demean the believers who drink poison but to simply suggest that with the exception of rare occasions, such poisons are not sufficiently lethal to kill.[1]

Likewise, fire handling of various sorts is an ability that most people have. Like fire walking, it is possible to do under most circumstances and need not be imbued with a religious significance. For instance, Danforth (1989) has noted how the religious significance of fire walking has been transformed into what is now an American fire-walking movement motivated by diverse interests, some religious, some spiritual, and some secular. An interesting parallel to fire walking is the treading on serpents. While much rarer than handling serpents, it does occur in serpent-handling churches.[2] The justification for this is Luke 10:19: "Behold, I give unto you power to tread on serpents and scorpions, and over all the power of the enemy; and nothing shall by any means hurt you" (KJV). Again, trance states may facilitate such activities, but they are not necessary. However, with respect to handling or treading on serpents, the issue is more complex.

We have already noted that handlers identify two ways in serpents are handled: by faith or by anointing. Some handlers admit to doing both; that is, they sometimes handle by faith and sometimes by the anointing. In addition, there is a sense in which all handling is by faith insofar as one must believe and have faith in the power of the anointing. However, that individuals who have faith wait for an identifiable experience of anointing is crucial for suggesting the possibility of a physiological state of some sort, whether hypnotic-like, dissociative, or euphoric. In chapter 9 we provide from handlers themselves a global description of meaning in the experience of the anointing. Here it is sufficient to note that the range of possible physiological indicators for individuals is large. As the Reverend Pack stated, "Everybody that feels the anointing of God, I think, probably feels it somewhat different. It depends on how God deals with that individual person. Some get a tremendous physical anointing that I've heard them say, 'I get numb.' Some say, 'I have a tingling sensation. Particularly in the hands.' I don't think any two people probably get anointed alike" (cited in Burton, 1993, p. 140).

We concur with Wacker's (2003) summary of the literature on trance and tongues speaking in that both dissociative states and cultural cues interact to allow individuals to know when and how to enter into, control the depth of, and exit from a given trance state. We further believe that handlers who seek the anointing do the same. It is likely that serpent handlers, who are repeatedly conditioned to the fear of serpents, have this fear reduced as they enter into an anointed state (Williamson, Pollio, & Hood, 2000). Those who handle by faith alone perhaps have less of a conditioned fear of serpents and thus require less of anointing to do what remains problematic—for what makes serpent handling different from handling fire or drinking potentially lethal poisons is the simple fact that serpent striking behavior is unpredictable, as is the amount of venom injected and the resistance of the person bitten. Thus it requires faith or anointing to take from the box or from another believer what is an unpredictable outcome.

It is this unpredictability that we think links serpent-handling churches more strongly to Otto's (1917/1928) analysis of the holy than to mainstream Pentecostals who, as Anderson (1979, p. 10) claims, wish to possess and be possessed by this power. For the power itself, like the serpent, awakens a primal ambivalence that is the central core of all religion. While Otto (1917/1928, p. 8) identifies "creature-feeling" as a feature of the numinous, it is our contention that serpents are uniquely empowered as creatures to elicit a sense of creature-feeling in persons. Fear and/or awe appear to be universal human reactions to serpents, probably for sound evolutionary reasons (sign value) and enhanced by the serpent's symbolic value. It also is the case here that insofar as Otto's "creature-feeling" is inherent in the numinous, Pentecostals who handle serpents are both attracted to and repelled by the serpent as both a sign and a symbol of the power of their God. Often we have heard it preached, "It is a fearful thing to fall into the hands of the living God" (Heb. 10:31, KJV).

In his extensive work on serpents, Mundkur (1983) has marked out these relations in almost all cultures that gave way to cults that venerate the serpent. Of course, serpent-handling churches do not worship serpents, but they do handle them in a ritual that seeks a sense of anointing to empower them to be obedient to Jesus' command. Howey (1926), in his study of cultural snake mythologies, suggested that the "encircled serpent" primarily signified perfection and deity, and he committed a chapter to anecdotes illustrating the power of fascination and awe it commands from both humans and other animals. It is of particular interest here to note the fascination and awe or fundamental reactions aroused in humans in response to the Holy (Otto, 1917/1928).

In Otto's well-known work, *The Idea of the Holy* (1917/1928), God is viewed as a nonrational suprareality—nonrational in the sense that God transcends all comprehension by rational thought or human logic—who exists above all religious concepts, which, based on previous experience, are meant to understand and relate to him. At best, any "idea" of this "numen" is awakened in "creature-feelings" that are realized in two extraordinary sensations captured in the expression "mysterium tremendum." While experience of the numen involves an ineffable "mysterious" quality, it also provides a sense of awe, overwhelming power, and an urgent energy, all of which contribute to an aura or "tremor" that simultaneously entices and repels. These dual qualities, which are both daunting and fascinating, are thought to unite as a "strange harmony of contrasts" in the experience of the numen:

> The daemonic-divine object may appear to the mind an object of horror and dread, but at the same time it is no less something that allures with a potent charm, and the creature, who trembles before it, utterly cowed and cast down, has always at the same time the impulse to turn to it, nay even to make it somehow his own. The "mystery" is for him not merely something to be wondered at but something that entrances him; and beside that in it which bewilders and confounds, he feels a something that captivates and transports him with a strange ravishment, rising often enough to the pitch of dizzy intoxication; it is the Dionysiac-element in the numen. (Otto, 1917/1928, p. 31)

While serpent handlers are seldom credited with either a sophisticated theology or a sense of ritual deeply rooted in Scripture, Anderson (1979, p. 10) is right to credit Pentecostals with seeking both to be both possessed by and to seek possession of the numinous. If serpent handling is perceived by many people to be less than rational, it is proper to suggest that it may indeed be more than merely rational. There is another convergence point identified by Otto, much as we identified the serpent as a merging of sign and symbol. Otto identified it as a human response to the divine. J. W. Harvey, translator of the original 1917 German work, *Das Heilige*, stated it this way: "The primary fact is the confrontation of the human mind with a Something, whose character is only gradually learned, but which is from the first felt as a transcendent presence, 'the beyond,' even where it is also felt as 'the within' man" (1917/1928, p. xv). Without pressing the issue further, it is sufficient to point out that insofar as the serpent is a merging of sign and symbol, so are fear and awe merged in a tangible way in the ritual that most identifies the serpent-handling churches and suggests that, as with mainstream Pente-

costalism, these renegade churches of God seek in their own way to possess and to be possessed by what they understand to be the Holy Ghost.
It is shortsighted to dismiss this yearning as merely ecstatic religion
(Lewis, 1971), although it is indeed ecstatic. What has gone unnoticed by
such scholars of the serpent-handling churches is that Otto (1917/1928)
explicitly focused on Mark 16. He spoke of "signs following" (p. 176)
and devoted an appendix to "signs following" as well (Appendix VII,
pp. 212–16). Here Otto finds Jesus' "exalted spiritual power over nature"
(p. 176). He properly notes, with respect to the gift of healing of Jesus,
that it is possible as a heightened and intense capacity that lies dormant in
human nature in general (p. 214). This is precisely what handlers believe
not only with respect to healing but also with respect to the handling of
serpents. Serpent handlers believe that Jesus has given them this power
over nature, power over the lowly yet deadly serpent. It should make us
pause and consider what we might learn from a tradition too often
ridiculed for a ritual that is little understood. Otto reminds us of Mark
16:20: "And they went forth, and preached every where, the Lord working with *them* and confirming the word with signs following." Serpent
handlers use this verse to affirm that Jesus and the apostles handled serpents.[3] Although we find no historical documentation that early Christians handled serpents, it remains an intriguing possibility (Tomlinson,
1959). Regardless, there are Christians today who handle, and they must
be judged by criteria that permit them a fair hearing. They would argue
that the criteria must come from Scripture itself, from what is inherently
holy—not from any external source. This is the application in a living
tradition of the principle of intratextuality (Hood et al., 2005, chap. 5).
Otto (1917/1928, p. 177) has made a similar case for judging religions by
criteria that transcend mere secular claims to functionality: "The criterion of the value of a religion as religion cannot ultimately be found in
what it has done for culture, nor in its relation to the 'limits of reason' or
the 'limits of humanity' . . . nor in any of its external features. It can only
be found in what is the innermost essence of religion, the idea of holiness
as such, and in the degree of perfection with which any given religion
realizes this."

   Our discussion of trance with respect to tongues speaking and handling is not intended to suggest that dissociative states undermine the
experience of the holy. Indeed, it is just the opposite. Taves (1999) has
traced the history of the debate between those who would deny the
validity of religious experiences, such as tongues speaking, because they
could be produced by natural ("trance") means, and those who would

deny that trance states could produce genuine ("supernatural") religious experiences. Taves notes that William James added to the natural/supernatural debate by providing a third alternative, natural states that are also genuinely religious states. Our use of the merging of symbol and sign in the serpent allows for a similar view. While handlers would not want to identify their anointing as a naturally induced yet genuine religious state, the scientist can reject a "supernatural" view and still respect the genuineness of religious experience. Handlers seek to possess and be possessed by the Holy Ghost. Believers are likely sensitive to cues that permit them to enter into a state that they are assured is a genuine sense of a supernatural presence. Social scientists may not confirm the supernatural presence, but this supernatural state does have a thematic structure that makes it distinct. Insofar as we include Pentecostalism as a specific instance of ecstatic religion (Lewis, 1971), we are reminded of what Wacker (2003, pp. 56–57) adroitly perceives as a delicate balance between a primitive impulse to be possessed by the Holy Ghost and a pragmatic impulse to be guided by the external culture at appropriate times and places. While Wacker applies this to the phenomenon of tongues speaking, we hope that we have shown its applicability to the handling of serpents as well. If one grants a wisdom to this tradition, it is not only that the anointing empowers believers to handle and express a primitive impulse that is as well a response itself but also that it guides them in making a pragmatic adaptation that allows their tradition to continue within a culture that remains hostile to their most exceptional ritual.

CHAPTER 7

Extemporaneous Sermons in the Serpent-Handling Tradition

Contemporary Christian serpent handlers share with other Christian fundamentalists the love of what they claim is "the Word." Preachers are "God called," not seminary trained. Their knowledge of the King James Bible is extensive and deep; this is true even of preachers who might be considered illiterate. There is a powerful oral tradition in which the Bible is preached and memorized. Preaching is unscripted; notes are never used. Typically a pastor of a church will ask, "Who has the Word?" The person who is moved to preach will approach the altar, Bible in hand, and speak. There is but one criterion each church demands: the preacher must "stay within the Word."

In this chapter we provide a descriptive understanding of the phenomenon of serpent handling on the basis of the rhetoric in sermons commonly given by preachers at church services in which serpent handling takes place. We collected and analyzed spontaneous sermons during ongoing worship services (for methodology, see Appendix 3). The set of sermons discussed here took place during services at times when serpents were handled or just thereafter. We attended a serpent-handling congregation in northern Georgia on various occasions from January 1995 through March 1996. During this period, segments of the services that included extemporaneous sermons were videotaped by permission. We selected for study eighteen sermons that were most descriptive of serpent handling. All eleven preachers who delivered these sermons were male. (Females are not allowed to preach in the serpent-handling tradition.)

The preachers included the pastor of the Georgia congregation and various other ministers who had practiced the signs the night of their sermons.[1] As is typical of serpent-handling churches, sermons were impromptu and free associative in nature, lasting from a few minutes to over an hour. Each sermon was carefully transcribed verbatim, and the resulting text was used to obtain our thematic analysis described below.[2]

Because most sermons were relatively brief, from five to ten minutes, all themes were not required to appear in each sermon, as is the usual requirement for interpretive analysis (e.g., see Pollio et al., 1997). For present purposes, it seemed reasonable to require themes to have been noted in more than 75 percent of the sermons considered. In addition, any given thematic meaning defining the experience of serpent handling, derived from this procedure, could not be contradicted by the content of any sermon for it to be considered critical to the meaning of the overall practice.

THE SERMONS

Interpretive analysis of the various sermons indicated that the experience of religious serpent handling is an embodied event emerging from the context of Pentecostal worship. The services in which these sermons were given included intense singing, shouting, dancing, glossolalia, and prayer, all common features of Pentecostal worship, and, with the exception of glossolalia, characteristic of Holiness worship as well (Synan, 1997; McCauley, 1995). In this context of ongoing activities and related sermons, the phenomenon of serpent handling emerges in relation to a particular awareness of the body that serves to affect the meaning of the event for the person. The body is the modality through which the handlers experience this sacred world and God (see McGuire, 1990).

From the present analysis of sermons, five themes were noted to characterize the first-person experience of serpent handling. The diagram in chart 1 presents the themes and suggests that the meaning of serpent handling, as expressed in sermons, emerges as a pattern related to experiences of the body that serves to provide a context of understanding in the existential world of the handler. All themes are felt in the body, and the encounter is experienced as a direct phenomenon, without reflected thought. As suggested by the lines used to connect the various themes, relationships among and between themes are fluid within the experience of serpent handling; all, however, are consequential to the central theme of God moving on the believer. Each of the major

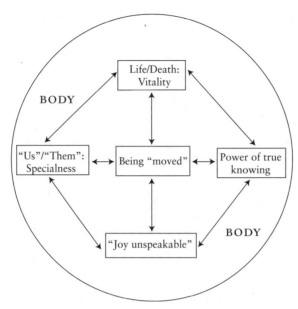

Chart 1. The thematic pattern of described meaning in the experience of serpent handling as derived from the rhetoric in sermons given on the topic after handling serpents. From Williamson & Pollio, 1999, p. 209. © 1999 Society for the Scientific Study of Religion. All rights reserved. Reprinted by permission.

themes and subthemes of the experience is outlined below with brief excerpts from various sermons to illustrate its sources.

Theme I: Being Moved . . . the Feeling of God

Central to the activity of handling serpents is the experience of God moving on the person. In the context of a service, many activities take place: praying for the sick, singing fervent songs, dancing to intense music, and preaching of personal convictions; however, it is agreed that no one goes inside the serpent box without first feeling God move in a convincing way. How that moving is discerned differs from individual to individual, although each of the preachers emphasized the need to feel God move personally before any attempt to take up a serpent. Their words clearly describe this powerful experience:[3]

> The Lord moved on us while we was a cleaning them [serpent boxes] and got to handling them and everything. . . . Brother, once you get into this,

and get a little taste of this victory . . . how sweet it is . . . there's just one way to go . . . and that's straight ahead! (S9–1)

[The TV news reporter] wanted me to come outside and talk to him, and he began to ask about taking up serpents. . . . That lady, she asked about the women that took up serpents in here, what kind of training they had [laughter]. . . . They think there's a gimmick to it. Brother B, I don't care what the Lord does, somebody's going to look for a gimmick, Brother B, a sleight of hand or something. I said, "Hey, there ain't no kind of training to do it," Sister C. I said, "The best thing to do is get down on your knees and cry out to God, push your plate back for three or four days till you find the answer." And when you find the answer, that begins to get on you. . . . Brother D, when you began to praise the Lord, and that begins to get upon you. And when it gets on you, you can't wipe it off of you. That begins to get upon you, you can't walk out from under it, and you know that the Lord's moving on you, then that's the time to [take up serpents]. (S5–2)

The experience of the anointing—or feeling the Lord move—is curious, and preachers describe it in various ways. In terms of personal manifestation, some descriptions openly shared its bodily affect when being moved to handle; others were more guarded and did not describe it directly. As will be shown, the experience of feeling God move on the person is linked to other themes that emerge.

Theme II: "Life"/"Death" . . . the Feeling of Vitality

In their preaching, the ministers regularly addressed and affirmed the reality of death. On many visits to serpent-handling services, a caution often heard from the pulpit was, "There's death in that box"; hence life takes on a certain vitality, becoming more pronounced and accentuated in its sacred confrontation with death. Some of the preachers handled serpents as they preached and expressed full awareness of the potential for death. In addition, the experience of being bitten holds meaningful interpretations that range from lack of congregational prayer in the course of handling to personal disobedience when told by God to put the serpent down to God's wisdom in using the incident as a testimony to unbelievers in revealing the genuine danger and divine protection afforded those who obey his Word.

Two preachers experienced serpent bites at the times of their sermons: one was bitten only minutes beforehand, and the other was struck between sermons while singing a song. If one was bitten, the consensus was that survival is in God's hand; no mention of medical intervention was made in either case. The following excerpts illustrate clearly the handlers' awareness of death and its implications.

But, Boys, I don't care about this old flesh. Boys, I'll keep taking up serpents cause the Bible says, "The signs shall follow them that believe." . . . It
ain't nothing more than a shortcut to the other side. (S2–1)

[Immediately after being bitten] Through these serpent bites, he'll take care
of us. . . . Don't worry about me. Don't cry over me when I leave this
world. Rejoice. I'm gonna be with Jesus. (S7–1)

I'd love to take that serpent up, if God moves. . . . If he don't, I'm just
gonna leave him right there in the box. Amen, Thank God. One end of it's
got a head, and the other one's got a tail . . . and that head part's what's
gonna bite. (S1–4)

These men experienced a full awareness of potential death related to
their practice, yet there was a vitality emerging within the confrontation
that they "love" (S1–4) to experience. They reach inside the serpent box
as the spirit moves and experience the vitality of spiritual life overcoming death within a sacred community and locale.

Theme III: "Us"/"Them" . . . the Feeling of Specialness

The preachers made constant reference to themselves as "us" and to others who did not handle serpents as "them." Such distinctions included
"we"/"they," "God's children"/"the world," and "ours"/"theirs." In each
case, they experienced themselves as favored by God and sanctioned as
true believers by virtue of their obedience to the mandate of serpent handling. As a pattern, the "us"/"them" theme emerged as figural in terms of
three subthemes, each lending a feeling of specialness to the "us" group.

Subtheme A: Obedience. Those obeying the scriptural mandate to
take up serpents experience themselves as having crossed over a line to
full obedience and thus becoming recipients of the blessing and favor
that follow. On the other hand, the "them" group will not believe or
obey—hence they fail to merit God's blessing and may be eternally lost.
True believers, however, make the ultimate sacrifice and live in full obedience to God.

[Jesus] said, "These signs shall follow them that believe." And, if you
believe it, Boys, you're gonna do it. And if you don't do it, I believe it with
all my heart that you'll die and go to hell. (S2–1)

No matter what it takes, I'm gonna do what the Lord wants me to do.
(S11–1)

The Bible says, "They shall take up serpents." Honey, it means what it
says, and says what it means. . . . It won't change for me. It won't change

for you, Amen, thank God. . . . Some folks, Amen, thank God, they go in around, thank God, where they preach you can get there any way. Amen, thank God. But we're gonna have to go the Bible way. Amen, thank God. The Word of God's right. (S1–3)

Subtheme B: The Sign of True Believers.   The sermons indicate that serpent handling is considered a literal indicator of God's genuine people. An analogy shared in one sermon likened the Bible to the map book of a trucker. It may indeed show the route to a destination, but signs are needed along the road to confirm the validity of the map. Hence serpent handling confirms the Word of God in the life of the believer and publicly indicates the rightness of his (the preacher's) walk. More important, the sign is an indicator of how God can richly bless people if they believe and fully obey the biblical command. Such a meaning is implied in an excerpt that follows a reprimand to an overly zealous TV crew for disrespectful conduct and obtrusive maneuvers while filming serpent-handling activities:

> When people see the Lord move on you, then they can say they've seen something move. Whenever I began to see this, I didn't see them people handling them snakes. What I seen, I seen God moving in them. I seen the Lord moving in people . . . you come up here and you just handle that snake just to be handling that snake, that don't prove nothing. . . . If the Lord's moving on you, thank God, somebody can see that, and they'll know there's something real about that. When I seen that move on them, I wanted that. It wasn't so much handling that snake. That wasn't it, thank God, but I wanted to see the Lord move . . . and I wanted to feel the goodness of God. I didn't care nothing about handling that snake, but I wanted to feel that . . . that moved on them. (S1–6)

It is not simply the handling of serpents that is the sign of distinction—in fact, some preachers expressed an awareness that counterfeiters may occasionally handle serpents with success. What is of more significance is the observed manifest power of God on the handler, which is felt to be the true mark transcending even the act itself so as to become the distinguishing feature of belief.

> There's more to this than just handling a serpent. It ain't nothing to handle a snake, but it takes a believer to take up serpents. . . . I've seen homosexuals handle snakes. That ain't no big thing. But when the power of God gets into it, when the power of God gets into it, then it's gonna edify. It's gonna edify. (S11–1)

Subtheme C: The Established versus the "Sugar-Coated."   Members of the in-group, qualified by obedience and performance of the signs, see themselves as spiritually mature and "established" in the Word. They boldly stand without compromise for what the Bible says regarding signs of the believers. On the other hand, they view their counterparts as preferring and settling for a "watered-down" or "sugar-coated" gospel that cultivates immaturity and unbelief. Of course, the mature stand fast in belief and practice all of God's Word.

> I'm surprised some of the churches ain't got rubber snakes in them. Amen, thank God. I am. I'm surprised. They try to imitate every other way. They do! The devil, amen thank God, he'll try anything and everything to counterfeit for everything the Lord's got. . . . He's a counterfeiter. The true thing's gonna stand. (S1–3)
>
> God's children is gonna be standing. Brother, he said when he'd come back he'd find faith on the earth. Somebody's gonna be standing and doing that word. (S8–1)
>   Some of them try to say that . . . I don't believe that like that. I don't see that like that. . . . You know what? People has sugar-coated this thing around trying to please to somebody—sugar-coated. We've had to pet people, amen, thank God, we've had to pamper them. . . . Just give them the word. (S1–1)

As a group, serpent handlers characterize themselves as fully obeying the Bible, manifesting the sign of true believers, and being firmly established in the truth of God's Word without compromise. When handling serpents, these three qualities lend a unique feeling of specialness—as an "us" group privileged by God.

Theme IV: The Power of True Knowing

Although the actual words *true knowing* did not appear in the various sermons, they convey an idea that harmonizes the three subthemes below. Serpent handlers, especially those new to the practice, speak of their experiences in such a way as to indicate a kind of ineffable knowledge or meaning that surpasses rational understanding; that is, they have encountered true knowledge and are convinced of its impact on their lives.

Subtheme A: True Knowledge of Being "Somebody."   Although this subtheme is similar to the "Us"/"Them" theme, the manner in which it appeared in the sermons was distinct. The feeling of specialness associated with the "Us"/"Them" theme involves a sense of achievement centered on a decided obedience to the Bible—a manifest enactment of the sign and a visceral stance for the "truth." In the present subtheme, true knowledge of being "somebody" is recognized by virtue of one's acceptance by God. Whereas the former is earned by personal effort and achievement through obedience, the latter is the consequence of unmerited grace, a part of the experience in which one feels lifted from insignificance by a power greater than the self—a humble feeling that one is "somebody" based on connection to God. The preachers indicated quite positive self-perceptions in their sermons but always in relation to God's merciful favor and not to themselves.

> Somebody said, "Preacher . . . ," said, "you act like you're better than somebody." I am! Hey, I'm a child of the King! I'm better than any sinner man that walks the streets. Do you hear me now? I'm not any better than my brothers and sisters . . . now you follow what I'm saying . . . I'm not lifting [handler's name] up. I'm lifting God up. (S6–1)

> Let me express something to you tonight. God never took the time to make a nobody. I've said that repeatedly. God never took the time to make a nobody, and you are a somebody. Everybody here is a somebody in the sight of God. (S10–1)

Subtheme B: True Knowledge of "Understanding." Preachers who handled serpents reported that God had broadened their "understanding" of truth and had revealed the real way of life to them that would otherwise have been inaccessible. They also spoke of such revelation as an ongoing process.

> I want to stand up and thank the Lord for everything he's done for me. God moves on you and more everyday. He doesn't leave you in the dark. He opens your understanding. I want to thank God for that. You know, he'll move you on up and in. (S4–1)

> We might back up. . . . We might just get disgusted, "Well, I ain't gonna go back around those snake-handlers no more." You better stay in the Truth. You better not hear that devil . . . You better stay in the Truth. If God has put you into the Truth, you better stay there. (S3–1)

> Thank God. I said he blessed me tonight. If you knowed what I knowed, you'd raise your hands and you'd thank him tonight. (S11–1)

Subtheme C: True Knowledge of the "Good Way." In their sermons, the preachers did not speak of "good" as describing their own dispositions but rather as characterizing their changed way of life as revealed by God. They viewed their present lives as serpent handlers as the "good way" in comparison to their former ways in the world.

Oh . . . this is a good way. This is the best thing that could ever happen to you. (S1–3)

This is a good way. That's what this thing is founded on. It's on love and nothing else. (S11–1)

The Lord moved on us while we was a cleaning them [serpent boxes] and got to handling them and everything . . . and it came to me, Brother pastor, there ain't no way back. . . . There ain't no looking back. . . . There ain't nothing back there. . . . Brother, once you get into this, and get a little taste of this victory . . . how sweet it is . . . there's just one way to go . . . and that's straight ahead! (S9–1)

Those who handle serpents preach in their sermons about experiencing a unique kind of power that only true knowledge can give: knowledge of a personal significance made possible by God, enlightenment concerning hidden spiritual truth, and the good life to experience while on earth.

Theme V: "Joy Unspeakable"

In reference to their experiences of serpent handling, preachers spoke of "joy unspeakable" that accompanied the remarkable event. Most acknowledged prior experience with "worldly" activities, including alcohol, drugs, and sex, although the pleasure deriving from such experiences had no comparison to the ultimate joy found in the practice of their religion. The joyful feelings, however, were almost always attributed to the experience of God while handling rather than to the act of handling the serpent itself.

This feeling that you got . . . the world didn't give it to you, Brother [name]. Amen. This Holy Ghost you got, the world didn't give it to you. . . . If folks—people would have told me thirty years ago that I'd be handling rattlesnakes, I'd told them they was crazy. . . . But this feeling that comes on you . . . I tell you, it'll make you do some strange things. . . . Joy unspeakable and full of glory. (S1–6)

I was trying to describe to my son, Amen, glory to God, when he was by the house the other day, I said, "Son," I said, "I want to tell you it's a wonderful feeling to take up a serpent." . . . But you can't explain it. You can't tell me how it feels. I've got to experience it for myself. (S6–1)

When a handler takes up a serpent as moved by the spirit of God, there is an ineffable sense of joy accompanying it that transcends any found in the world. It is this unspeakable joy that connects with, and to, the other themes and captures the apex of the serpent-handling experience.

Based on information contained in the present set of sermons, the ritual of religious serpent handling is undertaken only after the person experiences a movement of God on the corporeal body, which is often referred to as "the anointing." Handlers reported an unmistakable bodily sensation that provides a sense of knowing when it is time to reach for a serpent inside the box or from another person. It is felt by some to be compelling in the sense that "you can't wipe it off of you . . . [and] . . . you can't walk out from under it" (S5–2). For others, the moving of God is not so commanding as to usurp personal will; indeed, it requires these individuals to "learn to yield ourselves to God [so] we'll know when to move" (S6–1). When the anointing does move on the handler it relieves worry and fear about the immediate situation. As God is felt to move on the body, the serpent handler loses personal concern for danger and feels fully prepared to obey God in fulfilling the biblical mandate to take up serpents.

It seems probable that the most compelling theme to emerge in these sermons is the handler's awareness of life and death and the subsequent feeling of vitality it provides. In a context made sacred by Scripture, serpent handlers are very much aware of the reality and potentiality of death through the presence of poisonous serpents. In fact, S11 told in his sermon of a revival he had attended in Kentucky where another believer prophesied to him that he would "have the fangs laid to you." He recalled that earlier the same week he had hunted and caught several rattlesnakes for worship services without being harmed, yet he later sat in the evening service of the revival replaying in his mind the words of the so-called prophet, wrestling with the possibility of their truth. Feeling God move on him, however, he felt courage enough to pray silently, "Lord, I'm gonna find out if it was you [speaking through the man]." Obeying the spirit, he took up serpents that very night, despite the warning of injury and possible death, without any bodily harm. Commenting on the "victory" God gave him over the serpent, he declared, "The devil can't do nothing God won't let him do" (S11–1).

Rather than deny the reality of death, the serpent handler confronts it openly when he feels the moving of God to take up the poisonous serpent. It is through this very act that the embodied feeling of God negates the fear of death for the handler—hence the threat of death is transcended and gives way to a vitality of spiritual life that is experienced as an ineffable kind of "joy unspeakable and full of glory" (S1–6). Given the powerful, spiritual meaning of this experience, as it relates to death, there is little wonder that S11 continued in the tradition after the loss of his wife—or that other believers, including S11's parents, continue now in the faith after the fact of his death from a serpent bite. Indeed, it was no great surprise when we watched the faithful of the tradition respond to the moving of God and take up poisonous serpents at S11's graveside service. In this otherwise somber context, the stark reality of death was confronted and transcended once more on the basis of a meaningful religious experience that bridges for them the temporal with the eternal. Those who had gathered at the graveside left knowing that S11's death was much less a loss than a far greater victory attained through the literal practice of his faith.

Through the literal taking up of a serpent comes an awareness of feeling kinship with a select group special to God, for it is indeed the consequence of a decided obedience to his Word. It is "us" who are willing to fully comply with *all* the express words of Jesus, not "them" who pick and choose from among Scriptures what is appealing and conducive to their compromising way of life. In the words of one preacher:

> They take out what sounds good to them, but Jesus told John, said, "Take ye it and eat it," talking about that little book. . . . But when it begins to cut down deep they back up and they don't want it. . . . Boys, it don't change for me. It don't change for you. The Word of God means what it says, and it says what it means. (S8–1)

Membership in this favored group is also marked by the very fact that they take up serpents—a sign made visible not only by the virtue of taking them up but also by a notable manifestation of God's spirit on the believer in a very convincing way. The group who practices all the mandates of Scripture further knows itself to be selected because of a spiritual maturity not found among those who do not. In fact, concerning those who had once stood strong on the doctrine of serpent handling but have since weakened, another handler declared, "They ain't stable. They ain't rooted. They ain't grounded. . . . [They are] just like a ship out on the sea, and they're tossed about by every wind of doctrine" (S1–3). Serpent handlers, by their complete devotion to the Scripture, see themselves as a unique group given to full obedience that is honored by God. This awareness, however, is not prideful: "You get exalted, and God can't do nothing. But if you get down on them knees and cry out to God, we'll see God move" (S7–1). Indeed, the road to God is paved with humility.

In the experience of handling serpents, there comes a certain power of true knowledge. The handler no longer feels himself an unworthy creation of God but one who comes to a knowledge of being graced and valued by God and deemed worthy to participate in the signs of true believers. In fact, it is felt that no matter "how little you feel like you are, how big you think you are, God still can use you" (S1–1)—if only one has an obedient heart. Through practicing the signs, the handler discovers a deeper revelation of spiritual knowledge that has been found in no other way. After handling his first serpent, one young man stated, "You don't know the way until he shows you the way. You can't do when you're ignorant" (S4–2). The best possible life to live is one that knows the fullness of God through following the signs; even in the most difficult of times, "this thing will do you to depend upon" (S5–2).

It has been through the practice of religious serpent handling that these persons have become aware of such knowledge as this that has changed their lives in profound ways. This theme of true knowledge weaves together with all the others and contributes to indescribable feelings of joy, blessedness, gladness, goodness, peace, victory, wonder, and greatness, all of which transcend feelings experienced from pleasures in the corporeal world and are "better felt than told." Hence the structured pattern of themes found to emerge from the sermons concerning serpent handling is directly felt by these practitioners as an embodied experience connected in meaningful ways to their complete religious tradition—including, especially, their understanding of life and death.

The phenomenon of serpent handling may be described, in a global description, as an experience of the body being moved on by a pattern of special meanings in the broader context of Pentecostal worship. When feeling a particular moving of God in or on their bodies, persons take up serpents in that sacred context, consciously confront death, and thereby come to encounter a renewed vitality in their present spiritual life. In taking up the serpent, the person feels a particular specialness to God that gives him or her distinction from all others who refuse the scriptural mandate. In addition, the person experiences an empowerment of true knowledge that is reflected in a transformed significance of self, in spiritual understanding, and in an enlightened enactment of the good way of life reserved to those who take up serpents. Finally, the experience of taking up serpents culminates in a "joy unspeakable and full of glory," an ineffable feeling that escapes precise description but was sometimes referred to as "a bubbling in my soul" (S1–4). The phenomenon of religious serpent handling is a powerful, direct body experience charged with personal and religious meaning for the people who engage in this practice.

The structure and meaning of religious serpent handling emerging from the present analysis seems appropriate and plausible for the texts of the sermons studied; however, the use of extemporaneous sermons may present some limitations. One possible limitation is that all the participants in this study were preachers, whereas not only preachers handle serpents. Nevertheless, it should be remembered that preachers circumscribe and predicate the religious language used by others to interpret and legitimate their experiences within the tradition. A second possible limitation is that sermons given in the context of worship tended to reflect certain rhetorical devices often lacking in precise descriptions. For example: What is it like to experience "joy unspeakable and full of glory" (S1–4)? What does it mean to "know that the Lord's moving on you" (S5–2)? In the context of ongoing worship, there was no opportunity to solicit clarification of such descriptions, as might be done in an interview. On the other hand, given the direct experience of serpent handling just as sermons were given—or immediately beforehand—it would be difficult to ascertain how much descriptive material might be lost in interviews distant in time from the actual phenomenon of experience. Nonetheless, these concerns should be considered in evaluating present results.

In addition to its substantive findings, the present study would seem to have implications for social scientists who study the serpent-handling tradition. First, contemporary psychology continues to pursue an objective, or third-person, perspective in which theoretical neutrality is meant to free the researcher from bias and help him or her to discover "objective truth" about the subject of investigation. Since truth, but especially religious truth, may be thought of as perspectival, it seems unnecessary to maintain an outsider approach to religious phenomena, and an important contribution of a phenomenological approach might be to shift psychological inquiry from a strict third-person perspective to one in which the first-person perspective is recognized. Thus, in addition to observing religious serpent-handling practices from a distance, as objective psychology would do, phenomenological interpretation allows the researcher to see the world as the religious practitioner sees it, unaffected (as far as possible) by theories external to the context of the practitioner's belief and experience. In this blending of perspectives, a more complete picture of the phenomenon, a more exacting truth of

religious serpent handling than would be otherwise possible, is likely
to emerge. As Wulff (1998) has suggested, discovering the richness of
religious experience requires the inclusion of such methodological
approaches that are qualitative in nature. Our explication of the qualitative methods we employ is presented in Appendix 3.

Although the structure of meaning as derived from our analysis of
sermons is illuminating and substantiated by relevant texts, we found it
helpful to conduct direct phenomenological interviews with serpent
handlers and collect additional descriptions of personal experiences,
which are presented in chapter 8. Since extensive field research has
noted that approximately 30 to 35 percent of handlers are women, we
included female participants in these interviews, as well as handlers
from different geographic locations and nonpreaching believers who
have taken up serpents. As we show in chapter 9, these interviews also
provided an opportunity to explore the specific experience of anointing
that was characterized in the present set of sermons as "God moving on
me"; furthermore, we come to see the meaning in the distinction of
what some preachers have referred to as handling serpents "by faith
alone." In the words of one preacher, handling serpents "is the *best*
thing that could ever happen to you" (S1–3). We hope to bring to light
through the use of phenomenological methods an empathic understanding of serpent handling as experienced by believers.

As mentioned above, it is significant to note that since the collection
of the sermon data one of the preachers, John Wayne "Punkin" Brown
(S11), a renowned minister in the tradition, was fatally bitten by a timber rattler while preaching in a revival service on October 3, 1998. The
thirty-four-year-old refused the offer of medical aid and died within several minutes. His twenty-eight-year-old wife, Melinda Duvall Brown,
had died from a rattlesnake bite received during a serpent-handling
homecoming service only three years earlier. What appears on the one
hand to be tragedy to the secular world is underscored on the other as
an affirmation of the rich meaning this tradition holds for those who
live (and die) in the faith. The Brown family, including the deceased
Melinda and Punkin, are among the three serpent-handling families
whom Brown and McDonald (2000, pp. 2–125) have allowed to tell
their own stories. The parents of their beloved Punkin, Peggy and John
Brown, who have custody of the five children of Melinda and Punkin,
tell the story of their continuing faith, as does Punkin's brother, Mark
Brown. We mention this here not only to prepare for our discussion of
near-death experiences in a later chapter, but also to affirm the sincerity

and power of those who not only preach the Word but also follow its signs as God grants them an understanding that those outside the faith often fail to appreciate. A major part of this failure is probably the inability or refusal to consider the possibility that a ritual that maims and kills can also liberate and save. We explore this paradox in chapter 10. Ironically, one of the persons scheduled to be interviewed by us was John Wayne "Punkin" Brown, whose death remains near to us and whose family has helped us to understand the powerful faith that sustains families whose members have died while practicing the signs.

CHAPTER 8

The Experience
of Handling Serpents

In this chapter we focus exclusively on what it is like to handle poisonous serpents by using a particular phenomenological method, one that allows handlers to freely explore and describe in an open-ended interview what their specific experiences have been in handling serpents.[1] In chapter 7 we explored the meaning of serpent handling based on what is publicly proclaimed in sermons. Here we study its meaning based on what believers have to say as they reflect on their experiences in the context of personal interviews. Our main focus is on handling that, in the words of believers, granted them "victory" over the serpent. Thus most of the handling described in this chapter did not involve bites. However, even when focusing on successful handling, there is a sensitivity to the possibility of bites, maiming, and death. If "there is death in the box," then handling always takes place in the context of possible harm. The serpent in the box becomes the serpent in the hand in a ritual that handlers sustain on the basis of faith and their own understanding of Mark 16:17–18.

THE CONTEXT OF HANDLING EXPERIENCE

Here we use interviews with seventeen religious serpent handlers.[2] The participants described 105 specific encounters with serpent handling—almost all involving personal experiences of taking up serpents. On rare occasion, a participant described an experience of seeing another believer handle a serpent. Of these 105 different events, 78 were experienced in worship that occurred during a church service, 22 were experienced in worship outside the church service context but in the presence of others (i.e., after the close of a service at church, at the place of employment, in the woods, on the roadside, or in homes), and 5 were experienced in private worship without others in attendance (i.e., at home or in the woods). All interviews were conducted with handlers we have known for several years so that rapport had already been established. The interviews took place in churches, in the handlers' homes, or, in one case, at a motel and lasted from approximately one to two and a half hours. In all cases the interview continued until both participant and interviewer were convinced that all that the handler could express about the meaning of handling had been exhausted.

Most of the seventeen handlers took up serpents as part of their worship. Most serpent handling took place during church services at which believers, and often unbelievers, were gathered for the worship of God. The phenomenon of serpent handling usually occurred as congregants would (in their words) "get in" the worship of the service and participate fully in a focused manner. One participant gave a generalized description of such a meeting that eventually leads to manifestations of the sign:

> It's like the whole service changes. The whole environment changes. Everybody seems to want to get in when the Lord begins to move. The service may be a little tight. People have not got their minds together, but when the Lord begins to move a little bit, then everybody gets their minds together. Everybody'll get their minds together, then you can begin to get in. You feel things kind of loosen up. . . . [E]verybody begins to get in a little bit. Stand up, raise their hands, praising the Lord. When everybody does their part in a church service, then it's obviously going to get easier. It's like you take one person, maybe pulling a rope, pulling a heavy object. It's extremely hard, but when you get two or three or four or five or eight or ten more, then obviously, it's going to get a little easier. So when everybody tries to press in, then it gets easier for you to press in. . . . [T]here's times I've had to press in myself and try to get the Lord to move. The Bible said in Psalms, David said to praise him on the stringed instruments and high-sounding cymbals. Praise him in a dance. Sometimes you just got to praise the Lord a little bit before the Lord will really begin to move. . . . You just feel it. (H16)[3]

As noted above, and in descriptions contained in various other protocols, the experience of "getting in" a worship service involves willful participatory singing, hand-clapping, dancing, praying, and shouting—all of which are typical expressions of traditional Pentecostal-type worship that focus congregants on God (Synan, 1997). Here we again emphasize the central commitment of handlers to a more generalized Pentecostal worldview but one that includes, rather than excludes, Mark 16:17–18. Worship services that resulted in serpent handling were described by some participants as including personal effort to remain focused on God. For example:

> Seemed like the service—I really began to get in. I mean I really began to get my mind on God. I thought about, you go out to service, and you can get your mind on God, [or] you can let your mind scatter. It's easy for you to get your mind off of God. You've got to have your mind fully on God, and if you don't keep it that way, you begin to look around at this one— maybe somebody sitting around here, somebody across the church house. Or you may get your mind on something back at home—get your mind completely off of God. But I'm talking about getting your mind completely *on* God and letting Him just take your mind and began to teach you and tell you, "[Interviewee's name], now's the time for you to carry out my signs." (H15)

Although serpent handling occurred in situations other than in services at church, all such events were understood and described by participants from the context of their larger Pentecostal tradition of worship that emphasizes a direct encounter with God—whether experienced inside or outside a regular church service. These encounters involved either a more common experience of feeling God in the body or a less frequent sense of knowing his presence through faith.

AN ANALYSIS OF MEANING IN THE EXPERIENCE OF HANDLING

Our interpretive analysis of the interviews found that the phenomenon of serpent handling emerges primarily as a sacred, embodied event from the larger ground of Pentecostal-type worship. The meaning of this experience can be understood and represented as a gestalt-type pattern involving four interrelated themes: (1) "Wanting to Do," (2) "Death," (3) Connection with God, and (4) "Fear"/"Victory." As suggested by chart 2, meaning in the experience of serpent handling emerges as a pattern of themes related to experiences of the body, which, in turn, serves to ground them in corporeal existence by providing a context in which they are understood. In the sacred arena of worship, an awareness of one's own body was described as a major context in taking up serpents, although other contexts, such as others, world, and time, were also noted to lesser degrees.

CONTEXT OF WORSHIP

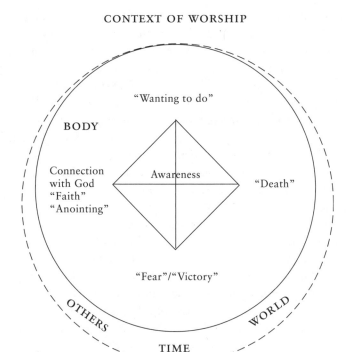

"Wanting to do"

BODY

Connection
with God   Awareness
"Faith"   "Death"
"Anointing"

"Fear"/"Victory"

OTHERS   WORLD

TIME

CONTEXT OF WORSHIP

Chart 2. The thematic structure of meaning in the religious experience of handling serpents.

The experience begins with participants feeling a desire of "wanting to do" the sign; most often this involves an awareness of the need for obeying the Word of God. While sensing this desire, participants are keenly aware of the potential for death through the presence of the serpent. Through a focus on God, however, they experience a connection with God, described as "faith" and/or "the anointing" and thus are enabled to confront "death" through the taking up of the deadly serpent. If harmed by the serpent, or if the connection with God ceases, an experience of "fear" returns; if unharmed while handling the serpent—which does not necessarily mean without receiving a bite—participants reported intense feelings described as "victory." Although idiographic differences exist within this structure of meaning, its thematic pattern emerged consistently across all seventeen protocols in which experiences of serpent handling were described.

In terms of other existential contexts that come into awareness (see chart 2), God is experienced through connection as an Other, although people also enter into the Other awareness in different ways, for example, through the taking up and handing over of serpents, the laying on of hands, the observance of fellow handlers. Death also is experienced as an Other in the form of a fearful enemy who threatens one's life and must be overcome. As serpent handling takes place, the context of world comes into awareness in varying degrees—from a full consciousness of worship music and other environmental surroundings to a diminished awareness of anything but God. Except when harmed, time is transcended in the handling of serpents, especially when victory is experienced.

Each of these themes is felt in the participant's body, not thought and represented, and the experience is direct and unreflected. As suggested by the connecting lines in chart 2, relationships among and between the themes are fluid within the experience of serpent handling. None of the themes are independent, and none are uniquely bounded. As one theme comes to the forefront of awareness, all others shift momentarily to the periphery of consciousness, where they merge with, and provide support for, the theme currently in focus. This continues in the experience until the flow of consciousness brings another of the themes into primary awareness, pushing all others to the periphery where, they, in turn, interplay and provide support for the focal theme currently attended. Interdependent as such, all four themes are simultaneously present and co-constitute for participants the general meaning of the experience of serpent handling. Each of these major themes and subthemes of the experience is outlined below, with brief excerpts from various protocols to illustrate the specific ways in which participants described them.

Theme I: "Wanting to Do" (the Word of God)

All participants described feeling a "desire" or a "need" to take up serpents. With the exception of two young female participants, whose families were active in the tradition long before their own times of conversion, all participants specifically described an awareness of wanting to obey the Word of God in relation to their handling—desiring "to be a doer of the Word and not a hearer only" (H12). All seventeen participants, however, expressed a basic desire of wanting to practice the sign and used descriptive words or phrases such as "want[ed] to [do]"

(H1, H5, H6, H7, H8, H9, H10, H11, H12, H13, H14, H15, H16, H17); "I wanted more" (H8); "desire[d] [to do]" (H3, H6, H15, H16); "I need to be doing" (H6); "just started gnawing at me inside" (H2); "I had every intention of doing it" (H4); and "like to [do]" (H5, H6). (Codes in parentheses indicate specific participants.)

The the seven participants who had no relatives initially involved in the serpent-handling tradition reported that they had heard from others about the practice and had read about it in the Bible, at which time they described experiencing a desire to respond to the mandate as obedient believers. For example, one young preacher told of his conversion to the practice:

> I remember reading the signs, one night—the actual Scripture, Mark 16:18. I remember reading that one night. And I remember it was like all through my sleep that night. I was quoting that Scripture: "They shall take up serpents. They shall take up serpents. And if they drink any deadly thing, it shall not harm them." And when I woke up that morning, I was quoting that Scripture. It was just like all through my sleep, the whole night, that Scripture was there. And then, it wasn't long . . . I had a made-up mind that I was going to do that. So I did. . . . I went to the man that I knew had been there—down to [a local serpent-handling church]—and I asked him if he'd go with me that night, and he said, "Yeah, we'll go." And I had—on the way down there—I had every intention of doing it. (H4)

At one level, it seems difficult to distinguish between the handler's immediate awareness of obeying the Scripture when practicing serpent handling and his (cultural) disposition for being, at all times, an obedient believer who practices the sign. Despite this ambiguity, when asked to describe their experiences, all participants disclosed a conscious desire to obey the scriptural command. Whether given as a justification for their handling or as a present aspect of awareness in their experience of handling, it remains as part of their experience as described and serves to provide meaning for the event.

When asked what was meant by stating that he "had to" take up serpents, one participant said:

> You have to believe it. It's in the Bible. If you believe it like you ought to, you will go where it's being done. You'll desire to go and see it being done. And if you go to that place, at some point God's going to move on you to do it. You may do it. You may not. If you don't, that's just between you and God is all I know. But I believe at some point, I believe God will move on you to do it, and I believe at some point, if you really believe it, and you're going and seeing it done, and you go to a church where it's being done all time, at some time, you're going to desire to do it. (H16)

Another participant described how the biblical mandate inspired in him a desire to handle but also how it came up inside him and took over, giving him faith and courage to handle the serpent:

> I had a good feeling, but I had a little fear. But I said, "It's in the Bible. It's in the Scriptures." . . . I knew it was right. And I wanted to do it. . . . As you move into this and begin to deal with it, when the Scriptures began to move out to you, and you begin to read it, and it begins to come in to you . . . them Words will just come up in you. . . . [I]t just takes me over. I mean it's just a wonderful feeling. He said it's bread come down from heaven. You know, we can eat of it. When that's coming up to me, I'm eating. I'm eating of the Word. I'm drinking his blood, and believing every Word he said. (H1)

As they reflected on the first time they took up serpents, other participants described similar experiences:

> [A] man had found it [the serpent] inside the plant where I was working, and I remembered the Scripture—the Word of God—coming to me then, and the Lord speaking to me and said, "Don't you believe my Word?" And I reached down and picked it up and carried it and put it outside. (H4)

> And I said, "Lord, you told me I *shall,* and that *shall* means *shore enough.*" And I said, "I'm just a baby in this," and I said, "I'm just gonna take you at your Word." So the next thing I knew I went up there and I had a serpent in my hand. (H8)

In the context of a worship experience, the taking up of a serpent involves an awareness of "wanting" to handle serpents, primarily as an obedient response to the expressed command in the Bible. In the words of one participant, "It's what the Bible said. You shall take up serpents *if you believe.* They say it's proving your faith. . . . No, I'm not proving my faith. I'm proving to God I'm *doing* what God wanted me to" (H12).

From an interpretive analysis of the protocols, it seems difficult if not impossible for participants to separate "believing" from "doing." These two terms appear to them as one and the same—believing *is* doing. As Bible believers, they experience a desire to obey the last command of Jesus before his departure from earth. During this practice, they are aware of wanting to do what Bible believers "ought" to do—that is, "take up serpents."

Theme II: "Death"

In the serpent-handling context, an awareness of "Death" is always present; this awareness was described by all seventeen participants. The possibility of being bitten is ever present, belying popular stereotypes that handlers are in some sense secure in the knowledge that they cannot be hurt. We have never met a handler who did not understand that serpents mean death. No handler believes in a magical ability to handle without harm. While some handle from faith alone and others handle only when anointed (see chapter 9), neither faith nor anointing assures immunity from bites. All seventeen persons whose interviews are discussed in this chapter, with a single exception (H2), had attended church with acquaintances who subsequently died from serpent bites when practicing the sign. Nine participants (H3, H5, H6, H7, H9, H11, H12, H15, H17), three of whom were relatives of the deceased (H7, H12, H17), voluntarily mentioned these individuals in their interviews. Eight participants (H3, H5, H6, H7, H9, H11, H12, H15) described their presence at services in which these individuals received fatal bites. Three participants (H5, H9, H12), in fact, had handled the same serpent that delivered the lethal bite, and one of them (H12) described handling the same serpent *after* the death of its victim, his own sister. Another participant (H11) described the service in which he had provided the serpent that fatally bit Charley Hall, a renowned serpent-handling minister of yesteryear, and told of his difficult feelings both during and after the incident. One participant (H15) described taking up serpents at the graveside of a close friend who had died of a serpent bite—an event that took place just two days before his own interview. It was evident that participants were keenly aware of death as a constant presence.

I mean, it's like you take up death in your arms and just hold it there and not worry about it. (H1)

I just went right on over and took it from him. . . . It just happened all of a sudden like that. He moved that way cause He knows I'm scared to death of them. (H6)

He got bit by an eastern diamondback in church, and he stayed here at my house until about one or two o'clock in the morning. His wife kept calling and talking to him, and she finally talked him into going to Chattanooga to the hospital, so we carried him up there, and he died about seven o'clock the next morning. (H7)

I had danger in my hand—had death in my hand. (H8)

That serpent that bit me was given to me, and we took it home. . . . It scared me. It really, really scared me. We were all praying one night. We had the snake box . . . and they opened the box up, and took that serpent out. . . . Scared me to death. I could see it biting everybody in the house. It really frightened me. (H9)

[My first experience of handling serpents] was at a service in Johnny Holbrook's—the man that was serpent bit and died—it was at his church. (H13)

Like I said the other night, when you take those things out, you've got your life laying there in your hands. I mean, when you're looking at that thing, you're looking at your life because it can bite you, and if God don't intervene, you're gone. I mean it can take you out, and it don't take a day or two, it can take you out the very minute it bites you. (H14)

Anytime you handle one, it could bite you, and it might could be your last bite. (H16)

It's instant death. . . . You better make sure that you're not hypocriting—that you're living a good clean life—because when you take up that serpent, you stand a chance of being bitten and dying. (H17)

As indicated by these excerpts, the element of deadly serpents at church and personal knowledge of their capabilities loom large among participants. Their awareness of potential harm and death is present each time the serpent box is opened—whether the person participates as a practitioner of the faith or as a concerned observer.

Of the seventeen participants, twelve (H1, H4, H5, H7, H9, H10, H11, H12, H13, H14, H15, H16) had experienced serpent bites when obeying the scriptural mandate and provided descriptions of such events—three (H4, H11, H12) of which were described as near-death situations. Among these encounters, H4 provided the most detailed account and afforded the most insight, perhaps because he was only twenty-four years old and had relatively recently converted to the tradition. As a newly converted preacher, only two and a half years into the faith, H4 was conducting a tent revival on the rural property of a fellow believer. After having already handled a copperhead, he felt moved to take up a canebrake rattlesnake, while preaching, which struck his wrist, injecting sufficient venom to produce immediate physiological reactions. Without his consent, the property owner eventually summoned emergency medical help, which transported the victim to the nearby hospital. Despite surgical and antivenin interventions, his vital organs began failing, and he received a dismal prognosis. H4 slowly recovered, however, and returned to the practice of serpent handling a few months later. His detailed description of facing what he thought at the time was his own death appears in chapter 10.

In addition to the twelve accounts of actually encountering the fangs of the serpent, four participants described dreams in which they themselves or others were bitten. One participant who had never experienced a bite remarked, "Sometimes, it's like when I lay down and go to sleep, I have dreams of people getting snake bit, or if I'm in a service with somebody when they get snake bit, that puts a fear upon me—not only me, but other people that's around me" (H8). Thus death is a major concern as believers go to the box or accept serpents from one another.

Theme III: Connection with God

All participants spoke of being connected with God and of discerning his "voice" in direct ways—a spiritual connection through which they were enabled to take up serpents. One participant described feeling a specific bodily reaction when experiencing God giving him clear directions for the handling of a serpent:

> When those chill bumps come up, I know that God is there. I know that the spirit is there. And you feel it. You just feel it, and you just have to do what it wants you to do. And I had to go in the box and get that serpent out and handle it. . . . He'll tell me which one to take out. He'll tell me what to do when I take them up, and he lets me know when it's time to put them up. . . . It's just something that just sits right down on you. Have you ever just all at once wanted to go somewhere and you knew that—you just got up and started getting ready to go? Well, that's the way the spirit does you. All at once you just know. (H14)

Other participants described similar experiences involving a connection with God in which he was both felt and heard:

> I felt the protecting spirit of the Lord there with me. And then when it left, I then put the serpent back up. It was as if to say, "That's enough now. I've let you do it." (H3)

> When you feel that come down—"He's [the serpent's] not going to hurt you. Now you can do my will." It'll all work out. Demons will be casted out, and serpents will be handled. (H5)

> I felt the spirit of God move on me to do it, and . . . I don't believe I would have got bit if I would have obeyed the Lord and did what he told me to do when he told me to put that serpent up. (H10)

> If you feel that the Lord has took you over, then he's going to lead you—if you'll let him lead you—'cause you can hear the leading of the spirit. You can hear the voice of God. (H11)

On the other hand, experiencing a connection with God and receiving instructions does not always involve specific emotional reactions. Participants also described serpent-handling experiences in which such communication was experienced in the absence of feelings: "And God says, 'You can go up there and take that serpent out and there won't be no harm to you.' Whether I feel anything, I'll hold on to that faith, and I'll come up here because God spoke to me, and I can do those things" (H11). When the issue was raised, participants were asked to describe what it was like to hear the voice of God. One individual responded:

> It's kind of hard to explain. . . . He'll talk to you all the time, and unless you're listening, you won't know it. . . . You can't hear him with your ears. You've got to hear him with your heart. You'll hear him from within you, talking to you, and he'll verbally talk to you just like I'm talking to you. He'll tell you, and you'll *know* because you'll have that feeling of love. (H9)

Another participant said that immediately after receiving a serpent bite he heard the voice of God in a similar manner—but this time to comfort his subsequent fear: "It's just like my conscience spoke to me, 'You're alright.' It sounded like my voice. It was like God was speaking, but it was using my voice" (H1).

In describing her experience of hearing God, a female participant took exception to being labeled crazy by unbelievers and to being accused of hearing "audible voices" on such occasions. When God speaks to her, she explained, "It's almost like you're thinking . . . an intuition . . . a gut feeling . . . you just *know*" (H17). However communication with God is experienced among participants, it involves a certain connection with God such that they feel enabled to take up poisonous serpents and to do his will. Further analysis of the protocols indicated that the theme "Connection with God" is characterized by two subthemes, "Faith" and "Anointing," either of which enables the handling of serpents.

Subtheme A: "Faith." All seventeen participants included in their descriptions a distinct reference to handling serpents by "Faith," although two, H2 (a male) and H6 (a female), had never actually done so. Participant H2, however, described ingesting strychnine, the fourth sign of Mark 16, by faith; this description did not differ in structure from those rendered by other participants who had handled serpents by faith. When asked what it was like to take up serpents by faith, participants gave strikingly similar descriptions, all marked by a present awareness of simply believing God for the ability to carry out the sign at the moment of the event. The basis for this faith was generally described as a personal belief that the perceived imperative of Mark 16 ("*shall* take up serpents") may also be understood as an enablement ("*can* take up serpents")—that is, an ability to "handle them at any time just because it's what the Word said" (H16). When he was asked to say more about this type of handling, one young preacher described an experience that occurred at his home:

> Handling it by faith, with God speaking to you . . . I've talked to the Lord, and the Lord tell me I could. I've asked the Lord, I said, "Lord, can I take that up?" You know, "I'd sure like to take that up. Can I take that serpent up?" And the Lord's told me, said, "Yeah, I'll let you take it up." . . . So I went ahead, and I did it. To me, the Word of God says it. The Word of God didn't say, "I'll let you take them up [only] on the anointing," or "I'll let you drink the deadly thing on the anointing." . . . I believe that you can take them up on faith without the anointing being there all the time. (H4)

Another participant described a unique way in which faith works within him when taking up serpents by such means:

> Now by the faith, they can be handled—*if* you've got the faith. . . . The way I do it . . . I get a picture in my mind—and I'm talking to the Lord all at the same time—of the cross, and it's sticking out of the ground, and I'm looking at the base of it. And as I start up, I see the blood on it, and by the time I see the blood running down it—I never get to his feet—I reach out and let that blood run right on my hands—and you're talking to the Lord—and when you see that blood on your hands, reach right down and pick him [the serpent] up and let him crawl in that blood, and he'll never bite you. But if you get your mind off that blood and look over at where they're snapping cameras at you standing there, he'll see you, and he'll bite, and kill you. As long as you've got that blood, and you don't see nothing else but that blood, he won't touch you. Now that's the way I've done it. . . . The faith is *you*. The faith is: "God, I *know* you'll let me do it. You said it. I believe it. I'm willing to do it. If I live or die, I'm going to do it." (H5)

As may be seen from these excerpts, and from other protocols as well, handling serpents by faith is based on a present belief, or knowing, that it can be done—that God has given "permission" to do the sign through a specific awareness of connection with him. This type of enablement involved no feeling of God on the body but was a more cognitive type of response to the scriptural mandate—perceived as the "permissive will of God" (H12). The descriptions of participants regarding the emotional aspects of this experience are well represented by H15's pointed remark, "On faith, I don't feel nothing." In contrast to H5 (quoted above), some participants described the possibility of experiencing a serpent bite, and even of potential harm, when handling by faith, but in such cases the same faith that enabled the handling would also be sufficient to sustain them if they did not waver in their belief. When telling of handling by faith, some participants described various degrees of fear experienced during the practice—for example: "a little fear" (H1); "still had fear" (H3); "feel fear" (H5); "a little leery" (H13); "quite a bit nervous" (H4); "had fear" (H7); and even "no fear" (H15). Other participants did not mention fear when handling by faith.

Subtheme B: "Anointing" ("God Moving on Me").   Although serpents may be handled by faith alone, all participants stated a preference for taking up serpents on the basis of what was described as the "Anointing." This is a central aspect of handling that we discuss fully in chapter 9. However, here it emerges as a subtheme in which the distinction between handling by faith alone is contrasted to handling by the anointing. In the words of one participant:

> I don't guess there's really no [particular] time to do it, if you're doing it by faith. You just do it. I really believe anybody should wait on the spirit of God to do it. (H10)

This "waiting" was mentioned by all participants in their descriptions of serpent handling and was always used with reference to anticipating a "moving" of God on or in the person—an embodied connection with God experienced as the anointing, which reportedly gave handlers a remarkable ability to take up serpents, as well as to carry out other signs.

It is noteworthy that when asked to describe how they felt the anointing, six of the seventeen participants indicated they were reexperiencing it at that moment, and this was evidenced not only by their own reports but also by observed physical gestures and affect. In each of these cases, the individuals needed a few moments before the interview could resume. One participant recalled his most memorable experience of anointing during a visit to a local revival. Concerning this event, he rendered one of the most complete and illuminating descriptions of the anointing found among the protocols. Because of its richness, a version of this account is presented below, though in condensed form.

> I was handling the serpent, and God began to move on me. . . . It was something that you could raise your hands, like this right here, and you could begin to feel that come from another world—just like you was touching heaven . . . the pearly gates. . . . I just feel it begin to move upon me right now [participant begins to cry]. . . . It felt just like rain. . . . [I]t would

start like maybe just at the top of my head. It's just like you would be standing in just a small drizzle of rain, and it would just sprinkle. . . . The more I'd reach my hands, the more I'd feel. . . . I began to just look up and let God take my mind, blocked everything out from all around me, and said, "God, here I am. Just whatever you want me to do . . . ever how you want to move on me, here I am." . . . [He] takes your mind, just like he's talking to you. You just quit [talking to him], and it's like he keeps on. . . . It's just like you're standing out in a small drizzle of rain. . . . I can feel it just a little bit, and before you know it, I'm soaked and wet. I'm just covered with the spirit of God—the anointing of God. . . . The power of God began to move on me, and I thought that there was no harm. . . . [I]f I just held on to that serpent . . . I believe the power of God would have killed it. . . . [A] fellow was sitting in front of me . . . [who] never cared a lot for me . . . God began to wipe my mind and never let enter what that man thought about me—or what nobody thought about me. . . . It's something you just can't explain. . . . You begin to try to tell somebody just how good how it feels, and you just can't tell them. (H15)

The experience of the anointing is a complex phenomenon and deserving of an in-depth thematic analysis that we provide below. For now—and for this participant in particular—it seems that the experience of the anointing involves four basic aspects of meaning, all of which are directly felt in the body: (1) God moving on him, (2) a diminished awareness of surroundings, (3) indescribable good feelings, and (4) a compelling sense of empowerment when handling the serpent. As we shall see in chapter 9, a focused study of the anointing produced a global pattern of themes that somewhat varies with and is more nuanced than those expressed here in this idiosyncratic description. However, those themes observed above may serve as a template in the present analysis to highlight similarities in the experience of the anointing that emerged across all protocols.

Based on his description, the anointing was felt by H15 as "God began to move upon me"—an experience reported by all other participants in this study. This "moving" was described as a body sensation that felt like rain, first on his head and then over his entire body. Other participants variously described this body sensation as a warmness, numbness, tingling, goose bumps, chills, and chill bumps (H3, H5, H6, H7, H8, H9, H13, H14, H15, H17), or as electricity, energy, juice, excitement, a stirring, fire, and pressure (H1, H4, H6, H8, H11, H12, H15, H16). Some participants described physiological responses involving increased heart rate, sweating, a quickening, a shaking, trembling, dancing, weakness, walking, running, and crying (H1, H2, H4, H6, H8, H10, H11, H13, H14, H15). The experience of being moved on also was described by H15 as being taken over or controlled by God for some divine purpose—the controlled object, in this case, being his mind. All other participants gave similar descriptions of feeling taken over when the anointing comes. For example, one participant spoke of losing control of his body to God as a "puppet . . . [with] . . . God pulling all the strings" (H16). One participant always experienced the anointing moving on him to take up serpents through losing control of his feet: "And then I said, 'Lord, I don't know where these feet are going, but they look like they're going to go up there.' That's when I just let them go. The Lord was pulling me and urging me. . . . If my feet don't move, I don't go. . . . I've got to know it's God" (H2). With the arrival of the anointing, participants felt it as a moving of God on them, marked by particular body sensations and some sense of lost control.

H15's description indicated that the anointing also related to "another world"—one that involved a diminished sense of awareness or a blocking out of his surroundings to some degree. Concerning the immediate context, all participants described their awareness of being present in varying degrees. Asked if she was aware of surroundings when describing an experience of anointed handling, one participant remarked, "Yes you are, but you're not focused on it. It's just kind of on your peripheral vision" (H17). When describing his experience, H16 expressed a similar awareness to the context: "You see everything, and you know what's going on." On the other hand, H3 described her experience as involving a "darkness" one encounters such as when "fainting." Others described being present to the immediate context in various degrees within this range when experiencing the anointing.

In terms of emotion, H15 described his experience as one involving a "good" feeling—a feeling that could not be adequately communicated to others. These "indescribable" feelings also were mentioned by all participants in their descriptions of the anointing. For several participants, the feelings were experienced as a "high" that far surpassed any comparison with alcohol or drugs. "Joy" also was used to describe the experience of good feelings, as well as "laughter."

Participants further described various feelings of "peace" and the absence of worry. One participant said, "At that time, it was just like I was covered. It was like a fan on me here just a blowing, and there wasn't nothing in here but peace. . . . No worry. There wasn't nothing on my mind but just feeling the Lord" (H8).

The good feelings that accompanied the anointing were commonly described as a "perfect love" that was "unconditional." In sum, these various descriptions of emotions experienced with the anointing can be understood only as an estimate of a very moving experience that transcends adequate description. As we mentioned earlier, a common expression among serpent handlers regarding this type of experience is, "It's better felt than told."

The most compelling feature of the anointing, and the most important one for the present context, is the sense of empowerment that accompanies the experience; this experience was described by H15 as "the power of God." Feeling "soaked and wet" with the anointing, he experienced empowerment to such an extent that he felt (1) protection—"no harm"—from the serpent, and (2) power to carry out the will of God—to handle the serpent—in an uncontested way. Connected with God through the anointing, participants described an enablement to take up serpents characterized by experiences of protection and power to do the will of God.

As for the feeling of "protection," it relates to experiencing the theme of death in the context of poisonous serpents, which understandably elicits the sense of fear—not only in those who would handle them, but also, to some degree, in believers who witness the practice. As the anointing is experienced, however, all participants reported a sense of "protection" (H3, H5, H9, H12) or "insurance" (H15) that lessened or removed altogether any fear related to the serpent. The anointing provides the person with a feeling of being "covered" (H3, H4, H8, H16), "safe" (H5, H6, H17), "alright" (H1, H7, H14, H16), or surrounded by a "hedge" (H2, H8, H9, H10, H11, H12) or a "shield" (H12, H15) from the explicit danger of the serpent; it was also described as being taken care of by the protective "hand" of God (H5, H9, H13). Since the participant is completely "covered" by the anointing, the sense of fear is eliminated, thereby allowing for the perceived will of God to be done. Participants indicated their loss of fear and feeling of protection in the anointing as follows:

> It's just something taking over in you to do that, and when he gets on you, then you're ready. When the spirit of the Lord gets on you, it's a wonderful feeling. It's joy. I mean, it's like you take up death in your arms and just hold it there and not worry about it. . . . There's no fear there when God takes over. (H1)

> It's like a warmth that comes over you, and it's like you feel in your heart it's alright to take up the serpent. And when you reach out there to take the serpent, you know what's going on . . . yet the Lord's in full control. . . . His presence may not be very strong upon you, but yet you can feel his presence—that he's protecting you. And then it's like you can feel it—as

quick as it came—you can feel it start to leave. And that's when you know to put the serpent back up 'cause you don't want to get within yourself 'cause that will get you hurt. (H3)

We were at church one night, and they had a big box of copperheads up behind the pulpit, and the Lord was moving. I had two of them in my hands, and two of the brothers kept taking the serpents out and piling them in my hands. And I had about twenty-two copperheads in my arms. There were whole heads going everywhere and . . . I didn't have any fear whatso-ever of getting bit, nothing hurting me. It was just a calm feeling. . . . I wasn't worried about anything at that point. (H9)

At that point, I had no fear, no fear whatsoever. . . . When you accept that anointing, all fear goes. You have no fear because you're right there in the palm of God's hand and you're going to be okay. (H17)

Some participants agreed from personal experience that feeling the anointing was no guarantee against being bitten while handling ser-pents, although if bitten, when anointed, there would be no harmful consequences—no ill effects. For example: "I've never been bit *and* hurt when I was anointed by God to take up a serpent. I don't believe he's that kind of God. I've been bit and hurt, but not when I was anointed to take up serpents" (H7). Hence the experience of the anointing pro-vides the obedient with a felt sense of protection that removes the fear of harm and enables them to obey God in taking up serpents.

In addition to feeling protected from harm, participants experienced through the anointing an enablement of the "Power to Do" the will of God. They reported that when handling serpents through the anointing, it was the power of God working through them that brought success. For example, when asked how she felt about knowing she had handled a deadly serpent with impunity, the participant quickly replied, "I didn't do it. The Lord did it" (H17). The following excerpt contains a description of one participant's first experience of handling a serpent.

They had serpents out everywhere, but I was in the spirit. I didn't realize they had took out the serpents, and I just kind of froze in my tracks, in a sense, and I was just amazed—actually. I could just see the power of God moving. I was just amazed at these serpents being bound by the power of God, you know. And the next thing I knew, my feet was kind of headed right on up to the people. I said, "Lord, I don't know where these feet are going, but it looks like it's going up there to those serpents." I said, "I'm trusting you in all this." And so I went right amongst the people and took the serpent out of one of the brothers' hand, and I looked at that serpent—it was a big rattlesnake—it was a very large rattlesnake—and I just said, "I bind you in the name of the Lord Jesus Christ." And that serpent just straightened out just as straight as a rod, and I handed him back, and I came back to my seat, and I said, "What did I just do?" I really didn't have that much control over it because the Holy Ghost, the spirit of the Lord, just came upon me to show me that I could, and he took over my vessel because I've always tried to be a willing vessel. If the spirit's moving, I try to follow. (H2)

As described, the participant's awareness was, first, of God's power moving through other believers to manifest the sign and, second, of God's power moving on him to handle a serpent. He perceived that his ability to come forward, to handle the serpent, and to "bind" it from harm came from an enablement of power through the anointing—that is, through a manifestation of God working in him, as a yielded "vessel," to fulfill his immediate purpose. Other participants described their experiences of empowerment to handle in similar but nuanced ways:

In the Bible, the Lord tells us we have power over the devil. When you take up a serpent, it gives you a feeling and lets you know the Lord did give me the Holy Ghost. I do have power over the devil. But you have to make sure it's God before you do it. (H6)

Whether I reach and get it from you or I get it from the box, I've got the same anointing. . . . [Y]ou might want to call it "taking a risk," but you're not taking a risk when you've got the power of God on you. You're in warfare with the devil, and you're depending on God to be there when you take them up and being there through the whole thing. (H12)

Then when he began to move upon me with his anointing power from heaven. . . . It's hard to explain. There's no way to explain what it feels like when I say he anointed my soul and let me carry out the signs. (H15)

Participants described an awareness of their ability to handle serpents successfully through the power of God working in and through them. For some, like H6, the experience of anointing not only provided a feeling of sufficient power for practicing the sign; it also provided an overall sense of feeling powerful—an empowerment that also annihilates fear and makes one feel invincible to harm.

In their connection with God, some participants described their experiences of faith and anointing as though they were aspects of a continuum. In a portion of his interview, for example, a highly experienced participant was asked what it was like to experience faith at the moment of faith handling.

H12: Well, it's just a feeling you've got. You're coming in with the feeling. You get a feeling—like you're obeying the feeling. And

which I think that the anointing is the spirit of God. So I feel like
I'm obeying God—doing what God wants me to do.

Interviewer: When you're obeying God, is that the faith part or the anointing
part?

H12: It's both. See, without faith, it's impossible to please God, and
the anointing is just the spirit of God moving within the faith. In
other words, it's a generating power.

Interviewer: A generating power?

H12: A generating power. Like a generating power 'cause God is really
moving and getting bigger all the time, seems like. Of course, he's
the same God all the time. But it just seems like when it starts, it
starts off light and easy, and then it gets like bigger and bigger, but
it's no heavy pain or nothing like that. It's just a heavy feeling.

For this participant, the experience of connection with God is such that
it begins primarily with faith—a basic belief in God's Word combined
with a desire to obey it—which is then gradually increased in magnitude
through a generating quality of the anointing. It is important to note that
in earlier descriptions of the anointing this participant was aware of no
fear at all when fully anointed to handle serpents and claimed to have
never experienced a single bite under such a condition. He described this
type of experience as a "comfortable feeling" that starts in his abdomen
and rises to his arms and hands and finally to his head: "When it gets up
to here [his head], I feel fine now. There's nothing going to happen"
(H12). On the other hand, he also reported that all 125 of his bites
occurred when handling within a range of experiences, from handling
only by faith up to handling when partially anointed (i.e., when he felt it
only in his arms and hands). When bitten on such occasions, he sometimes felt a subsequent hesitancy or need to "wait on God a little more."
He elaborated, "To me—now other people may feel differently—I feel
like I want to slow down. Maybe I'm getting a little ahead of God. . . .
I'm doing things out of the will of God—when God's not really there,
not your protector, right then. And you're going mostly by faith—in serpent handling—and you get ahead of God." For this participant, connection with God begins first with a faith experience—a felt desire to
obey God's Word—and some hesitancy concerning the lack of protection. With the onset of anointing, however, the sense of protection is felt
to increase continually until full anointing is sensed in the body, at which
time full protection is felt from all harm. According to H12, his failure
to wait for the completion of this dynamic, between faith and anointing,
sometimes has resulted in serpent bites and harm.

At least nine other participants described a similar relationship between faith, the anointing, and feeling protected when handling serpents. For example:

> It starts with faith. You've got to have faith to do anything. . . . Then the spirit begins to move. . . . You've got to move from faith. See, that's how we start, by faith. . . . Fear will move away when that anointing comes down. Like when I start in myself, there might be a little fear there, but if you wait till God *really* moves, then there's no fear. You don't fear death. (H1)

> There's been times I took them up on faith. He let me know, "It's alright." And I've took them up on faith and not feeling nothing, and then that anointing would begin to come by. . . . At any given time, I'm just waiting on the Lord to begin to anoint my soul, and when he begins to anoint my soul, then you just don't care what the serpent does. You just get to a point that you'll let them crawl, let do what they want to do. (H15)

Hence participants described feeling an enablement to handle serpents when connected with God through faith or anointing, or in some relationship involving the two, although protection from fear of harm or death was most often experienced during encounters of the anointing. At such times, according to one participant, "It'll all work out. Demons will be casted out, and serpents will be handled" (H5).

Theme IV: "Fear"/"Victory"

The major theme "Fear"/"Victory" was experienced by participants across all contexts of serpent handling. Based on participant descriptions, the experience of fear may be described as inverse to the experience of victory. For example, where fear is experienced as predominant, there is little or no sense of victory; with the experience of "complete" or "good" victory, fear is not sensed at all. "Fear"/"Victory" merges with the theme Connection with God.

Among all who assemble for worship, the presence of poisonous serpents is an abiding reminder of death, whereas the serpents' role in the "sign" itself makes them a physical threat to any who take them up. The presence of fear was described by all participants at some point when handling serpents. In experiencing a connection with God (especially on the basis of the anointing), feelings of fear are "overcome," leading to the "successful" handling of the serpent without harm and the concomitant experience most often described as "victory."

I was handling it, and I was testifying, and its head was laying in my hand. Had good victory. . . . [Can you tell me what victory is?] It's feeling that anointing and knowing everything's alright. (H16)

The Lord moved on me, and I had a courage. . . . It was like a boldness of a lion. I mean it was like a courage of a lion. . . . I come up over the rail that night, and . . . went in on that western [diamondback rattlesnake], and I got him out. . . . So that's one of the greatest experiences, probably, that I've ever felt in serpent handling—is knowing that there's something that is so . . . so mean, but the Lord gives you victory over it—that you're able to handle it without getting bit. (H4)

I just had that feeling again. You know, you can feel the Holy Ghost move, and like . . . it's excitement . . . and I just felt like he wanted me to do it. He was showing me I could have the victory over the devil. . . . Well, after I gave it back to [a congregant], I just went to the place where I was standing and just thanking God that, again, he let me do something like that and took care of me while I was doing it, not letting me get hurt, and just blessing me so. (H6)

I was talking to the Lord: "Thank you, Lord, for giving me the victory." He was giving me victory over those copperheads. I mean, there were legions of devils right there in my arms, and the Lord was giving me victory and the power over them. . . . When the Lord moves and you have a serpent, it's just like a baby. It's just like a dishrag. It can't do nothing. When God's got control of it, it's helpless. (H9)

Concerning her first experience of taking up serpents, one participant gave a lengthy, detailed description of experiencing the anointing so strongly that she lost awareness of her surroundings and even of the serpent she held. She reflected on her experience:

An awesome experience. I mean God had full control, and I guess, you know, he knew I was so scared of the serpent—the snake—and he knew I was scared to reach there and take him up and hold him and everything, and that he just—the first time, he just had to—I call it—wipe me out, so I wasn't aware of what I was doing, [in order] to be able to experience his love and his feeling. . . . I really don't know how to explain it. . . . It was like I entered into a darkness. . . . [W]hen I realized what was going on, and I was coming out of this darkness, I was happy. I was shouting. I was praising the Lord cause he gave me the victory over this. (H3)

For all participants, the word *victory* helps to capture various feelings that were described as being similar to those of someone who has conquered a formidable adversary—in this case, the foiling of the devil and his malevolent forces. Such a feeling of victory was described as different from the feeling of "Power to Do," which is experienced with the "Anointing." Whereas "Power to Do" stems from feeling sufficiently equipped for spiritual battle with the adversary, "Victory" is a feeling of celebration over the battle having been won—sometimes even experienced in advance of the confrontation with the serpent. Participants were asked to elaborate on the feeling of victory.

> I was happy. . . . I was praising the Lord that he let me experience this feeling, because to myself, I had accomplished something for him, to be able to do one of his signs. . . . The more that you can accomplish for him and do for him, it just feels like your spirit's uplifted. . . . It's a joyful experience. (H3)

> It's good. It's like that you've been satisfying to the Lord—that you've done something of his approval, because he's watching out for you. . . . But just to take something so aggressive, the Lord will stop the mouth of something so aggressive—something so mean. It's a good feeling. It's like that you're at a satisfactory point for the Lord. . . . It's like a goal accomplished. (H4)

> Victory is having power over anything—coming out on top. That's the way it is. See, if you win a war—the victory of the war—you've got the victory. . . . It's victory I feel like I've got over serpents when I handle them and don't get bit. I feel like, "I've got victory over that devil." . . . I feel good when I'm handling them. (H12)

> Whew! It felt good. I could have went through the top of the church. . . . When you get the victory over that serpent, [you can] throw him back in that box. . . . God overtook him. (H14)

It is important to note that participants sometimes received serpent bites when anointed and feeling the victory, but there were no physical consequences. In such cases, the bite was experienced as "a sign from God. . . . It proved to other people how real God is" (H15). In this way, it is felt that unbelievers, expecting to see unfortunate consequences of a serpent bite, were shown instead that God is among the believers—an experience of victory indeed.

Participants reported a variety of meanings when a serpent bite and harm occurred. Harm sustained from a bite was described as a sign to prove the danger of the serpents to unbelievers and skeptics (H1, H8, H9, H15, H16, H17); chastisement for disobedience (H2, H3, H8, H10, H16); pride (H11); carelessness (H3); misinterpretation of the anointing (H6, H8, H10, H11, H12); unspecified sin (H5, H9, H10, H12, H13, H14, H16); suffering on behalf of another (H4, H11); a personal lesson in the virtue of suffering (H12, H14); the will of God (H5, H6, H12, H13); an occurrence for unknown reasons (H4, H7, H10, H11, H16). Regardless of the meaning inferred, effort was made to overcome the subsequent feelings of fear with victory.

One participant (H3) said that she was "scared" when she witnessed a fellow believer being bitten because she knows "what they [serpents] can do." Along with other believers who were present, she "got to praying for him, and the Lord moved in it" to such an extent that victory was finally obtained for the victim over the bite. When asked what "getting the victory" was like in that context, she replied:

> It feels good that the Lord has moved on something that you're asking him for—that he has healed someone that's sick, if you've been praying for someone that had been sick and going through a lot of torment. . . . [I]t puts another step on the devil, you know, to get victory over him. It brings him down just a little bit more every time we can pray through to God and God hears us. It just pushes him out that door a little bit more. (H3)

When asked to describe the experience of feeling troubled for the victim and then helping him pray through to victory, she said:

> It's a painful experience in your heart. You're hurt 'cause you know, when that happens, it can lead to death, okay? It hurts you, like you've already lost a loved one. It hurts 'cause you know what can happen, and you just start praying with everything you've got, "Lord, hear me," you know, "hear this prayer. See the need that we need right now." And then when it finally overcomes that one—the Lord moves upon it—and you start feeling good within your heart again, you know the Lord's moved on it and took care of it. . . . It's just joy . . . Victory and joy . . . Victory. (H3)

Although she felt the presence of death, the participant experienced fear as vanishing when God was felt to move (anointing) and to bring feelings of joy—victory. Asked if the physical appearance of the bite changed after the experience of victory, she said: "It looks the same. You just know the Lord's gonna take care of it. . . . It don't matter if it's swelled humongous or if it don't swell at all. If you know without a shadow of a doubt the Lord's moved in it and you stand upon that, and that faith, and believe in that. It's gonna be alright." After the experience of victory, the victim reportedly suffered no pain from the bite, although he did experience some swelling of tissue. The occasion of the bite and the victory achieved were experienced by believers as a sign to onlooking unbelievers for the purpose of confirming the viability of the serpents—observed in the swelling of tissue—and of God's power to heal—so noted by the testimony of no pain. In the context of even a harmful serpent bite, subsequent feelings of fear can be overcome by experiences of victory.

On the other hand, the feeling of victory obtained after the event of a harmful bite can be lost again by refocusing on the severity of the injury with doubt—hence, the return of fear. For example, after receiving a serious bite and returning home with symptoms, H7 was visited by a believer who laid hands on him and prayed for his recovery. He described what happened as the believer was praying:

> I came up off the couch just like I had never been snake bit, or nothing like that. And I sat around there for about, I guess, probably three hours and wasn't feeling the effects of it at all. I mean, it was over with . . . and some of them kept sitting around talking about what it [the bite] was supposed to do, how it was supposed to affect you, how it was suppose to do this, and how it was supposed to do that, and I got to listening to them, and I just thought, "How bad am I bit?" And I looked down, and when I looked at my finger, it was like I got bit all over again. It set in to burning again, and I never did get victory over it again. (H7)

For H7, and others like him, the experience of victory obtained when bitten can be ephemeral unless "you stand upon . . . that faith, and believe" (H3).

As described, "successful" handling can be experienced through victory in any of three situations: (1) the serpent does not bite, (2) it bites but without harm, or (3) it bites with harmful consequences. The critical factor for this is the way in which the "Fear"/"Victory" theme is experienced. Drawing collectively from his experiences of serpent handling, one participant described the meaning of victory for himself:

> If you get bit and it don't hurt you, you've got that much victory over it. If you get bit and it hurts you, and you don't die—by a rattler especially—you've got victory over it even if it *did* hurt. . . . I've always got the victory. . . . [I]f you've got fear, you've got doubt there. It's the same way with a serpent bite. . . . Victory's not fear. To get victory, you've got to keep praying, and believing that God's going to take care of everything. And he's *going* to take care of everything. He don't leave you out in the thin air. And if you die, well then, that's God's will . . . [So victory is . . .] . . . overcoming fear. (H12)

In summary, the experience of serpent handling, as described by participants, involves a structure of meaning characterized by a pattern of four interdependent themes. This pattern involves a feeling of "Wanting to Do" the sign, in obedience to the scriptural mandate, and an awareness of "Death" through the use of poisonous serpents. Through a felt Connection with God (obtained either on the basis of "Faith" or the "Anointing"), an enablement to take up the serpent is experienced in which feelings of "Fear" are overcome by feelings of "Victory" ("Fear"/"Victory"). As Connection with God remains, the serpent is handled with impunity (regardless of physical outcome), and "Victory" is experienced in terms of feelings of spiritual celebration.

From the perspective of participants themselves, the experience of taking up a serpent begins with an awareness of wanting to do what God has expressly commanded in his Word—that is, take up a poisonous serpent. Through the presence of the serpent, however, an awareness of death and potential harm is experienced on the basis of fear for one's safety. Amid this conflict—between wanting to obey God and fearing for personal harm—the person becomes aware of focusing on God and thereby experiences connection with God, either through faith or the anointing, sometimes both. On the basis of an experience of faith—that is, by actively believing that the Bible says believers *can* take up serpents—the person feels a confidence that relieves fear and provides a sense of God's permission to proceed to take up the serpent. In experiencing the anointing, the person feels God "move on" him or her, particularly on the basis of sensations on or in the body that are felt to strengthen in magnitude until all sense of fear is expelled from awareness and replaced by exuberant feelings of victory and protection from danger. In this felt connection with God, the person experiences the lessening (or complete loss) of fear and feels enabled (or empowered) to obey God in the taking up of the poisonous serpent. As long as connection with God remains, the person handles the serpent without harm (even if bitten) and becomes aware of celebratory feelings of victory and a renewed sense of vitality experienced as a foretaste of eternal life.

Because of validity issues concerned with the above description that we abstracted from participant interviews, we sent it to three serpent handlers and asked for their independent evaluations as to whether it accurately captured their own experiences of handling serpents. In other words, we wanted to see if we had "gotten it right." Two of these handlers had participated in this study; the third had refused to participate in this study because of previous unfortunate experiences with researchers and interviewers. After careful consideration, all three of the serpent handlers agreed that the above description depicted their own experience of serpent handling as well as could be captured in language.

The experience of handling serpents is infused with spiritual significance that affects the meaning of life for practitioners in a much broader context—an important aspect often overlooked by previous investigations concerning this subject. This understanding is made possible only by taking into account what participation in the practice means from the participants' point of view.

TOP: Believers fellowshipping outside the Old Rock House Holiness Church (1997) before the service begins. (Photo: Ralph W. Hood Jr.)

BOTTOM: A pastor transporting serpents in locked boxes. (Photo: Jeffrey Schifman)

TOP: Serpent boxes, the "deadly thing" (strych-nine), anointing oil, and the Word of God. (Photo: Ralph W. Hood Jr.)

RIGHT: Being obedient to the command of Jesus to "take up serpents." (Photo: Ralph W. Hood Jr.)

LEFT: Preaching while doing one of the signs. (Photo: Ralph W. Hood Jr.)

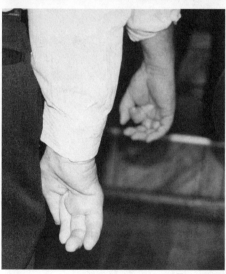

BOTTOM: The hands of the faithful who have been maimed by bites from their years of obedience in practicing serpent handling. (Photo: Ralph W. Hood Jr.)

RIGHT: Drinking the "deadly thing," in this case, strychnine. (Photo: Ralph W. Hood Jr.)

BOTTOM: Another obedient believer handling a serpent. (Photo: Ralph W. Hood Jr.)

Handling a serpent through the anointing. (Photo: Ralph W. Hood Jr.)

TOP: The once-infamous Dolly Pond Church of God with Signs Following in Birchwood, Tennessee. Years after serpent handling had ceased in the community, the property was purchased by the Church of God of Prophecy (COGOP), which built a modern facility alongside the old structure. Weeks after the picture was taken, the building was torn down by the COGOP, as if to rid itself of its historical association with serpent handling. (Photo: Ralph W. Hood Jr.)

BOTTOM: Sitting safely in the back of the church, a child handles a rubber serpent— a symbol of the future of a religious tradition whose hope rests largely in transmitting its faith across generational lines. (Photo: Ralph W. Hood Jr.)

CHAPTER 9

The Experience
of the Anointing

Anointing, like tongues speaking, may be linked to trance states. However, "trance" does little to describe the experience of anointing, a central experience in serpent-handling churches. Anointing is a common experience among Pentecostals, whether or not they handle serpents. In the existing research literature, there is little that deals specifically with the anointing experienced among Pentecostals—let alone serpent-handling churches. Also, as we noted previously, conceptualizing the anointing or tongues speaking in terms of changes in mental states or chemical levels suggests a causal analysis that bypasses the question of what the experience of anointing is like and what meaning it has in the believer's life. Neglecting the perspective of the anointed person would seem to produce an incomplete picture of the phenomenon. From a psychological point of view, it would seem that a more complete understanding must include a rigorous description of what the experience is like from a first-person perspective—that is, from the perspective of the anointed worshiper. This concern is the focus of this chapter. The material presented here is derived from the interviews of eleven of the seventeen serpent handlers who provided detailed descriptions of what it was like to experience the anointing.[1]

Individual interviews were scheduled at the convenience of participants and conducted at locations they suggested. We began each interview with the question, "Can you think of a time that you have taken up a serpent and tell me about that in as much detail as you possibly can?"

From this starting point, the interviews continued for approximately one and a half hours. In every interview, without exception, the participant raised the issue of handling serpents on the basis of the anointing, at which time questions were asked to seek a more complete description of what that experience was like. At the conclusion of all interviews, each participant expressed satisfaction that his or her descriptions of the serpent-handling experiences were as complete as possible.[2]

THE CONTEXT OF THE ANOINTING

Handlers have a clear sense of what it means to be anointed. As with Pentecostals in general, the phenomenon of anointing emerges largely as an embodied event. In most descriptions, the anointing was experienced in church services that also included intense praying, singing, shouting, dancing, and preaching, all of which express the emotional aspects of Holiness-Pentecostal worship that are integral to the faith (Synan, 1997; McCauley, 1995). Within this nexus of activities, the phenomenon of anointing was described to emerge as a particular awareness of the body that served to contextualize the way in which God was directly experienced by the person. Serpent handlers, like many other Holiness-Pentecostal believers who do not handle, all share a faith that is "better felt than told."

An Analysis of Meaning in the Experience of the Anointing

The experience of anointing was characterized by our interview participants in terms of five overlapping themes. The diagram presented below in chart 3 is meant to suggest that the anointing emerges as a pattern of themes related to experiences of the body, which, in turn, serve to ground each of the themes in corporeal existence as well as to provide a context in which they are understood. This diagram represents the pattern of themes that emerges within the direct experience of anointing among religious serpent handlers.

These themes emerge primarily from the existential ground of body, although the grounds world, others, and time are also experienced. As indicated in chart 3, an awareness of one's own body was described as the major context for the anointing; world, others, and time were noted to lesser degrees. The triangle circumscribed by the three uppermost themes represents those most directly related to the body. What this means is that the onset of anointing is experienced in terms of a partic-

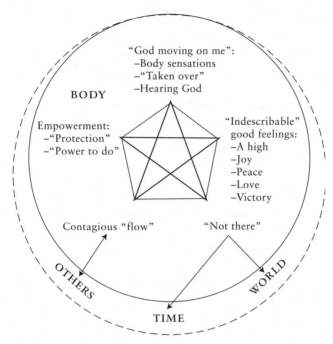

Chart 3. The pattern of themes that emerges within the direct experi-
ence of anointing among religious serpent handlers. © 2000. From
"A Phenomenological Analysis of the Anointing among Religious
Serpent Handlers," by W. P. Williamson, H. R. Pollio, and R. W.
Hood Jr. Reproduced by permission of Taylor & Francis Group,
LLC, www.taylorandfrancis.com.

ular body sensation usually described as "God Moving on Me." This
experience was characterized as involving invincible feelings of Empowerment as well as "Indescribable" Good Feelings—both of which were
reported as directly experienced in the body.

In addition, participants described the experience of "Not There"—a
theme that captured an encounter in which awareness of the immediate
surroundings was diminished in varying degrees. As other worshipers
enter into awareness, the phenomenon of the anointing is experienced as
a Contagious Flow that spreads to others in the context of worship. As
suggested both by its position in chart 3 and by the lines connecting it
with each of the other themes, the theme "God Moving on Me" was central to the experience of anointing and directly related to all other themes
experienced. In this regard, it is important to note that the interconnec-
tedness between and among the themes indicates their fluidity within the

experience of anointing and that none is mutually exclusive. Participant descriptions indicated that the various themes were experienced as direct, felt, and unreflected and not as thought, represented, or conceptualized. Each of the major themes and subthemes of the experience is outlined below, with brief excerpts from various protocols to illustrate the specific ways in which participants described them.

Theme I: "God Moving on Me"

In each of the protocols, participants described the onset of anointing as a sense that God was moving on them in a profound way. As one participant put it, "You know when the Lord is moving on you. You know, there's no mistaking it" (A9).[3] When telling of an experience of serpent handling, another participant noted, "That power that moves on me— a lot of people, they call it 'the anointing'" (A4). When asked to say more about feeling God move on them, participants described a core of three consistent subthemes.

Subtheme A: Body Sensations.   The participants' experience of feeling God move on them always began with a physical body event sensed in various personal ways:

> I've been just like that [hand trembling]. I wasn't nervous from being scared. It's the spirit of God. . . . I knew I wasn't nervous or scared. It had to be God moving in me. (A1)

> It don't just—BOOM!—hit you all at once. You feel just like warm water begins to run all over you real slow. (A5)

> I can usually feel it in my head, just like a crawling, tingling sensation. It just goes from the top of your head to your toes. Like I said earlier, I heard people call them goosebumps, tingly feelings, and it's just—you can't be still. I can't be still when I feel the Holy Ghost moving. (A6)

Other participants spoke of sensations in the feet (A2), dancing and crying (A8), or feeling "quickened" (A11).

Subtheme B: Taken Over.   As God is experienced to move on the person, there is a sense that he or she is being taken over by God for some divine purpose. As one participant remarked, "It's like something takes over the carnal mind" (A4). Another said it this way: "I began to lose control of my hands and stuff, and something else was beginning to take over my body" (A5).

Subtheme C: Hearing God.   The anointing not only makes itself known by various feelings in the body and by the sense that it has taken over bodily activities such as taking up a serpent or laying on hands for prayer; participants also reported experiencing God speaking to them in comforting or directive ways. When asked what it was like when God spoke to him on one occasion of anointing, one participant said, "It's just like my conscience spoke to me, 'You're alright.' It sounded like my voice. It was like God was speaking, but it was using my voice. But I knew I was alright" (A1). When anointed, participants are careful to listen for the voice of God to indicate the proper time when such activities are to begin and when they should stop. Such neglect may be costly in terms of missing God's will, which could result in loss of life. In experiencing God move on them, participants feel its onset in terms of various physical sensations, experience some loss of self-control, and hear God communicate with them in meaningful ways concerning his will.

Theme II: Empowerment

With the experience of God moving on them, participants reported finding themselves sensing an empowerment through the anointing. Empowerment was felt in two specific ways: through feelings of "Protection" and through feeling a special "Power to Do" what was needed at the moment for God.

Subtheme A: "Protection."   Whether the situation involves handling serpents or drinking poison, the experience of anointing provides the individual with a feeling of being "covered" (A3, A8) or surrounded by a "hedge" (A2, A8, A9, A10) from the explicit danger of these or *any* encounters. Hence the person's sense of fear is eradicated under the anointing, thereby allowing the perceived will of God to be done. In talking of his experience of anointing when handling a serpent, one participant said, "There's no danger, cause you're *safe*—actually feel the hands of God reach down and touch you. My Lord! You can very easily walk into the fiery furnace, like the Hebrew children done it" (A5). Some participants agreed from personal experience that it was possible to receive a serpent bite while under the anointing—in fact, a few had actually been bitten at such times—but none believed that a bite experienced under the circumstances of the anointing would result in any harmful consequences or ill effects. Hence the felt protection, while anointed, allays fears of harm and death among participants. As described by one handler, these issues are of no concern when feeling the anointing: "The spirit of God moved on me out there, and I honestly didn't care whether I got bit or not. I mean, it didn't matter to me" (A7).

Subtheme B: "Power to Do."   In experiencing this empowerment, participants reported being infused with whatever power is necessary to perform the will of God at the time of anointing—whether it be to take up serpents, drink poison, cast out devils, or heal the sick. When asked how he felt in knowing he was successfully handling a poisonous serpent, one participant said: "It had a feeling of power of knowing that the Lord would give you the power to do things like that. It really gives you a feeling of power that He gives me—That devil's subject unto you. It just makes—It's a feeling of power" (A9), For this participant, the experience of anointing not only provides a feeling of sufficient power to perform one of the signs, his awareness of that ability also contributes to an overall sense of feeling powerful—an empowerment that also annihilates fear and makes the person feel invincible to harm.

Theme III: "Indescribable" Good Feelings

When speaking of the anointing, every participant referred to an awareness of "good feelings." When asked to say more about these sensations, all had difficulty and struggled to find satisfactory words to describe them adequately. These sentiments of ineffability are probably best represented in the words of this participant:

> It's hard to . . . I've never had anything make me feel like that, so I can't put it in human words, or I can't find anything. . . . There's nothing in this life, right here, nothing in this world that this world contains to be able to explain that or how it makes you feel. You know, some could use, "Well, it's better than drugs" . . . but I couldn't even use that to explain it because it's—it's nothing like drugs—it's—it's beyond anything that I've ever experienced. So, you know, you can't use drugs to explain it. You can't use a ferris wheel to explain it or a ride at the amusement park. The only way I know to explain it: it's the alpha, omega, the beginning, the end, the first, and the last. That's what it is. . . . It's the alpha and omega, the beginning, the end, the first, and the last. It's all in all. That's what the anointing is . . . It's *God*. (A4)

Although each participant noted that the good feelings of the anointing were indescribable, they attempted to describe them in language that best captured the experience for them. The major theme "Indescribable" Good Feelings was given further explication in terms of five subthemes—each of which was present in the descriptions of from six to ten participants. The observation that all subthemes were not described by each person suggests the range of variation among participants in terms of how the major theme was personally experienced.

Subtheme A: Being "High."   One feeling that participants described in their experiences of the anointing was being "high." In their protocols, some participants disclosed they had engaged in alcohol and drug use before conversion; thus being high was a meaningful metaphor for comparison with an experience they felt transcended adequate description.

> I can't describe what it feels like, but all I can tell anybody is, you know, you can imagine the best feeling you've ever had. I don't care if you've been high on liquor, or cocaine, or marijuana, or whatever high you've been on, you can multiply that by 10,000 times 10,000, and you still—you still wouldn't be able to come up with what this feels like. I mean that is just how great it is. (A10)

Subtheme B: "Joy."   "Joy" was the most frequently used description of the good feelings experienced when anointed. It was often used in conjunction with other words to enlarge its effect and significance, for example, "burst of joy" (A3), "joy bubbling up" (A7), "great joy" (A9), and "joy unspeakable" (A8, A10). Expressing this joy another way, one participant remarked, "I've felt the presence at times when I could do nothing but just laugh—just laughter. Nobody said nothing. I was just under the control of laughter" (A2).

Subtheme C: "Peace."   As participants encountered the anointing, they also reported experiencing feelings of "Peace"—the kind of peace that makes one aware of "no cares" (A3), "comfort" (A5), "satisfaction" (A7), "calm" (A9)—an abiding relief from worry. In describing an experience of taking up a poisonous serpent under the anointing, one participant said, "I mean, it's like you take up death in your arms and just hold it there and not worry about it" (A1).

Subtheme D: "Love."   Feelings that accompanied the anointing also were described as "perfect love," as one participant put it. When asked to elaborate, he said:

> Well, you know how it is when you love somebody, alright, like your wife or your children—the love that you have for them. But nothing else matters. And you have so much love for one person, it doesn't matter what happens.

> If you lose everything in your life—even your life—then God . . . that's how
> much love he has. And it's just kind of hard to describe the feeling. (A9)

According to this description, the experience of perfect love is an awareness of feeling supremely loved as a person who is most precious—for
example, feeling treasured as a beloved spouse or child—without any
conditions. In recalling their experiences of the anointing, some participants referred to themselves as God's children who were uncondition-
ally loved by him.

Subtheme E: "Victory."   Participants used the word *victory* to describe
how they felt about being on the winning side—that is, on God's side—
in a divine battle against Satan. For them, much of the difficulties experienced in daily life are due to the malevolent forces of the devil whose
aim is to do battle against the children of God. This feeling of victory
that comes from the anointing is distinct from that of power discussed
under the theme Empowerment. With the infusion of "Power to Do,"
the believer encounters a feeling of enablement for the purpose of
engaging in warfare against the devil. On the other hand, victory
involves feelings of celebration in advance of the battle already known
to be won. In describing this feeling, one participant said, "It's like a
goal accomplished" (A4). In the case of witnessing the healing of a
serpent bite in which the pain had abated but the physical swelling was
still present, another participant said it this way: "It makes you feel
good. . . . I call that getting the victory over it. You know, it puts another
step on the devil, you know, to get victory over him. It brings him down
just a little bit more every time we can pray through to God and God
hears us. It just pushes him out that door a little bit more" (A3).
Whether the anointing is experienced while taking up serpents, drinking
strychnine, or healing the sick, success was reported to provide participants with an awareness of victory, a celebrated good feeling beyond
adequate description.

   Although all participants related that good feelings were difficult to
articulate, each attempted to describe them in terms most appropriate
for her or him. The five subthemes that emerged from the analysis of
these efforts should not be construed as an "abstracted essence" of the
good feelings experienced but only as approximations of experiences
that were described as ineffable. As one participant rightly put it, "You
can't explain what it feels like. All you know is it feels like something
you've never felt before" (A10).

Theme IV: "Not There"

The experience of anointing also was described as involving a diminished awareness of the surrounding context. One participant stated, "You just get to the point where you just don't—you know, like that you're not there" (A1). In describing his own experience of anointing, another participant declared, "I mean I was just in another orbit" (A2). Still others, while anointed, reported not being so far removed from the world around them:

> You could hear the music and the shouting. You could hear everything around you, but yet, it was like it was in a distance. (A3)

> It just seemed like the only two people there were us. I just didn't even realize that other people were around me. (A6)

When anointed, the range of awareness to surroundings differed among participants, although it is clear that whatever they were experiencing was much more compelling than other activities in or features of their environment. Their description of the experience of anointing was such that it simply did not allow them to be fully present to other aspects of the situation. In fact, the return of full awareness to the surroundings was seen as marking the lifting of the anointing and the end of the experience: "The next thing you know, I was right back to my mind again, and it was gone" (A5).

Theme V: Contagious Flow

The moving of God is experienced as an infectious flow that may spread from one individual to the next, often but not exclusively through the medium of physical contact.

> I could just feel something just start moving on me from somebody having their hand on me. And it was like going from person to person. (A6)

> She laid her hands on my head, and it just went all through my body. (A7)

Although this flow of the anointing is often felt through touch, its transfer is not restricted to this modality. Some participants described situations in which they experienced the flow of the anointing spread over a congregation without physical contact: "It was just a special anointing that moved in here. A love moved in here, and I mean it overtook everybody—not just me" (A8). Whether the flow of the anointing is experienced on the basis of personal touch or by simple presence in a context where it is felt to manifest, there is a contagious sense of connection that "flows from deep down within" (A4).

A GLOBAL DESCRIPTION OF MEANING
IN THE EXPERIENCE OF THE ANOINTING

Taken together, the pattern of themes emerging from the present set of protocols provides a global description of the anointing as follows: The experience begins primarily with feeling the moving of God on the person, which is felt in terms of various body sensations, a sense that God is taking control, and the hearing of God's directive voice. With this experience, there is a profound sense of empowerment that infuses a feeling of protection from all harm, combined with a feeling of being sufficiently empowered to do the will of God at the present moment. This experience is such that the person feels drawn away in varying degrees and no longer feels fully present to the immediate surroundings, date, or time; yet the person feels a flow that radiates through contact with others as they come into awareness. Indescribably good feelings—variously approximated as a high, joy, peace, love, and victory—are felt from the onset of the anointing and continue to linger after the experience lifts.

THE MEANING OF ANOINTING
IN LIGHT OF TRANCE STATES

We have discussed the claims of researchers regarding the necessity of trance states for both tongues speaking and the anointing. In regard to the hypothesized role of trance in the experience of anointing (Kane, 1974b, 1982; Schwarz, 1960), or to its presumed relationship to neurological correlates (Burton, 1993; Schwartz, 1999), we have attempted here to offer some context of meaning regarding the phenomenon others have observed. For example, the meaning of invincibility to noxious stimuli experienced by participants in hypnotic studies (Kane, 1982) would seem to be different from that experienced by anointed serpent and fire handlers in a religious context, although the same psychophysiological processes might be involved. Not surprisingly, similar EEG patterns (Burton, 1993) and neurological processes (Schwartz, 1999) can be found in various contexts, although the meaning of these observations differs as a function of context—especially for religious serpent handlers. In this chapter we have explored the first-person experience of participants from reports of their encounters with the anointing and, by so doing, have attempted to enlarge the understanding of this phenomenon in terms of the religious context from which it emerges. It is in this way that phenomenological inquiry can be used to inform the findings of other approaches.

It is of interest to note that all investigators, including ourselves, have seen the same phenomenon. However, while other researchers have been intent on making causal claims as to possible altered states of consciousness, our focus here has been on the religious sense of the encounter. However, the descriptions emerging from our phenomenologically based study of the anointing are clearly not idiosyncratic but have been observed by other investigators who have been guided by other approaches. It seems that the commonalities of such cross-theoretical observations lend a certain measure of "generalizability"—in terms of a core experience—to the present findings concerning the anointing, particularly among religious traditions, that give it emphasis as a personal experience. Such generalization, however, should be made with care and with particular concern for the unique ways in which the phenomenon presents itself to the individual in his or her specific religious context. We think a more complete psychological understanding of the anointing must take seriously the tradition in which it occurs, and personal narratives must be understood from that perspective (Gergen, 1992). In this sense we hope we have given the serpent handlers a fair hearing.

BEYOND CAUSAL CLAIMS

Our description of the anointing brackets any claim as to its proximate or ultimate "cause." Instead we find it useful to describe the experience of anointing in relation to the existential grounds of body, world, others, and time, which are often thought to contextualize all human experience (Pollio, Henley, & Thompson, 1997). In the theme "God Moving on Me," there is a primary awareness of the body; moreover, participants mark the arrival of the anointing based on how their bodies feel at a given moment—whether noted by tingling sensations in specific parts of the body, warm sensations, trembling (quickened) body parts, tears, or other notable manifestations. In the experience of God moving, the body is felt to be taken over, and body parts, such as feet and hands, move without personal volition in response to a mind spoken to or impressed by God for the engagement or disengagement of a certain activity. The body provides an experience of an empowerment to act and feels the flow of the anointing through physical contact with other people and in the holding of poisonous serpents. While anointed, and even afterward, sensations of the body are described as being intense, joyful, carefree, perfectly loved, and victorious over every opposition.

Though the anointing is largely an embodied experience, this awareness of the body occasionally gives way to an awareness of other existential grounds. For example, the experience of "Not There" describes a relationship with the physical world in which the participant is aware of not being fully present to the immediate surroundings—an awareness of being shifted to another world, a realm more spiritual in nature. When feeling empowered through the anointing, participants become aware that they can act on the world—on serpents, poison, the devil—and, at such times, feel protected from any potential harm it poses. The ground of other people comes into awareness through a felt intimacy with God—the ultimate Other—and through physical contact with other people in the context of worship. In the latter case, awareness of others may be experienced either as a contact for the transfer of anointing or as equals who share an intimate moment of spiritual connection and blessing (see Buber, 1970).

The existential ground of time is marked in participants by an awareness of critical moments in the experience of anointing. It is recognized (a) when the anointing begins—"It starts from the top of my head and moves down" (A9); (b) when it directs a specific activity to be done—"You don't have any doubts about it. Well, it's time to go in the [serpent] box" (A4); and (c) when it lifts—"I guess, you know, the Lord didn't say it was time to put it [the serpent] up. It was just . . . like I knew" (A3). There is also an important temporal quality associated with the experience of good feelings. According to participants, the experience of anointing is marked by an embodied sense that God is moving on them, a felt Empowerment that protects and enables, elated feelings of the body that are beyond description, a diminished awareness of present surroundings, and an infectious flow that spreads to others. With the lifting of anointing, however, these phenomena disappear, with the exception of good feelings, which extend beyond the experience of anointing itself, leaving a kind of residue of the experience. As one participant described, "[It] makes you want to come back Wednesday night for service . . . Friday night . . . [and] Sunday night" (A11). Indeed, the experience of good feelings encountered with the anointing transcends the enabling experience itself and takes on a quality that significantly enhances life for the participant—a quality that, when felt dissipating, inspires the person to return and reexperience the anointing again and again.

In the phenomenon of the anointing, the person's primary awareness shifts among the major grounds of experience. With the onset of anointing, the themes "God Moving on Me," Empowerment, and "Indescribable" Good Feelings emerge primarily from the person's awareness of the body; the presence of the anointing is known by how the body feels in various ways. The experience of "Not There" comes to the forefront of awareness when the individual experiences not being fully present to his or her immediate surroundings in the context of worship. The ground of others emerges as the anointing spreads from person to person. Time is marginally noticed with anticipation of the anointing's arrival, the timing of its directives, and the notice of its departure, although good feelings persist for a time even after the anointing is no longer felt. No particular ground, when central to awareness, excludes all others; rather the ground presently attended only moves the remaining contexts to the periphery of consciousness until another comes into primary focus, as in figure/ground perception. In the experience of anointing, awareness of the body is predominant, though fluid shifts of attention also bring the world, others, and time to the forefront at particular moments. What is important here is that *how* each ground is experienced contributes to the meaning of the anointing as directly and unreflectively experienced.

When the procedure used in this study is followed, far from being "unscientific," it produces a description well illustrated by one participant in summarizing the profound meaning of the anointing in his own life:

> It's better than anything I've ever experienced in *this* life. The anointing is better than anything I've ever felt. . . . I've been through good things, and I've been through bad things in life, and I'd rather have the anointing than to have any of it. . . . I'd rather be poor and feel the anointing, as to be a great king and not have that anointing. And that's the way I truthfully feel about it. (A4)

This description stands as as an exemplar of what Kvale (1996, p. 298) defines as methodologically grounded objective knowledge of an interpersonally negotiated world as experienced and understood by those who live it. Hence, to seek an understanding of the anointing requires that we approach it from many different perspectives, including those of natural science seeking to make causal claims. However, such claims are insufficient to provide an understand of the anointing. A more contextualized experiential approach such as we have provided here is required.

CHAPTER 10

Near-Death Experience from Serpent Bites in Religious Settings

In this chapter we place near-death experiences by serpent bite (NDBs) in religious settings in the context of what has become known as near-death experiences (NDEs). We do this for two reasons. First, the conceptual issues in NDEs are directly relevant to the religious beliefs of serpent-handling churches, particularly with respect to human immortality. Second, the claim to prototypical NDEs widely reported in the popular literature lacks clear empirical support. It is not, for instance, typical of NDBs from serpent bites in religious setting by believers who handle. Thus it may be that NDEs are influenced by the beliefs of those near death. Beliefs may be a particularly salient determinant of NDEs when they are firmly grounded in a religious worldview and even more so when that worldview includes a ritual that believers know can kill. We begin with a conceptual overview of issues in NDEs, in particular, as they apply to serpent handlers.

CONCEPTUAL ISSUES IN NDE RESEARCH

The history of NDE research illuminates serious conceptual issues that determine how one is to evaluate various research strategies and findings. Three conceptual issues are especially relevant to evaluating the empirical literature on NDE. These issues are the definition of *death,* the problem of definition and measurement of *near-death,* and the metaphysical assumptions within which the phenomenology of NDEs can be variously illuminated. We briefly address each of these in turn.

It is obvious, as Badham (1997) has noted, that if one declines consideration of specifically religious claims (such as the resurrection of Christ) reported experiences of having actually returned from death are false. In Badham's words (1997, p. 2), no one who has "totally died" has ever returned to give evidence of life after death. Serpent handlers are likely to correct Badham and add at least the biblical example of Lazarus, but Badham's point remains. The conceptual limit of death is that once it occurs life is over. However life is defined, when it is technologically impossible to revive a person, then and only then is that person dead. By definition, no person experiences death and returns to tell the story. While we are not claiming that philosophical assumptions require that immortality be denied, we are claiming that the process of dying is a complex one. Serpent handlers in Appalachia tell many stories of those who died and were raised from the dead (see Hood, 2003a). However, from an empirical scientific perspective, when finally acknowledged death is a judgment that no additional activities can resuscitate the person. Thus, by definition those who "return" were close to or near death. The irony is that, as Blose (1981, p. 59) has noted, the hypothesis of survival of bodily death is empirically testable but only "asymmetrically. Allowing its truth, should it be true, but not its falsity, should it be false, to be learnt." Historically, NDE became the paradigm for claiming the truth of Blose's asymmetrical hypothesis. Serpent handlers accept this asymmetrical hypothesis as well but ground it firmly in the belief that one will realize the truth of this assertion when he or she dies.

In *Human Immortality: Two Supposed Objections to the Doctrine* (1898), James offered competing metaphysical options for evaluating human immortality. He noted that if one assumed that the brain *generates* consciousness, then death likely can be seen as the cessation of consciousness and hence life. However, if one assumes the brain *transmits* consciousness, then the brain's demise need not alter the existence of consciousness and hence immortality is possible. James argues that both metaphysical options are consistent with the empirical facts; hence immortality is a card still in play. This becomes crucial when we evaluate the conceptual issues that cloud NDE research, for even from a scientific perspective immortality is a conceptual possibility.

DEFINING AND MEASURING "NEAR-DEATH"

If death is the final declaration that nothing more can be done to resuscitate a person, then being near death is in part defined by approaching that limit. Several investigators have noted the immense value of having medical (physiological) indicators of organ states effectively monitored to indicate that death is near (Noyes & Kletti, 1976; Rodin, 1980, 1981; Sabom, 1981). Others have relied on human anticipation of death, noting that NDEs can occur in the face of intense fear (Noyes & Kletti, 1976). We consider their research below, but first we must note that the field of NDE research is clouded by conceptual and empirical confusion as to precisely who was "near death." For instance, often included in NDE research are subjects who have attempted suicide, even if their attempts led to widely different physiological consequences (Greyson, 1983) and even if the intent was other than death (Hood, 1970, 1971). Anticipating that one is near death and actually being clinically near death are largely orthogonal phenomena. Without some clear guidelines for "near death," judging "anticipated death," as we shall see with serpent handlers, raises the same issues that cloud judging the severity or sincerity of suicide attempts (Hood, 1970, 1971). It is not necessarily the case that suicide attempts intend death, nor is it the case that near-death encounters necessarily produce NDEs (Greyson, 1990).

If "near-death" has yet to receive a definitional consensus among researchers, it is not surprising that its assessment and measurement also remain problematic. Two approaches have been especially pronounced in the empirical literature on NDE.

In his widely popular work, *Life after Life* (1975), Moody identified fifteen criteria common among NDEs. Unfortunately, these criteria mix phenomena occurring during the NDE (such as a panoramic life review) with consequences or effects of the NDE (such as a reduced fear of death). In a sequel (Moody, 1977), he added an additional four criteria of NDE (also see Greyson, 2002, p. 318). It is important to note that no experience reported by any of Moody's subjects fulfilled all nineteen criteria.

Moody's criteria have been used as "checklists" to measure the extent to which a reported NDE fits the phenomenological template he identified. Further, there are problems with the linking of NDEs and out-of-body experiences (OBEs) insofar as not all NDEs incorporate OBEs, nor are OBEs necessarily more frequent in NDEs (Alvarado, 2002, p. 184). Further, corroboration of events "witnessed" during OBEs raises concerns relevant to our discussion of metaphysical issues below.

While the consequential criteria identified by Moody are aftereffects of NDEs, the criteria that best identify the experience are derived from Moody's own assessment of the phenomenology of NDEs. The most frequently cited criteria, or phenomenology, of NDEs have been woven into a thematic narrative of an idealized NDE. It includes going through a dark tunnel, typically toward a luminous white light; a panoramic review of one's life; the return to one's body if the NDE included an OBE; and images of spiritual beings identified by the nearly deceased's own faith tradition. Other criteria are common to a wide range of experiences, such as experiencing peace and quiet, or believing that one has supreme knowledge. Some are obviously only possible in a medical setting (where Moody collects most of his data) such as remembering being officially pronounced dead (Moody, 1975, 1977; Greyson, 2002, pp. 317–19).

Moody's criteria can be used to see if reports of NDEs correspond to criteria that he identifies from his participants, but the checklist is simply one way of defining NDEs by a form of construct validity—for example, the researcher's subjects rate their own NDE on the criteria that Moody has identified as common to the event. A more rigorous approach has been proposed by Greyson (1983) and has resulted in a scale for measuring NDEs. Greyson solicited responses from members of an association that promotes NDE research. They responded to an initial list of 80 criteria of NDEs culled from the phenomenology literature. These items were reduced to the 40 most commonly cited criteria and then further reduced to 33 items by eliminating those that were redundant and confusing. This resulted in an initial 33-item scale. The 33-item scale was administered to sixty-seven individuals, all describing NDEs (some more than one) that occurred from 9 months to 72 years before they completed this scale, which yielded a mean elapsed time, between the NDE and completion of the scale, of 17.9 years (Greyson, 1983, p. 371). Most NDEs occurred as a result of complications during surgery or childbirth but also included suicide attempts and sudden natural events such as anaphylactic reactions. Using unspecified means, Greyson produced a final NDE scale consisting of 16 items, measuring cognitive, affective, paranormal, and transcendental dimensions, each with 4 items. Greyson's scale is not necessarily related to the now-classic paradigm of NDE that has become identified with Moody's typology— the movement through a tunnel to a bright light where spiritual beings aid in a life review (uncommon in NDEs of children [Bush, 1983]). The consequential experience of being sent back from a place where one is bathed in a luminous light and knowledge is the assurance that this OBE will be recalled as a mandated return from death to complete some significant work left undone. Greyson's scale includes items familiar to

NDE researchers and partisans but in ways that are less doctrinaire. For instance, his cognitive dimension includes the question "Did scenes from your past come back to you?" His affective dimension notes such items as "Did you have a feeling of peace or pleasantness?" His paranormal dimension asks, "Did you seem to be aware of things going on elsewhere, as if by ESP?" Finally, his transcendental dimension asks such things as "Did you seem to enter some other, unearthly world?" (Greyson, 1983, pp. 372–73). Thus Greyson's NDE scale takes the phenomenology of NDEs seriously while constructing a reasonable measurement instrument that at least is conceptually open to empirical refinement (e.g., via factor analysis). At this point in the research, it is best to view both Moody's criteria and Greyson's scale as providing useful phenomenological criteria that suggest the multidimensional nature of NDEs and the likely independent physiological correlates to be found for aspects of what is clearly not a unitary phenomenon.

Further support for deconstructing the only apparent unitary nature of NDEs comes from historical studies. Zaleski (1987) has explored NDEs in the context of a religious imagination that has been fostered throughout Western culture. Her comparative study of medieval and contemporary NDEs is expanded to include "other-worldly journeys" that reveal variations in social construction over time. To cite but one example, experienced journeys to an underworld or hell (common in medieval traditions) have been gradually minimized, if not eliminated, and are all but excluded from NDEs in reports from contemporary Westerners. The rare citing of a negative phenomenology of NDEs or of negative aftereffects of NDEs (Greyson, 1992) is largely lost in the unitary narrative of both a positive experience and positive transformative effects. Likewise, Segal's (2004) massive study of experiences of "life after death," as a function of a religious imagination created in the interplay between a socially constructed image of an afterlife (often religiously described), becomes incorporated into individual experience that it helps to shape if not create. What constitutes all such NDEs is less their unitary nature than their self-authenticating nature for those who experience them. Thus the ontological issues become paramount, both for those who have NDEs and for those who wish to explain their real power to transform individuals as due to the working of the human imagination in a specifically and ever-varied socially and culturally constructed context. Serpent handlers are ideal subjects insofar as their life centers on a faith and a ritual practice that confronts death at both its sign and its symbolic levels.

METAPHYSICAL CONSIDERATIONS

It is clear that two distinct ontological assumptions among NDE researchers guide two distinctive research trajectories. One assumes that a dying brain succumbs to "toxic psychoses" that are produced by testable and identifiable physiological processes. As such, the ontological claims to having a life beyond death are ignored in terms of the conditions that generate such *illusions*. To the extent that they are solely intrapsychic phenomena, the claim to have transcended death is a not only an *illusion* (akin to a fantasy or daydream) but if claimed to be "true" becomes a *delusion*. Thus the partisan claims of having empirical verification for life after death, for particular religious worldviews and for other dimensions of reality, are simply ignored; evolutionary and physiological psychology becomes the explanatory bedrock on which social and cultural psychologists can analyze the appeal of a religiously informed imagination that must work within the confines of what can be revealed and confirmed by a scientifically understood neurophysiology. Even the commonality of NDEs (Gallup & Procter, 1982) is not evidence in favor of the reality claims of those who have them.

At the other extreme is the assumption that NDEs are akin to travelogues (Zaleski, 1987; Segal, 2004). Persons have died and seen another dimension or world in which the ontological commitments of a scientific worldview are found to be but limits to be transcended. Rather than discredit the ontological claims of an out-of-body experience, NDE researchers have placed phrases in surgical rooms likely to involve patients near death—hoping to see if the recovered patient "looking down" can report not only the standard visions of medical personnel but the secret and unexpected word or phrase as well (see Fenwick & Fenwick, 1995). While some accept the methodological soundness of such research designs, others see this as curious pandering to a suspect metaphysics that places near-death research in the domain of pseudoscience (Alcock, 1981).

If there is an irony in NDEs, it is that scientific explanations have returned to the body. It is in physiological processes that many locate the true cause of NDEs. Every aspect of an NDE has likely explanations in the normal physiology of a dying body. Rather than provide evidential force for an afterlife or human immortality (Hick, 1980), NDEs are but adaptive ways the body yields to its impending extinction. Rodin (1980, 1981), a physician who has had a profoundly positive NDE, argues that it was simply a toxic psychosis brought about by oxygen

deprivation. Persinger (1994) supplements this explanation by attributing much of an NDE to right hemispheric invasion of left hemispheric
functions facilitated by oxygen deprivation. Carr (1982) argues that
most phenomena reported in NDEs can be accounted for by sensory
isolation and limbic lobe dysfunctions brought about by extreme stress
and correlated elevated endorphin levels. Visual phenomena are largely
dismissed as hallucinations or as imagery common under sensory isolation conditions (Hood & Morris, 1981; Hood, Morris & Watson,
1990; Persinger, 1994).

For every claim to a body-based explanation of imagery phenomena
experienced near death, counterclaims have been made. It appears that
no single physiological factor is a necessary requirement for the many
phenomena associated with NDEs. For instance, Sabom (1982, p. 178)
documented *elevated* oxygen levels in patients undergoing NDEs. This
was verified by blood samples and documented by medical charts. This
is inconsistent with claims to "toxic psychoses" produced by oxygen
deprivation. Others have noted that NDEs do not correlate well with
independent clinical criteria of being physically near death (Noyes &
Kletti, 1976). Many have noted that, by Moody's own admission, his
phenomenological rendering of a unitary, ideal-type NDE is largely a
function of "overorganization" of the data (Moody, 1975, pp. 23–25).

It seems futile at this stage of knowledge to seek a unitary physiological explanation for what is not a unitary phenomenon. At this juncture
Segal's conclusion is a good caution: "It seems almost sure that the NDE
is but another jump to an optimistic conclusion based upon physiological processes we do not understand" (2004, pp. 723–24).

Likewise, the effort to construct a master narrative for NDEs must
yield to the need for further explorations of what people experience in
anticipation of death (Zaleski, 1987, p. 123), both near and far (Segal,
2004). In this spirit we suggest that for at least two reasons the study of
serpent handlers is suggestive for near-death research. First, as both
Shiles (1978) and Osis and Haraldson (1986) have noted, culture shapes
even the "constants" identified in NDEs. One obvious example is that
the figures "seen" are culturally identified: Shiva appears in NDEs in
India; Jesus, among Christians in the West. Likewise, as McLaughlin and
Malony (1984) have noted, rated importance of religion correlates positively with depth of NDEs. Serpent handlers are ideal subjects to study
in that they have a coherent belief system that for them epitomizes strong
religious belief and practice involving a ritual identified by outsiders in
such terms as "bizarre" and "fanatical" (Hood, 1998). Thus to study a

subculture with well-articulated religious views should help to illuminate the social and cultural structuring of their NDEs. Second, that serpent handling occurs within a subculture in which maiming and death regularly occur assures that serpent handlers practice a ritual with a clear foreknowledge that they might be maimed or killed. Thus not only do handlers practice a ritual in which fear of serpents must await the experience of anointing to be overcome (discussed below), but even in the overcoming of that fear, the reality of a serious bite elicits the anticipation of death among those who are knowledgeable about what serpents can do. They have seen loved ones maimed and killed. That few seek medical treatment for bites allows us to access a sample of persons whose NDEs are much more akin to early NDE research such as Albert Heim's with accidents from falls in the Alps (see Noyes & Kletti, 1972). Like Heim, we seek to explore the descriptions of individuals who in high-risk settings have experienced the likelihood of death but survived.

SERPENT HANDLERS AND THEIR NDBS

The ultimate inability to predict serpent-striking behavior assures a wide range of perspectives on why someone is bitten. Further, given the complexities of serpent-striking behavior, variations in serpent venom (copperheads vs. rattlesnakes, etc.), and variations in the amount of venom injected in any given strike, handlers have developed complex theologies to explain outcomes (Hood, 1998; Williamson, 2000; Williamson & Polio, 1999). Of interest here is the simple fact that all handlers are aware of and most have been witness to severe bites to fellow believers that have maimed and killed. Thus when handlers are bitten they can both reasonably anticipate the severity of their wounds and realistically anticipate the likelihood that they will die. Our study took advantage of these facts in conducting interviews with thirteen handlers, all of whom had been severely bitten, who anticipated death and yet survived, most without any medical treatment, to describe their experiences. Because most did not receive medical treatment, we cannot document how clinically near death they were. However, all clearly described having anticipated imminent death.

PARTICIPANTS AND METHOD

We identified thirteen handlers who had anticipated death after suffering severe bites from handling serpents during church services. They came from churches in Alabama, Georgia, Kentucky, Tennessee, and West Virginia. Ages of participants ranged from early twenties to early seventies. All were male, and nine were preachers in the tradition. The elapsed time from actual near-fatal bite to interview varied from four years to approximately thirty years.

The method used for collecting data on serpent bites was the phenomenological interview (see Appendix 3). For the first portion of the interview, participants were asked various questions about their knowledge of the serpent-handling tradition and their personal histories within the tradition; the second portion focused on the experience of bites. At this point, the interviews were unstructured, nondirected, and concerned only with obtaining a thick description of what the participant was aware when experiencing what he thought was a fatal serpent bite in the context of practicing his faith (an NDB). The initial question was the same for each participant: "Can you think about the time you experienced what you thought was a fatal serpent bite and describe it for me in as much detail as possible?" For approximately thirty to sixty minutes (depending on the number of such bites an individual received), participants described their experiences from the moment of being struck through the hours that followed. The only other questions asked by the interviewer were those concerned with obtaining clarifications on descriptions that seemed ambiguous or unclear at the time.[1] After collection, each of the thirteen interviews was transcribed verbatim to a protocol text for a thematic analysis of the NDBs as explained in Appendix 3.

THEMATIC STRUCTURE OF NDES FROM SERPENT BITES

Our methodology focused on the phenomenology of being bitten and deriving an agreed upon (by researchers and participants) thematic structure that describes the meaning of the NDE from a serpent bite in the participants' life world (see Williamson, 2000, pp. 197–98; Williamson, Pollio, & Hood, 2000; Williamson & Polio, 1999). Four themes emerged from the analysis, which we identify in the participants' own words as: (1) "It 'Hit' Me"; (2) "Fear"/"Victory"; (3) "Suffering"; and (4) "Backtracking"/Surrender.

Theme I: "It 'Hit' Me"

The first theme that emerged across all handler protocols was a description of the sudden, unanticipated recognition of being struck by the serpent in a way that differed from experiences of less serious bites. This bite was perceived as being more severe than others on infliction. Instead of being "bitten," most participants declared that they were "hit" by the serpent. For example, one participant said:

> I had two big rattlesnakes. . . . [O]ne of them just reached over, just as easy, like it was nothing. Then, bam! . . . A little voice said, "You're gonna die over this one." (D6)[2]

Another participant was handling next to a woman who also was handling when the unexpected happened:

> I had my hand like that, and she [another handler] turned and when she did, it bit me on the arm. It struck me. I saw it and felt it at the same time, when it *hit* me. So I took it from her and put it up and went back to where I was standing to see what was going to happen. I knew I was hurt. I knew it. (D13)

Still, another participant described the unusual force of his bite:

> It just reached over and *hit* me. . . . They heard it all the way in the back of the church. It was just like a fist *hit* me. It *hit* me that hard. (D2)

Eleven of the thirteen participants had experienced multiple serpent bites over their histories as handlers. However, when experiencing a bite thought to be potentially fatal, they instantly perceived it was more forceful and aggressive in its delivery.

Theme II: "Fear"/"Victory"

This theme began with an initial "fear" of dying from the bite that eventually gave way to what some described as "victory," or overcoming the fear of death. After experiencing a serious bite, one participant described his need for connection to the continuing worship of believers inside the church as being crucial to overcoming his fear of death:

> It [death] was a possibility. I thought this could be the end of it. That is might be the one that takes me on. But I knew if I could feel that spirit, as long as I could feel that spirit moving, I knew I would live. So I went down to the guy's house [to rest], and, man, they [believers] were up there [still inside the church on the hill] . . . and I could hear them praying, and I could feel the Lord move on me . . . and I knew I was going to suffer, and I also knew that things would work out somehow. I didn't know how they were going to work out. I really didn't know if I was going to live or if I was going to die, but at that particular point when I felt the Lord move on me, I didn't care, because I figured either way I would be with him. (D10)

Another participant described his experience with fear and victory in this way:

> Victory is not fear. To get victory, you've got to keep praying, and believing that God's going to take care of everything. And He's going to take care of everything. He don't leave you out in the thin air. And if you die, well then, that's God's will. (D2)

Participants did not always move sequentially from fear to victory but sometimes oscillated between the two experiences on this continuum based on the degree to which they felt the anointing or God moving on them. However, all described an awareness of victory over the fear of death as the eventual outcome in processing their way through the experience.

Theme III: "Suffering"

The experience of anticipated death among handlers was most often accompanied by an awareness of intense physical suffering. The following excerpt is characteristic of most descriptions rendered.

> Well, you just lay there and suffer, you know. Then, well you always think, meditating and praying, all the time you're snake bit, wanting the pain and stuff to go away. . . . How the snake bite was hurting. That's about all you think of, you know. (D1)

Three of our participants were hospitalized (only one by his own choice). The others awaited and anticipated death while church members prayed that God's will would be done. Among the well-documented immediate proximate effects of serpent bite are pain, hemorrhage, swelling, breathing difficulty, temporary blindness, and periods of unconsciousness. All these characteristics of suffering were described in the experiences of our participants in varying degrees. Still, like other reports of NDEs, even with suffering there can be intense peace, as described by one participant:

> I knew I was going out. I couldn't talk. They kept praying and praying. I just told them to leave me alone. I was in the most beautiful place that I ever saw in my life. There wasn't nothing there that wasn't white. I can't describe the white. The whites [here] aren't nothing to the white of this city I saw. It was one big castle after another. . . . It was like transparent glass. It was beautiful, just like a drift of snow. I can't tell how white it was. I wish I could have told them to leave me alone. I would have, cause I was at rest. I was at peace, but they kept praying till I came back. (D12)

Theme IV: "Backtracking"/Surrender

In experiencing the aftermath of a potentially fatal bite, participants first described a sense of "backtracking," or reflecting on their lives, to understand the cause of the bite and how it came about. In processing through this experience, they described a sense of coming to terms with the probability of death by surrendering to the ultimate will of God. The following description is illustrative.

> I began to talk to the Lord. I said, "Lord, is there anything I need to do? Maybe like just ask you, if I've ever done anything to you, to forgive me." You'll just start *backtracking* to see if you owe anybody anything or you need to fix anything. I felt like everything was clear. I turned my face to wall the best I could, and I said, "Well, Lord, I know I'm going out." . . . [M]y mind [was] like leaving me. I said, "Well, Lord, if I wake up in the morning, I'll still be the pastor out there, and if I ain't, I hope I'll meet with you." (P4)

While panoramic life reviews have long been identified with NDEs, among serpent handlers they take the unique form of trying to understand the reason for being bitten and seeking highly individualistic explanations, as illustrated in the following excerpt.

> I just felt like I wanted to handle it, and I went the box and got it and it bit. . . . You search your life. . . . See, you search yourself. How come? Most of the time when you get right down to it you will find that there is a purpose. . . . There is always a purpose for everything. . . . A lot of times we handle serpents, maybe, we might not be right where we ought to be, and we get bit and we see what that problem is: we're not there [where we ought to be]. (D12)

Some participants attributed the bite to their disobedience or sin, others to not being anointed or simply being distracted by bystanders or curiosity seekers. Some described their belief that they spared others from harm by taking over an unruly serpent, or that the bite was a test of their faith.

Backtracking is linked to an eventual surrender to the outcome of the bite—whether survival (with likely maiming) or death. As D10 earlier noted, "It [death] was a possibility. I thought this could be the end of it. . . . I really didn't know if I was going to live or if I was going to die, but at that particular point when I felt the Lord move on me, I didn't care, because either way I figured I would be with the him." When anticipating death from a serpent bite, participants became aware first of reflecting on their lives to search for reasons for the infliction, then of resolving any conflicts with God or others that came to mind, and finally of surrendering to the ultimate will of God and even to death.

A GLOBAL (NOMOTHETIC) DESCRIPTION
OF NDES FROM SERPENT BITE

Together the above themes form a thematic structure that handlers who have survived bites accept as sufficiently describing their individual experiences. While we need not create a single master narrative for all NDEs, within more narrowly triggered specific NDEs they together provide what we will term a *global meaning*. Within the geographically isolated and fairly restrictive theological boundaries of the Jesus' Name handlers, the themes described above interconnect to form a coherent narrative. We might summarize it as follows.

Near-death by serpent bite involves a structure of meaning characterized by four interdependent themes. This structure involves a feeling of being "hit" by the serpent in such a way that the strike is experienced as extremely serious, likely to maim or kill. The experience of overcoming fear by "victory" is encountered first, by a sense of losing life in the face of doubt, and later as a confidence that whatever the outcome, it is God's will. Soon after envenomation, intense "suffering" occurs: pain, swelling, blurred or lost vision, breathing difficulties, and loss of consciousness in varying degrees. Anticipating death, the stricken believer "backtracks" over his life, contemplating both the reason for and the finality of his bite. Fear of the anticipation of death may be relieved by visions of luminous places in which the believer is contented to remain. Ultimate victory is experienced in the eventual acceptance of both the serpent bite and its outcome as God's will for the obedient believer, whether it means full recovery, maiming, or death.

While this global meaning emerges from across all protocol texts of our interviews, we do not propose it either as a master narrative or as a full explication of NDEs from serpent bites in religious settings. It is, however, a useful heuristic summary that illuminates the individual variations in the experience of being near-fatally bitten in a subculture that over the years has created a religious framework within which to understand the phenomenon. Moreover, it illuminates how maiming and death from handling in perceived obedience to God's will interacts with obvious physiological conditions to create a meaningful experience (Hood, 1998).

AFTEREFFECTS OF NDES FROM SERPENT BITES

Our research, like much of the NDE research, is heavily weighted toward its positive aftereffects due to the problem of subject mortality. That is, by soliciting persons who had NDEs from serpent bites and remain within the tradition, those who left because of bites or even entire churches that eliminated the ritual because of bites are ignored (Williamson & Hood, 2004). Thus, not surprisingly, among the thirteen survivors of NDBs we interviewed, all subscribe to a common structure of meaning that emerges from the survival of their experience. The structure is simple and coherent. The survivors are resolute in that, by being obedient to the Word, they simply affirm that they are indeed signs following believers; their beliefs are followed by practice of the signs of Mark 16:17–18, which include the command to take up serpents. It is a simple act of obedience that defines a tradition in which, as many have said, the imperative to take up serpents does not include assurance that one will not be bitten. As one elderly participant, claiming hundreds of bites in his long career and with body maimed but faith unyielding, put it:

> If [a serpent] bites you and takes you away from here, why, that's fine. I don't care. That's the way I want to go anyhow when I die. But I'm in no big hurry for it. . . . I told them I wanted them to have church when they put me away, just like we have church . . . taking up serpents . . . that's what I want. I want to be rolled in here[,] . . . them have church over me, and handle serpents. . . . What I really want is people to get in when I'm laying there. I want it just like we're having church and I want it to be real spiritual. I want some of them to sing when they're wheeling me out, "I Won't Be Coming Back Anymore." (D2)

Such resolution as this bespeaks the power that some find in a tradition that reckons the potential for maiming and death as but a small sacrifice for being obedient believers of their Lord.

CONCLUSION

Our approach has been to place the anticipation of death from serpent bites in the larger context of research on NDEs. Rather than seek a single, ideal master narrative of NDEs, the variation of these experiences, both across culture and over time, suggests less uniformity than many have proposed. Even our thematic structure is not meant as a master narrative.

Like all NDEs, those resulting from serpent bites in a religious setting cannot be accepted uncritically as evidence for an afterlife by those outside the tradition. Still, the power of what we have identified as Blose's (1981) "asymmetric" hypothesis remains, and surely is an option as James's discussion of the metaphysical objections to immortality is consulted. NDEs provide both comfort in the anticipation of death and a powerful transformation about feelings and fear of death. As we have argued in chapter 5, handlers literally take death into their hands and are victorious regardless of the outcome. Repeatedly, it is said by handlers, "It says 'they shall take up serpents'; it does not say they shall not get bit." Phenomenologically oriented approaches are essential for clarifying the nature of a faith that can accept all possible consequences of the religious handling of serpents. For instance, it is clear from our analysis of NDEs from serpent bites, intense fear is elicited and then overcome by a largely cognitive appeal to a faith tradition that makes any outcome of an obedient act "God's will." Furthermore, the intense suffering makes it clear that the peace that is found in this experience does not override the physiological realities of the painful effects of venom. Thus one should not expect a single unifying physiological explanation for all NDEs any more more than one should expect a single master narrative purporting to transcend culture and history. What we can anticipate is collaboration among diverse disciplines to piece together what clearly are varieties of NDEs, and of their causes and consequences as well. The serpent handlers provide a unique religiously based ritual that can provide a perhaps equally unique perspective on the role of religious beliefs in the interpretation of a religious ritual whose outcomes have important implications for the believer.

It may be that what appears to some people a simple and perhaps even naive faith is conducive and perhaps even necessary to religious experiences, especially the NDEs of the faithful. In Friedrich von Hügel's masterful study of Saint Catherine of Genoa, he notes that friends in attendance at her death asked if she wanted to speak. It is reported that she silently pointed with her right index finger toward the sky. "And her friends understood by this that she had to go and communicate in heaven" (von Hügel, 1923/1999, p. 215). When in 1998 Punkin Brown was struck and fatally bitten by a large rattlesnake, like Saint Catherine of Genoa, he raised his hand and pointed to the heavens. Then he said, "I'm going home."[3]

CHAPTER 11

Music among Serpent-Handling Churches

The serpent-handling churches share with the larger, mainstream Pentecostal denominations the use of music as an essential component in worship. At a typical serpent-handling meeting, it is most likely that instrumentals and singing will provide a prelude to the service as members enter the church and fellowship with one another. The importance of music is such that services rarely begin "on time" but usually whenever the musical prelude happens to end or, more often, as it swells and rises to a level that elicits participation from congregants to join in with singing. In such cases the music itself has blurred the boundary between the prelude and the service and has set the stage for all that will follow: prayer, preaching, and demonstrations of the signs. The immense significance of music, and its ability to move believers into a worshipful frame of mind, is highlighted by its absence on some occasions. When no musician (or one with little talent) is present, the service is likely to be very subdued and much briefer. Our data make it possible to compare powerful services accompanied by talented and expressive musicians and those that struggle in worship with musicians of sincere but limited abilities. What we have discovered from years of visits to numerous churches can be put succinctly: no music, no church.

Here we examine music in three ways. First, we provide a basic understanding of the music of serpent-handling churches based on descriptions of typical musicians, the type of instruments used, and the process through which music becomes a dominant factor of worship.

Second, we explore the existing literature relating to the music of serpent-handling churches to gain an understanding of how others view this phenomenon. Third, we present an analysis of the content of the music of serpent-handling churches based on an empirical analysis of videotaped songs during actual services.

ASPECTS OF SERPENT-HANDLING CHURCH MUSIC

Musicians in serpent-handling churches are of a varied sort and display differing levels of skill. We have witnessed and videotaped musicians ranging in talent from minimal to gifted. Most instrumentalists have had little or no formal training but learned to play by "ear" from family members or other church musicians. Children begin at early ages to sing and to play instruments in church services. After learning basic chords, most perfect their talents through trial and error by playing along with others as worship takes place. Whoever feels so inclined is typically welcomed and even encouraged by others to come forward, pick up (or sit down at) an idle instrument, and contribute to the production of music. This informal approach of "whosoever will" fosters participation among players and helps to ensure that a sufficient number of instrumentalists will be on hand at most church services.

Those who lead singing or supply special songs (e.g., solos, duets) also typically have little or no formal training but have grown up learning to sing in church. Aside from the more talented who have gained a reputation among the churches as song leaders, anyone may come forward and offer a special song, either voluntarily or solicited by the moderator. Although one church we frequently attended has mostly female instrumentalists and singers, men are usually responsible for providing much of the singing and musical accompaniment in a majority of the serpent-handling churches. The number and sequence of songs, both congregational and individual pieces, are largely spontaneous, as "prompted by God," and for as long as the "spirit leads." Singers sometimes face the wall, not the congregation, indicating that their singing is a form of worship unto God and not a performance.

In this participatory atmosphere, a variety of musical instruments may be played. The most common instrument, of course, is the guitar, including the acoustic, electric, and bass; several guitarists are usually present at any given service. Less common in small congregations are keyboard instruments such as the piano, organ, and synthesizer, which, even if present, may be played little or not at all. All kinds of percussion instruments will be found for use at any service, including various types of drums, tambourines, cymbals, maracas, and, of course, "ten-stringed instruments" (clapping hands). Tambourines and cymbals often are in good supply and may be passed from believer to believer in the course of singing. At one church we frequently attended, a musician with different-keyed harmonicas contributes to worship on a regular basis, although this instrument rarely was seen elsewhere. On occasion, a visiting musician may bring a mandolin, banjo, accordion, or autoharp but play only during a special song or at an invited time. Because of the informal atmosphere at church, most musicians feel free to bring whatever instruments they possess, for it is certain that opportunity will present itself to "play for the Lord."

The process through which a musical prelude commences and comes to command influence in a service is of particular interest. After the initial tuning of instruments, music often starts in much the same way as when jazz musicians begin to jam—each one playing off the others' offerings. Among the serpent-handling church musicians themselves, what sometimes begins as a cacophony of disordered notes and improvisations gradually rises to take on life as a harmonious entity that facilitates a spiritual connection between believers and their God. It is at this moment that those who have been gathering and visiting with each other are pulled away from casual interactions into a flow of music that has become synchronized and energized for worship. Worshipers slowly migrate toward the front of the church—men to one side and women to the other—to congregate around musicians and join in with the musical atmosphere. Much of the time (but not always) the music is up-tempo and compels believers to participate through singing, hand-clapping, and dancing. Its contagion is such that most people cannot remain passive observers; even the most reserved in the pews find it difficult to sit still without tapping a foot to the rhythm of music. It is at this point that all would agree: "Church" has begun—and may continue for two hours or more, according to the ebb and flow of music and its influence on testimonials, sermons, signs, and prayers.

MUSIC AND WORSHIP IN THE PENTECOSTAL TRADITION

The link between music and religious experience is well established and has a long history (Hills & Argyle, 1998; Lipe, 2002). The early Greeks believed that the harmonious structure in music was an empirical expression of the mathematical order of the universe (Lipe, 2002). This idea evolved during the Middle Ages into the belief that the very act of composing music could be understood as an imitation of divine creation itself. For this reason, it was felt that music was a reflection of the divine order and, as such, made possible a spiritual connection between the Creator and the listener. Hence the person who experienced music was thought to gain access to a doorway through which God could be encountered in an influential way. As Lipe (2002, p. 211) has observed, "There is a dynamism inherent both in music and in human life which can mirror and shape each other in a reciprocal manner." The interaction of these intrinsic qualities contributes to a compelling spiritual influence cross-culturally among religions in various ways: Judaism and Christianity incorporate singing into worship as a practice in spiritual preparation for worship; Islam sings the text to facilitate religious experience; Eastern religions often chant sacred texts and make use of instruments to access spiritual domains; and African religions make use of song and dance to enter the realm of ancestors and deities. Music is widely viewed as a facilitator of religious experience (Hills & Argyle, 1998).

How that music relates to religious experience has been the concern of some investigators. Observing that both musical and religious experiences evoke intense emotional responses, Hills and Argyle (1998) found that both types were related to certain affective and mystical qualities but that those experienced in music were reported as more intense. Lipe (2002) surveyed the literature that connected music, spirituality, and health and derived from her assessment a model of music experience that outlines its function in relation to spirituality and health. Accordingly, music serves the central function of personal transformation in terms of (1) bringing into concrete experience that which is abstract (e.g., beauty, wholeness); (2) actualizing the experiences of death and rebirth; and (3) bringing a sense of order out of chaos. In addition to the central function, there are three secondary functions that are thought of as hierarchical in their work toward achieving personal change. Secondary function I of music is concerned with the elicitation and support of transpersonal experiences—for example, connection with God, altered states of conscious, images and affect, self-transcendence, and spiritual yearnings. Such transpersonal experiences enhance secondary function II, which is related to individuation—the process of achieving self. At this realm, music may function to bring into awareness various abstract ideas and symbols (or archetypes, in Jungian terms) that become concretized in personal experience and available for integration in the process toward change. Secondary function III elicits and facilitates the experience of healing at three levels: (1) the intrapersonal, which may involve an altered perception of one's situation, modified physiological and emotional responses, comfort and reassurance, and reinforced tendencies toward growth and healing; (2) the interpersonal, which is concerned with effective communication and a fostered sense of community; and (3) the communal/global, in which music facilitates healing a group that has experienced a common trauma or tragedy. Whereas Hills and Argyle (1998) are concerned with clarifying the experience of affect shared by both musical and religious experiences, Lipe (2002) has provided a useful theoretical model to explain how it is that music serves an important function in the process of spiritual growth and health concerns. As we shall see, music among serpent-handling churches not only brings about spiritual transformation by establishing a perceived connection with God; it also facilitates almost all aspects of worship, from healing to handling.

Other studies have been concerned with music and its role in religious experience. Among Protestant churches, including a Pentecostal one, Price and Snow (1998) concluded that music and physical movement, along with other factors, contributed to dissociative states consistent with our discussion of trance. Here it is noteworthy that often, as believers handle serpents, others are playing music, perhaps facilitating the experience of anointing. Unwin, Kenny, and David (2002) studied the effects of group singing on emotion under experimental conditions and found that for a group that performed singing and another that only listened to the performance, significant increases in positive affect were reported, but there were no significant differences between the groups. Hence simply listening to singing done by groups may be just as effective in elevating mood as the act of singing itself, which is consistent with the simultaneous occurrence of handling by some believers and the singing and playing of instruments by others. Concerned with Pentecostal music and its effect on mood and subsequent religious experience, Miller and Strongman (2002) conducted two experimental studies, one of which took place in the context of a worship service. They found in reports of mood assessed before the service, immediately after the musical portion in the service, and after the entire service was concluded that participants indicated an increased positive mood *after* experiencing the music. This positive mood continued even after the service was over. The second experiment, involving a Pentecostal group from the first study and a secular group from a community choir, found that after listening to fast and slow selections of both secular and sacred music, Pentecostals were more likely to report higher levels of positive affect (as measured by scales described as energetic and awesome) and lower levels of negative affect, but only for sacred music. The researchers concluded that characteristics of Pentecostal music—such as rhythm, tempo, repetition, intensity, and dancing—provide structure for dissociative states and physiological arousal, which then are given subjective cognitive appraisal in the social context of lyrical meanings and guidance by worship leaders. This is consistent with Wacker's (2001, pp. 108–14) observation that music has been used in Pentecostal churches since their beginning as a means of regulating the ebb and flow of emotion expressed by the congregation. From Protestant hymnals, Young (1926) categorized 2,922 songs on the basis of twelve implicit psychoanalytic themes, the most dominant being an infantile yearning for the perfect earthly father (33 percent) and, closely related, a yearning for future reward (25 percent). Although the above studies are indirectly related to serpent-handling church music, they do contribute to a larger context for understanding the relationship between music and religious experience— something of primary importance in Pentecostal denominations in general and in serpent-handling churches in particular.

As important as music is to serpent-handling church services, it is surprising that it has been given little attention in the literature. Most of the studies that have made serpent-handling services the focus of investigation have at least mentioned the phenomenon of music to provide a context for the more popularly researched ritual of serpent handling. For example:

> The service begins spontaneously and informally with the congregation singing a stirring hymn to the accompaniment of four to five (and sometimes six) electric guitars, a flattop guitar to two, clashing cymbals, tambourines, piano, organ, and drums. . . . There is much handclapping and foot stamping. Usually several hymns are sung and the communicants get "happy" (the anointing of God falls), which is similar to "holy roller" or tent revivals. Some of the communicants completely follow the Holy Spirit: some dance, others jump up and down, some turn around and around in a circle, while others very quietly offer-up praises unto the Lord. . . . The "anointing" moves for twenty to thirty minutes and then one of the male communicants will go toward the serpent box which sets on the church platform in the pulpit area. He unlocks and removes the lid of the box and pulls out the serpents. (Rowe, 1982, pp. 48–49)

Similar descriptions, some in more or less detail, have been offered by others (e.g., Ambrose, 1970; Kane, 1974b; La Barre, 1962/1974; Miller, 1977; Moore, 1986; Van Hoorebeke, 1980).

There are a few studies that do in fact give closer attention to serpent-handling music. With an interest primarily in the Appalachian religion, Dickinson (1977) produced an excellent videotape consisting of various church-related activities and rituals among various denominations and sects of the region without commentary that included significant excerpts of serpent-handling church music. Concerned with fire handling among serpent-handling churches, Kane (1974b) considered the characteristics of music as being a possible source for inducing dissociative states associated with the ritual but rejected music as the only explanation in view of the multiplicity of other contributing influences—psychological, physiological, social, and cultural. Thus music is but one component, though an essential one, that contributes to the overall experience of worship in serpent-handling churches—and particularly to the practice of the signs, including, of course, serpent handling.

Schwartz (1999) offered a pictorial digest of a small group of serpent-handling congregations in eastern Kentucky and included one chapter based on a first-person description of his own experience of their music. He draws from music history, scientific literature, and his conversations with serpent handlers to weave together a better understanding of their music and its relationship to serpent and fire handling. Intrigued by the transformed worldview experienced by serpent-handling believers, Stekert (1963) observed that abandoned worldly behaviors (e.g., singing country music, dancing, and even telling folktales) are only suppressed and emerge in the context of serpent-handling church services in disguised forms as country gospel music and dancing in the spirit.

Van Hoorebeke (1980), a communications major, studied rhetorical aspects of worship in a serpent-handling congregation, one component of interest being music. She suggested that music serves as "a form of indirect suggestion" (p. 95) for believers that leads to a desired level of emotional response, according to the circumstances encountered in worship at a specific time. In fact, she concluded, it serves as an important auditory channel of communication between leaders and the audience, and even among members of the audience itself, to accommodate the needs of the given moment. Finally, in perhaps the study most related to ours, Moore (1986) performed an analysis of serpent-handling church songs based on social deprivation-compensatory theory as applied to the "stationary poor" of Appalachia and the contextual problems of lower socioeconomic status. He suggested four categories of songs that enable believers to compensate for material and social lack: songs concerned with (1) condemnation of the established world order, (2) escapism, (3) hardship and suffering, and (4) a multi-faceted nature—that is, songs that fit into more than one category. According to Moore, the singing of such songs, in the context of ampli-fied accompaniment and dancing, allows for a cathartic-type experience that results in higher self-esteem for believers.

Of all the studies cited, only two are given to a categorization of songs based on empirical data. Young (1926) made use of Protestant hymns to formulate categories. Although his sample was impressively large, it was drawn from songs in hymnals, not songs actually sung by congregations; furthermore, they were not songs that appear with any frequency among serpent-handling churches, which rarely use hymnals. We have found that most serpent-handling churches use and maintain handwritten or typewritten songbooks that contain songs handed down from generation to generation. Moore (1986) did in fact investigate music among serpent-handling churches, although it is unclear how much time was spent in research or how many songs were included in his study. A final concern of both these studies is related to the reductionistic approaches used to understand the meaning of music. Young (1926), using psychoanalytic theory, came to view the singing of songs as a neurotic ritual through which a return to repressed infantile longings for the safety, comfort, and protection of a father is experienced and relieved in an unwitting manner, whereas Moore (1986), drawing from deprivation-compensatory theory, reduced the meaning of singing among serpent-handling churches to an attempt to alleviate frustration that stems from lack of social resources.

Our own view is that reductionistic interpretations of the effect of music ought to be limited in scope, especially when the centrality of music in the history of Pentecostalism is recognized. It is not unreason-able to entertain the notion that music may mean precisely what believ-ers say it means. In the words of one believer, "Music in church is a way of beginning a service, and getting your mind focused on God, to praise and worship him as he wants us to" (pers. com.). Accepting this description at face value, we present in the remainder of this chapter a much more holistic view of music among serpent-handling churches based on an understanding of the meaning of songs in the context of the believers' own world and spiritual values.

AN ANALYSIS OF SERPENT-HANDLING CHURCH MUSIC

Much has been reported in the popular media and in the social sciences that has contributed to a pejorative stereotyping of serpent-handling churches and the perpetuation of an Appalachian "otherness" that contrasts much too often with mainstream America (Birckhead, 1993; also see Sweet, 1996, for an assessment of how bluegrass music has contributed to perpetuating this stereotype). In this context, there have been uncritical judgments that fail to appreciate the depth and meaning of music in this religious tradition. What follows is neither myth nor speculation but an analysis of songs based on empirical data we have collected from our field research.

Our analysis is based on the general thematic meaning of words in the songs, using a method similar to that explained in Appendix 3. The combination of words and melody allows a spiritual connection between the believer and God in worship. As one believer stated:

> Music is where it's at. The music gets the people stirred up. The song gets everybody's mind on the Lord. . . . It's the text that is most important. It's the words that get the people's mind on the Lord. . . . The music is inspirational. It clears my mind and gets my mind on the Lord. Sometimes the words of a song fit your situation and the music lifts you up. . . . The song's text is the word of God. (Quoted in Schwartz, 1999, pp. 41, 42)

This believer easily could have spoken for others in serpent-handling churches; her words ring true in that believers often say that God speaks to them personally through their music. We offer a basic analysis of songs in an attempt to present a better understanding of the role of music in the typical service as well as the meaning it provides believers in everyday life.

Method of Collection

Almost all the videotapes of church services housed in the Hood-Williamson Research Archives for the Serpent Handling Holiness Sects contain music, often instrumental solos as well as individual and collective singing. For this chapter, we selected eighty-eight services from a collection of videotapes that spanned seven years, 1994 to 2000, inclusively.

The two-hour (or sometimes two-hour-and-twenty-minute) videotapes contained most if not all of the services, which included meetings of individual congregations that had gathered for local worship and multiple congregations that had gathered for homecomings. Homecomings are events at which several congregations come together to support a single church, usually over three days, beginning with a Friday night service and ending with a shared meal after a late-morning Sunday service.

Our attendance at these services involved numerous visits to six congregations in four southern states: three churches in northern Georgia, one in northern Alabama, one in eastern Kentucky, and one in West Virginia. Attendance at the homecoming services used in this analysis ranged from 30 to 120 believers, whereas attendance at local church services numbered from 10 to sometimes 90, the average attendance being from 15 to 25. Numerous visits, diverse locations, and different types of services contributed to a large database of songs with a rich variety of form and content.

DESCRIPTIVE ANALYSIS OF THE MUSIC

A descriptive analysis of the recorded music data from these eighty-eight services found a total of 1,114 songs (this number reflects the omission of instrumentals—i.e., the performance of a musical selection without singing). The average number of songs per service was 12.66, and most services (about 68 percent) included from 8.34 to 16.98 songs (SD = 4.32). The largest number of songs in a single service was 24, whereas the least number was 4. There was no service that lacked music.

To gain a sense of the temporal importance of music in a typical service, an individual church service was selected and analyzed in terms of the amount of time devoted to singing. The service was attended by nineteen people (most of whom were children) and lasted 3 hours and 14 minutes from beginning to end. Congregants sang 16 songs. These songs were accompanied by as many as three guitarists (all males) at different times. The songs totaled 53 minutes and accounted for over 27 percent of the time spent in service.[1] Among the singers were three adult males who sang a total of 8 songs, and five females (two of them children), who also sang 8 songs. The congregation often would join in the singing. The average time per song was 3 minutes and 20 seconds, whereas the range of time for songs was from 40 seconds to 5 minutes and 45 seconds. The duration of songs is typically longer at homecoming services than at individual church services such as this. For example, it is not uncommon for a song at homecomings to last 10 minutes; one of the most popular songs among serpent-handling churches is "Little David, Play on Your Harp." It was sung at one homecoming for 25 minutes. At well-attended homecomings (more than a hundred people in attendance), more singers are present, and believers tend to sing a more songs for longer periods in anticipation of a highly emotional collective worship.

TABLE 5. CATEGORIES OF SONGS
AND PERCENTAGES [N = 342]

Categories	Percentage
Comfort/Mercy/Deliverance [n = 98]	28.6
Heaven [n = 93]	27.2
Witnessing/Evangelization [n = 44]	12.9
Jesus Songs [n = 21]	6.1
Praise/Thanksgiving [n = 19]	5.6
Consecration [n = 15]	4.4
Empowerment [n = 14]	4.1
Identity [n = 13]	3.8
Serpent Handling [n = 13]	3.8[a]
Holiness/Separation [n = 12]	3.5

[a] Almost all songs having verses regarding serpent handling or strychnine drinking have other, more dominant themes, e.g., Holiness/Separation from the World, Praise/Thanksgiving. However, since they refer to serpent handling, they were categorized as such in the present analysis.

Song Categories

To better understand the meaning and role of serpent-handling church music, songs were organized into categories based on general content of meaning. Among the 1,114 songs on video, 71 were eliminated from consideration for reasons of inaudibility or their offering by visiting choirs from non-serpent- handling churches. Among the remaining 1,043 songs, there were 342 different ones. When attention was given to common themes expressed by lyrics, songs were categorized into ten distinct groups that seemed to capture their general meanings.

Table 5 presents the ten categories and the number of songs each contains. Among these categories, those represented with the most songs were Comfort/Mercy/Deliverance, Heaven, and Witnessing/Evangelization, which together accounted for 68.7 percent of all songs. Almost 29 percent of songs (98) were concerned with the dominant theme Comfort/Mercy/Deliverance. These are songs that expressed for believers the reality of experiencing God and their faith as reassurance in the face of problems and the existential concerns of life. For example, "He'll Ride Out Your Storm" offers encouragement that God will be there with the believer in midst of life's greatest problems to offer comfort and support until they are resolved. "I Can't Make It on My Own without God" expresses belief in the need for total dependence on God not only at church but also in everyday life. From personal testimonies in a typical service, it is evident that many believers have experienced life difficulties that could not be resolved by themselves or with the help of others. In such situations, they describe an eventual turning to God that resulted in what was experienced as a merciful resolution and a felt need for continued dependence on God, without whom life would be unmanageable. Still another song, "Go Down, Moses, Down to Egypt Land," draws on the Old Testament story of Israel's miraculous deliverance from Egyptian bondage as an analogy to a strengthened faith that God, in like manner, will provide contemporary believers with deliverance from personal bondages, both literal and spiritual, in the present world. Clearly, these songs, and others of the group, reflect the ways in which God is experienced by believers at critical times in life and how it is that such experiences, when captured in song, serve as a continuing testimony of hope and assurance that the God of their religion is one of action who cares for his own in a personal way.

More than 27 percent of our sample (93) were concerned with Heaven. Of great importance to serpent handlers is the belief that the present world is not all there is to existence; heaven, with all its riches and comforts, is perceived as a future reality for the believing. As in most other churches, members differ in terms of earthly possessions and social status. Some of the more educated members have occupations or successful businesses that supply more than sufficient income for providing the comforts of middle-class living as well as the necessities. Those who are less fortunate and live from week to week or month to month survive on meager incomes to "make ends meet." However, for those at both extremes of the social spectrum, and others in the middle, a common meeting ground for faith is the belief that the promise of heaven is the ultimate goal that makes all else on earth pale in comparison. It is in this that their religion serves them great existential value in place of concern for achieving worldly riches, fame, or even acceptance—for serpent handlers, because of their unique beliefs and practices, are among the most marginalized, misunderstood, and rejected religious groups.

Simply the titles of a few Heaven songs are adequate to describe the encouragement for future hope that comes to believers through their music: "After a While, It's All Gonna Be Over"; "Beulah Land, I'm Longing for You"; "(I'll Have a New Home) Designed by a King"; and "Nothing Can Hold Me Here, I'm Headed Home." In the context of meaningful music, believers feel drawn away from physical and social maladies, persecutions, or even desire for worldly success to a concern with heaven, which is a reality for believers that is of far greater significance than what this temporal world affords. As one song puts it, whatever the sufferings and trials of this present life, "Heaven will be worth the journey when I get there." This type of music affords transcendence of the present moment through an ephemeral glimpse into what is believed to await the faithful beyond this life.

Witnessing/Evangelization, the third largest category of music, accounted for about 13 percent (44) of the songs. As is typical among most Holiness-Pentecostal sects, serpent-handling churches do little outside their regular services in the way of organizing to evangelize their communities. Rather they rely on what is experienced as immediate manifestations of God during worship to convince unbelievers of their lost condition and need for salvation. The emphasis is on encountering the presence of God in worship, at which time songs become an effective medium for witnessing to others about merciful blessings for the obedient and future judgment for the disobedient and lost. Consider the lyrics of "Born Again":

> Born again, free from sin,
> I'm happy night and day.
> Makes me shout, there's no doubt.
> I know that I've been born again.
> (Traditional)

The verses describe a personal experience of being lost and without hope of salvation. On turning from sin to God, the author reports experiencing the crisis conversion of a second birth in Jesus, one that is spiritual and leads to the happiness expressed in the above refrain. Other songs emphasize in a testimonial way the goodness of God as experienced by believers and an improved quality of life: "God's been good to me, He's been better to me than any other thing I know"; "I've got my foot on the rock, and my soul is satisfied"; "This feeling that I have, the world didn't give it to me, The world didn't give it, and the world can't take it away."

Songs sung as a way to witness and evangelize sometimes convey a message of doom and judgment for the unrepentant of heart. The words of a popular song, "House of Gold," illustrate this meaning:

> (Refrain) I'd rather be in a deep, dark grave,
> And to know that my poor soul was saved,
> Than to live in this world in a house of gold,
> And deny my God and lose my soul.
>
> (Verse 1) Some people steal, they cheat and lie,
> For this world's wealth, what it can buy.

But don't they know on the Judgment Day,
That gold and silver will melt away.

(Verse 2) What good is gold and silver, too,
If your poor heart's not good and true.
Oh, Sinner, hear me when I say,
Fall down upon your knees and pray.
                    (Hank Williams, as sung by believers)

We have observed on numerous occasions that when the song is sung at
the time of an "altar call," unbelievers, backsliders, and other seekers
respond to the message by coming forward for prayer. As suggested by
the size of the Witnessing/Evangelization category, a number of songs in
each service are given to this type of message, which may result in the
appearance of an "altar service" at any given time with prayer for salvation and deliverance by the laying on of hands. As such songs are
sung, opportunity presents itself for enlisting new converts to the tradition, for reclaiming those who have strayed from fellowship, and even
for rekindling the flame among believers as they reflect on their own
experiences of salvation and blessings.

The remaining 31 percent of songs were distributed among seven other
categories. Over 6 percent (21) of songs could be described as Jesus Songs.
This category was characterized by up-tempo songs with repetitive words
that typically addressed the nature of Jesus or blessings he bestows on
believers. For example, the title, "Ananias, Tell Me What Kind of Man
Jesus Is," is the central lyric repeated in the course of one up-tempo song.
Its verses supply various responses that also are repetitive to the plea:
(1) "He's a healing man," (2) "He's a Holy Ghost man," and (3) "He's a
saving man." Other songs of this group with repetitive lyrics are "Jesus Is
That Rock, He's That Solid Rock," "Can't Nobody Do Me Like Jesus,
He's My Friend," and "God Is God, and Jesus Is His Name." As suggested by these examples, believers are reminded of who Jesus is and what
he means to them, based on personal experiences. In singing such songs,
they are brought into connection not only with what they have experienced with Jesus at earlier times but also with current needs they feel can
be met in the context of a presently sensed healing or saving Jesus.

Praise/Thanksgiving accounted for 5.6 percent (19) of songs. These
songs were largely concerned with offering praise to God or with thanking him for various blessings received by believers, consisting primarily
of up-tempo and repetitive refrains with add-on verses. A few titles are
sufficient to provide understanding of their meaning: "I Don't Know
What You Came to Do, But I Came to Praise the Lord"; "I Feel Like

Praising, Praising Him"; "I've Got So Much to Thank Him For"; and "You Ask Me Why I'm Thankful." As a believer reflects on personal blessings, he or she often finds a song to express thanks to God. In this context, the entire congregation may be reminded to reflect on their own blessings and join in with singing.

Songs concerned with Consecration accounted for 4.4 percent (15) of our sample. This group included songs that express a commitment to serving God, a desire to be closer in relationship to God, or a concern with doing his will. "Deeper, Deeper in the Word of God" is a song with repetitive verses that express a dominant theme among serpent-handling churches, that is, the centrality of the Bible and the need to be rooted and grounded in God's word. The lyrics of another song, "I Shall Not Be Moved," proclaim a dedicated stance in service to God, one in which a return to the old life is no option. An old song that has been passed down through the tradition is "Keep Your Hand on the Plough, Hold On," which encourages believers to remain committed to faith without waivering. For believers, songs of Consecration serve as a reminder that the Christian journey is one that requires dedication and faithfulness despite the temptations and trials of life.

About 4 percent (14) of the songs had the common theme of Empowerment. In living the Christian life, believers often speak of the need to rely on the power of God on a daily basis. As is the case with all Pentecostals, serpent-handling churches live in a world in which Satan is believed to be real and to be the primary force of evil. Not only is Satan understood as the fundamental cause of all evil in the world, he also is believed to have personal interest in overcoming each individual believer as part of the overall plan in his war against God—hence the interpretation of negative personal experiences as trials, persecutions, and tribulations. For this reason, believers commonly confess to being under attack from Satan and express the constant need for God's power to resist and overcome him. Various songs describe this power, its need and effect. As an example, note the words of a popular traditional song among serpent-handling churches:

> We've got the power in the name of Jesus.
> We've got the power in the name of the Lord.
> Though Satan rages, we will not be defeated.
> We've got the power in the name of the Lord.
> (Traditional)

The verses of this song elaborate on the theme of satanic warfare with which Christians must contend on a daily basis, although, as the refrain indicates, the ultimate victory is assured because of belief in the residence of God's power within the believer. Other songs in this category include "I've Got the Holy Ghost"; "Holy Ghost Power"; "God's Not Dead, He's Still Alive"; and "Fire, Fire in My Bones." In singing songs of Empowerment, believers are able to reconnect with a believed reality in which the power of God is available for personal experience and daily living.

Almost 4 percent (13) of songs were in the category Identity. These songs expressed the personal identity of being a follower of Jesus, or the fact of meaning or purpose in life based on being a Christian. One song, whose melody and beat are based on the once-popular country hit, "I'm Proud to Be an Okie from Muskogee," was sung often by one believer and aptly illustrates the theme:

(Refrain) I'm glad to be a Christian, hallelujah.
I'm glad to know my name is written down.
I'm proud to know that Jesus is my savior.
And someday I'll wear that robe and crown.

(Verse 1) I don't smoke marijuana, I don't have to.
I don't take no trips on LSD.
I've been born again of the spirit.
And most of all he's done set me free.

(Verse 2) There'll be no thieves and robbers up in heaven.
They'll have no place up there at all.
Everybody will be the bride of the savior.
And Jesus is the greatest one of all.

                                    (Traditional)

An Identity theme is clearly reflected in the titles "I'm a Child of the King, Yes I Am"; "I'm a Soldier in the Army of the Lord"; and "Lord Jesus, I'm a Lord Jesus Man." As believers sing these songs, they not only declare to others who they are but also remind themselves of their own identity and of the benefits associated with being in special relationship to God.

Although Holiness/Separation is an important theme among serpent-handling churches, songs pertaining to this category accounted for less than 4 percent (12). Among serpent-handling churches, holiness not only means complying with various guidelines and abstentions that outline what is viewed as appropriate Christian behavior but also includes guarding oneself from too close associations with others of the world, for fear of being enticed away from the faith or of being tempted to compromise the holiness way of life. Songs in this category express the fact of holiness for believers or the need to live righteously and free from sin. A favorite among serpent-handling churches illustrates this theme quite effectively:

(Refrain) Crying holy unto the Lord, Crying holy unto the Lord.
If I could, I surely would
Stand on that rock where Moses stood.

(Verse 1) Lord, I ain't no sinner now, Lord, I ain't no sinner now.
For I've been to the river, and I've been baptized.
Lord, I ain't no sinner now.

(Verse 2) Sinner run and hide your face, Sinner run and hide your face.
Run to the rocks and hide your face.
Find your soul a hiding place.

(Traditional)

In this song the idea of holiness is associated with the biblical account of Moses' experience of seeing God and is earnestly coveted by believers, whereas sinfulness is outright condemned and judged as forever banned from the presence of God. Other songs also concerned with this theme are "I Want to Live Where God Can Use Me," "I'm Going on with Jesus Just the Same," "I'm Traveling This Highway," and "They Call Me a Holy-Roller." It should be noted that some songs containing the Holiness theme have been assigned to other categories as well. For example, a popular song among serpent-handling churches titled, "I'm a Holiness Child," was included in the next category because of verses referring to serpent handling. In whatever song it is found, however, the Holiness theme proclaims for believers their special standing in relation to God as a holy people.

The final category is Serpent Handling, which accounts for nearly 4 percent (13) of songs. Although fewer in number, songs in this group were among the most frequently sung, understandably so. Practicing all the signs of Mark 16 is what has given serpent-handling churches attention, even at the international level, and notoriety. Not only do they preach on the subject often—particularly in the presence of visitors and even curiosity seekers—they also sing about the sign, often with abandon. Most songs in the category are not about serpent handling per se but typically are concerned with other more dominant themes, with a verse or phrase about the ritual added in. The song below was written by a handler to highlight the biblical basis for the signs practiced by believers and also to defend the doctrinal stand on Oneness in the Godhead, as opposed to the more popular Trinitarian view. Often called "the Mark 16 song," it includes more references to the practice of serpent handling than most others.

(Verse 1) There's many things in this old world that I can't understand.
But there's one thing that I surely know—I'm guided by his hand.
I'll do the signs of Mark 16 just like he told me to.
Cause it's alright with me, Lord, if it's alright with you.

(Verse 2) I'll speak in tongues and heal the sick and cast the devils out.
I'll take up serpents, drink the poison, sing and dance and shout.
I've been baptized in Jesus' name just like he told me to.
Cause it's alright with me, Lord, if it's alright with you.

(Verse 3) They call us Jesus-only, They'll turn their back on you.
But believe in one God only is all that I can see.
I believe your whole word, Jesus, just like you told me to.
Cause it's alright with me, Lord, if it's alright with you.

(Traditional)

Most Popular Songs

Of the 1,043 songs in our sample, certain songs were sung much more
frequently than others. Table 6 presents 11 songs that believers sang
most often in their church services, along with their frequencies and category membership.

The most popular song was "I'm a Child of the King, Yes I Am,"
which occurred twenty-nine times in our sample. An up-tempo song, its
inclusion in the Identity category suggests it serves as a constant
reminder to believers of their immediate and special-felt relationship to
God as children of a royal and holy King:

I'm a child of the King, Yes I am, Yes I am.
I'm a child of the King, Yes I am, I know I am.
I belong to the Lord, Yes I do, Yes I do.
I'm a child of the King, Yes I am.

(Traditional)

In addition to the above refrain, verses refer to the believed reality of
heaven as a goal and rejection of the world's attempt to change the plain
meaning of the Bible in such a way as to conform to modernity, an issue
to which serpent-handling churches take great exception. The song
allows believers to express a claim for themselves as being unique and
special to God while living in a world that rejects and marginalizes them
on the basis of their belief in and obedience to his expressed commands.

The second most popular song occurred twenty-eight times and shares
membership with others in the category Comfort/Mercy/Deliverance.

TABLE 6. MOST POPULAR SONGS
BY FREQUENCY AND CATEGORY [N = 1,043]

Song Title	Frequency	Category
"I'm a Child of the King"	29	Identity
"God Knows All about Us"	28	Comfort/Mercy/Deliverance
"King Jesus, Won't You Hear Me When I Pray"	23	Comfort/Mercy/Deliverance
"Little David, Play on Your Harp"	23	Serpent Handling
"John Tells of That City"	22	Heaven
"God Don't See Me with His Eyes"	18	Comfort/Mercy/Deliverance
"[The] God of the Mountain"	16	Comfort/Mercy/Deliverance
"Talking about a Good Time"	15	Serpent Handling
"Crying Holy unto the Lord"	14	Holiness/Separation
"Do, Lord, Do Remember Me"	14	Heaven
"I'm Tired of You, Devil"	14	Comfort/Mercy/Deliverance

NOTE: The combined frequency of the above songs accounts for approximately 21% of all 1,043 songs.

The lyrics of "God Knows All about Us, and God Understands," are rich with meaning and worthy of review:

(Refrain) God understands. He knows all about us.
He knows all our hopes, and he knows all our plans.
He's willing to help us, if we will just follow.
God knows all about us. Yes, God understands.

(Verse 1) I've walked with my Lord, through sunshine and darkness.
I cannot forsake, his love or command.
Temptations are great, but God's love is greater.
God knows all about us, yes, God understands.

(Verse 2) I know of his love. I know of his healing.
I know of his power, he's given to man.
Without faith in God, our life would be hopeless.
God knows all about us. Yes, God understands.

(Verse 3) When troubles appear, and life has no meaning,
Be washed and be cleansed, in the blood of the Lamb.
Then your life will be brighter, and there'll be no more sorrow.
God knows all about us. Yes, God understands.

(Traditional)

As believers sing the song, multiple meanings emerge with which they connect while living in a difficult world. Verse 1 describes a continuing relationship with God, in which both sunshine and darkness have been experienced and in which temptation has been overcome by God's personal love and understanding. Verse 2 acknowledges the experience of God's love and power, without which life would be meaningless. Verse 3 relates to those who are presently struggling with meaninglessness in life and offers words of encouragement: God knows all details about the person and situation; and he is willing to provide personal help and purpose in life for any who will heed the call. Given the basic existential themes of the song, it is not difficult to understand its popularity and frequency in serpent-handling churches. What greater comfort can there be in a difficult and sometimes meaningless world than belief that an omnipotent God knows one personally, fully understands one's plight without need for explanation, and truly desires to help in the situation? Such is the comfort that believers enjoy each time the song is sung.

Two up-tempo songs shared the third most popular ranking by occurring twenty-three times each. One, "King Jesus," also suggests the theme Comfort/Mercy/Deliverance. Words of the refrain pose the question "King Jesus, won't you hear me when I pray?" and then go on to inform Jesus, "I'm down here in trouble, [so] send an angel by my way." The verses present various problematic contexts in which the best remedy is to call on Jesus for help. The second song, "Little David, Play on Your Harp," falls into the category Praise/Thanksgiving but also contains verses that encourage believers in their faith regarding two important biblical signs: serpent handling and strychnine drinking.

(Refrain) Little David, play on your harp, hallelu, hallelujah.
Little David, play on your harp, hallelu.

(Verse 1) Well little David, was a shepherd king.
He could play a harp, and he could sing.

(Verse 2) David-David, was a shepherd boy.
He killed a lion, and danced for joy.

(Verse 3) Well Noah stepped out, with a Bible in his hand.
He preached to people, there's trouble in the land.

(Verse 4) Well God told Noah, to build an ark,
Of gopher wood, without the bark.

(Verse 5) Didn't it rain? Didn't it pour?
Forty days, from door to door.

(Verse 6) Well all the beasts, that lived in the field,
They had to die, cause man wouldn't yield.

(Verse 7) Well there's the ark, on the mountain so high,
Cause Noah looked up, to God in the sky.

(Verse 8) Well God gave Noah, a rainbow sign.
It won't be water, but fire next time.

(Verse 9) Well up in heaven, around God's throne,
My name is written, a cornerstone.

(Verse 10) Moses, Moses, what's in your hand?
Well, it's a serpent, not a sinner man.

(Verse 11) Well I believe, in the Bible signs,
Taking up serpents, and drinking strychnine.

(Traditional)

This song represents an important characteristic among serpent-handling churches: the oral tradition of adding verses to songs as seems fitting. First, its refrain is a simple repetition of worship and praise to God. Two verses offer information about David that provide a context for the refrain. Several verses are concerned with the Bible story of Noah and God's judgment upon the earth in the form of a flood. Finally, verses are added that refer to the signs of serpent handling and poison drinking. Since the nature of this song is to flow and extend from itself, it is likely that other verses have been created and added from time to time. One of our video recordings of this lively song was more than 25 minutes long, during which time numerous serpents were handled by a company of believers at a homecoming. This instance and others illustrate the song's potential for declaring to unbelievers the compelling practices of the tradition and for reinforcing these rituals among believers themselves.

The remaining songs of popularity represent the categories Heaven and Holiness/Separation, which, together with Identity, Comfort/Mercy/Deliverance, Praise/Thanksgiving, and Serpent Handling, reflect themes that seem most important to serpent-handling churches in the sense that they are sung most frequently at church. In the context of worship, whatever needs are experienced by believers and unbelievers alike can connect and resonate with themes suggested from a variety of songs. Music serves as an effective medium that not only expresses the singer's feelings and thoughts but also allows the listener to relive and share with the singer the emotion conveyed (Seashore, 1938). This is especially important in a serpent-handling service, given its participatory nature. As voices rise in song, believers experience what is perceived as a connection with God—who is sensed as the savior, provider, and comforter described in lyrics—and with each other as comrades who journey together in a secular world with a common need for affirmation as followers of Jesus.

OBSERVATIONS AND CONCLUSION

To come to a better understanding of music in serpent-handling churches, it is important to consider what believers themselves say it means. When asked what music meant to her, DT responded, "Music in church is a way of beginning a service, and getting your mind focused on God so we can praise and worship him as he wants us to" (pers. com.). Music provides a way for believers to connect with their God. And, as stated earlier by another believer, "The song's text is the word of God" (quoted in Schwartz, 1999, p. 41), which makes the theme of the song important in that connection. Given this, it seems our categorization of songs is useful for understanding something about the role of music in that connection without being reductive (Moore, 1986; Young, 1926).

Among the ten categories in our analysis, nearly 70 percent of songs in our sample were represented in three groups: Comfort/Mercy/Deliverance, Heaven, and Witnessing/Evangelization. The way in which believers experience their lives and the nature of their particular situation at the moment seem relative to the music (Van Hoorebeke, 1980). As believers experience the need for comfort, mercy, or deliverance, songs that relate to these needs afford connection with God in such a way that comfort, mercy, or deliverance is experienced. If the need to become more focused on heaven and its rewards is present, music with that type of meaning allows a connection with God such that eternity becomes experienced as a present reality. At the attendance of unbelievers or skeptics at service, songs that convey the goodness and blessings of God or that even pronounce judgment on the wicked may provide a connection that leads to the revival of believers or salvation of the lost. As one believer put it, "The music fits your mood," and by doing so, it provides a doorway through which a spiritual connection with God can be experienced as a reality.

Issues raised by other research are relevant to these findings. Lipe (2002) has suggested that music serves a central function in personal transformation. Although our study does not directly inform the theory, the nature of our categories suggests that personal change can and does take place, particularly in the context of songs that convey witnessing or an evangelistic appeal. Although it is likely that numerous factors in the context of a serpent-handling church service are involved in the conversion experience, music plays no small role in facilitating transcendence as the listener hears its message and senses the presence of God (secondary function I). For example, in such songs as "House of Gold," abstract ideas about eternity may become a personalized concrete reality demanding some type of appropriate response (secondary function II)—typically in terms of repentance and salvation. Finally, intrapersonal, interpersonal, and communal/global issues related to transformation may be connected with the experience of serpent-handling church music (secondary function III). Of particular interest is how that music aids in sustaining the practice of serpent handling among a community of believers in the face of death from a bite. For instance, as we discussed above, we attended the graveside service of a young minister who had died only minutes after being bitten. As believers gathered beside his coffin in the very context of death, they began singing and moments later experienced connection with God such that boxes were opened and serpents were handled. As Lipe (2002) has suggested, music can serve a function in facilitating healing in a community that has experienced trauma at some level. In view of these issues, Lipe's theory might be useful in further investigations of music in serpent-handling churches.

In conclusion, as believers gather for worship, music provides a means for unifying scattered minds and for shifting attention from surrounding distractions to a focus on God. The music rises as participants join the singing, which allows for a spiritual connection in which God may be experienced in ways related to the meaning of lyrics. The effects of group singing that Unwin et al. (2002) observed in an experimental context also can be observed among serpent-handling churches: singing affects not only the emotion of participants but also that of others who remain seated in the pew. The final result is that all are moved by the experience of the music. In the words of one believer, "The music doesn't pump up the Spirit. Our music has a tradition that is passed down from one generation to another. . . . Singing helps you get your mind on the Lord so the Lord can work through you. God can anoint the music, and then the music anoints the members" (quoted in Schwartz, 1999, p. 41).

Finally, the central role of music in serpent-handling churches is not different from its role in major Pentecostal denominations. One need not postulate that music induces trance states, even though it can likely facilitate them. As we noted, believers learn how to enter into and exit from such states and thus have some degree of control. Music is clearly used to facilitate all aspects of worship, not simply trance states, and is integral to the tradition. However, one must not lose sight of the fact that not only the nature of the music but also the content of the songs contribute to a tradition that likely needs its music as much as it needs its serpents.

CHAPTER 12

Serpent Handling and the Law

History and Empirical Studies

Despite the fact that serpent-handling churches are part of the biblically based Pentecostal tradition and that they are most prominent in what many refer to as the mountain region of the "Bible belt," local governing bodies and state legislatures have sought to prohibit their central ritual. In this chapter we explore the history of legislation against serpent-handling churches and the success of this legislation in appellate courts. We then investigate both rational and prejudicial reasons for opposition to serpent handlers and discuss a study in which the presentation of factual information regarding serpent-handling churches alters people's opinions on whether laws banning serpent handling override one's religious freedom to practice his or her beliefs, even at the risk of harm.

HISTORICAL CONSIDERATIONS: SUCCESSFUL LEGISLATION AGAINST SERPENT HANDLING

As early as 1918, C. F. Noble wrote in the *Pentecostal Advocate,* "I have heard of many being bitten by snakes, *some dying,* others having arms taken off" (p. 2; emphasis added). Our earliest documented death is that of Jim W. Reece, sometime before 1922. Whether or not the reference to maiming and many deaths in 1918 is hyperbole, the suggestion is clear that other Pentecostal groups recognized the danger of serpent handling and likely had an empirical basis for this view in deaths that occurred but were not reported by the media. As mainstream denominationally oriented Pentecostal churches struggled with Mark 16, only the renegade churches maintained a commitment both to its literal interpretation and to the practice of serpent handling in the face of documented maiming and deaths.

As Pentecostal groups debated the issue of serpent handling in their own publications, local and national newspapers began to run stories on the practice of handling, especially when bites occurred. For instance, the *Birmingham News,* on September 16, 1934, referred to an upcoming convention of "Holy Rollers" and noted their curious practice and their willingness to let serpents bite them as a test of their faith (Holy Rollers, 1934). In 1936 the *New York Times* reported H. T. C. Anderson's death by serpent bite (Faith service, 1936). The tendency of newspapers to only report on services in which bites or death occurred served to sensationalize serpent handling. Furthermore, the reports stereotype believers and misinterpret their central ritual (Birckhead, 1997; Hood, 1998). For instance, serpent handling is *not* a test of faith. This stereotyping continues and is, we believe, one of the reasons that legislation banning serpent handling has been so successful.

In reviewing the history of laws against serpent handling, we were struck both by the curious reasoning used to persuade legislatures to ban the practice and by the reasoning of appellate courts that upheld convictions handed down by the lower courts in both criminal and civil cases. As we discuss below, the courts had little factual information on which to base their decisions. For now, we want to acknowledge what we think is obvious: few Americans are likely to willingly endorse a religious practice that can bring harm to believers. It is implicit in a commonsense view that religion must be "good" and should not condone rituals that can maim or kill. While this is a reasonable position, it also can be viewed as a prejudice. Why cannot religion legitimately endorse a practice that can maim or kill? One needs but acknowledge Kierkegaard's (1843/1986) assertion that to understand Abraham's willingness to obey God's command to sacrifice Isaac is to deny faith in favor of explanations, whether psychological (e.g., Abraham is mad) or ethical (e.g., Abraham is unethical). Kierkegaard notes that to acknowledge Abraham as a true knight of faith is accept a *teleological suspension of the ethical.* Something like this, we suggest, is necessary to acknowledge that despite the fact that serpent handlers are injured and killed, their faith may be both sincere and valid.

By their very nature, religious sects stand in opposition to the larger culture. This opposition includes tension not only with respect to acceptable religious practices but also with respect to the reasons that would legitimate such practices. The tension between practice and belief is one recognized by the courts. However, the courts have held that although handlers have absolute constitutional protection of their beliefs, the same protection does not apply to their practices.

In the early reporting of bites and deaths, public concern was raised for the welfare of handlers as well as for the welfare of believers. Laws against serpent handling vacillated between protecting church members or handlers or both. However, it is our contention that, given little factual knowledge about serpent-handling churches and the long history of media stereotyping, lawmakers were easily persuaded that serpent handling needed to be banned. In addition, the ability of Appalachian states to pass laws against serpent handling was aided by national publicity, especially that associated with the endangerment of children. In the early years of serpent handling, children did handle. There is no documented death of a child from handling, but a widely circulated photograph of a child touching a serpent added to the media frenzy surrounding serpent-handling churches in the late 1930s (Burton, 1993; Kane, 1979; Rowe, 1982).[1]

Even more serious was the widely publicized serpent bite of a six-year-old girl, Leitha Ann Rowan. She was bitten as a serpent was passed around her church in rural Georgia. Her mother hid her for seventy-two hours, but other family members then brought Leitha to the sheriff's office. She was examined by a physician, although the parents refused medical treatment. Leitha recovered without permanent damage, despite a *New York Times* article (Snake-rite leaders, 1940) claiming that she was dying from a copperhead bite. Her father, Albert Rowan, and the church pastor, W. T. Lipton, were arrested on charges of assault with intent to commit murder, which the sheriff said would be elevated to murder charges if Leitha died. On the previous day the *New York Times* (Snake bitten child, 1940) had identified the serpent as a "copperhead moccasin" and reported that the sheriff said it had also bitten eight other members. There were no explicit laws against serpent handling in the United States before 1940. It is likely that the national publicity surrounding Leitha's bite contributed to Georgia passing one of the harshest laws against the practice.

The first law against serpent handling was passed in Kentucky in 1940. It was stimulated by a complaint from John Day, of Harlan, Kentucky, who was offended when his wife began handling serpents at the Pine Mountain Church of God in Pineville, Kentucky. He had three men arrested for breach of the peace, a common way to discourage handling before legislation explicitly banning the practice (Vance, 1975, pp. 40–41). In June 1940 the Kentucky legislature passed the first and only law against handling serpents in a *religious* setting. While other states would quickly follow suit, none made reference to religious settings, nor did any include what Kentucky banned: not serpents, but the use of any reptiles in a religious service. The Kentucky law reads as follows: "Any person who displays, handles or uses any kind of reptile in connection with any religious service or gathering shall be fined not less than fifty ($50.00) nor more than one hundred dollars ($100.00)" (Snake handlers, n.d.). Two things are curious about the first law against serpent handling: (1) it presumably includes serpents under "reptiles," a broad classification that encompasses such harmless organisms as frogs and lizards; and (2) the ban specifically applies to religious settings or gatherings and hence not to secular events. Its focus on religious services would appear to violate religious freedom. This is clearly the view of serpent handlers (see Hood, 2003a). The statue was challenged in *Lawson v. Commonwealth* (Snake handlers, n.d.). Tom Lawson and other believers were convicted under the Kentucky statute of displaying and handling serpents and then appealed their conviction. In upholding the conviction, the appellate court cited *Jones v. City of Opelika,* a U.S. Supreme Court decision that affirmed the absolute right to freedom of religious *belief* but not the constitutional right to religious *practice.* In part, it said, "Courts, no more than Constitutions, can intrude into the consciences of men or compel them to believe contrary to their faith or think contrary to their convictions, but courts are competent to adjudge the acts men do under color of a constitutional right, such as freedom of speech or press or the free exercise of religion and to determine whether the claimed right is limited by other recognized powers, equally precious to mankind" (Snake handlers, n.d.).

Lawson v. Commonwealth reveals a zeitgeist that would assure that, with the exception of West Virginia, Appalachian states, in which handling was publicly exposed by the media, found it easy to pass laws against handling. Furthermore, the laws without exception were supported by appellate court decisions.[2] Handlers would be allowed to believe but not to practice. The states claimed overriding or competing interest. But how could they know?

Probably the most documented discussion of state laws against serpent handling focuses on the state of Tennessee. Burton (1993, chap. 5) has analyzed the history of serpent handling in the Tennessee courts and also has produced two documentary films with the assistance of Thomas Headley on the practice of serpent handling and legal action, primarily following deaths at Carson Springs (Burton & Headley, 1983, 1986). J. B. Collins (1947), a reporter for the *Chattanooga News Free Press* documented serpent handling at the church in Dolly Pond, just outside the city of Chattanooga. Tennessee is interesting because, of its two appellate court decisions upholding laws against serpent handling, one was a criminal conviction and the other was a civil conviction.

Tennessee is unique among states with serpent handlers in that one of its local newspapers is linked to the family that owns the *New York Times*. Thus much of the media coverage of serpent handling reached a wide audience as the *New York Times* often carried articles of handling, especially when associated with bites and death. The local Chattanooga papers, the *Chattanooga News Free Press* and the *Chattanooga Times,* also carried many articles on serpent handling at Dolly Pond and, later, at Carson City. As is typical, the coverage was linked to deaths at these churches.

In 1945 Lewis Ford was bitten at the Dolly Pond Church of God with Signs Following just outside Chattanooga (Ford, rattler's victim, 1945). J. B. Collins (1947, p. 17) wrote that more than twenty-five hundred people attended Ford's funeral at Dolly Pond. Other deaths occurred the same year, but not at Dolly Pond. Anna Kirk, a pregnant woman, was bitten in West Virginia, and both she and her preterm child, who was born just after the bite, died. The deaths were reported in the *New York Times* (Tennessee preacher, 1945). While handling serpents in a home in Daisy, Tennessee, Clint Jackson was fatally bitten (Collins, 1947, p. 23). In Cleveland, Tennessee, home of the international headquarters of the Church of God and just thirty miles from Chattanooga, eighteen-year-old Harry Skelton was bitten and died. His death was reported in the *Chattanooga Times* (Snake bite, 1946). Five days later Walter Henry, handling the same serpent that killed Skelton, was fatally bitten. Fred Travis wrote of these deaths in the *Chattanooga Times* (Bradley baffled, 1946). Finally, to continue this saga of deaths from serpent bites within a brief two-year period, Henry's own brother-in-law, Hobert Williford, handled a serpent at Henry's funeral, was bitten, and also died. The *Chattanooga Times* carried the story under the heading, "3rd Snake Cultist Dies in Cleveland" (1946).

The massive publicity concerning the serpent handling at Dolly Pond and Cleveland, as well as the deaths from serpent bites in surrounding states, made it easy for lawmakers in Tennessee to propose a bill banning handling. Tennessee's law was *not* modeled after Kentucky's, and the Tennessee law, not Kentucky's, became the model other states followed. Tennessee's law made no reference to religion. It simply made it illegal to "exhibit, handle, or use any poisonous or dangerous snake or reptile in such a manner as to endanger the life or death of any person" (Snake handlers, n.d.). A second difference from the Kentucky law is that specific reference is to snakes or reptiles that are *dangerous*. The law made handling a misdemeanor punishable by a fine of from $50 to $100 or six months in jail or both (Burton, 1993, p. 75).

The Tennessee law was challenged by believers at Dolly Pond, who, despite the law's passage in April 1947, continued to handle serpents. Publicity surrounding Dolly Pond (some of which referred to it as "Folly" Pond) made it an easy target for enforcement of the new law. In August 1947 Tom Harden, five female handlers, and six other male handlers were arrested. All but one were convicted. On appeal to the Tennessee supreme court the decision of the lower court was upheld. As Burton (1993, pp. 80–81) notes in his discussion of this case, two issues were asserted by the court: (1) the practice is inherently dangerous; and hence (2) the state has an overriding interest such that, while religious belief is protected, the religious practice of handling is constitutionally denied. As we discuss below, Tennessee judges would take different views on whether the phrase "any person" in the Tennessee law was absolutely inclusive and thus *included* the handler or whether it was to be interpreted as "any other person," thus *excluding* the handler. The difference would become significant when Tennessee civil law was applied to two deaths at the Carson Springs church in eastern Tennessee in 1973.

In a well-documented case, two handlers at the Holiness Church of God in Jesus Name in Carson Springs died.[3] The massive publicity surrounding these two deaths paralleled that surrounding Dolly Pond more than a quarter of a century earlier. The pastor of the church, Alfred Ball, and a well-known handler and former pastor of the church, Liston Pack, were ordered by the circuit court in Cocke County not to handle serpents. The irony is that the handlers who died, Allen Williams Sr. and Buford Pack, had done so after drinking strychnine, not handling serpents. Neither the Tennessee law nor any other states' laws banning handling make reference to drinking poison.[4] Both Ball and Pack were convicted under Tennessee civil (common) law. Despite the conviction, handling continued, as documented by Kimbrough and Hood (1995). The district attorney for Cocke County banned both poison drinking and serpent handling at Carson Springs, declaring them a "public nuisance." This is the first explicit ban on poison drinking directed at serpent handlers.[5] Ball and Pack ignored the injunction, and with much publicity surrounding the Carson Springs church, both were convicted, fined (ironically, differing amounts: $150 for Pack and $100 for Ball) and given twenty days in jail. The exact unfolding of subsequent events need not concern us here (see Burton, 1993, pp. 74–81). What is of concern are the appeal and the fact that it failed.

The Court of Appeals of Tennessee found that the law declaring handling a public nuisance was "unconstitutionally broad" (Burton, 1993, p. 78). The law was modified to allow consenting adults to handle, as long as they did so in a manner that did not endanger other persons. The reasonableness of this modification (in our view) is that consenting adults can (a) handle serpents and (b) be in the presence of those who handle serpents even if they do not wish to handle. This would seem to balance both concerns, that of the absolute freedom of religious belief and that of a conditional freedom to practice one's religion so long as others are not endangered.

Experienced researchers know that church members and observers are not endangered by others who are handling serpents. There is no documented case of a nonhandling member being bitten by a serpent handled by another believer. Members and visitors may sit far back, away from the area in which serpents are handled if they so choose. Unfortunately (again in our view), an appeal to the Tennessee supreme court resulted in overturning the appellate court, simply asserting that handling is *inherently dangerous* and that others present are, at a minimum, aiding and abetting. Thus both handlers and nonhandlers who are observing the practice create, in the supreme court's view, a "public nuisance." Thus, like Kentucky, Tennessee has consistently ruled against handlers in the final view. Only Tennessee has successfully challenged handlers on the basis of both criminal and civil law. An attempt to appeal to the U.S. Supreme Court failed; the court refused to hear the appeal.

Other states have banned serpent handling. Virginia banned handling in the same year as Tennessee, 1947. North Carolina followed in 1949, then Alabama in 1950. In all these states the issue is whether handling is dangerous to self (apparently obvious) or to others (e.g., nonhandlers). Legislatures and courts have had little real knowledge of serpent-handling churches and therefore have little basis on which to judge whether serpent handling is dangerous to others. As noted above, there is no record of a nonhandler ever being bitten; churches take precautions to ensure the safety of those who do not handle.

Within the serpent handling tradition, occasional efforts by pastors to place restrictions on handling to assure additional safety have failed because of the fierce autonomy of those who handle. Few handlers will accept "regulations" on how they handle. As they believe they are moved on by God, handlers do not want God's will regulated. One effort that failed was briefly known as the Morris Plan. Pastor C. D. Morris of the Faith Tabernacle in LaFollete, Tennessee, proposed to rope off an area of the church in which handling would occur. He further proposed there could be only one handler at a time and that each handler must obtain a serpent from the box; no handler could "hand off" to another person. The effort to impose a structure failed. All efforts to structure handling have consistently failed. The basic rule that cuts across all churches is simply, "When you handle, be sure God is in it."

Two states have not only banned handling but also have banned handlers from preaching their beliefs, something that seems obviously unconstitutional to us (Hood, Williamson, & Morris, 2000). Both Georgia and North Carolina have made handling and the "inducement to handle" a violation of law. After stating that "intentional exposure to venomous reptiles" is illegal, North Carolina's 1949 law went on to sanction any attempt to "exhort" or use "inducement to such exposure" (Burton, 1993, p. 81). The second state to ban serpent handling, Georgia, went furthest of all. Its 1941 law making handling illegal also, unlike most states, made it a felony. Further, it made it illegal to encourage or induce anyone to handle a serpent. Thus in North Carolina and Georgia even preaching from Mark 16:17–18 could be interpreted as a violation of state law. Moreover, the Georgia law was extreme in stating that if handling or the preaching of handling ("inducement") resulted in the death of any person, the guilty person "should be sentenced to death, unless the jury trying the case should recommend mercy" (cited in Burton, 1993, p. 81; Hood, Williamson, & Morris, 2000). Georgia was unsuccessful in getting convictions under its law (no appellate decisions have occurred), and the law was omitted during the 1968 rewriting of the Georgia state code. However, as with the North Carolina law, it reflects attitudes that not only infringe on religious practice but on the right to religious belief as well. It is a vacuous claim to state that one can have a religious belief but cannot exercise his or her constitutional right to preach that belief.

A final state, Alabama, deserves consideration here. Not only does it continue to house some significant serpent-handling churches, but it illustrates the case that even as states create, modify, and repeal laws against serpent handlers, serpent handlers continue to be prosecuted under a variety of other laws. Alabama first banned serpent handling in 1950. Like Georgia, Alabama made handling a felony, and like all states except Kentucky, no reference was made to a church or religious gathering. It simply stated, "Any person who displays, handles, exhibits, or uses any poisonous or dangerous snake or reptile in such a manner as to endanger the life or health of another shall be guilty of a felony" (Snake handlers, n.d.). Punishment was to be from one to five years in prison. As with all states, despite laws against handling, the practice continued. Often in states where handling has had strong subcultural support, local authorities have refused to press charges and juries have refused to convict when cases were taken to court. In 1953 Alabama revised its law by reducing handling to a misdemeanor with a penalty of up to six months in jail or a fine of from $50 to $150. In 1975 specific laws against handling were deleted when Alabama rewrote its state code (Hood et al., 2000). However, the repeal of specific laws against handling does *not* mean handlers cannot be persecuted. Alabama has laws against reckless endangerment (a class A misdemeanor) that ban "conduct which creates a substantial risk of serious physical injury to another person" (Snake handlers, n.d.). It also has a menace law (a class B misdemeanor) that states, "A person commits a crime of menacing if, by physical action, he intentionally places or attempts to place another person in fear of imminent serious injury" (Snake handlers, n.d.). Appellate courts have upheld the application of menacing or reckless endangerment laws to serpent handling.[6] Thus, as with the 1973 Carson City convictions in Tennessee, even without specific laws against serpent handling, other laws, both criminal and civil, can be used to arrest those who try to practice their faith.

As a final consideration of legislation against serpent handling, West Virginia provides the best counterexample. West Virginia is the home of several serpent-handling churches, some of which have long histories of notoriety. The most famous is the Church of the Lord Jesus in Jolo, McDowell County.[7] It began with a series of house church meetings conducted by Bob and Barbara Elkins in the late 1940s and was formally established as a church in 1956 with the construction of its first church building, which was the time it gained notoriety as a serpent-handling church (personal interview with Dewey Chafin, September 5, 1998; Brown & McDonald, 2000). Barbara Elkins had begun handling when she witnessed George Hensley handling serpents in West Virginia in 1935. Because of their receptivity to media, the Jolo church and its handlers became major media figures. Jolo gained added media attention when Barbara Elkins's daughter, Columbia Gaye Chafin Hagerman, received a rattlesnake bite while she handled in the Jolo church in 1961. She refused medical treatment and died at her parents' home four days later. In an interview in *People* magazine, Barbara said of Columbia: "She handled snakes quite awhile, and this was the first time she'd been bitten. We asked if she wanted us to take her to the doctor, but she said no. She wanted God to do what he wanted with her" (Grogan & Phillips, 1989). Media attention focused on Jolo and handling churches in other parts of West Virginia such as the Scrabble Creek Church of All Nations in Fayette County. This church became famous for allowing videotaping of its services, including the widely distributed film *Holy Ghost People* (Boyd & Adair, 1968). It also was the focus of the study by Tellegen, Gerrard, Gerrard, and Butcher (1969), which demonstrated with the Minnesota Multiphasic Personality Inventory (MMPI) that members of the Scrabble Creek Church were if anything healthier than control members of a Methodist church in the same locality.[8] This fact was widely reported in the region's newspapers (e.g., Snakehandlers mentally, 1968).

Given the publicity surrounding Columbia's death in West Virginia, legislatures introduced a bill to ban the practice of serpent handling. Barbara Elkins and others from West Virginia churches testified that they would continue to handle serpents even if a law were passed against the practice. In February 1963 the West Virginia House of Delegates passed a law that would make the handling of poisonous serpents a misdemeanor. Penalties were to be fines from $100 to $500 (House okays ban, 1963). However, publicity surrounding the proposed ban and active support from those sympathetic to West Virginia's powerful history of churches that endorsed serpent handling eventually won the day. The state's Senate Judiciary Committee refused to act on the bill. Since that refusal, West Virginia has made no other efforts to pass legislation against serpent handling.

The case of West Virginia is instructive for the psychological insights it provides into attitudes toward handling. We explore this below in two ways. First, we look at an empirical study that suggests that even when there is reasonable disagreement on support for serpent handling, prejudice is often also involved. Second, we look at a study that successfully changed attitudes toward handling by providing factual information about the practice.

ATTITUDES TOWARD SERPENT HANDLING:
A PSYCHOLOGICAL INVESTIGATION

Over the years we have supplemented our field research with other methodologies in order to more fully understand serpent handling. One concern has been with the rejection of handling by those who have little factual knowledge about the tradition. Another concern has been that even those familiar with the tradition often are so strongly opposed to the practice that they are blinded by its positive aspects. In the former case, factual knowledge can reduce opposition to the tradition. One example that might be useful here is cited in Burton (1993) with regard to the Tennessee supreme court declaration that "the practice [of handling serpents] is too fraught with danger to permit its pursuit in the *frenzied atmosphere* of an emotional church service, regardless of age or consent" (cited in Burton, 1993, p. 80; emphasis added). Such loaded adjectives suggest lack of control and endangerment of others, which is certainly not characteristic of serpent-handling services. Not only is there no confirmation of a nonhandler being bitten during a service, but the powerful emotions expressed are best seen as religiously orchestrated, not "frenzied."

To illustrate the second point noted above, believing handlers are often harassed by nonbelieving friends and family. For instance, Jeff Hagerman of the Jolo, West Virginia, church—despite having been bitten many times—declared, "I praise God for all my bites. . . . I desire for my kids to be in this one day" (Snake handlers don't, 1991, p. A1). However, Hagerman's two brothers are nonhandlers and have been arrested more than once for disrupting services at Jolo in an effort they believe is in Jeff's best interest—the abandonment of handling. However, Hagerman has been quoted as saying, "I plan to have a lot more [bites]. . . . I love handling serpents" (Snake handlers don't, 1991, p. A1). These comments were made the same year another death occurred from a serpent bite in the Jolo church: that of Ray Johnson. Our point here is simply that disagreements over handling can be due to prejudices against the validity of religious rituals that can maim and kill and that these prejudices may mask other legitimate motives for concern, such as love and reasoned opposition to the practice. We decided to explore this in an empirical study.

Empirical Study 1: Prejudicial Judgments
Concerning Serpent Handlers

In a series of studies, we explored individuals' reactions to religious conversion based on a hypothetical Bible study of the Gospel of Mark.

We created six different vignettes concerning a fictitious male named "Bill" whom we said rediscovered his faith after becoming involved in a Pentecostal church. We went on to say that Bill renewed his enthusiasm in a variety of ways—not the least of which was his commitment to the signs that Christ said would follow those who believe.

Using six different groups to evaluate the six different vignettes, we explored how participants would evaluate the conversion of our hypothetical Bill based on whether they thought Bill's conversion was (a) legitimate, (b) likely to be long-lasting, (c) well grounded, or (d) unfortunate. One of the six vignettes referred simply to "Bible study" as a general control. Each of the other five referred to one of the five signs of Mark 16. A general template for all six vignettes is presented below; the italicized terms, enclosed in parentheses, indicate how the vignettes varied.

TEMPLATE

Bill has rediscovered his faith as an adult as a result of being involved in a Pentecostal church. His renewed enthusiasm expresses itself in a variety of ways, not the least of which is his firm commitment to the signs that Christ said would follow those who believe. In particular, he is active among those in his church who *(handle snakes; drink poison; speak in tongues; cast out demons; lay hands upon the sick; study the Bible)*. Bill often talks to others about how his practice of *(handling serpents; drinking poison; laying hands upon the sick; casting out demons; studying the Bible)* has renewed and strengthened his faith. He is confident that he will never again participate in any church that does not enthusiastically endorse *(the handling of serpents; the drinking of poison; laying hands upon the sick; casting out demons; speaking in tongues; studying the Bible)*.

Each vignette was included in a questionnaire packet containing items that allowed us to obtain a wide variety of information about the participant, including age, sex, religious orientation, and the importance of religion to the him or her. We used this information to make sure that our participants were themselves religiously committed and that religion was a salient part of their own lives. Note that we asked participants to judge Bill's conversion experience, based not on their own religions but on Bill's. Let us compare two vignettes and indicate how they were to be rated.

SERPENT-HANDLING VIGNETTE

Bill has rediscovered his faith as an adult as a result of being involved in a Pentecostal church. His renewed enthusiasm expresses itself in a variety of ways not the least of which is his commitment to the signs Christ said would follow those that believe. In particular, he has been active among those in his church who *handle snakes*. Bill often talks to others about how his practice of *handling snakes* has renewed and strengthened his faith. He is confident that he never again will participate in any church that does not enthusiastically endorse *snake handling*.

BIBLE STUDY (CONTROL) VIGNETTE

Bill has rediscovered his faith as an adult as a result of being involved in a Pentecostal church. His renewed enthusiasm expresses itself in a variety of ways not the least of which is his commitment to the signs Christ said would follow those that believe. In particular, he has been active among those in his church who *study the Bible*. Bill often talks to others about how his practice of *studying the Bible* has renewed and strengthened his faith. He is confident that he never again will participate in any church that does not enthusiastically endorse *Bible study*.

Each of the six different groups of participants in our study received and rated only one specific vignette that was randomly assigned. Using a rating scale from 1 to 5 (with 1 being "strongly disagree" and 5 being "strongly agree"), the results were as we had predicted. As a general overall statement, Bill's conversion was perceived as less legitimate, poorly grounded, and unlikely to be long-lasting. It also was found to be unfortunate when linked to the most controversial signs of Mark 16, namely, serpent handling and the drinking of poison.[9]

This finding may seem obvious. However, additional assessments suggest more than mere reasonable disagreement with religious beliefs and practices. We also included in our questionnaire packet a measure of prejudice. This measure allowed us to assess participants' prejudice based on three dimensions: (a) stereotyping, (b) negative emotional reactions against a group, and (c) behavioral avoidance. Thus our assessment of prejudice includes a behavioral indicator (avoidance of handlers), an affective indicator (negative emotional reaction to handlers), and a cognitive factor (stereotyping of handlers).

Certainly people can disagree with handling and poison drinking on a variety of very reasonable grounds. But as we have noted throughout this book, so can a reasonable argument in favor of these practices be made. Thus disagreement and agreement can be based on a rational dialogue. However, the use of appropriate statistical procedures to analyze the low acceptance of conversion—when attributed to either serpent handling or the drinking of poison—revealed that, independent of rational rejection, prejudice plays a significant role in coming to such conclusions. People who reject serpent handlers also stereotype them, have negative emotional reactions to them, and seek to avoid them.[10]

Thus our empirical study reveals a more complex picture of attitudes toward serpent-handling churches. Our findings are suggestive of the history of legal retaliation against the tradition that began in 1940 and that continues today with the creative use of various laws, whether or not they are directly linked to serpent handling. Note that our treatment of the history of serpent handling within the Church of God and the Church of God of Prophecy entails the use of sophisticated theological arguments that were used to argue for the validity of all five signs and the reasonableness of their being followed.

Our concern always has been that debates over the reasonableness of the practice are clouded by the prejudice that a ritual that can main and kill cannot attract reasonable believers. This is the prejudice we think we have uncovered. It assumes that *bizarre,* a term often used to stereotype serpent-handling churches (Birckhead, 1993, 1997), must be matched by equal stereotyping of the believer, despite all the evidence to the contrary (see Hood et al., 2005, chap. 8; Tellegen et al., 1969). Could such prejudices be removed, and, if so, would attitudes toward serpent handling and the law be changed? We approached these questions in a further empirical study.

Empirical Study 2: Changing Stereotypical Views of Serpent Handlers

Given that serpent-handling churches are most prevalent in Appalachia, they share the religious landscape with other Pentecostal groups that have never endorsed the practice or that once endorsed the practice but later abandoned their support in the face of maiming and deaths. However, also powerful in this region of the United States are other fundamentalist and Evangelical groups that, despite their support for religious liberty in the abstract, have been unlikely to support the religious rights of unconventional believers (Jelen, 1999; Wilcox, Jelen, & Leege, 1993). Furthermore, despite recent concern of sociologists of religion with popular media-supported stereotypes of new religious movements, often identified as "cults" (Bromley & Shupe, 1981; Richardson & van Driel, 1991), no investigators have included what is the most legislated against religious ritual, serpent handling, in their concerns for the constitutional protection for religious groups who endorse sectarian practices.

Given the prejudice against serpent-handling churches demonstrated in the studies above, our concerns focused on changing attitudes toward serpent-handling churches. In particular, we wished to consider changing stereotypical views of serpent handlers. How could this be done?

Our procedure was to make two sets of videotapes regarding serpent handling. One tape included footage of actual services, including handling and poison drinking, along with preaching and testimonies of believers as to why they worship as they do. Another (control) tape included an equivalent amount of footage of actual services but without handling or drinking of poison; nor were there testimonies included regarding belief in these practices.

The videotapes were presented to three groups of viewers, after which time each group completed a posttest that measured their attitudes toward handlers. One group saw the control tape; the other two (experimental) groups saw the tape of actual handling and poison drinking, as well as testimonies supporting these practices. The control group and one of the experimental groups took a pretest that measured their attitudes toward handlers before viewing their respective tapes. The second experimental group did not take a pretest. As described above, all three groups viewed their respective tapes and then took the posttest. This research design ensured that if the two experimental groups did not differ on the posttest, then we could reasonably infer that the pretest did not sensitize viewers to please the experimenter by changing their attitudes toward handlers after seeing the tape. As we shall see, both experimental groups (pretest/posttest and posttest-only) did not differ in their prejudice scores on the posttest, and thus what social scientists call "expectancy effects" did not account for the changes. In view of this, any changes in the stereotyping of serpent handlers, as reflected in posttest prejudice scores of both experimental groups, would likely be due to viewing factual information about serpent handlers presented in the videotape.[11]

All participants completed a questionnaire similar to the one discussed in the first study (Hood et al., 1999), this time with the focus on the stereotyping aspect of the prejudice measure. The control group and one experimental group took these measures prior to viewing any tapes. These two groups also responded to questions about whether the handlers were sincere in their faith and whether handling should be legal. All three groups then completed the same questionnaire items, once they had finished viewing the tapes.

As anticipated, our results were encouraging in that persons presented with factual information from handlers themselves in their religious context changed their views. Before viewing the tape, all groups felt handlers were insincere and that laws against the practice should exist. However, both experimental groups that saw the explanatory tape changed their minds, felt handlers were sincere, and felt that handlers should have a legal right to the practice of their beliefs. A reasonable inference is that these changes were due to the documented decline in stereotyping in that both experimental groups saw the tape with handling and testimonies explaining the practice.[12] Thus allowing handlers to express their own views in the setting of their ritual is an effective counter to the dominant media stereotyping of these believers. As expected, viewers of the control tape did not change their attitudes regarding what they perceived as the insincerity of handlers and continued to support laws against the practice. Not surprisingly, the maintenance of these beliefs was likely rooted in the fact that their stereotyping on the prejudice measure remained constant. Thus only actually seeing handling in its religious context, combined with explanations from handlers themselves, serves to reduce stereotyping and to change attitudes. We do not expect others to convert to handling serpents, but we do argue that it is only when others are knowledgeable about the tradition and its beliefs that they will allow handlers to practice what they believe.

The results of our study are encouraging. The opportunity to see the practice of religious serpent handling in its proper context, to hear sermons justifying the practice, and to listen to testimonies of handlers allows for changes in attitudes in three important ways. First, it reduces stereotypes concerning handlers. Second, in a country committed to religious freedom, it allows the viewer to use the same criteria the U.S. Supreme Court uses to test the sincerity of religious belief (Hammond, 2001); viewers come to see handlers as sincere believers. Third, unlike the courts in the cases cited above regarding handling, our viewers came to believe that sincere believers ought to have the right to practice their faith. That a consenting believer might be bitten, maimed, or even killed gives the state no compelling reason to deny the practice. This is the authors' belief and the belief of handlers as well. In the words of one pastor, "If you don't believe in handling, pray for those who do."

BACK TO THE LARGER SOCIAL CONTEXT: HANDLERS AND THE LAW

Given our success in changing attitudes toward serpent handling, it is apparent that once handlers are understood in their own context, the "bizarre" nature of their practice dissipates and gives way to an understanding of what can be seen as a legitimate religious practice. It is only when removed from this context of meaning that serpent handling requires pathological or other discrediting forms of explanation. La Barre's (1962/1974) classic armchair psychoanalysis of a lone serpent-handling preacher is a striking example. Attending few if any services himself, La Barre relied heavily on field notes of graduate students to produce his analysis of serpent handling as the acting out of sexual repression. The fallacy of this generalized analysis is balanced by Schwartz (1960), a psychiatrist who visited services and conducted psychiatric evaluations of handlers, which revealed no psychopathology. Likewise, the finding of Tellegen and his colleagues (1969), who used the MMPI with members of one of West Virginia's largest and most controversial serpent-handling churches, revealed that, if anything, handlers were overall more psychologically healthy when compared to a Methodist control church in the same region. As noted earlier, this finding was played up in local papers in the Appalachian region with immense delight (Snake-handlers mentally, 1968).

Our point is simply that religious serpent handling, when taken in the sacred context of worship, emerges as an understandable religious ritual experienced by believers who are in every sense of the word sincere people simply trying to express a faith that demands a particular form of life.

In our studies, that uninformed control participants remained prejudiced in their stereotypical view of handlers is not surprising, and, we suggest, contributes to our understanding of the ability of legislatures to oppose serpent handling beginning in the 1940s. Legislatures, informed at best by media reports, were far removed from the understanding afforded when the practice is embedded in a proper religious context. It is unlikely that the states' claim to an overriding "compelling" interest would carry much weight if the sincerity of handlers in terms of both belief and practice was acknowledged. On the other hand, the states' conspicuous tolerance for numerous activities in the secular world that entail the risk of maiming and death—from hang-gliding to rock climbing to football to NASCAR racing—seems curious. Cannot believers die from their faith as legitimately as others die in high-risk secular activities that are deemed legal?

What we suggest from the studies discussed in this chapter and our analyses throughout this book is not that one uncritically affirm serpent handling—only that the tradition receive a fair hearing. Indeed, handlers scrutinize their Bible and even differ among themselves on various matters of religious belief. All they assert is that there is no privileged understanding that can be applied to them outside the context that they themselves recognize as ultimate.

We have called this the principle of intratextuality and have developed it for all fundamentalisms that rely on a scared text, from Protestants to Muslims (Hood et al., 2003). If we can change views in a quasi-experimental context that assures handlers a fair chance to express their beliefs, it is a compelling argument against the unfortunate reliance on media reports that accentuate, stereotype, and sensationalize the unique practices of marginal groups (Fiske, 1993). The willingness to be exposed to conditions that allow one to understand such marginal groups would appear to be a necessary first step to giving serpent handlers a fair hearing. Although such a hearing may find neither agreement nor acceptance from those committed to differing views, the resulting judgments can be based on reason, not prejudice. With their King James Bible and their admiration for the U.S. Constitution, serpent handlers ask for nothing more (see Hood, 2003a).

Epilogue

The Hood-Williamson Research Archives for the Holiness Serpent Handling Sects of Appalachia is a rich source for exploring the rise and fall of churches and the tension within the tradition. For instance, twenty-three DVDs from July 1994 to July 2002 document the decline of one of the most powerful Jesus-only serpent-handling churches in Georgia, the Church of the Lord Jesus Christ, pastored by Carl Porter, who died in 2006 of natural causes. Porter died expelled from his own church and disgraced in the eyes of many within the tradition. The reason is simple enough: his wife of many years divorced him, after which time he took a second wife, who is a daughter of a powerful serpent-handling family, the Elkinses, who are associated with probably the most filmed and well known serpent-handling church, the Church of the Lord Jesus. The DVDs document Pastor Porter's attempt to continue to pastor his church. One can see one of Carl Porter's own sons, in his own struggle to stand for what he believed was right, preach against his father's refusal to step down as pastor and literally preach him from the church. The loss of Carl Porter's authority due to the rebellion of his church members is in part a testimony to his effective preaching against double marriage in years past—a case of being hoisted with his own petard. His second marriage failed quickly. Remarriage to the same woman also failed. Until his death, Carl Porter lived within sight of a church that he built and owned but could no longer preach in. Ironically, he rented out the church to a congregation that for some time placed a sign outside the church that read, "We do not handle serpents."

Continuing efforts to revive the Georgia church through several new pastors have not as yet succeeded. As mourners gathered at Porter's funeral in his former church, they remembered his early work in the tradition, although a second-generation serpent-handling preacher, whose own father had died practicing the signs, was careful not to "preach him into heaven." Porter lies buried in the front yard of his once-famous church, beside his mother and father whom he had converted to serpent handling many years before.

It is a well-known fact that all religious traditions, including Pentecostalism, have a dark side. However, we have chosen not to focus on such matters in the serpent-handling tradition for a clear and deliberate reason. The tradition has not been fairly presented by many scholars and public media, nor have the believers been allowed to speak for themselves. However, there are some exceptions to this fact that are worth noting here. Brown and McDonald (2000) investigated three serpent-handling families—the Elkinses and their church in Jolo, West Virginia; the Browns and their church in Marshall, North Carolina; and the Cootses and their church in Middlesboro, Kentucky—and allowed the handlers to speak for themselves. Before publication of their book, they allowed the interviews of individual family members to be edited by the interviewees themselves to assure that their views were properly expressed. Another exception is *Serpent Handling Believers*, Thomas Burton's 1993 major study of the tradition. He included an autobiographical piece by Anna Prince (pp. 108–25), the daughter of a serpent handler and the sister of Charles Prince, one of the tradition's most charismatic preachers, who died from a serpent bite in 1985. Burton (2004) also wrote a balanced and respectful book exploring reactions of the serpent-handling community and others involved in the widely covered trial and conviction of Glenn Summerford, a serpent handler who was found guilty of assaulting his wife with serpents kept on their property.

This trial was the initial reason Dennis Covington (1995, pp. 21–44) became aware of this tradition and wrote a popular book, *Salvation on Sand Mountain*. While the book is interesting, it is more the spiritual journey of the author himself than a fair representation of the serpent-handling tradition (Hood, 1995). Others, especially the electronic media, have more than tarred this tradition with revelations of its dark side, often exaggerated and sometimes fabricated. We wanted to avoid this temptation to sensationalize a tradition that needs understanding, which may be gained by shedding light on its beliefs and practices instead of searching in the shadows to further discredit a tradition whose cultural support is minimal.

Occasionally, a dark side of the tradition emerges that becomes central and cannot be avoided. For instance, in the process of collecting interviews and footage for a documentary film, two filmmakers followed a young serpent-handling preacher for what began as an interest in documenting the personal life of a young minister in the tradition; an unexpected turn of events in the preacher's life culminated in a series of crises that eventually led to his arrest and guilty plea to molestation charges.[1] The encounter and ultimate outcome of this unfortunate situation was neither intended nor sought by the filmmakers but was simply a consequence of attempting to document the positive aspects of a tradition whose dark side is surely no worse than that of any other tradition.

THE CURRENT STATE OF SERPENT-HANDLING CHURCHES

We are often asked how many churches handle serpents and what their membership is. No one knows the actual number of handling churches, even less the actual number of handlers. There are several reasons for this. First, churches rise and fall with remarkable rapidity. The "church" can be any building or home where two or more people can gather. We have documented churches in abandoned gas stations in Alabama, in isolated trailers throughout Appalachia, and in homes deep within the many hollows of the Appalachians. Even handlers do not know how many churches there are or how many believers handle serpents.

Another difficulty is "backsliding." Typically, a backslid believer is likely to stop attending church and also to stop handling serpents. The cause of backsliding is the adoption or readoption of any prohibited behavior of the church—from adultery to smoking or "snuffing." Churches differ in what they define as specific sins, and there is no consensus across the tradition, although all would identify themselves as belonging to the Holiness tradition. One church may allow smoking; another may not. Fierce autonomy is the rule. Jolo is infamous to some for its "double married" members; the Kingston church, as we noted above, refused to endorse its pastor when he became double married. Such differences allow the tradition to continue by fragmentation. A church that attempts to introduce a ban on smoking will likely cause dissension and eventually lead to a split as the smokers create a new church down the road or up the hollow. The church may comprise as few as three members, and it will take time for news of "another church" to travel and reach the ears of other discontented believers who may come along and join.

A third factor is that, given the legal actions taken against this tradition, churches do not "announce" their presence. Handlers learn by word of mouth of another church. By the time some people learn of the new church it is gone because of the inability to attract support from the community or other believers.

A fourth factor is that some handlers travel hundreds of miles to attend a serpent-handling church. Many circulate among several churches. Throughout Appalachia on any given night, there is bound to be a church someplace having service and handling serpents, and not simply in Appalachia. We have documented handling serpents in California in the 1980s in several private homes. Churches exist or have existed in the southeastern United States and in parts of Canada. Most are unknown and poorly documented. It would be foolish out of hand to claim the absence of handling in any state or region of the United States. However, the tradition is most firmly established in the Appalachian region and in what we refer to as powerful "hub" churches. These have included the Church of the Lord Jesus Christ in Kingston, Georgia, now in decline, and the Church of the Lord Jesus in Jolo, West Virginia, now but a shadow of its former glory. However, current powerful hub churches exist in Middlesboro, Kentucky (the Full Gospel Tabernacle in Jesus Name church linked to the powerful Coots family), and on Sand Mountain in Macedonia, Alabama (the Old Rock Holiness Church, long pastored by Billy Summerford). These are among the "Oneness" or "Jesus-only" Holiness-Pentecostal tradition churches, with which we have had the most experience in our research and which are heavily documented in our archives. However, we also have documented from our field investigations a significant number of serpent-handling churches in the "Trinitarian" Holiness-Pentecostal tradition. For example, we have visited on different occasions the Sanctuary Holiness Church, a congregation of about one hundred fifty members who meet each Sunday morning in a large, well-furnished, upscale structure on the outskirts of Berea, Kentucky. The church was founded several decades ago by the Eades family, and the current pastor is Harold Eades. Another much smaller Trinitarian church we have attended is the Bill Moore Branch Holiness Church, located just outside of May King, Kentucky, whose present pastor is Wendell Bates. Several decades ago, Pastor Loyd

Collins (now deceased) established the Little Colley Holiness Church, another small Trinitarian congregation near May King, which is now led by his son Walter. With the assistance of longtime evangelist Ron Hensley, a former pastor of the Rella Holiness Church (founded by the well-known Lee Valentine), and Verlin Short, Williamson was successful in constructing a list of some thirty-three Trinitarian churches, most of which are located in Kentucky but also in Michigan, Indiana, Tennessee, Alabama, and Georgia. Most of these Trinitarian churches are associated with a founding family that has served as the hub.[2]

We use the term *hub* because every such church has "spokes" that create a "rim" that defines the possibility of the rise and fall of additional churches, created, however briefly, by dissatisfied members of a hub church. Few of these "rim" churches survive for long; often their failure simply means that the formerly dissatisfied members return anew to their hub church.

While hub churches tend to be large by serpent-handling church standards, this seldom means more than one hundred members. Usually no records are kept, and one becomes an implicit member of a particular church by regular attendance and by agreement with the basic theology of the pastor. Among the many variations among serpent-handling churches are debates over baptism. All demand immersion, preferably in a nearby stream or river, but one can listen to interesting debates over whether one must be baptized in the *name* of the Father, Son, and Holy Ghost—which are considered de facto to mean Jesus, Jesus Christ, the Lord Jesus, or the Lord Jesus Christ (depending on the preacher's own theology)—or simply in the *name of the Father, Son, and Holy Ghost*. As mentioned above, the churches that use the former baptistic prescription are "Jesus-only" churches or are sometimes called "Oneness" churches, whereas those that use the latter prescription are called Trinitarians. Variation among the Jesus-only tradition on which *version* of the "Jesus" baptistic prescription to use has been the point of much dissension and has led to the establishment of a new church more than once. Other variations of doctrine exist and are the fodder of intense biblical debates. It would be wrong to assume that the unity shared among believers with respect to handling serpents assumes any more unity than that! Serpent-handling churches are fiercely independent; they remain churches of rogues and renegades and wonderfully proud of being "God's peculiar people," as we have heard many a preacher claim.

Another issue is that it is not true that all members of serpent-handling churches handle serpents. All members *believe* in handling, but some have not yet been called by God to do so or have not yet experienced sufficient anointing to practice the sign. Probably on average, 15 percent of church members handle. Overall, more men than women handle. However, even here, generalizations must be cautiously interpreted. For instance, the church at Jolo, West Virginia, was noted for its many female handlers; some, as documented in the archives, continued to handle even after being maimed by the practice. Others readily "go to the box" and take serpents out, rather than wait for men to hand them serpents, as is more typical in other churches. A look at the list of deaths from serpent bites in Appendix 1 shows that many more men than women have died from bites. We attribute this to the simple fact that, across the tradition men handle serpents much more frequently and in greater numbers than do women.

We are happy to leave the issue of the number of churches and handlers vague. It is a tradition that is like a stream running deep at times, going underground, and emerging at unanticipated places. The one thing of which we are certain is that the tradition will not die. As we conclude this book, the Jesus-only churches at Middlesboro and Sand Mountain—as well as several Trinitarian churches in eastern Kentucky—stand strong. Little gems of churches persist at such places as Del Rio, Tennessee, where Jimmy Morrow pastors the Church of the Lord Jesus Christ, and at Marshall, North Carolina, where John Brown pastors the House of Prayer in the Name of Jesus Christ. They are not growing, but they are safe havens for these families and their friends and for roving believers who wish to handle serpents. These churches will survive and are potential larger hub churches of the future. For now, the small number of members, likely no more than fifteen or twenty, includes as least as many children as adults, and that also secures the future of the tradition. Furthermore, despite small numbers, the passion of these believers is perhaps best evident in people like Pastor Jimmy Morrow. More than once, he has told us, he has preached to an empty church, ever anticipating that God might send a believer in need. He refuses to not have church, regardless of the number in attendance. He also meets on both Saturdays and Sundays.

SERPENT-HANDLING FAMILIES: THE MAINTENANCE OF THE FAITH FROM WITHIN

If what we have called hub churches help to sustain the tradition, associated with hub churches are powerful families, long established in

Appalachia. We do not want to stereotype these families as "clans," but it is true that blood and belief mix to sustain the practice of serpent handling. There are many families now with third- and some with fourth-generation handlers. Passed down from fathers and mothers to sons and daughters and to cousins and aunts, serpent handling grows and maintains itself from within. With relatively large families (three or four children are most common), handlers continue to sustain the tradition through their children. Furthermore, handlers are likely to marry other handlers, and this further sustains the tradition. There are sometimes adults who convert to serpent handling from other religious faiths, but the real strength and source of growth of this tradition is from within. Who has read Mark 16:17–18 and then sought out a serpent-handling church? Few if any, and most likely none. But those raised in the tradition will have heard Mark 16:17–18 repeatedly preached and the signs modeled. While young children are not now allowed to handle, we have seen them sit with their rubber snakes in church as they watch their mothers and fathers handle real ones.

Powerful names that sustain the faith are linked to what outsiders see as the ultimate tragedy of the practice of handling: death. Oscar Pelfrey died at Big Stone Gap, Virginia, from a bite in 1968. The church no longer endorses handling, but his now-aged son, Bill Pelfrey, handles and preaches the doctrine that his daughter and her husband also practice. Jimmy Williams died at Carson Springs in 1975 from practicing one of the signs. His son, Alan Williams, continues the practice of the signs of Mark 16 and is one of the more powerful evangelists for the faith, as he leads his own wife and children in the tradition. Likewise, despite the 1961 death of her daughter, Columbia Hagerman, at the Jolo church in West Virginia, Barbara Elkins handled until her death by natural causes at the age of eighty-four. Her other children are among the most well known handlers, and they have passed on the tradition to a fourth generation.

Perhaps most indicative of the power of families to sustain this tradition is the Brown family. The head of the family, John Brown, has a church in Marshall, North Carolina, the House of Prayer in the Name of Jesus Christ. As discussed more fully in chapter 7, one of his sons, John Wayne "Punkin" Brown, died while preaching a revival at Macedonia on Sand Mountain in Alabama at the Old Rock House Holiness Church, pastored by Billy Summerford. Punkin's wife had died from a serpent bite three years earlier at the homecoming service of the Full Gospel Tabernacle Church in Jesus Name in Middlesboro, Kentucky.

The church was (and is still) pastored by Jamie Coots, from a powerful second-generation serpent-handling family. A brief look at the Brown family can do much to promote an understanding of the role of families in sustaining a tradition that refuses to succumb, despite legal pressures to abandon its central ritual, if not the belief. Much of our brief description is from material in our archives and from Brown and McDonald's (2000) useful text in which the Brown family is one of three families that consented to explain their faith in their own words, uncontaminated by the outsider's views.

John Brown Sr., a delivered alcoholic, was converted to the faith by Liston Pack at the then-famous Carson Springs Holiness Church of God. He witnessed Jimmy Ray Williams Sr. (who later would die at this church from drinking strychnine) handling a serpent. A few weeks later John went with Buford Pack (who drank the same strychnine as Williams, in addition to being bit by a serpent, and died the same night) to hunt a serpent to take to church. Buford handled the serpent, but John waited another month until he was moved to do so (Brown & McDonald, 2000, p. 63). This began a long career, interrupted by a brief period of backsliding, in which John Brown Sr. rose to become one of the most respected handlers in the Oneness serpent-handling tradition. His wife, Peggy, also handles but much less frequently, and only when moved to do so. She says she has handled about twelve times in more than thirty years (Brown & McDonald, 2000, p. 43). She has never been bitten.

John and Peggy were to be eclipsed by their firstborn son, John Wayne Brown Jr., or Punkin. Raised in the tradition and anxious to handle, he quickly became the most powerful evangelist in the Oneness tradition. At eighteen he married Melinda Duvall whom he met at a Kingston, Georgia, church homecoming. She had been raised in a serpent-handling family and had begun handling at the age of fourteen (Brown & McDonald, 2000, p. 65). Their young marriage was marked by turmoil and tragedy, ending in divorce but then remarriage that held great promise. We need not explore all this here. It is covered sufficiently elsewhere (Brown & McDonald, 2000, pp. 23–35). Punkin and Melinda returned to church; they prospered with spiritual riches but saw increasing material poverty. In rapid succession they had four additional children, including a set of twins. Punkin's reputation as a preacher was attested even by Covington (1995), who deceitfully "converted" to the faith to obtain material for his widely popular but unfortunately distorted report on this tradition (see Hood, 1995, for a critique).[3] He described Punkin as "the handlers' equivalent of a mad monk" (Hood, 1995, p. 209) and went on to spread rumors that were damaging to Punkin's reputation that need not be repeated here (see Covington, 1995, pp. 208–9; for reaction, see Brown & McDonald, 2000, pp. 28–29, 11–117). What Punkin did have was a powerful preaching style that eclipsed his father's. He is arguably the greatest preacher in the tradition since George Hensley. Fred Brown, a reporter who has written numerous newspaper articles about this tradition, stated that Punkin was the only handler he had witnessed who came close to the charisma and religious intensity possessed by Charles Prince, who died from a lethal serpent bite at the Apostolic Church of God in Greensville, Tennessee, in 1985.[4] John Brown Sr. said of his deceased son, "He was not only an evangelist, but he was an apostle of the church. The apostle's job was to establish the church and to work signs and miracles and wonders" (Brown & McDonald, 2000, p. 65). Few who witnessed Punkin preach would deny he did this admirably.[5] It is perhaps irony, if not God's will, that Punkin, like the two other major charismatic preachers of his tradition (George Hensley and Charles Prince), was to die practicing the signs in which they all believed.

It was at the 1995 homecoming in Middlesboro, Kentucky, that Punkin handled a large timber rattlesnake and then handed it to Melinda, who was signaling she wanted to handle it.[6] She was bitten, fatally, as it turned out. Although her death occurred in Kentucky, a custody battle for the Brown children, involving the maternal grandparents, ensued in Tennessee where Punkin lived. The children were initially removed from Punkin, but in October 1995 full custody was given to Punkin on the condition that the Brown children could not attend a church where serpents were handled, nor could they even be outside a church where serpents were handled. The judge ruled that children were endangered if in the church and even if outside, given that serpents had to be transported into the church. The court affirmed it had an obligation to protect children from potential harm.[7]

It is well known that Punkin violated this injunction.[8] This was to be used against the Brown family three years later, in 1998, when Punkin was bitten and died while preaching a revival at the Sand Mountain church. While none in the Brown family believe Punkin's death was from a serpent bite—he died so quickly—the coroner's official ruling was death by serpent bite. Thus, within three years, both wife and husband died from practicing a faith that the Tennessee courts had long ago said ought to be unlawful because it made the believers' children orphans.[9]

An additional custody battle for the Brown children, again involving the maternal grandparents, explicitly used the fact that Punkin had taken his children to services where serpents were handled. The judge cautiously warned John and Peggy that joint custody of the Brown children with Melinda's mother would be based on strictly enforcing the ban on the children ever being present at a service where serpents are handled. John and Peggy have honored this injunction, despite their belief that it is wrong.[10]

At Punkin's funeral, near the old Carson Springs church, John Brown Jr. was buried beside Melinda. At the graveside service, John Brown Sr. and Mark Brown, Punkin's brother, both handled serpents, as did many others in attendance. Despite two deaths in their family, neither father nor surviving son deny the Word. The Old Rock House Holiness Church, where Punkin was fatally bitten, and the Full Gospel Tabernacle in Jesus Name, where Melinda was fatally bitten, remain two of the most powerful contemporary serpent-handling hub churches. John Brown Sr. has returned more than once to preach at Sand Mountain but without his grandchildren. Mark Brown follows in his famous brother's footsteps. His preaching style is more subdued than his brother's, and unlike Punkin, who often handled simply on faith, Mark, like his mother and father, waits on the anointing. Ordained as a preacher by his father at the Marshall church, Mark and his serpent-handling wife, Shell, continue the tradition, practicing the signs and confirming the Word. Mark, like his father, has on occasion returned to Sand Mountain to preach and practice the signs. Melinda and Punkin's five children are nearly matched by Mark and Shell's four. John and Peggy now have complete custody of the five orphaned grandchildren. Among these nine grandchildren, it is more than likely that some will become handlers. It is also more than likely that they will seek mates who handle serpents.

At Jimmy Morrow's 2006 homecoming in Del Rio, Tennessee, Hood witnessed a gratuitous act remarkable for this tradition. John Brown Sr. was invited to come to the final Sunday homecoming service. The church agreed not to have serpents present so that Punkin's children could be present. As church began with song and rejoicing, neither John nor Peggy nor the children of Melinda and Punkin were there. However, as music and song continued, light came across the room from an open door. Peggy, John, and all but one of the orphaned grandchildren came in. The church greeted them, and as Peggy and the children took a seat,

John Brown Sr., as is customary for preachers, shook hands with every-one and took a seat. As the service continued, he felt moved to preach a sermon. In the power reminiscent of Punkin, he preached with passion from the Gospel of Mark 16. To the congregation and to the children of Melinda and Punkin, he preached the Word. "No man, no government can deny the right of the faithful to do as God commands," he exhorted. He said that it was an abomination to God and a reluctant acquiescence from this church that no serpents were present; if orphaned children could witness the ritual by which their parents had been called to heaven, they would at least know that it was God's Word, preached to them and this congregation by their grandfather, such that one day they too, as consenting adults, would be free to be obedient if they so choose. Our guess is that among the grandchildren of Peggy and John are the seeds of a tradition that continues precisely because of the power of families to transmit a faith that cannot be easily understood in reductive explanatory categories often favored by social scientists. Some equiva-lent of Kierkegaard's teleological suspension of the ethical is needed to provide an appreciation of a tradition in which handling serpents at the risk of maiming and death can be nevertheless religiously meaningful. Our hope is that what we have presented in this book helps to facilitate such an appreciation and underscores the right of a tradition, rooted in what they know to be God's Word, to continue not only to preach but also to practice what they believe.

As long as people read the King James Bible, there will be some who will take the plain meaning of Mark 16:17–18 to heart. It is even more assured that in small, isolated churches scattered throughout Appalachia there will be preachers who model the practice of handling serpents for others to emulate. Both in the King James Bible and in practice there are able prompts for the taking up of serpents and the drinking of the "deadly thing." The tradition survives and will continue to do so both because of the text and because, however small and scattered the believ-ers, this faith has now firmly established itself as a *faith tradition*.

Deaths by Serpent Bite

NAME	YEAR	STATE	SOURCE
1921–1930			
1. Jim W. Reece	Prior to 1922	Alabama	*Church of God Evangel,* *13*(36), September 9, 1922, p. 2
1931–1940			
2. Shirley Hall (female)	1930s	Kentucky	Oral history as confirmed by Verlin Short
3. Lois Guire	1931	?	*Cincinnati Enquirer,* August 16, 1931
4. Unknown man	1934	Alabama	Oral history
5. Alfred Weaver	1936	Florida	*Tampa Morning Tribune,* May 5, 1936, p. 1; *New York Times,* May 5, 1936, p. 25
6. Reverend T. Anderson	1936	Virginia	*New York Times,* September 28, 1936, p. 18; *New York Times,* October, 1936
7. Mrs. Jeffie Smith	1938	Georgia	*Atlanta Journal,* August 5, 1940, pp. 1, 3 (prosecution story two years after Smith's death)
8. Birchel Arnett	Late 1930s	Kentucky	Oral history
9. Sanders (male)	1940?	Kentucky/ Tennessee	Oral history as confirmed by Jimmy Morrow

NAME	YEAR	STATE	SOURCE
10. Jim Cockran	1940	Kentucky	Oral history (Kane, 1979, p. 66)
11. Martha Napier	1940	Kentucky	*Corbin Times*, August 25, 1940, p. 1
12. Robert Cordle	1940	Virginia	*New York Times*, September 22, 1940
13. James Couch	1940	Kentucky	Oral history

1941–1950

NAME	YEAR	STATE	SOURCE
14. Maudie Lankford	1944	Kentucky	Oral history
15. John Hensley	1944	Virginia	*Newsweek*, August 21, 1944
16. Jesse Coker	1944	Kentucky	Oral history
17. George Coker (father of Jesse)	1945	Kentucky	Oral history
18. Anna Kirk's baby—died at birth[1]	1945	Virginia	*New York Times*, September 5, 1945, p. 25
19. Anna Kirk (mother)—died hour after giving birth	1945	Virginia	*New York Times*, September 5, 1945, p. 25
20. Lewis Ford	1945	Tennessee	*Chattanooga Times*, September 9, 1945
21. B. A. Parker	1946	Tennessee	*Chattanooga News–Free Press*, March 30, 1947
22. Clint Jackson	1946	Tennessee	*Chattanooga Times*, July 15, 1946
23. Harry Skelton	1946	Tennessee	*Chattanooga News–Free Press*, August 27, 1946
24. Walter Henry	1946	Tennessee	*Chattanooga News–Free Press*, August 26, 1946
25. Hobert Williford[2]	1946	Tennessee	*Chattanooga Times*, September 5, 1946, p. 13
26. Charles Haley	1946	Tennessee	Oral history
27. Harvey Bell	1948	Tennessee	*Chattanooga Times*, August 10, 1948

1951–1960

NAME	YEAR	STATE	SOURCE
28. Ruth Craig	1951	Alabama	*New York Times*, July 17, 1951; *Chattanooga News–Free Press*, July 11, 1951, p. 15
29. Harvey Howard	1952	Kentucky	Oral history
30. Velma Parker	1954	Alabama	Oral history (Vance, 1975, pp. 116–17)
31. Jim Gifford	1954	Alabama	*Chattanooga News–Free Press*, June 14, 1954, p. 1

NAME	YEAR	STATE	SOURCE
32. Reece Ramsey	1954	Georgia	*Chattanooga News–Free Press,* August 13, 1954, pp. 1, 5
33. Bertha Smith	1954	California	Oral history (La Barre, 1962/1992, p. 46)
34. Anna Marie Covington Yost	1955	Tennessee	*New York Times,* August 31, 1955
35. George Hensley	1955	Florida	*Chattanooga Times,* July 25, 1955
36. Lee Valentine	1955	Bitten in Alabama, died in Kentucky	*Chattanooga News–Free Press,* August 15, 1955
37. Jack Graham (Johnny Cadwell Graham)	1957	Georgia	Jack Graham, list in *Valdosta* (GA) *Times,* January 29, 1957, p. 14 (as cited in Vance, 1975, p. 45); Johnny Cadwell Graham, list in *Saturday Evening Post,* September 28, 1957, p. 156
38. Eli Sanders	1958	Kentucky	Oral history as confirmed by Verlin Short
39. Unknown woman	1958	West Virginia	Oral history
40. David Henson	1959	Alabama	*Birmingham Post-Herald,* July 27, 1959, p. 1
41. Loyd Hill	1960	Georgia	*Valdosta Daily Times,* August 29, 1960, p. 1

1961–1970

NAME	YEAR	STATE	SOURCE
42. Sally Hall	1961	West Virginia	*Logan Banner,* August 10, 1961
43. Columbia Hagerman	1961	West Virginia	*Bluefield Daily Telegraph,* October 15, 1961
44. Brother Wilson	1960s	West Virginia	Oral history
45. Sister Payne	1960s	West Virginia	Oral history
46. Robert Ely	1965	Kentucky	Oral history
47. Charles Lane	Mid-1960s	Virginia	Oral history
48. Dan Powers	1967	Kentucky	Oral history
49. James Saylor	1967	Kentucky	Oral history (Kimbrough, 1995/2002, p. 149)
50. Jean Helton Saylor	1967	Kentucky	Oral history (Kimbrough, 1995/2002, p. 150)

NAME	YEAR	STATE	SOURCE
51. Howard Lane	Prior to 1968	Virginia	Oral history as confirmed to Thomas Burton by Penelope Lane (Howard was her husband's uncle)
52. Oscar Pelfrey	1968	Virginia	*Louisville Courier-Journal*, October 24, 1968
53. Jim Helton	1968	Kentucky	Oral history
54. Johnny Newton	1968	Kentucky	Oral history (Kimbrough, 1995/2002, p. 151)
55. Raymond Hayes	1968	Kentucky	Oral history as confirmed to Thomas Burton by Flora Bettis (Kimbrough 1995/2002, p. 151)

1971–1980

NAME	YEAR	STATE	SOURCE
56. Ersaline Meadows	1972	Alabama	Oral history (Vance, 1975, pp. 3, 125–26)
57. Alfred Leon Parsons	1972	Georgia	*Atlanta Journal*, September 28, 1972, p. 2A; *Valdosta* (GA) *Times*, September 27, 1972, p. 1; *Chattanooga Times*, July 26, 1973
58. Beulah Van Bucklen	1972	West Virginia	*Charleston Daily Mail*, September 25, 1972
59. Larry Burgess	1972	North Carolina	*News and Observer*, October 4, 1972, p. 5
60. Shirley Wagers (male)	1973	Kentucky	*Louisville Courier-Journal*, November 5, 1973, p. 1
61. Richard Williams	1974	Ohio	*Chattanooga Times*, December 19, 1973, p. 7
62. Tallamade Adkins	1974	West Virginia	*New York Times*, October 23, 1974
63. Lonnie Richardson	1974	West Virginia	*New York Times*, October 23, 1974
64. Frank H. Wagner	1976	West Virginia	*Kingsport Times*, August 31, 1976, p. 48
65. Curtis Mounts	1976	West Virginia	*Birmingham News*, May 21, 1976
66. Berlin Barbee	1976	Georgia	*Chattanooga Times*, October 25, 1976
67. Aaron Long	1978	Kentucky	*Louisville Times*, June 1, 1978
68. Roy Leon Johnson	1978	Virginia	Oral history as confirmed by Bud Gregg

NAME	YEAR	STATE	SOURCE
69. Wayne Thornton	1979	Georgia	*Whitesburg Mountain Eagle,* September 8, 1980
70. Claude Amos	1980	Kentucky	*New York Times,* September 17, 1980, p. B10

1981–1990

NAME	YEAR	STATE	SOURCE
71. John Holbrook	1982	West Virginia	*Louisville Courier-Journal,* September 13, 1982
72. Mack Wolford	1983	West Virginia	*Louisville Courier-Journal,* August 30, 1983
73. Richard Barrett	1984/1985	Georgia	Oral history as confirmed by Carl Porter
74. Charles Prince	1985	Tennessee	*New York Times,* August 20, 1985
75. Shirley McLeary	1986	Kentucky	*JC Press Chronicle,* February 15, 1986
76. Charley Hall	1987?	Alabama	Oral history as confirmed by Billy Summerford and Joe Short
77. Wayne Short	1989	Kentucky	Oral history as confirmed by Verlin Short
78. Arnold Loveless	1990	Georgia	Oral history as confirmed by Carl Porter

1991–2000

NAME	YEAR	STATE	SOURCE
79. Mark Daniels	1990s	Kentucky	Oral history as confirmed by Verlin Short
80. Jimmy Ray Williams Jr.	1991	Tennessee	*Chattanooga Times,* July 16, 1991, p. B5
81. Garland Ray Johnson	1991	West Virginia	Oral history as confirmed by Dewey Chafin
82. Dewey Hale	1995	Georgia	Oral history as confirmed by Carl Porter
83. Kale Saylor	1995	Kentucky	*Louisville Courier-Journal,* September 10, 1940, p. 7
84. Melinda Brown	1995	Kentucky	*Knoxville News-Sentinel,* August 10, 1995
85. Daril Collins	1997	Kentucky	*Knoxville News-Sentinel,* December 17, 1997
86. John "Punkin" Brown Jr.	1998	Alabama	*Lexington Herald Leader,* October 6, 1998
87. Daryl Fee	2000	Virginia	Oral history as confirmed by Verlin Short and Jimmy Morrow

NAME	YEAR	STATE	SOURCE
2001–2006			
88. Dwayne Long	2004	Virginia	*Bluefield Daily Tele-graph,* April 15, 2004
89. Bruce Hill	2005/2006	Georgia	Oral history as con-firmed by James Wade
90. Linda Long	2006	Kentucky	*Lexington Herald Leader,* November 8, 2006 (www.Kentucky.com)

NOTES

We have relied on research from Kane (1979), Vance (1975), and Kimbrough (1995/2002). We are especially grateful to Thomas Burton for access to his own records of deaths and for reviewing our final list as presented above. Two handlers within the tradition were especially helpful, Pastor Jimmy Morrow and Verlin Short.

With respect to the first reported incidence of death by serpent bite, we found a note of importance in the early autobiography of James Benton Ellis (1976, pp. 67–71), in which he discusses serpent handling and states, "One man, who had been bitten 230 times without harm, was finally bitten one time and died within thirty minutes" (p. 70). We assume this is Jim W. Reece but cannot be certain. In addition, the reference to being bitten 230 times suggests the frequency with which handling occurred—not only by this man but no doubt by many others. Thus we might anticipate additional undocumented bites within the tradition. If we assume that handling began around 1890, as Morrow claims (Hood, 2005), then, if Reece's is the first death talked about and he is also the man to whom Ellis referred, we can document deaths by decades as follows: 1891–1900, none documented; 1901–10, none documented; 1911–20, none documented; 1921–30, 1 death; 1931–40, 12 deaths; 1941–50, 14 deaths; 1951–60, 14 deaths; 1961–70, 14 deaths; 1971–80, 15 deaths; 1981–90, 8 deaths; 1990–2000, 9 deaths; and 2001 to the present (2006), 3 deaths.

Our best guess is that the media did not begin to document deaths by serpent bites until after 1930, although it is likely that deaths occurred with the emergence of serpent handling from the 1890s but were unreported. There are different ways we can estimate the number of unreported deaths from religious serpent handling that likely occurred in the decades preceding the 1930s. One way is to observe the minimal number of deaths that were reported by the media in the decades after the 1930s and assume that at least that number occurred as unreported in the decades before the 1930s. For example, the minimal number of deaths on record as reported per full decade is 8 (1981–90 and 1991–2000). For the four decades preceding the 1930s (1891–1900, 1901–10, 1911–20, and 1921–30), that would be 32 (4 × 8) unreported deaths that might have taken place. Another way to estimate the number of unreported deaths is to take the average number of deaths per full decade for which there is documentation (from 1931 to 2000) and calculate their average for estimating unreported deaths in the four decades prior to 1931 (1891–1900, 1901–10, 1911–20, and 1921–30). The average number of reported deaths for that period of decades is 12.3 (SD = 2.6), which means that there could have been 49.2 (4 × 12.3) unreported deaths before 1931. On the other hand, if we include the decade in which Reece is likely to have been killed (1921–30) in calculating an average of reported deaths per decade from 1921 to 2000, we have an estimate of 10.9 (SD = 4.7) deaths, which would suggest that 32.7 (3 × 10.9) unreported deaths took place from serpent handling in the three decades preceding 1921. A final reasonable estimate is that an average of one person per year dies from handling serpents in religious settings; if we consider a period of serpent handling from 1891 to 2006, this would suggest that 115 people have died from the practice since its known beginning. One death per year seems fairly constant, despite the waxing and waning of handling in Appalachia. Most scholars begin the history of serpent handling with Hensley around 1907 (Burton, 1993). However, Morrow's narrative history of his Jesus' Name tradition claims handling began much earlier, closer to 1890 (Hood, 2005). Regardless of where one begins the history of serpent handling, it is highly unlikely that there would be any decade of handling without deaths.

We have argued that the media began documenting deaths only after the tradition gained notoriety from maiming and deaths. If we are correct, oral histories are essential to completing the early history of the tradition and to documenting deaths by serpent bites, especially because there are so few written records. It is also likely that, in absolute numbers, more believers handled in the early years of the tradition. If so, the simple fact of increased frequency of handling would contribute to a greater likelihood of bites, maiming, and death (Hood, 2003a). Thus Ellis's comment about a man being bitten hundreds of times before he was finally stricken with death is instructive and suggestive.

1. We should note that Thomas Burton has suggested that Anna Kirk's baby (#18) should not be included in this list because had the mother suffered from terminal cancer instead of a serpent bite, the baby's death would not be listed as the result of cancer. However, we felt that Anna's (#19) bite from handling a serpent was the direct cause of the baby's untimely death and thus have included it here.

2. In the *Chattanooga Times*, on September 3, 1946 (p. 15), an article titled "3rd Snake Cultist Dies in Cleveland" reported that Hobart Wilson died from a snakebite on September 2. He was handling a serpent and was bitten while attending a funeral service for Walter H. Henry, who had died from a serpent bite. In a later issue of the same newspaper, an article discussing the same incident begins "Hobart Wilson [sic] . . . ," indicating a recognition that the name published in the earlier issue was not correct but, curiously, left that way. A photograph we have recently obtained of the deceased man's headstone clearly shows that both the first and last names were incorrectly reported in the paper. The headstone reads: "Hobert Williford."

Deaths by Poison

NAME	YEAR	STATE	SOURCE
1. V. A. Bishop	1921	Texas	*Evangel*, 12(19), 1921, p. 1
2. Martha Mullins	1947	West Virginia	*Christian Century*, December 10, 1947, p. 1518
3. Earnest Davis	1947	West Virginia	*Time*, 50(10), p. 25 (September 8, 1947)
4. Ball Body	?	West Virginia	Oral history as confirmed to Thomas Burton by Dewey Chafin (Jolo, WV)
5. Kenny Johnson	?	West Virginia	Oral history as confirmed to Thomas Burton by Dewey Chafin (Jolo, WV)
6. Unnamed woman #1	1940s?	Tennessee	*Saturday Evening Post*, September 28, 1957, p. 156
7. Unnamed woman #2	1940s?	Tennessee	*Saturday Evening Post*, September 28, 1957, p. 156
8. Jimmy Ray Williams Sr.	1973	Tennessee	*Knoxville News-Sentinel*, April 9, 1973, p. 1
9. Buford Pack	1973	Tennessee	*Knoxville News-Sentinel*, April 9, 1973, p. 1

NOTE: We are deeply grateful to Thomas Burton for his assistance in reviewing and contributing to this list.

The Phenomenological Interview and Hermeneutic Techniques of Interpretation

In this appendix we discuss a unique methodology that was used in the studies presented in this book, including those concerned with the extemporaneous sermons and personal interviews and their interpretive analyses. For our analysis of extemporaneous sermons (chapter 7), the videotaped sermons were transcribed and then analyzed by a hermeneutic technique to reveal the thematic structure of meaning concerning serpent handling. Our interviews employed a phenomenological method of interview and the same hermeneutic technique to reveal the thematic structure of meaning in successful serpent handling (chapter 8), the experience of being anointed (chapter 9), and near-death experiences from serpent bite (chapter 10). Our methodology is not commonly used in the psychology of religion, so we present both a philosophical justification and a methodological exposition for our phenomenologically based interviews and our hermeneutic method for determining the thematic structure of meaning derived from these various experiences.

PHILOSOPHICAL CONSIDERATIONS OF EMPIRICAL RESEARCH

We begin by noting that David Wulff (2003) has identified the psychology of religion as "a field in crisis." Less pessimistic but still provocative is the claim by Emmons and Paloutzian (2003) that the psychology of religion is in need of a new "*multilevel interdisciplinary paradigm*" (p. 395; original emphasis) to replace the older measurement paradigm identified by Gorsuch (1984). The need for the multilevel interdisciplinary paradigm proposed by Emmons and Paloutzian (2003) raises issues that Koch and Leary (1985, pp. 935–50) suggested are an emerging consensus in general psychology. Included in that consensus are the limited applicability of experimental methods and an increasing awareness of the philosophical presuppositions contained in research methods.

To this we add the recent argument by Brinkmann (2006), heavily influenced by the philosopher Wittgenstein, that psychology is best conceived as a noncausal enterprise in which what is truly psychological is the *reason for* and not the *causes of* actions. Thus Brinkmann calls for a "depsychologized psychology" where the central conception is that mental life is lived in the space of reasons rather than in the space of causation (p. 1). This echoes the critical response by Belzen and Hood (2006) to the call for a new interdisciplinary multilevel paradigm for the psychology of religion. They suggest that methodological issues are crucial for what more than one scholar perceives as a "field in crisis" (Wulff, 2003). They contrast the methodological assumptions of an empiricist-analytic psychology with a hermeneutically oriented psychology and note that if the focus is on hermeneutic psychology it may require psychology in general and the psychology of religion in particular to, in Wulff's terms (2003), "start over."

The Hermeneutic Tradition

Hermeneutics is an old tradition, deriving from the question of how to interpret texts (especially sacred texts like the Bible). Friedrich Schleiermacher (1768–1834), whom many consider the forefather of the psychology of religion, first systematically outlined hermeneutic reasoning. It has developed into a much more embracing philosophical approach, from which principles for research in the social and human sciences have been derived. One seeks not to predict and control as in empirical-analytic-based causal psychologies but rather to understand. Understanding necessarily entails capturing the lived meaning of experience from the experiencer's perspective.

Belzen and Hood (2006, p. 16) have noted that modern psychology has co-opted the term *empirical*. It is defined to mean experimental methods linked to measurement and statistical analysis purporting to uncover causal mechanisms. Thus many psychologists refuse to accept phenomenology and hermeneutic methods because they are not "empirical." This is a curious distortion of the term's original meaning. As Belzen and Hood (2006, p. 17) have observed, in the original, Aristotelian sense, *experiential* (Latin) is *empereia* (Greek). The original Aristotelian sense implies a return to "data" in the original sense of the word. The word *data* is derived from the Latin *datum,* as that which is given, versus *factum,* as that which is made. Therefore, along with recognition of the central role of language and discourse, hermeneutic and phenomenological methods work with actual lived experience. Phenomenological and hermeneutic research does not try to "bring about" experience in a controlled laboratory setting but proceeds from what is "given" already (e.g., autobiographies, letters, participant observations in real-life situations, and narratives provided by interviews). This is *empirical* research and ironically requires, as Brinkmann (2006) rightly notes, the "unpsychologizing of psychology." The goal is to expose the *reasons for* and *meaning of* lived experience.

If the move is to avoid causal claims it is a mistake to view the avoidance of causal claims as "nonempirical" or "unscientific." The term *hermeneutics* derives from Greek mythology where Hermes was commissioned by the gods to present their messages to humanity. In fulfilling this mission, Hermes was obliged both to relate their words verbatim and to supply an interpretation that rendered them clear and meaningful to recipients. As Bleicher (1980/1990) notes, hermeneutics viewed its task as involving two concerns: deriving the precise meaning of a word, phrase, or text; and locating implicit directives expressed on the basis of metaphor and other symbolic forms. Because of its focus on language and its implications for human understanding, hermeneutics has become a philosophy of interpretation as well as an empirical method for use by social scientists (Bleicher, 1980/1990; Hood & Belzen, 2006; Kvale, 1996; Gadamer, 1976; Gergen, 1992; Pollio et al., 1997; Polkinghorne, 1989; Valle, King, & Halling, 1989; Van Manen, 1990).

Hermeneutic methods vary in particulars but share a set of procedures best outlined by Gadamer (1960/1986). As summarized by Belzen and Hood (2006, p. 15), Gadamer's procedures include the following:

1. Exploration within a hermeneutical circle: interpretation begins on the basis of preliminary, intuitive understanding of the whole. This guides the understanding of the parts, leading to a judgment about the whole. This judgment then can be tested anew on a study of parts. This is a cyclic process that never ends. It may entail the rejection of the initial intuition as based upon insights achieved in the process of interpretation. Understanding is therefore always finite, limited, and provisional.

2. The discovery of internal relationships: one looks for meaningful relationships within actions and occurrences. External relationships (like correlations or law-like relationships sought in analytically oriented empirical research) are insufficient to reveal meaning.

3. A focus upon individual cases: emphasis is on the understanding of individual cases, whether this understanding can be generalized or not. The unique is sought, not simply generalized tendencies across cases.

4. The merging of horizons: there is a difference between the knowledge/ understanding of the researcher/interpreter and the subject of study. When understanding increases, the discrepancy between both horizons diminishes.

5. Application: all understanding is in the present. Written texts and human narratives are taken seriously in their claim to truth. These claims are applied in the present situation. Truth is always contextual and in time.

As the philosophical defense of qualitative methods continue, psychologists can ill afford to simply assert an untenable definition of psychology as an empirical, causal discipline (Belzen & Hood, 2006; Brinkmann 2006; Wulff, 2003). Neither can they assert that nonlaboratory studies are nonempirical. As Neisser (1976) has argued, psychology is more ecologically valid the more it is involved with real-world, nonlaboratory studies.

OUR METHODOLOGY

Given our commitment to the lived experienced of the serpent-handling tradition, we will outline the specific procedures we used to interview handlers in the real-world context of the practice of their faith. Our procedures parallel and in some instances expand the assumptions of Hood and Belzen (2006) with respect to hermeneutic methods in general and to their application by Belzen (1999) to conversion among the *bevinderlijken* in particular (Belzen, 1999; Hood & Belzen,

2006, pp. 21–24). Below we discuss our methodology in two areas: the phenomenological interview and the hermeneutic method of textual analysis.

The Phenomenological Interview

The methodology we used in chapters 7 through 10 can be traced most directly to research procedures developed at Duquesne University in the 1970s and 1980s (Giorgi, Fischer, & von Eckartsberg, 1971; Giorgi, Fischer, & Murray, 1975; Giorgi, Knowles, & Smith, 1979; Giorgi, Barton, & Maes, 1983). In general, these procedures involve collecting descriptions of experiences from participants and then analyzing the resulting texts (Giorgi, 1970, 1971). The actual interviewing is more directly linked to phenomenology, and the interpretation of the transcribed interviews involves hermeneutic techniques. It is this balance of phenomenological and hermeneutic methods that is both controversial and unique.

As noted in the relevant chapters, interviews were conducted in churches, homes, and settings where the participants were comfortable. In addition, interviews occurred only after several years of participant observation with these persons in their worship services. Our interviews were dialogical, a two-way interaction in which we explored in depth the meaning of the object of interest (e.g., anointing, handling serpents, near-death experience). Here the focus is phenomenological.

In the context of phenomenology, the use of any method always involves a choice thought to provide the best access to the phenomenon of concern. As noted by both Kvale (1996) and Gergen (1992), narratives often are useful in gaining first-person descriptions of lived experiences, and Pollio et al. (1997) have suggested the appropriateness of an open dialogic encounter in which the participant is helped by the interviewer to construct a descriptive narrative of the phenomenon at hand. To understand the nature of phenomenological interviewing, and its subsequent hermeneutic interpretation, it is necessary to present a concise overview of its procedures. Generally, our phenomenological procedures involve the researcher with three major steps: (1) determining the initial question, (2) participating in a bracketing interview, and (3) engaging in phenomenological interviews with selected participants. (The resulting transformation of these interviews into texts and the analysis of their meaning and thematic structure will be discussed later.)

The Initial Question.   Once dialogue is chosen as the method for collecting descriptions in a particular study, the first concern involves an attempt to formulate an appropriate opening question for the interview. Since the specific question chosen will direct the ensuing conversation, it is important to make sure that it is sufficiently open to allow for multiple ways of taking it up in the interview. Van Manen (1990) has suggested that the process of coming to terms with this question begins with wondering "what something is really like" (p. 42) and evolves to a point where "we live this question[,] . . . we 'become' this question" (p. 43). It is only from such a vital sense of the question that the researcher is sufficiently prepared to pursue a specific phenomenon.

It is a common practice for researchers to bring proposed opening questions to a phenomenology research group where they are assisted by others in clarifying their research interest and helped in structuring the specific interview question to be used. Because "why-questions" have been found to lead the participant away from the phenomenon toward an explanation of its origins or mode of operation, phenomenological interviewing is based on the use of "what-questions"—that is, concern for what the experience was like for the participant (Pollio et al., 1997). In the case of the phenomenon of fear, for example, one question might be, "Can you tell me about a specific time that was fearful for you?" Responses to this question might focus on describing a significant personal event in which fear was experienced in a meaningful way. The opening question, phrased in terms of a specific episode, not only begins the interview but also serves as a constant point of reference for talking about the phenomenon of interest.

The Bracketing Interview. Phenomenological philosophers such as Husserl and Merleau-Ponty have noted that the so-called natural attitude must be relinquished in order to consider the perspectival ways in which a phenomenon is experienced. To clear the ground of preconceived notions as to what a phenomenon may mean, an initial bracketing interview is conducted in which the interview question is posed to the researcher (Pollio et al., 1997; Williamson & Pollio, 1999). The immediate issue of importance here concerns the specific meanings the researcher brings to the phenomenon of study. An examination of this awareness is critical since it is designed to make possible a coming "to the things themselves." Although it is impossible to bracket one's presumptions entirely, what is possible is to keep them in the forefront of awareness so as to enable the researcher to be mindful of his or her presuppositions when conducting interviews with participants.

The Phenomenological Interview: General Considerations. Because our phenomenological interview method is that developed over many years by Howard Pollio at the University of Tennessee at Knoxville, we discuss his general method first, then focus on our specific interviews.

In Pollio's technique, once an initial question has been formulated, and related preconceptions acknowledged, the researcher moves toward a selection of participants for the interviews (Pollio et al., 1997). It is from such dialogic encounters that first-person descriptions of a phenomenon will be obtained and interpreted in coming to some description of the meaning of the experience in question. In a phenomenological study, there are relatively few restrictions on the selection of participants. As the goal of investigating lived experience is not generalizability but interpretive clarity, random samples are not a consideration (Polkinghorne, 1989). Two criteria for selecting participants are (1) they must have experienced the phenomenon under investigation, and (2) they must be able to provide an articulate description of the experience. Aside from these requirements, the number of participants chosen is determined by the richness of descriptions obtained during the interviews (Pollio et al., 1997). Interviews continue until the process ceases to render further variation of the phenomenon—typically ten to fifteen interviews—although no specific restrictions apply. Concerning the issue of variation, the procedure of focusing on a specific phenomenon in a variety of personal interviews (contexts) is thought comparable to Husserl's more personal technique of "imaginative variation," in which the phenomenologist himself or herself imagines and reflects on the event in a variety of contexts.

There are certain dynamics of a phenomenologically motivated interview that are also noteworthy (Pollio et al., 1997). Once an initial question is posed, the interview is unstructured, open-ended, and largely directed by the participant. In this way, a certain freedom is granted the participant to locate frames of reference both for the researcher and for himself or herself. It also provides an opportunity for the participant to discover such important issues as the attitude of the researcher toward the participant and the phenomenon, both of which might affect the encounter. It must be remembered that the encounter also is an experience, one that respects the participant's privileged perspective. Because of the conversational quality of the interview, "leading questions" that can distract from the emergence of descriptive data are unnecessary and avoided; dialogue is encouraged to flow freely, weaving together details of the experience without interruptions from an agenda. Questions that emerge within the flow—say, for purposes of clarity or proper understanding—connect the researcher and the participant and serve to promote the quality of the descriptions produced. Once obtained, such descriptions supply a rich data source for interpreting the meaning of the phenomenon under study.

Keen (1975) has acknowledged three criticisms levied by traditional psychologists against verbal reports of the type deriving from phenomenological interviews. First, such reports are thought to be replete with subjective biases and therefore offer little contribution to psychology as a science. What this criticism seems to miss is that obtaining a wide variety of personal experiences surrounding a particular phenomenon is precisely the goal of phenomenology. The traditional methodological concern over subjective bias is rooted in the positivistic assumption of an objective truth beyond the context of dialogic encounter (Gergen, 1992; Kvale, 1992). Since knowledge emerges from social discourse, any description emerging from a dialogic encounter is considered the experience of the participant and serves to present the concrete phenomenon at hand (Pollio et al., 1997).

A second objection centers on concerns for unconscious processes: because much behavior is thought to be rooted in the unconscious, participants are thought to be unable to render accurate reports of their engagements and activities (Keen, 1975). Without taking any final stance on the role of unconscious factors in human discourse, the phenomenological view is specifically interested in how a phenomenon is present to experience, and the interview process is concerned precisely with obtaining descriptions detailing the "what" of an experience rather than its "why" (Pollio et al., 1997). Thus what is described of an experience reveals what is currently meaningful about that experience to the participant.

A third criticism is that participants are assumed to disclose largely what they think researchers want to hear (Keen, 1975). In the context of a traditional psychological experiment, it is thought that the "subject" is keenly aware of being under scrutiny—and this may well be the case. In the context of a phenomenological interview, however, the nature of the relationship is such that the "subject" becomes a "participant," or even a "co-researcher" (Pollio et al., 1997). In this role, it is the participant, not the interviewer, who directs the interview and assumes the position of knowledgeable authority in terms of the experience. Because of a sensitivity to issues relating to the (admittedly incomplete) process of bracketing, the researcher is encouraged to take a nonjudgmental stance toward the participant and simply attempt to clarify descriptions of the experience rendered. In this way, problems regarding the demand properties of verbal reports are minimized by the nature of phenomenological inquiry as well as by the context in which the research dialogue takes place.

Another traditional concern involves the trustworthiness of data obtained from phenomenological interviews (Pollio et al., 1997). If personal experience is at least to some degree socially constructed, the matter of intercontextual coherence across various contexts of a particular experience is at issue, even among different conversations with the same participant. However, it is assumed that the same phenomenon will bear some resemblance in different contexts since day-to-day change in the personal field of experience is organized against the stabler backdrop of personal surroundings and culture (Berger & Luckman, 1966)—hence the expectation is for an experience to be supplied with reasonably consistent and coherent meanings. Further, the reconstruction of memory in present consciousness involves a temporal fusing of one's past knowledge of an experience with the present, one that integrates the newly constructed understanding into the context of personal history. Although the present meaning is nuanced, it is not radically transformed by the process (Gadamer, 1960/1975; James, 1890/1983).

The Phenomenological Interview: Specific Encounters. Individual interviews were scheduled at the convenience of participants and conducted at locations they suggested. Before the phenomenological interview began, a few basic questions were asked of all participants: age, vocation, number of years involved with serpent handling, and whether family members were believers in the tradition.

The initial question used to begin each interview was an open-ended one regarding the topic of our concern for this set of interviews: successful serpent handling (chapter 8), the experience of the anointing (chapter 9), or near-death experiences (chapter 10). (For the extemporaneous sermons [chapter 7], our hermeneutic methodology, discussed later, was applied to transcriptions of the recorded sermons.) For approximately one to one and a half hours, dialogue followed our initial question within the guidelines described above. As participants offered various details of their experiences, care was taken to ask for complete descriptions with regard to personal meanings, especially when details were ambiguous or couched in the terminology of the tradition. Concern also was given to helping participants articulate *descriptions* rather than *explanations* of their experiences. As emphasized above, our concern is with the meaning of lived experience. The phenomenological interview is crucial in providing the basic datum to be hermeneutically analyzed.

It is noteworthy that when giving detailed descriptions some of the participants reexperienced the phenomenon, especially the anointing, at that very time—as evidenced by verbal confessions, closed eyes, tears, facial expressions, and body gestures—to such a degree that a few moments were required before the interviews could resume. At the conclusion of all interviews, each participant confirmed that his or her descriptions were as complete as possible. All interviews were videotaped with the consent of participants. These unedited tapes are in the Hood-Williamson Research Archives.

Hermeneutic Considerations: Interpretation
of the Phenomenological Interview

Once an interview (or sermon, as in the case of chapter 7) has been completed, the material is transcribed verbatim into textual form (a protocol) that can be both privately and publicly read. Interviews were read aloud and analyzed for meaning. The analysis includes group interaction by researchers trained in dialogic procedures. This technique is unique to the procedures developed by Pollio (Williamson & Pollio, 1999).

Concern with presuppositions about the phenomenon is essential throughout the research process, especially during its interpretive phases. As each text is read aloud, group members are available as accountability partners to point out reactions to the unfolding text that seem to derive from personal bias and not from the text. In this way, preconceived theories and presumptions are noted and taken into account so as to allow the meaning of the phenomenon as presented in the text to emerge. As a dialogic group typically consists of eight to fourteen members, it affords multiple perspectives on the possible meanings of the text. The presence of others trained in dialogic methods also brings to the process accountability for any interpretation offered. Since the text is considered autonomous and sufficient to the experience, members of the group respond to various proposed meanings by asking the individuals posing them, "Where do you find that in the text?" Group members also attempt to ensure internal consistency of interpreted themes across passages, a safeguard against meanings that appear disjointed and out of context in regard to the complete text.

The sheer magnitude of a project can appear overwhelming to a single researcher, and the responsibility for interpreting texts on one's own can be a daunting task. In bringing texts to an interpretive group, the responsibility is distributed among members and does much to relieve personal doubts surrounding possible meanings arrived at by singular effort.

Before any interpretation is accepted, it must meet with the approval of all group members. It is always possible that dissenting opinions or reservations reveal some glimpse of the participant's experience yet unclear to the group. As group dialogue continues, such differences are freely considered and discussed until a common understanding of the protocol is reached.

In an interpretive group of this type, written texts take on a lifelike quality as each passage is read aloud by members designated to read specific parts. At appropriate breaks in the reading, members react to what has been read and negotiate proposed meanings. This process of group interpretation contributes significantly to a clear description of the personal experience presented in the protocol.

An essential tool of textual interpretation involves an ongoing attempt to relate parts of the text to its overall meaning—the so-called hermeneutic circle (Kvale, 1996; Belzen & Hood, 2006; Williamson & Pollio, 1999). As an interpretation for a single passage or remark is proposed, reflections on meanings derived from earlier passages are considered simultaneously for consistency of understanding. The analysis of any text invariably involves a circular pattern of determining the meaning of a part that affects the meaning of the whole, which, in turn, bears on the meaning of the individual part. This process of going back and forth strengthens internal consistency and the interdependency of emerging themes as they lead toward an overall meaning for the text.

The use of hermeneutic interpretation extends beyond an idiographic description for a single participant to other protocols describing the same phenomenon so as to produce a "global meaning" or a "nomothetic thematic description" (Pollio et al., 1997). At this level, the process includes interpreting the meaning of each text in the context of all others; such extension is not for purposes of generalization but to improve the researcher's understanding of the phenomenon as described in different contexts. In considering all protocols, a pattern of themes tends to emerge and constitute the meaning of the phenomenon as experienced. Valle and colleagues (1989) have compared such a consistency of themes across contexts to a melody transposed to different keys: Although the piece can be played in a variety of keys, the melody is immediately recognized by the familiar sound of its note structure regardless of key. This does not mean, however, that the interpretation of an experience has been exhausted or closed in any way by the structure of nomothetic meaning, since the meaning of a phenomenon is always open to reinterpretation as unique variations emerge from specific participants and contexts of experience. As Belzen and Hood (2006, p. 19) have observed of hermeneutic methods in general, they are open-ended and ultimately depend on human judgment.

A WORD ON VALIDITY

It is of constant concern to psychology that a study render "valid" results. In agreement with Giorgi (1975), Pollio and his colleagues (1997) have argued that validity for research of this type depends primarily on the degree to which a reader may take up the findings of a study and see what the researcher saw from his or her investigation. The issue is extended to include a consideration of the particular evidence in the text that is used to support the specific interpretation offered and the quality of understanding attained. The point of agreement between researcher and reader is not absolutely essential, although the quality of textual evidence presented for the interpretation is imperative. Likewise, Hood and Belzen (2006) have noted that while one can speak of inter-researcher reliability insofar as different researchers using similar methods reach similar conclusions (interpretations), ultimately, "Certainty is not achieved but is replaced as an aim by the acceptance of the best possible interpretation, which ultimately remains a human judgment" (p. 19).

The concern for the quality of the evidence presented and the conclusions reached treats validity as a judicial-like process (Pollio et al., 1997). The validity of phenomenological interpretation does not rest on a direct correspondence to some reality experienced by the participant. Instead, it is determined by the degree of evidence brought forward by the analysis and by whether the thematic structure discovered illuminates the experiential world described by participants. Such evidence can be determined both methodologically and experientially. From a methodological perspective, appropriateness and rigor are weighed against the claims of understanding provided by the investigation. The experiential factor of validity is determined by whether the structure offers insight into the phenomenon—a condition best understood as plausibility and illumination. If the reader is able to understand relationships between the interpretation and the evidence, an interpretation may be considered plausible. Illumination may be experienced when the structure of meaning presents the phenomenon in a new light such that the reader comes away with a new and/or enlightened perspective. If a structure is both plausible and illuminating, it has a resonating quality that brings about a different view of the experience. Given these considerations, it is possible to judge a phenomenological investigation as "valid" if its method is appropriate and rigorous and if its interpretation is plausible and illuminating. The combination of phenomenological interviews (including the initial bracketing interview) and the hermeneutic interpretation that follows (based on consensus in a dialogic group) allows for what Belzen and Hood (2006, p. 19) suggest are reasonable criteria by which to judge qualitative techniques' "transparency of method" that is "true to reality" as holistically experienced. "Transparency of method" means that the method used contains no deceit and is openly expressed both to the subject and to the reader. Likewise, being "true to reality" means providing a description of experience that the subject accepts as true to his or her own understanding. A further indicator that these criteria are fulfilled is Gadamer's assertion that when hermeneutic interpretations are true to reality, the understandings of researcher and subject of study merge if not coincide (cited in Belzen & Hood, 2006, p. 15). We hope that our analyses of extemporaneous sermons, the experiences of serpent handling and the anointing, and near-death experiences in a religious setting do just this. Handlers who have read these chapters satisfy us that our efforts have not been in vain.

Notes

PREFACE

1. The Hood-Williamson Research Archives for the Holiness Serpent Handling Sects of Appalachia is described on-line at UTC Lupton Library: University Archives (Special Collections), www.lib.utc.edu.

CHAPTER 1. "THEY SHALL TAKE UP SERPENTS"

1. The Church of God and the Church of God of Prophecy began as the same sect in the late 1800s and continued as a small denomination until 1923, when General Overseer A. J. Tomlinson, a strong supporter of serpent handling, was ousted from power over leadership issues (Conn, 1996). With Tomlinson's leave, less than one-third of the church membership and ministry followed and eventually became known as the Church of God of Prophecy. As we shall see in chapter 2, almost all the evidence for serpent handling is found in the Church of God's official publication, the *Church of God Evangel*, although a few instances are found in the Church of God of Prophecy's own organ, the *White Wing Messenger*, after the separation occurred in 1923.

2. There is scholarly debate as to whether the latter passage of Mark 16 (vv. 9–20) appears in the original manuscript, although serpent-handling churches—and other fundamentalists—counter this claim with a proclamation that divine providence has resulted in the present canon of Scriptures, which may be faithfully trusted as the infallible Word (see chapter 4 below; Carden & Pelton, 1976). In this sense, serpent handlers are what Hood, Hill, and Williamson (2005) refer to as intratextualists. Intratextuality is the principle that, in the case of Christianity, the Bible must be understood in the plain meaning of the text. In this sense, "They shall take up serpents" means precisely that.

We are grateful to Thomas Burton for giving us a reference to an article by Davenport (1966) concerning a change that occurred in the translation from the Tyndale to the King James Version Bible. An interesting fact noted by Davenport is that the King James Bible of 1611 corrects an error in William Tyndale's 1534 Bible that concerns Mark 16:18. The Tyndale Bible incorrectly stated that believers "shall kill serpents" (pp. 47–48), an error that the King James Bible corrected in rendering the phrase as "they shall take up serpents." According to Davenport, in one text version, the Greek is *kai en tais khersin opheis arousan,* which Davenport translates as "in their hands shall lift up snakes"; and in another version, the Greek is *opheis arousing,* which Davenport translates as "shall lift up snakes" (p. 48). Last, Davenport notes that Saint Jerome rendered the Greek as *serpentes tollent,* which Davenport translates as "they shall raise up snakes" (p. 48).

3. Thomas Burton also has video footage archived as the Burton-Headley Tapes in the Appalachian Archives, East Tennessee State University, Johnson City.

CHAPTER 2. THE HISTORY OF PENTECOSTALISM ABSENT THE SERPENT

1. Wacker (2003, chap. 1) gives numerous delightful examples of the early Pentecostal belief that glossolalia was an actual miraculous speaking of a cultural language that the believer did not know. Obviously, it was fairly quickly learned that glossolalia, even among believers, was not an actual spoken human language.

2. The major biblical text from which the Pentecostal doctrine of tongues is derived states: "And they were all filled with the Holy Ghost, and began to speak with other tongues, as the Spirit gave them utterance" (Acts 2:4). Other biblical texts also are used by Pentecostals to legitimate the doctrine (e.g., Isa. 28:11; 33:19; Mark 16:17; Acts 2:11; 10:46; 19:6; 1 Cor. 12:10, 28; 14:5, 6, 18, 22, 39).

3. The original name of the publication, the *Evening Light and Church of God Evangel,* was shortened to the *Church of God Evangel* after one year and is commonly referred to simply as the *Evangel.*

CHAPTER 3. THE MEDIA AND THE MAN

1. Jimmy Morrow identified the *Life* magazine as a "1940 copy" in his own oral history. We were able to track down the precise date. Morrow's oral history is always accurate in terms of general details. He has no desire to identify precise dates, but his oral history and those of others to come are essential to a complete understanding of the serpent-handling tradition.

2. Based on a telephone interview Williamson (2000) had with J. B. Collins, October 22, 1999, the information that Collins (1947) published about Hensley's conversion to serpent handling, which we discuss in this chapter, came directly from personal interviews conducted with Hensley.

3. This psychological interpretation relies heavily on Sundén's (as presented by Holm, 1995) role theory that Holm (1991) has also found useful for understanding tongues speaking among Pentecostals.

CHAPTER 4. SERPENT HANDLING ENDORSED BY THE CHURCH OF GOD

1. Identical names, while common, do not imply a central organizational structure. Serpent-handling churches are fiercely independent, and few have a stated creed or articles of faith. Of course, they all assert the validity of Mark 16:17–18. As we shall see later in this chapter, they also have a theology that articulates a scriptural basis for their practice of all the signs.

2. The practice of serpent handling is not limited to Appalachia, for as families migrated to other regions of the country in search of employment, they took with them their religion and established small congregations in which they could continue the practice of their faith. In many of these areas, especially the Southeast, states and communities either have or have had laws and local ordinances that explicitly forbid practice of the ritual (see Hood, Williamson, & Morris 2000 for a more detailed discussion of this issue). One notable exception is West Virginia, where the late Barbara Elkins, a noted matron and defender of serpent handling, thwarted attempts to pass a law by testifying before the state legislature concerning her convictions of the truth about the practice and the case of her own daughter who had received a fatal bite when handling a serpent.

3. For the first known media accounts of serpent handling in the Church of God, see articles that appeared in the local newspaper: "Religion and Snakes" (1914); and "Snakes in Demand: Church of God Adopts New Stunts to Prove Presence of the Power" (1914).

4. Also see Schreiter (1985, pp. 1–21) for an interesting discussion on the process of how local theology is developed within a specific faith tradition. The ethnographic approach of his context model seems most appropriate here; it involves the struggle of a group to make sense of the gospel—that is, in terms of related issues such as the Scriptures, salvation, worship, and the presence of God—in its changing cultural context.

There also is evidence that some members of the Church of God practiced the fourth sign of Mark—the drinking of the "deadly thing." State Overseer George T. Brouayer (1921) reported that Church of God evangelist V. A. Bishop died as a result of practicing the sign of drinking poison. It seems, however, that manifestations of this sign were quite rare, possibly because the sign is prefaced in Mark 16 with the conditional word *if.* We have found from our field research that for this reason drinking poison is not considered a specific mandate among contemporary serpent-handling sects, as are the other four signs, but rather an optional practice that true believers may manifest at the bidding of the spirit.

5. Williamson (1995) did a preliminary analysis of 123 articles on serpent handling found in the Church of God between the years 1910 and 1952, most of which were reports of the practice among local congregations. From this research, a bibliography of the articles was donated to the Church of God Pentecostal Research Center, Cleveland, Tennessee, where it is available to scholars. The *Church of God Evangel* has been the official voice for the Church of God (Cleveland, Tenn.) since its first publication in 1910. The initial name, the *Evening Light and Church of God Evangel,* was soon shortened to its present name, the *Church of God Evangel.*

6. Two of the 89 articles were accounts of serpent handling already reported in other articles by other persons. Hence there were actually 87 reports of different meetings at which the sign was practiced. The duplicated reports were not included in the analyses that follow, except where indicated, e.g., locations of serpent handling.

7. A single report from Arizona was not one of a physical handling but of a woman intensely fearful of snakes who, when experiencing God and speaking in tongues, sat fearlessly beside a rattlesnake that had crawled alongside her during a Bible devotion. She attributed her success in the event directly to fulfillment of the third sign in Mark 16 and reported "such victory for a week after that . . . [that she] . . . seemed as if [she] would almost leave the earth at times" (Mull, 1921, p. 4). Some years later, a similar event was reported in the *White Wing Messenger* (Wright, 1939), in which the three-year-old daughter of a Church of God of Prophecy member was observed at play to attempt to put an object into the mouth of a copperhead snake. After a neighbor killed the snake, a Baptist minister remarked that the child must have "charmed the snake." However, the mother praised God and concluded that "the Lord locked its jaws so it couudn't [sic] bite" (p. 3). The article was titled, "Child Receives No Harm from Copperhead," which appears to be a reference to serpent handling as a biblical sign.

8. There is no evidence to suggest that Jernigan ever handled serpents but only that he preached as a young evangelist in a revival at Silver Point, Tennessee, where a rattlesnake was handled by John Yates, who was himself a Church of God minister. The report was written by fellow minister S. F. Beard (1924), who briefly served as Arkansas State Overseer during part of the 1929–30 Assembly year (see Conn, 1977, table 44).

9. Charles W. Conn, the noted but apologetic historian for the Church of God, relegated the practice of serpent handling to a single footnote in his first edition of *Like a Mighty Army* (1955). Its occurrence was described as a "morbid digression" practiced only by "independent, irresponsible, neighboring congregations" (p. 191), an opinion not much changed in his revised edition (Conn, 1977) some twenty years later. In his "definitive" edition (Conn, 1996, pp. 167–170), he acknowledged the fact of serpent handling in Church of God history, as well as George Hensley's ministry, yet condemned its practice as a damaging spectacle that transformed "sanctuaries that should be places of refuge into places of endangerment and death and into sideshows of the bizarre" (p. 170).

10. Clark (1942) appears to not have been the author of "Kentucky Rules against Snakes," but to have reprinted it from another source as editor of the *Evangel*.

11. The last report found of serpent handling in the *Evangel* was published by Gladys Roberson (1935). The last supportive article of the sign as a legitimate Pentecostal manifestation was by Myrtle Whitehead (1943).

12. To identify a serpent-handling "theology" is not to assert that there is an equivalent to a written church dogma to which handlers have access. Churches keep no records, nor do they articulate a theology in written form. However, they do struggle to develop a cohesive and comprehensive biblically based interpretation of serpent handling, and this, we claim, is an oral equivalent to a

serpent-handling theology. It also balances the stereotypes that scholars who study fundamentalists have leveled against them, including their anti-intellectualism and assumed ignorance (see Hood et al., 2005, chap. 8).

More recently, in 1995, we attempted to arrange a visit to the church building erected by the infamous Dolly Pond Church of God with Signs Following, the sect that reestablished serpent handling in Grasshopper, near Birchwood, Tennessee, during the 1940s (see Collins, 1947). The building was purchased for use years later by the Church of God of Prophecy, after it had abandoned the practice of serpent handling. Although the current pastor was well acquainted with one of us, he was not a little distressed to learn of our interest in the historical significance of the building and thus categorically denied us the opportunity to inspect the facilities. As though serpent handling somehow could be purged from the Church of God's (and the Church of God of Prophecy's) past, he declared his congregation's intention of *burning* the historically tainted structure to make room for the new one under construction beside it. Although the building was not burned as promised, it was torn down to the foundation the following year and no longer stands as an important landmark in American religious history.

CHAPTER 5. THE SERPENT

1. In two states, Georgia and Alabama, violations of the original laws involved felonies, which were later reduced to misdemeanors and finally deleted altogether from their codes in the 1970s. The practice of their religious faith by believers continues to be in violation of state codes in Kentucky, Tennessee, Virginia, and North Carolina as misdemeanors, though rigorous enforcement of these statutes has abated in recent years, most likely because early prosecutions—some of which led to acquittals—brought understanding to the context of serpent handling as a legitimate, though unpopular, religious belief when examined more closely, as in courtrooms. Although there are accounts of children who handled serpents and were sometimes bitten in the early history of the tradition (see Hood et al., 1999), there is no death on record concerning children who handled. Contemporary serpent handling churches do not allow minors to handle serpents in their worship services; it is restricted to those who are at least eighteen years of age. The age requirement is moot in states where the practice is illegal. We discuss the laws against serpent handling fully in chapter 11.

2. Many of these bites are captured on DVD. Services with bites are identified in the Hood-Williamson Research Archives of the Holiness Serpent Handling Sects of Appalachia, Lupton Library, University of Tennessee at Chattanooga.

3. A church video of Punkin Brown's fatal bite was confiscated by police and then obtained by TV stations and widely aired. This video is in the Hood-Williamson Research Archives of the Holiness Serpent Handling Sects. Brown died quickly, leading his father and others to believe it was not a death "in the signs, but rather due to a heart attack." Regardless, the proximate cause of death was the serpent bite (see Brown & McDonald, 2000, pp. 15–18).

4. All measurements of venom reported here are in dried form. It should be noted that there is some degree of variation among researchers concerning venom yields (see Pinney, 1981).

5. Information reported with respect to bites and deaths in this present discussion are not concerned with those that have occurred within the serpent-
handling tradition but only (so far as we know) with those that have occurred
in secular contexts.

6. Pinney (1981) has estimated the storage of venom to range from 370 to
720 milligrams.

CHAPTER 6. TRANCE STATES

1. There are wide individual differences in tolerance for strychnine. We took
a sample from the altar of a church in 1995 and had it tested by an independent
chemical laboratory. It was certified to contain 54 milligrams per liter. Depending
on the amount drunk, it is possibly a lethal dose, but unlikely. Schwarz (1960)
had tested strychnine that was drunk by two believers. It contained strychnine
sulfate in magnitude 43.5 milligrams per liter. He estimated the amount drunk by
the two believers was 80 milliliters, which would be an amount of strychnine of
at least 17 milligrams (assuming each drank an equal amount).

Strychnine can produce convulsions and be fatal in amounts as little as 5 milligrams. As Schwarz (1960) concluded, relative to the strychnine he witnessed
being ingested by two believers, "such an amount by way of the method and
time of administration might have been sufficient to produce convulsive, or
either toxic and/or possibly even lethal effects" (p. 425). Thus while handlers
drink mixtures of poisonous substances they believe might be fatal, in most
cases the successful drinking indicates that the dosage was not sufficient to be
lethal. However, the documented cases of death by poison drinking is a test to
the sincerity of the believers whose poison is indeed, like the serpent, a sign of
possible death.

2. The Hood-Williamson Archive identifies DVDs in which the treading
upon serpents occurs.

3. As discussed in chapter 4, serpent handlers do not dispute the Gospel of
Mark. They accept the King James Bible. While much of Mark is "disputed" by
higher biblical criticism, conservative theologians have defended the entire text.
For instance, Frodsham (1946, pp. 263–68) was among the first to argue that the
Codex Freer contains all of Mark 16. This codex, along with Codex Alexandrius,
is used by those who defend the "later" verses in Mark. Regardless of the historical issues of the "disputed" Markan text, the meaning of the "signs following," as
noted by Otto (1917/1928) and serpent-handling believers, remains of relevance.

CHAPTER 7. EXTEMPORANEOUS SERMONS
IN THE SERPENT-HANDLING TRADITION

1. This included handling serpents and, in some cases, the drinking of
strychnine.

2. See Appendix 3 for a detailed discussion of this method. The sermons are
included as portions of entire services that are videotaped and housed in the
Hood-Williamson Research Archives for the Holiness Serpent Handling Sects of
Appalachia.

3. To protect the identity of the preachers, we used codes as follows: Preacher 1 is S1, Preacher 2 is S2, and so on. Since some preachers gave more than one sermon, an added hyphenated number is attached to each citation. For example, S1–1 indicates that the quote is from Preacher 1, sermon 1; S4–2 indicates that the quote is from Preacher 4, sermon 2. Our analysis uses the participants' own words, and all excerpts are rendered unedited with respect to the grammatical and linguistic structure used by the participants.

CHAPTER 8. THE EXPERIENCE OF HANDLING SERPENTS

1. See Appendix 3 for a discussion of our method for interviewing and determining the structure of meaning in the awareness of human experiences such as the handling of serpents.

2. All interviews for this study are housed in the Hood-Williamson Research Archives for the Holiness Serpent Handling Sects of Appalachia.

3. To protect the identity of the seventeen participants in this study, we assigned to each a code for reference instead of using their names. For example, Participant 1 is referred to as H1, Participant 2 as H2, and so on. Our analysis uses the participants' own words, and all excerpts are rendered unedited with respect to the grammatical and linguistic structure they used.

CHAPTER 9. THE EXPERIENCE OF THE ANOINTING

1. Appendix 3 describes the methodology used in this present study.

2. The interviews used in this analysis are housed in the Hood-Williamson Research Archives.

3. To protect the identity of the participants in this study, we assigned to each a code for reference instead of using their names. For example, Participant 1 is referred to as A1, Participant 2 as A2, and so on.

CHAPTER 10. NEAR-DEATH EXPERIENCE FROM SERPENT BITES IN RELIGIOUS SETTINGS

1. All thirteen interviews were videotaped with permission and are archived in the Hood-Williamson Research Archives.

2. To distinguish among participants and to protect their anonymity, we have coded their descriptions in the following manner: Participant 1 is D1, Participant 2 is D2, and so on.

3. The service during which Brown was bitten and died was captured on videotape by the church. The tape was confiscated by the local authorities, and a copy, anonymously given to the media, was aired on television. A copy of the TV footage from the church video is in the Hood-Williamson Archives.

CHAPTER 11. MUSIC AMONG SERPENT-HANDLING CHURCHES

1. The vast majority of time in this service was given to preaching. One preacher offered a sermon that lasted well over an hour; another preacher

followed with a sermon of much shorter length. Other parts of the service included testimonials by believers, seasons of prayer, and brief handling of serpents. Depending on the amount of time given to preaching, singing may account for over half of the time spent at a worship service.

CHAPTER 12. SERPENT HANDLING AND THE LAW

1. As noted above, Ana Kirk handled while she was pregnant. She was bitten, and both she and her child died. The widely circulated picture of a child touching a snake was first published in the *St. Louis Dispatch*, September 11, 1938, p. D10.

2. The most complete listing of court cases involving serpent handling is in Burton (1993, p. 204).

3. As mentioned earlier, Burton and Headley (1983, 1986) produced two documentaries on serpent handling at Carson Springs. In these films, they address the legal cases involving the preachers Alfred Ball and Liston Pack.

4. Drinking poison can be and has been, in several court cases, interpreted as an act of suicide. In many states, including Tennessee, either suicide is illegal, or the aiding or abetting of suicide is illegal, or both. In this sense, drinking poison also is illegal and can be punished by legal action.

5. While many serpent handlers do not drink poison, all believers who drink poison also handle serpents. We know of no member of a serpent-handling church who only drinks poison.

6. For instance, Luther Hill was convicted of handling, and the Appellate Court of Alabama upheld the conviction (see Hill v. State, 88 So. 2d. 8860, Court of Appeals of Alabama, 1956).

7. After construction of their first church building in 1956, the Elkinses and their members selected as their first official pastor an African American, Winford Dickerson, who at the time worked in the community as a coal miner (personal interview with Dewey Chafin, September 5, 1998; Brown & McDonald, 2000). His selection was most likely because he was a recognized minister known to oversee other established (African American) churches in nearby towns and various parts of the region. During the few years of his Jolo pastorate, Dickerson was known to handle serpents among the members, although he did not take serpent handling to his other congregations (personal interview with Dewey Chafin, September 5, 1998). He later gave up the ministry to become a member of the West Virginia state legislature. The years with Dickerson at the helm of the Jolo church are important, since African Americans are seldom, if ever, represented in serpent-handling churches. Although we have had rare occasion to observe African Americans visiting, worshiping, and even sometimes preaching at serpent-handling churches, we have never seen any take up serpents to date; neither have we discovered documentation to confirm that they ever have—except for Dickerson.

8. The MMPI is the most widely used clinical instrument in clinical psychology and psychiatry to objectively measure and determine mental disorders.

9. Appropriate statistical tests supporting this claim are in Hood et al. (1999, pp. 101–2).

10. Further discussion of our prejudice measure and the appropriate statistical tests supporting its involvement in even rational rejection of handling and poison drinking may be found in Hood et al. (1999, pp. 99–100, 103–4).

11. Our present concern here is with stereotype only. Other measures of prejudice (negative affect and behavioral avoidance) are discussed in the original article (Hood et al., 2000, pp. 290–93). Our focus on stereotyping is linked to our concern discussed in this chapter that (a) the media have stereotyped handlers and (b) legislatures' and judges' knowledge of serpent handling is largely driven by the media.

12. This is a modified version of a Solomon four-groups design. The merits of this design and the statistical analyses supporting our conclusions are in Hood et al. (2000, pp. 290–93).

EPILOGUE

1. This documentary is titled *Heaven Come Down* and aired on the Sundance Channel. It is based on over one hundred hours of original footage that the filmmakers shot and eventually donated to our archives. It was directed by Gabriel Wrye and Michael Meese of 3420 Alta Place, Los Angeles, CA 90031.

2. To date, we have conducted limited field research at four Trinitarian serpent-handling churches in eastern Kentucky: Pine Mountain Church of God, Sanctuary Holiness Church, Little Colley Holiness Church, and the Bill Moore Branch Holiness Church. From our preliminary observations, it appears that although they are larger than "Jesus-only" churches, their worship tends to be less demonstrative, more formal, and less frequented by serpent handling—and sometimes only at an annual homecoming. In the above-mentioned churches, most have never seen another believer drink "the deadly thing." More research is clearly needed among Trinitarian serpent-handling churches.

3. After publication of *Salvation on Sand Mountain* (1995), Covington returned to the Old Rock House Holiness Church and asked forgiveness of the people he had maligned. Our archives contains footage of Covington at Sand Mountain, along with a well-known TV actor he had brought to the church. Our *guess* is that a movie or TV film was planned. Hood talked to the actor, who assured him that he was interested only in observing and understanding the power of these people. On the DVD the actor is clearly seen trying to hide his face when the camera turns toward him. Our own interest was, as always, simply to film ongoing services. We had not anticipated this actor being present, but the church had given us permission to film the service. If the intent was to make a movie, it was (or has not yet been) made.

4. Charles Prince's bite, his suffering of thirty-eight hours before dying, and his funeral are on DVD in our archives.

5. Our archives contain extensive footage of Punkin preaching and handling in many different churches.

6. The senior author was standing beside Melinda as she signaled for the serpent and as she then was bitten.

7. Note that we have argued in chapter 12 about the fallacy of this assumption. Even when serpents are present, children are not endangered.

8. Our archives have footage of Punkin's children at church services with serpents being handled.

9. We have discussed in chapter 12 the influential role "child endanger-ment" plays in stereotyping this tradition, as well as the assumption that rituals that risk maiming and death are not properly "religious"—this despite the fact that no child has ever died from a serpent bite (with the possible exception of the Kirk birth noted in chapter 12). As we also have discussed in chapter 12, children did handle early in the tradition, although they are not allowed to han-dle in contemporary churches.

10. John Brown explains his reasoning for supporting Punkin's decision to defy the injunction and for their own assistance in taking his children to churches while serpents were being handled (see Brown & McDonald, 2000, pp. 67–68).

References

Alcock, J. E. (1981). Pseudo-science and the soul. *Essence: Issues in the Study of Ageing, Dying, and Death, 5,* 65–76.

Alland, A. (1962). Possession in a revivalist Negro church. *Journal for the Scientific Study of Religion, 1,* 204–13.

Allen, E. R., & Swindell, D. (1948). Cottonmouth moccasin of Florida. *Herpetology, 4,* 1–15.

All need the Holy Ghost. (1910). *Evening Light and Church of God Evangel, 1*(5), 2.

Alvarado, C. S. (2002). Out-of-body experiences. In C. S. Cardeña, J. Lyn, & S. Krippner (Eds.), *Varieties of anomalous experience* (pp. 183–218). Washington, DC: American Psychological Association.

Ambrose, K. P. (1970). Survey of the snake handling cult of West Virginia. Unpublished master's thesis, Marshall University, Huntingdon, WV.

Ammerman, N. T. (1977). Golden Rule Christianity: Lived religion in the American mainstream. In D. D. Hall (Ed.), *Lived religion in America: Toward a history of practice* (pp. 196–216). Princeton: Princeton University Press.

Ammerman, N. T. (1991). North American Protestant Fundamentalism. In M. E. Marty & R. S. Appleby (Eds.), *Fundamentalisms observed* (pp. 1–65). Chicago: University of Chicago Press.

Anderson, C. T. (1924). Virginia for Jesus: Signs and wonders. *White Wing Messenger, 1*(8), 2.

Anderson, C. T. (1925). Great victory and power in Coeburn Camp meeting: Signs and wonders wrought: Rattlesnake caught. *White Wing Messenger, 2*(18), 3.

Anderson, R. M. (1979). *Vision of the disinherited: The making of American Pentecostalism.* New York: Oxford University Press.

Badcock, C. R. (1980). *The psychoanalysis of culture.* Oxford: Basil Blackwell.

Badham, P. (1997). *Religious and near-death experience in relation to belief in a future life*. Oxford: Westminster College, Religious Experience Research Centre.

Ballard, B. (1933). Bitten by snake—delivered: People are now reading their Bibles. *White Wing Messenger, 10*(21), 3.

Bataille, G. (1986). *Eroticism, death and sensuality* (M. Dalewood, Trans.). San Francisco: City Lights Books.

Beard, S. F. (1924). Old Tennessee still rising. *Church of God Evangel, 15*(31), 2.

Belzen, J. A. (1999). Religion as embodiment: Cultural-psychological concepts and methods in the study of conversion among "bevindelijken." *Journal for the Scientific Study of Religion, 38* (2), 236–53.

Belzen, J. A., & Hood, R. W., Jr. (2006). Methodological issues in the psychology of religion: Toward another paradigm? *Journal of Psychology, 140,* 1–28.

Berger, P. L., & Luckman, T. (1966). *The social construction of reality.* Garden City, NY: Doubleday.

Birckhead, J. (1993). "Bizarre snake handlers": Popular media and a Southern stereotype. In K. G. Heider (Ed.), *Images of the South: Constructing a regional culture on film and video* (pp. 163–89). Athens: University of Georgia Press.

Birckhead, J. (1997). Reading "snake handling": Critical reflections. In S. D. Glazier (Ed.), *Anthropology of religion* (pp. 19–84). Westport, CT: Greenwood Press.

Bleicher, J. (1980/1990). *Contemporary hermeneutics: Hermeneutics as method, philosophy and critique.* New York: Routledge.

Blose, B. L. (1981). Materialism and disembodied minds. *Philosophy and Phenomenological Research, 42,* 59–74.

Book of minutes. (1922). Cleveland, TN: Church of God Publishing House. .

Bowdle, D. N. (1999). Holiness in the highlands: A profile of the Church of God. In B. J. Leonard (Ed.), *Christianity in Appalachia* (pp. 243–56). Knoxville: University of Tennessee Press.

Boyd, B., & Adair, P. (Producers). (1968). *Holy Ghost people* [Film]. New York: McGraw-Hill Film.

Bradley baffled by snake problem. (1946, August 28). *Chattanooga Times,* p. 9.

Brinkmann, S. (2006). Mental life in the space of reasons. *Journal for the Theory of Social Behavior, 36,* 1–16.

Bro. George Hensley is conducting a revival. (1914). *Church of God Evangel, 5*(37), 6.

Bromley, D. G. (2007). On spiritual edgework: The logic of extreme ritual performances. *Journal for the Scientific Study of Religion, 46,* 287–303.

Bromley, D. G., & Shupe, A. D., Jr. (1981). *Strange gods.* Boston: Beacon Press.

Brouayer, G. T. (1915). Southside, Tenn. *Church of God Evangel, 6*(43), 3.

Brouayer, G. T. (1917a). Report from Ladonia, Texas. *Church of God Evangel, 8*(24), 4.

Brouayer, G. T. (1917b). Report. *Church of God Evangel, 8*(33), 2.

Brouayer, G. T. (1921). Died in the faith. *Church of God Evangel, 12*(19), 1.

Brown, F., & McDonald, J. (2000). *The Serpent Handlers: Three families and their faith.* Winston-Salem, NC: John F. Blair.

Bruce, A. B. (1979). The synoptic gospels. In W. R. Nicoll (Ed.), *The expositor's Greek New Testament* (Vol. 1, pp. 1–65). Grand Rapids, MI: Eerdmans.

Buber, M. (1970). *I and thou.* New York: Charles Scribner's Sons.

Bullinger, E. W. (1975). *A critical lexicon and concordance to the English and Greek New Testament.* Grand Rapids, MI: Zondervan Publishing House.

Burkhart, J. B. (1922). Fire was seen. *Church of God Evangel, 13*(1), 3.

Burton, T. (1993). *Serpent handling believers.* Knoxville: University of Tennessee Press.

Burton. T. (2004). *The serpent and the spirit: Glenn Summerford's story.* Knoxville: University of Tennessee Press.

Burton, T. G., & Headley, T. F. (Producers). (1983). *Carson Springs: A decade later* [Film]. Johnson City: East Tennessee State University.

Burton, T. G., & Headley, T. F. (Producers). (1986). *Following the signs: A way of conflict* [Film]. Johnson City: East Tennessee State University.

Bush, N. E. (1983). The near-death experience in children: Shade of the prison house re-opening. *Anabiosis, 3,* 177–93.

Cahoone, L. (Ed.). (2003). *From modernism to postmodernism.* Malden, MA: Blackwell.

Campbell, J. (1974). *The mythic image.* Princeton, NJ: Princeton University Press.

Campbell, W. D. (1974). Which is the real evil—snake handling or the established church? *Southern Voice, 1*(1), 41–48.

Capshaw, W. A. (1917). Erastus, N.C. *Church of God Evangel, 8*(31), 2.

Capshaw, W. A. (1922). Large serpent was handled. *Church of God Evangel, 13*(24): 3.

Carden, K. W., & Pelton, R. W. (1976). *The persecuted prophets.* New York: A. S. Barnes and Company.

Carr, D. (1982). Pathophysiology of stress-induced limbic lobe function: A hypothesis for NDEs. *Anabiosis, 2,* 75–90.

Chasseguet-Smirgel, J. (1986). *Sensuality and the mind.* New York: New York University Press.

Chavies, J. (1937). Covering news—revivals in North America: Signs following. *White Wing Messenger, 14*(10), 3.

The Church of God: Teaching. (1910). *Evening Light and Church of God Evangel, 1*(12), 3.

Clark, E. C. (1934). An exposition of Mark 16:18. *Church of God Evangel, 25*(28), 1.

Clark, E. C. (1942). Kentucky rules against snakes. *Church of God Evangel, 33*(31), 4.

Cobb, A. L. (1965). Sect religion and social change in an isolated rural community of southern Appalachia. Unpublished Ph.D. dissertation, Boston University.

Collins, J. B. (1947). *Tennessee snake handlers.* Chattanooga, TN: Chattanooga News-Free Press.

Conn, C. W. (1955). *Like a mighty army.* Cleveland, TN: Pathway Press.

Conn, C. W. (1977). *Like a mighty army* (rev. ed.). Cleveland, TN: Pathway Press.

Conn, C. W. (1996). *Like a mighty army: A history of the Church of God: Definitive edition.* Cleveland, TN: Pathway Press.

Cotton, C. (1910). Revival at Coalburg, Ala. *Church of God Evangel, 1*(9), 7.

Coulson, J. E., & Johnson, R. W. (1977). Glossolalia and internal-external locus of control. *Journal of Psychology and Theology, 5*(4), 312–17.

Covington, D. (1995). *Salvation on Sand Mountain: Snake handling and redemption in southern Appalachia.* Reading, MA: Addison-Wesley.

Cox, H. (1995). *Fire from heaven.* New York: Addison-Wesley.

Creech, J. (1996). Visions of glory: The place of the Azusa Street revival in Pentecostal history. *Church History, 65*(3), 405–24.

Crews, M. (1990). *The Church of God: A social history.* Knoxville: University of Tennessee Press.

Cutten, G. B. (1927). *Speaking in tongues: Historically and psychologically considered.* New Haven, CT: Yale University Press.

Dalley, Ms. D. (1921). Revival at Maryville, Tenn. *Church of God Evangel, 12*(45), 2.

Danforth, L. M. (1989). *Firewalking and religious healing: The Anastenaria of Greece and the American firewalking movement.* Princeton, NJ: Princeton University Press.

Daugherty, M. L. (1978). Serpent handling as sacrament. In J. D. Photiadis (Ed.), *Religion in Appalachia* (pp. 103–11). Morgantown: West Virginia University.

Davenport, G. (1966). Taking up serpents. In G. Davenport (Ed.), *The hunter Gracchus: And other papers on literature and art* (pp. 47–51). Washington, DC: Counterpoint.

Davidson, C. T. (1973). *Upon this rock* (Vol. 1). Cleveland, TN: White Wing Publishing House.

Dickinson, E. (1981). Eleanor Dickinson Pentecostal videotape and audiotape collection, 1967–77. Archives Center, National Museum of American History, Washington, DC. Gift of the artist.

Dittes, James E. (1971). Typing the typologies: Some parallels in the career of church-sect and extrinsic-intrinsic religion. *Journal for the Scientific Study of Religion, 10,* 375–83.

Ehrman, B. D. (2005). *Misquoting Jesus: The story behind who changed the Bible and why.* New York: HarperCollins.

Eigen, M. (1981). Comments on snake symbolism and mind-body relations. *American Journal of Psychoanalysis, 41*(1), 73–79.

Ellis, J. B. (1914). Oneonta, Ala. *Church of God Evangel, 5*(19), 8.

Ellis, J. B. (1976). *Blazing the gospel trail.* Plainfield, NJ: Logos International.

Emmons, R. A., & Paloutzian, R. F. (2003). The psychology of religion. *Annual Review of Psychology, 54,* 377–402.

Ernest, C. H. (1992). *Venomous reptiles of North America.* Washington, DC: Smithsonian Books,

Evans, A. D. (Ed.). (1943). *A. J. Tomlinson: God's anointed—prophet of wisdom.* Cleveland, TN: White Wing Publishing House.

Faith service snake-bite fatal. (1936, May 5). *New York Times,* p. 25.

Fenwick, P., & Fenwick, E. (1995). *The truth in the light.* London: Headline.

Finke, R., & Stark, R. (2001). The new holy clubs: Testing church-to-sect propositions. *Sociology of Religion, 62,* 175–89.

Fisk, S. T. (1993). Controlling other people: The impact of power on stereotyping. *American Psychologist, 48,* 621–28.

Ford, rattler's victim. (1945, September 9). *Chattanooga Times,* p. 1.

Fortune, R. F. (1924). The symbolism of the serpent. *International Journal of Psych-Analysis, 7,* 237–43.

Frazer, J. G. (1892/1955). *The golden bough* (abridged ed.). New York: Macmillan.

Freud, S. (1961). Beyond the pleasure principle (1920). (J. Strachey, Trans.). In J. Strachey (Ed.), *The standard edition of the complete psychological works of Sigmund Freud* (Vol. 18, pp. 3–64). London: Hogarth Press.

Frodsham, S. H. (1946). *With signs following* (rev. ed.). Springfield, MO: Gospel Publishing House.

Gadamer, H. G. (1960/1986). *Truth and method.* New York: Crossroad.

Gadamer, H. G. (1976). *Philosophical hermeneutics.* Berkeley: University of California Press.

Gaddy, W. C. (1926). Red hot gospel in mountains. *White Wing Messenger, 3*(1), 3.

Gallup, G., & Procter, W. (1982). *Adventures in immortality: A look beyond the threshold of death.* New York: McGraw-Hill.

George, B. (1987). *Added to the church: A Church of God membership manual.* Cleveland, TN: Pathway Press.

Gergen, K. J. (1992). Toward a postmodern psychology. In S. Kvale (Ed.), *Psychology and postmodernism* (pp. 17–30). London: Sage.

Gerlach, L. P., & Hine, V. H. (1968). Five factors crucial to the growth and spread of a modern religious movement. *Journal for the Scientific Study of Religion, 7,* 23–40.

Giorgi, A. (1970). *Psychology as a human science: A phenomenologically based approach.* New York: Harper and Row.

Giorgi, A. (1971). Phenomenology and experimental psychology: II. In A. Giorgi, W. F. Fischer, & R. von Eckartsberg (Eds.), *Duquesne studies in phenomenological psychology: Vol. 1* (pp. 17–29). Pittsburgh, PA: Duquesne University Press.

Giorgi, A. (1975). An application of phenomenological method in psychology. In A. Giorgi, C. T. Fischer, & E. L. Murray (Eds.), *Duquesne studies in phenomenological psychology: Vol. 2* (pp. 82–103). Pittsburgh, PA: Duquesne University Press.

Giorgi, A., Barton, A., & Maes, C. (Eds.). (1983). *Duquesne studies in phenomenological psychology: Vol. 4.* Pittsburgh, PA: Duquesne University Press.

Giorgi, A., Fischer, C. T., & Murray, E. L. (Eds.). (1975). *Duquesne studies in phenomenological psychology: Vol. 2.* Pittsburgh, PA: Duquesne University Press.

Giorgi, A., Fischer, W. F., & von Eckartsberg, R. (Eds.). (1971). *Duquesne studies in phenomenological psychology: Vol. 1.* Pittsburgh, PA: Duquesne University Press.

Giorgi, A., Knowles, R., & Smith, D. L. (Eds.). (1979). *Duquesne studies in phenomenological psychology: Vol. 3.* Pittsburgh, PA: Duquesne University Press.

Goodman, F. D. (1969). Phonetic analysis of glossolalia in four cultural settings. *Journal for the Scientific Study of Religion, 8*, 227–39.

Goodman, F. D. (1972a). Altered mental state vs. "style of discourse": Reply to Samarin. *Journal for the Scientific Study of Religion, 11*, 279–99.

Goodman, F. D. (1972b). *Speaking in tongues: A cross-cultural study of glossolalia.* Chicago: University of Chicago Press.

Goodman, F. D. (1988). *Ecstasy, ritual, and alternate reality.* Bloomington: Indiana University Press.

Gorsuch, R. L. (1984). Measurement: The boon and bane of investigating the psychology of religion. *American Psychologist, 39*, 201–21.

Grant, M. (1977). *Jesus: An historian's view of the Gospels.* New York: Charles Scribner's Sons.

Greyson, B. (1981). Near-death experiences and attempted suicide. *Suicide and Life-Threatening Behavior, 11*, 10–16.

Greyson, B. (1983). The near-death experience scale: Construction, reliability, and validity. *Journal of Nervous and Mental Disease, 171*, 369–75.

Greyson, B. (1990). Near-death encounters with and without near-death experiences: Comparative NDE profiles. *Journal of Near-Death Studies, 8*, 151–61.

Greyson, B. (2002). Near-death experiences. In C. Cardeña, S. J. Lyn, & S. Krippner (Eds.), *Varieties of anomalous experience* (pp. 315–52). Washington, DC: American Psychological Association.

Griffin, J. N. (1922). Report was false. *Church of God Evangel, 13*(36), 2.

Grogan, D., & Phillips, C. (1989, May 1). Courting death, Appalachia's old-time religionists: Praise the Lord and pass the snakes. *People*, p. 82.

Hagwood, N. B. (1916). Southside, Tenn. *Church of God Evangel, 7*(24), 2.

Hammond, P. (2001) American church/state jurisprudence from the Warren Court to the Rehnquist Court. *Journal for the Scientific Study of Religion, 40*, 455–64.

Harris, R. W. (1949). Snake-handling. *Church of God Evangel, 39*(47), 8–9.

Hassall, J. C. (1919). The serpent as a symbol. *Psychoanalytic Review, 6*, 296–305.

Headrick, W. (1918). Birchwood, Tenn. *Church of God Evangel, 9*(15), 2.

Heath, S. J. (1928). Signs following believers. *Church of God Evangel, 19*(30), 3.

He hath shed forth this which you now see and hear: Speaking in other tongues as the Spirit gives utterance the evidence of the baptism with the Holy Ghost. (1910). *Evening Light and Church of God Evangel, 1*(6), 3.

Heidegger, M. (1927/1962). *Being and time.* (J. Macquarrie & E. Robinson, Trans.). New York: Harper and Row.

Henderson, J. L., & Oakes, M. (1963). *The wisdom of the serpent.* New York: Collier.

Hensley, M. (1914). Ooltewah, Tenn. *Church of God Evangel, 5*(14), 7.

Henson, E. (1917). Erastus, N.C. *Church of God Evangel, 8*(35): 3.

Herzog, H. A., Jr. (1990). Experimental modification of defensive behaviors in garter snakes *(Thamnophis sirtalis). Journal of Comparative Psychology, 104*, 334–39.

Hick, J. (1980). *Death and eternal life.* San Francisco: Harper and Row.

Hills, P., & Argyle, M. (1998). Musical and religious experiences and their relationship to happiness. *Personality and Individual Differences, 25*(1), 91–102.

Hine, V. H. (1969). Pentecostal glossolalia: Toward a functional interpretation. *Journal for the Scientific Study of Religion, 8*(2), 211–26.

Hollenweger, W. J. (1972). *The Pentecostals.* Minneapolis, MN: Augsburg Publishing House.

Holm, N. G. (1991) Pentecostalism: Conversion and charismata. *International Journal for the Psychology of Religion, 1*(3), 135–51.

Holm, N. G. (1995). Religious symbols and role taking. In N. G. Holm & J. A. Belzen (Eds.), *Sundén's role theory—An impetus to contemporary psychology of religion* (pp. 129–51). Åbo, Finland: Åbo Akademi.

Holt, J. B. (1940). Holiness religion: Cultural shock and social reorganization. *American Sociological Review, 4,* 740–47.

Holy Rollers hold their annual assembly. (1934, September 16). *Birmingham News,* n.p.

Hood, R. W., Jr. (1970). Effects of foreknowledge of death in the assessment of suicide notes of intent to die. *Journal of Consulting and Clinical Psychology, 34,* 129–33.

Hood, R. W., Jr. (1971). Effects of foreknowledge of sex and manner of death in the assessment of suicide notes of intent to die. *Journal of Social Psychology, 84,* 73–80.

Hood, R. W., Jr. (1973). Hypnotic susceptibility and the report of religious experience. *Psychological Reports, 33,* 549–50.

Hood, R. W., Jr. (1995). Salvation on Sand Mountain: Snake handling and redemption in southern Appalachia. [Review of *Salvation on Sand Mountain*]. *Appalachian Heritage, Summer,* 54–56.

Hood, R. W., Jr. (1998). When the Spirit maims and kills: Social psychological considerations of the history of serpent handling sects and the narrative of handlers. *International Journal for the Psychology of Religion, 8*(2), 71–96.

Hood, R. W., Jr. (2003a). American primitive: In the shadow of the serpent. *Common Review, 2,* 28–37.

Hood, R. W., Jr. (2003b). The relationship between religion and spirituality. In A. L. Greil & D. Bromley (Eds.), *Defining religion: Investigating the boundaries between the sacred and secular.* Vol. 10 of *Religion and the social order* (pp. 224–64). Amsterdam: JAI, Elsevier.

Hood, R. W., Jr. (Ed.). (2005). *Handling serpents: Pastor Jimmy Morrow's narrative history of his Appalachian Jesus' Name tradition.* Mercer, GA: Mercer University Press.

Hood, R. W., Jr., Hill, P. C., & Williamson, W. P. (2005). *The psychology of religious fundamentalism.* New York: Guilford.

Hood, R. W., Jr., & Kimbrough, D. L. (1995). Serpent handling Holiness sects: Theoretical considerations. *Journal for the Scientific Study of Religion, 34*(3), 311–22.

Hood, R. W., Jr., & Morris, R. J. (1981). Sensory isolation and the differential elicitation of religious imagery in intrinsic and extrinsic persons. *Journal for the Scientific Study of Religion, 20,* 261–73.

Hood, R. W., Jr., Morris, R. J., & Watson, P. J. (1990). Quasi-experimental elicitation of the differential report of mystical experience among intrinsic and indiscriminately pro-religious types. *Journal for the Scientific Study of Religion, 29,* 164–72.

Hood, R. W., Jr., Morris, R. J., & Williamson, W. P. (1999). Evaluation of the legitimacy of conversion experience as a function of the five signs of Mark 16. *Review of Religious Research, 41,* 96–109.

Hood, R. W., Jr., Spilka, B., Hunsberger, B., & Gorsuch, R. (1996). *The psychology of religion: An empirical approach* (2nd ed.). New York: Guilford Press.

Hood, R. W., Jr., & Williamson, W. P. (1998, March). *Nuances of serpent bite death: Secular influences on theological perspectives.* Paper presented at the twenty-eighth annual meeting of the Society of Pentecostal Studies.

Hood, R. W., Jr., & Williamson, W. P. (2006). Near death experiences from serpent bites in religious settings: A Jamesian perspective. *Archives de Psychologie, 72,* 139–59.

Hood, R. W., Jr., Williamson, W. P., & Morris, R. J. (2000). Changing views of serpent handling: A quasi-experimental study. *Journal for the Scientific Study of Religion, 39,* 287–96.

Hopkins, E. D. (1919). Report. *Church of God Evangel, 10*(28), 3.

Horton, G. B. (1989) With signs following: " . . . They shall take up serpents." *Church of God Evangel, 79*(10), 19–21.

Horton, H. (1934/1975). *The gifts of the Spirit.* Springfield, MO: Gospel Publishing House.

House okays ban on snake rituals. (1963, February 14). *Charleston Daily Mail,* p. 1.

Howey, M. O. (1926). *The encircled serpent.* Philadelphia: David McKay.

Hudson, L. (1972). *The Cult of fact: A psychologist's autobiographical critique of his discipline.* New York: Harper and Row.

Hunter, H. D. (1988a). Serpent handling. In S. M. Burgess & G. B. McGee (Eds.), *Dictionary of Pentecostal and Charismatic movements* (pp. 777–78). Grand Rapids, MI: Zondervan Publishing House.

Hunter, H. D. (1988b). Tomlinson, Homer Aubrey. In S. M. Burgess & G. B. McGee (Eds.), *Dictionary of Pentecostal and Charismatic movements* (pp. 848–49). Grand Rapids, MI: Zondervan Publishing House.

Index to the roster of ministers: 1886–1921. (n.d.). Computerized document archived at the William G. Squires Library and the Dixon Pentecostal Research Center, Lee University, Cleveland, TN.

Jackson, P. (1936). We are living signboards. *Church of God Evangel, 27*(20), 3.

Jaffé, A. (1964). Symbolism in the visual arts. In C. G. Jung & M. L. von Franz (Eds.), *Man and his symbols* (pp. 230–71). New York: Doubleday.

James, W. (1890/1983). *The principles of psychology.* Cambridge, MA: Harvard University Press.

James, W. (1898). *Human immortality: Two supposed objections to the doctrine.* New York: Houghton-Mifflin.

James, W. (1902/1982). *The varieties of religious experience.* New York: Penguin Books.

Jelen, T. G. (1999). Dimensions of free exercise: Abstract beliefs and concrete applications. *Review of Religious Research, 40,* 349–58.

Johnson, B. (1963). On church and sect. *American Sociological Review, 28,* 259–70.

Jones, E. (1948). The theory of symbolism. In E. Jones (Ed.), *Collected papers in psychoanalysis* (5th ed.), (pp. 87–144). London: Baille.

Jones, E. (1961). *Papers on psycho-analysis* (5th ed.). Boston: Beacon Press.

Joslin, G., Fletcher, H., & Emlen, J. (1964). A comparison of the responses to snakes of lab- and wild-reared Rhesus monkeys. *Animal Behavior, 12,* 348–52.

Joyner, C. (1994). "Believer I know": The emergence of African American Christianity. In P. E. Johnson (Ed.), *African American Christianity* (pp. 19–46). Berkeley: University of California Press.

Jung, C. G. (1964). Approaching the unconscious. In C. G. Jung & M. L. von Franz (Eds.), *Man and his symbols* (pp. 18–103). New York: Doubleday.

Kane, S. M. (1974a). Holy Ghost people: The snake handlers of southern Appalachia. *Appalachian Journal, 1*(4), 255–62.

Kane, S. M. (1974b). Ritual possession in a southern Appalachian religious sect. *Journal of American Folklore, 88*(346), 293–302.

Kane, S. M. (1978). Holiness fire handling in southern Appalachia: A psychophysiological analysis. In J. D. Photiadis (Ed.), *Religion in Appalachia* (pp. 113–24). Morgantown: West Virginia University.

Kane, S. M. (1979). Snake handlers of southern Appalachia. Unpublished Ph.D. dissertation, Princeton University.

Kane, S. M. (1982). Holiness ritual fire handling: Ethnographic and psychophysiological considerations. *Ethos, 10*(4), 369–84.

Kane, S. M. (1984). Snake handlers. In S. S. Hill (Ed.), *Encyclopedia of religion in the South* (pp. 698–99). Macon, GA: Mercer University Press.

Kane, S. M. (1987). Appalachian snake handlers. In J. C. Cobb & C. R. Wilson (Eds.), *Perspectives on the South: An annual review of society, politics and culture* (Vol. 4, pp. 115–27). New York: Gordon and Breach Science Publishers.

Kane, S. M. (1989). Snake handlers. In C. R. Wilson & W. Ferris (Eds.), *Encyclopedia of southern culture* (p. 1330). Chapel Hill: University of North Carolina Press.

Keen, E. (1975). *A primer in phenomenological psychology.* Lanham, MD: University Press of America.

Kelhoffer, J. A. (2000). *Miracle and mission: The authentication of missionaries and their message in the longer ending of Mark.* Tübingen: Mohr Siebeck.

Kierkegaard, S. (1843/1986). *Fear and trembling: Dialectical lyric by Johannes de Silentio* (A. Hardy, Trans.). New York: Penguin.

Kildahl, J. P. (1972). *The psychology of speaking in tongues.* New York: Harper and Row.

Kimbrough, D. (1995/2002). *Taking up serpents: Snake handing in eastern Kentucky.* Mercer, GA: Mercer University Press.

Kimbrough, D., & Hood, R. W., Jr. (1995). Carson Springs and the persistence of serpent handling despite the law. *Journal of Appalachian Studies, 1,* 45–65.

Kirkpatrick, L. A., Hood, R. W., Jr., & Hartz, G. (1991). Fundamentalist religion conceptualized in terms of Rokeach's theory of the open and closed mind: New perspectives on some old ideas. *Research in the Social Scientific Study of Religion, 3,* 157–79.

Koch, S., & Leary, D. E. (Eds.). (1985). *A century of psychology as science.* New York: McGraw-Hill.

Kvale, S. (1996). *Interviews: An introduction to qualitative research interviewing.* Thousand Oaks, CA: Sage.

La Barre, W. (1962/1974). *They shall take up serpents: Psychology of the southern snake- handling cult.* Prospect Heights, IL: Waveland Press.

La Barre, W. (1972). *The Ghost Dance.* New York: Dell.

Laffal, J. (1965). *Pathological and normal language.* New York: Atherton Press.

Lapsley, J. M., & Simpson, J. G. (1964). Speaking in tongues: Infantile babble or song of the self? Part II. *Pastoral Psychology, 15*(146), 16–24.

Lee, F. J. (1925). The unruly member. *Church of God Evangel, 16*(25), 2.

Lewis, I. M. (1971). *Ecstatic religion: An anthropological study of spirit possession and shamanism.* Baltimore: Penguin Books.

Lipe, A. W. (2002). Beyond therapy: Music, spirituality, and health in human experience: A review of literature. *Journal of Music Therapy, 39*(3), 209–40.

Lippy, C. H. (1994). *Being religious American style.* Westport, CT: Praeger.

Lovekin, A. A., & Malony, H. N. (1977). Religious glossolalia: A longitudinal study of personality changes. *Journal for the Scientific Study of Religion, 16,* 383–93.

Lundin, R. W. (1991). *Theories and systems in psychology* (4th ed.). Lexington, MA: D. C. Heath.

MacRobert, I. (1988). *The black roots and white racism of early Pentecostalism in the USA.* London: Macmillan.

Maguire, M. (1981). Confirming the Word: Snake handling sects in southern Appalachia. Quarterly Journal of the Library of Congress *38*(3), 166–79.

Malony, H. N., & Lovekin, A. A. (1985). *Glossolalia: Behavioral science perspectives on speaking in tongues.* New York: Oxford University Press.

Marcuse, H. (1955) *Eros and civilization: A philosophical inquiry into Freud.* Boston: Beacon.

Martin, C. C. (1917). Hayesville, N.C. *Church of God Evangel, 8*(37), 2.

McCauley, D. V. (1995). *Appalachian Mountain religion: A history.* Chicago: University of Illinois Press.

McGuire, M. B. (1990). Religion and the body: Rematerializing the human body in the social sciences of religion. *Journal for the Scientific Study of Religion, 29*(3), 283–96.

McLain, T. L. (1910). The latter rain. *Evening Light and Church of God Evangel, 1*(1), 7.

McLaughlin, A. A., & Malony, H. N. (1984). Near-death experiences and religion: A further investigation. *Journal of Religion and Health, 23,* 149–59.

Miller, G. R. (1915). Report from Dividing Ridge, Tenn. *Church of God Evangel, 6*(44), 4.

Miller, K. A. (1977). Religious revitalization: The serpent handlers of Appalachia. Unpublished master's thesis, University of Cincinnati, Cincinnati, OH.

Miller, M. M., & Strongman, K. T. (2002). The emotional effects of music on religious experience: A study of the Pentecostal-Charismatic style of music and worship. *Psychology of Music, 30,* 8–27.

Mineka, S., Davidson, M., Cook, M., & Keir, R. (1984). Observational conditioning of snake fear in Rhesus Monkeys. *Journal of Abnormal Psychology, 93*(4), 355–72.

Minton, S. A., & Minton, M. R. (1969). *Venomous reptiles.* New York: Charles Scribner's Sons.

Minton, S. A., & Minton, M. R. (1980). *Venomous reptiles* (rev. ed.). New York: Charles Scribner's Sons.

Minutes of the eleventh annual Assembly of the Churches of God. (1915). Cleveland, TN: Church of God Publishing House.

Minutes of the fifteenth annual Assembly of the Church of God. (1920). Cleveland, TN: Church of God Publishing House.

Minutes of the sixth annual Assembly of the Church of God. (1911). Cleveland, TN: Walter E. Rogers Print.

Moody, R. A. (1975). *Life after life.* Covington, GA: Mockingbird Books.

Moody, R. A. (1977). *Reflections on life after life.* St. Simon's Island, GA: Mockingbird Books.

Moore, J. K. (1986). Socio-economic double entendre in the songs of the snake handlers. *Hymn, 37*(2), 30–36.

Mulkey, N. P. (1915). Soddy, Tenn. *Church of God Evangel, 6*(34), 3.

Mull, Ms. J. H. (1921). Signs that follow believers. *Church of God Evangel, 12*(33), 4.

Muncy, J. A. (1923). The power of God seems to be falling everywhere. *Church of God Evangel, 14*(41), 4.

Muncy, J. A. (1925). The Lord blessing Kentucky saints. *Church of God Evangel, 16*(30), 1.

Mundkur, B. (1983). *The cult of the serpent.* Albany: State University of New York Press.

Neisser, U. (1976). *Cognition and reality.* San Franscisco: Freeman.

Newman, E. (1955). *The great mother: An analysis of an archetype* (2nd ed.). (R. Manheim, Trans.). New York: Pantheon.

Nichol, J. T. (1966). *Pentecostalism.* New York: Harper and Row.

Noble, C. F. (1918, January 10). Christianity, man, and methods. *Pentecostal Advocate,* p. 2.

Noyes, R., & Kletti, R. (1972). The experience of dying from falls. *Omega, 2,* 45–52.

Noyes, R., Jr., & Kletti, R. (1976). Depersonalization in the face of life-threatening danger: An interpretation. *Omega, 7,* 103–14.

O'Neal, H. (Ed.). (1992). *General Assembly Minutes: 1906–1914: Photographic reproductions of the first ten General Assembly Minutes.* Cleveland, TN: White Wing Publishing House.

Osis, K., & Haraldson, E. (1986). *At the hour of death* (2nd ed.). New York: Hastings.

Otto, R. (1917/1928). *The idea of the Holy* (J. W. Harvey, Trans.). London: Oxford University Press.

Parrish, H. (1980). *Poisonous snakebites in the United States*. New York: Vantage Press.

Patterson, S. W. (1915). Report from Sobel, Tenn. *Church of God Evangel*, 6(38), 4.

Pavelsky, R. L., Hart, A., & Malony, H. N. (1975). Toward a definition of act and process glossolalia: Social, physiological, and personality determinants. Unpublished manuscript, Graduate School of Psychology, Fuller Theological Seminary.

Pedrini, L. N., & Pedrini, D. T. (1966). *Serpent imagery and symbolism*. New Haven, CT: College and University Press.

Pelton, R. W., & Carden, K. W. (1974). *Snake handlers: God fearers? Or fanatics?* Nashville, TN: Thomas Nelson.

Pentecostal Testimony. (1910). Manifestation of the spirit. *Evening Light and Church of God Evangel*, 1(17), 3–5.

Persinger, M. A. (1984). Striking EEG profiles from single episodes of glossolalia and transcendental meditation. *Perceptual and Motor Skills, 58*, 127–33.

Persinger, M. A. (1994). Near death experiences: Determining the neuroanatomical pathways by experimentalpatterns and simulation in experimental settings. In L. Bassette (Ed.), *Healing: Beyond suffering or death* (pp. 277–85). Beauport, Canada: Publications MNH.

Photiadis, J. D. (Ed.). (1978). *Religion in Appalachia: Theological, social, and psychological dimensions and correlates*. Morgantown: West Virginia University.

Pinney, R. (1981). *The snake book*. Garden City, NY: Doubleday.

Pitts, W. F. (1993). *Old ship of Zion: The Afro-Baptist ritual in the African diaspora*. New York: Oxford University Press.

Polkinghorne, D. E. (1989). Phenomenological research methods. In R. S. Valle & S. Halling (Eds.), *Existential-phenomenological perspectives in psychology: Exploring the breadth of human experience* (pp. 41–60). New York: Plenum Press.

Pollio, H. R., Henley, T. B., & Thompson, C. J. (1997). *The phenomenology of everyday life*. New York: Cambridge University Press.

Poloma, M. M. (1989). *The Assemblies of God at the crossroads*. Knoxville: University of Tennessee Press.

Poloma, M. M. (1998). Routinization and reality: Reflections on the serpent and the spirit. *International Journal for the Psychology of Religion, 8*, 101–5.

Poloma, M. M. (2003). *Main Street mystics: The Toronto blessing and reviving Pentecostalism*. Lanham, MD: AltaMira Press.

Poloma, M. M. (2006). Old wine, new wineskins: The rise of healing rooms in revival Pentecostalism. *PNEUMA: The Journal of Pentecostal Studies, 26*, 59–71.

Price, C. A., & Snow, M. S. (1998). Ceremonial dissociation in American Protestant worship. *Journal of Psychology and Christianity, 17*(3), 257–65.

Priest, C. (1938). Convention highlights: Eleven states report blessings: Power and progress. *White Wing Messenger, 15*(3), 2.

Pruyser, P. R. (1963). [Review of *They shall take up serpents*]. *Journal for the Scientific Study of Religion, 3*(1), 136–37.

Quinn, D. M. (1993). Plural marriage and Mormon fundamentalists. In M. E. Marty & R. S. Appleby (Eds.), *Fundamentalism and society* (pp. 240–93). Chicago: University of Chicago Press.

Reed, R. (1922). Serpent as phallic symbol. *Psychoanalytic Review, 9,* 91–92.

Religion and snakes. (1914, October 1). *Cleveland Herald,* p. 3.

Richardson, J. T. (1973). Psychological interpretations of glossolalia: A reexamination of research. *Journal for the Scientific Study of Religion, 12*(2), 199–207.

Richardson, J. T., & van Driel, B. (1984). Public support for anti-cult legislation. *Journal for the Scientific Study of Religion, 23,* 412–18.

Roberson, G. (1935). Snake handled at Odum, Ga. *Church of God Evangel, 26*(27), 9, 15.

Robertson, A. (1950). *That old-time religion.* Boston: Houghton Mifflin.

Robins, R. G. (2004). *A. J. Tomlinson: Plainfolk modernist.* New York: Oxford University Press.

Rodin, E. A. (1980). The reality of near-death experiences: A personal perspective. *Journal of Nervous and Mental Disease, 168,* 259–63.

Rodin, E. A. (1981). The reality of near-death experiences: A reply to commentaries. *Anabiosis, 2,* 15–16.

Roseneau, P. M. (1992). *Postmodernism and the social sciences: Insights, inroads, and intrusions.* Princeton, NJ: Princeton University Press.

Rousselle, R. (1984). Comparative psychohistory: Snake handling in Hellenistic Greece and the American South. *Journal of Psychohistory, 11*(4), 477–89.

Rowe, D. (1982). *Serpent handling as a cultural phenomenon in Southern Appalachia.* Unpublished master's thesis, East Tennessee State University, Johnson City.

Rubio, M. (1998). *Rattlesnake: Portrait of a predator.* Washington, DC: Smithsonian Institution Press.

Sabom, M. B. (1981).The near-death experience: Myth or reality? A methodological approach. *Anabiosis, 1,* 44–56.

Sabom, M. B. (1982). *Recollections of death: A medical investigation.* New York: Harper and Row.

Samarin, W. J. (1972a). Sociolinguistics vs. neurophysiological explanations for glossolalia: Comment on Goodman's paper. *Journal for the Scientific Study of Religion, 11,* 293–96.

Samarin, W. J. (1972b). *Tongues of men and angels: The religious language of Pentecostalism.* New York: Macmillan.

Samarin, W. J. (1972c). Variation and variables in religious glossolalia. *Language in Society, 1,* 121–30.

Samarin, W. J. (1973). Glossolalia as regressive speech. *Language and Speech, 16*(1), 77–89.

Samarin, W. J. (1974). [Review of *Speaking in tongues: A cross-cultural study of glossolalia*]. *Language, 50*(1), 207–12.

Sargant, W. (1949). Some cultural group abreactive techniques and their relation to modern treatments. *Proceedings of the Royal Society of Medicine, 42*(5), 367–74.

Schreiter, R. J. (1985). *Constructing local theories*. Maryknoll, NY: Orbis Books.

Schwartz, S. W. (1999). *Faith, serpents, and fire: Images of Kentucky Holiness believers*. Jackson: University of Mississippi Press.

Schwarz, B. E. (1960). Ordeal by serpents, fire, and strychnine. *Psychiatric Quarterly, 34*, 405–29.

Seashore, C. E. (1938). *Psychology of music*. New York: McGraw-Hill.

Segal, A. F. (2004). *Life after death: A history of the afterlife in Western religion*. New York: Doubleday.

Sheehan, T. (1989). *The first coming: How the Kingdom of God became Christianity*. New York: Vintage Books.

Shiles, D. (1978). A cross-cultural study of beliefs in out-of-body experiences. *Journal for the Society for Psychical Research, 49*, 699.

Shults, J. M. (1933). Signs followed believers. *White Wing Messenger, 10*(20), 1.

Simmons, E. L. (1939). Believers and signs. *Church of God Evangel, 30*(36), 4.

Simmons, E. L. (1940). Religion and snakes. *Church of God Evangel, 31*(14), 4.

Smith, D. S., & Fleck, J. R. (1981). Personality correlates of conventional and unconventional glossolalia. *Journal of Social Psychology, 114*, 209–17.

Snake bite is fatal to cultist: Another struck down by rattler (1946, August 27). *Chattanooga Times*, p. 9.

Snake bitten child remains untreated. (1940, August 3). *New York Times*, p. 28.

Snake handlers and the law. (n.d.). Retrieved June 6, 2006, from htt://members .tripod.com/Yeltsin/law/law.htm.

Snake handlers don't fear death. (1991, August 21). *Charleston Daily Mail*, p. 1A.

Snake-handlers mentally healthier. (1968, May 10). *Charleston Gazette*, n.p.

Snake-rite leaders fast. (1940, August 4). *New York Times*, p. 31.

Snakes in demand: Church of God adopts new stunts to prove presence of "The Power." (1914, September 17). *Cleveland Herald*, p. 1.

Spanos, N. P., & Hewitt, E. C. (1979). Glossolalia: A test of the "trance" and psychopathology hypotheses. *Journal of Abnormal Psychology, 88*(4), 427–34.

Spilka, B., Hood, R. W., Jr., Hunsberger, B., & Gorsuch, R. (2003). *The psychology of religion: An empirical approach* (3rd ed). New York: Guilford.

Stagg, F., Hinson, E. G., & Oates, W. E. (1967). *Glossolalia: Tongue speaking in biblical, historical, and psychological perspective*. New York: Abingdon Press.

Stark, R., & Bainbridge, W. S. (1979). Of churches, sects and cults: Preliminary concepts for a theory of religious movements. *Journal for the Scientific Study of Religion, 18*: 117–33.

Stark, R., & Bainbridge, W. S. (1985). *The future of religion*. Berkeley: University of California Press.

State high court to consider ban on handling snakes. (1975, March 13). *Chattanooga Times*, p. 29.

Stekert, E. (1963). The snake handling sect of Harlan County, Kentucky: Its influence on folk tradition. *Southern Folklore Quarterly, 27*(4), 316–22.

Stone, J. (1977). *The Church of God of Prophecy history and polity.* Cleveland, TN: White Wing Publishing House.

Stover, R. M., & Keffer, C. (1925). In the fight all over: A new church set in order: Having wonderful times in Virginia. *White Wing Messenger,* 2(2), 3.

Strom, A. J., & Malony, H. N. (1979, October). The use of Kirlian photography to assess altered states of consciousness and group differences between glossolalics and non-glossolalics. Paper presented at the annual meeting of the Society for the Scientific Study of Religion, San Antonio, TX.

Sullivan, J. L. (1938). God's power: Is yet the same. *White Wing Messenger,* 15(4), 3.

Svorad, D. (1957). "Animal hypnosis" (totstellreflex) as experimental model for psychiatry. *Archives of Neurology and Psychiatry,* 77, 533–39.

Swanson, G. E. (1978). Trance and possession: Studies of charismatic influence. *Review of Religious Research,* 19(3), 253–78.

Sweet, S. (1996). Bluegrass music and its misguided representation of Appalachia. *Popular Music and Society,* 20(3), 37–51.

Synan, V. (1971). *The Holiness-Pentecostal movement in the United States.* Grand Rapids, MI: Eerdmans.

Synan, V. (1988). William Joseph Seymour. In S. M. Burgess, G. M. McGee, & P. H. Alexander (Eds.). *Dictionary of Pentecostal and Charismatic movements.* Grand Rapids, MI: Zondervan Publishing House.

Synan, V. (1997). *The Holiness-Pentecostal tradition: Charismatic movements in the twentieth century.* Grand Rapids, MI: Eerdmans.

Taves, A. (1999). *Fits, trances, and visions.* Princeton, NJ: Princeton University Press.

Tellegen, A., Gerrard, N. L., Gerrard, L. B., & Butcher, J. N. (1969). Personality characteristics of members of a serpent handling religious cult. In J. N. Butcher (Ed.), *MMPI: Research developments and clinical applications* (pp. 221–42). New York: McGraw-Hill.

Tennessee preacher, Virginia woman dies of snake bites in rites of religious sect. (1945, September 5). *New York Times,* p. 25.

3rd snake cultist dies in Cleveland (1946, September 15). *Chattanooga Times,* p. 15.

Thomas, J. C., & Alexander, K. E. (2003). "And the signs are following": Mark 16.9–20. A journal into Pentecostal hermeneutics." *Journal of Pentecostal Theology,* 11, 147–70.

Tomlinson, A. J. Journal of happenings: March 7, 1901–November 3, 1923. Typed transcript of the original journal archived at the Church of God Pentecostal Research Center, Cleveland, TN.

Tomlinson, A. J. (1910). Supernatural occurrences—A little girl's experience. *Evening Light and Church of God Evangel,* 1(6), 1–2.

Tomlinson, A. J. (1914a). General Overseer's annual address. In *Echoes from the tenth Annual Assembly of the Churches of God* (pp. 6–18). Cleveland, TN: Church of God Publishing House.

Tomlinson, A. J. (1914b). Sensational demonstrations. *Church of God Evangel,* 5(38), 1–3.

Tomlinson, A. J. (1914c). The Assembly. *Church of God Evangel, 5*(45), 1–4.

Tomlinson, A. J. (1914d). Faith is developing. *Church of God Evangel, 5*(46), 1–3.

Tomlinson, A. J. (1914e). Extracts from an address. *Church of God Evangel, 5*(48), 1–3, 7.

Tomlinson, A. J. (Ed.). (1915). *Minutes of the eleventh annual Assembly of the Churches of God.* Cleveland, TN: Church of God Publishing House.

Tomlinson, A. J. (1916). Editorial notes. *Church of God Evangel, 7*(6), 2.

Tomlinson, A. J. (1922). Manifestations of the spirit. *Faithful Standard, 1*(6), 1–2, 12.

Tomlinson, A. J. (1930). Editorial. *White Wing Messenger, 7*(21), 1.

Tomlinson, H. A. (1968). *The shout of a king.* New York: Church of God, U.S.A., Headquarters.

Tomlinson, M. A. (1945). Signs following believers: A greater manifestation of the signs needed in these last days. *White Wing Messenger, 21*(23), 1–2, 4.

Tomlinson, M. A. (1956). The power of God brings results. *White Wing Messenger, 33*(29), 2, 14.

Tomlinson, M. A. (1959). Signs following believers: One of the 29 more prominent church teachings. *White Wing Messenger, 36*(35), 2, 14.

Tripp, P. S. (1975). Serpent handlers: A case study in deviance. Unpublished master's thesis, Georgia State University, Atlanta.

Unwin, M. M., Kenny, D. T., & Davis, P. J. (2002). The effects of groups singing on mood. *Psychology of Music, 30,* 175–85.

Valle, R. S., King, M., & Halling S. (1989). An introduction to existential-phenomenological thought in psychology. In R. S. Valle & S. Halling (Eds.), *Existential-phenomenological perspectives in psychology: Exploring the breadth of human experience* (pp. 3–16). New York: Plenum Press.

Vance, P. R. L. (1975). A history of serpent handlers in Georgia, north Alabama, and southeastern Tennessee. Unpublished master's thesis, Georgia State University, Atlanta.

Van Hoorebeke, K. (1980). The rhetorical paradigm in the service of the snake handling cult. Unpublished master's thesis, Western Illinois University, Macomb.

Van Manen, M. (1990). *Researching lived experience: Human science for an action sensitive pedagogy.* Ontario: University of Western Ontario.

von Hügel, F. (1923/1999). *The mystical element of religion: As studied in Saint Catherine of Genoa and her friends.* New York: Crossroad.

Wacker, G. (2003). *Heaven below: Early Pentecostals and American culture.* Cambridge, MA: Harvard University Press.

Walker, B. E. (1927). Signs will follow believers. *Church of God Evangel, 18*(36), 2.

Wall. R. A. (2003). A response to Thomas/Alexander *[sic],* "And the signs are following" (Mark 16.9–20). *Journal of Pentecostal Theology, 11,* 171–83.

We had the pleasure. (1914). *Church of God Evangel, 5*(40), 6.

Welch, M. R. (1977). Empirical examination of Wilson's sect typology. *Journal for the Scientific Study of Religion, 16,* 125–39.

Wellman, J. (2002). Religion without a net: Strictness in the religious practices of West Coast urban liberal Christian congregations. *Review of Religious Research*, 44: 184–99.

Whidden, M. T. (1910). Latter rain revival. *Evening Light and Church of God Evangel*, 1(1), 3.

Whitehead, M. (1943). Signs. *Church of God Evangel*, 34(40), 14.

Wilcox, C., Jelen, T. G., & Leege, D. C. (1993). Religious group identification: Toward a cognitive theory of religious mobilization. In D. D. Leege & L. A. Kellstedt (Eds.), *Rediscovering the religious factor in American politics* (pp. 72–99). Amonk, NY: M. E. Sharpe.

Williams, G. G. (1923). Mississippi revival: Great rejoicing. *White Wing Messenger*, 1(3), 2.

Williamson, W. P. (1995, March). An attributional basis of the Church of God's rejection of serpent-handling. Paper presented at the annual meeting of the Southeastern Psychological Association, Savannah, GA.

Williamson, W. P. (1999). *Foundations: Fitly joined together: Concise history, polity and doctrine of the Church of God of Prophecy.* Cleveland, TN: White Wing Publishing House.

Williamson, W. P. (2000). The experience of religious serpent handling: A phenomenological study. *Dissertation Abstracts International*, 6(2-B), 1136.

Williamson, W. P. & Hood, R. W., Jr. (2003, March). A preliminary analysis of music lore among Appalachian Christian serpent handlers. Paper presented at the annual meeting of the Appalachian Studies Association, Eastern Kentucky University, Richmond.

Williamson, W. P., & Hood, R. W., Jr. (2004a, October). A phenomenological perspective on encountering death from bitten religious serpent handlers. Paper presented at the annual meeting of the Society for the Scientific Study of Religion, Kansas City, MO.

Williamson, W. P., & Hood, R. W., Jr. (2004b). Differential maintenance and growth of religious organizations based upon high-cost behaviors: Serpent handling within the Church of God. *Review of Religious Research*, 46(2), 150–68.

Williamson, W. P., & Pollio, H. R. (1999). The phenomenology of religious serpent handling: A rationale and thematic study of extemporaneous sermons. *Journal for the Scientific Study of Religion, 38*(2), 203–18.

Williamson, W. P., Pollio, H. R., & Hood, R. W., Jr. (2000). A phenomenological analysis of the anointing among religious serpent handlers. *International Journal for the Psychology of Religion, 10*(4), 221–40.

Wood, W. W. (1965). *Culture and personality aspects of the Pentecostal Holiness religion.* Paris: Mouton.

Wright, C. (1939). Child receives no harm from copperhead. *White Wing Messenger, 16*(19), 3.

Wuest, K. S. (1973). *Wuest's word studies: From the Greek New Testament* (Vol. 1). Grand Rapids, MI: Eerdmans.

Wulff, D. M. (1991). *Psychology of religion: Classic and contemporary views.* New York: John Wiley.

Wulff, D. M. (1998). Does the psychology of religion have a future? *Psychology of Religion Newsletter: American Psychological Association Division,* 36.23(4): 1–9.

Wulff, D. M. (2003). A field in crisis: Is it time to start over? In H. M. P. Roelofsma, J. M. T. Corveleyn, & J. W. van Saane (Eds.), *One hundred years of psychology of religion* (pp. 11–32). Amsterdam: VU University Press.

Young, K. Y. (1926). The psychology of hymns. *Journal of Abnormal and Social Psychology,* 20(4), 391–406.

Zaleski, C. (1987). *Other-world journeys: Accounts of near-death experience in medieval and modern times.* New York: Oxford University Press.

Zinnbauer, B. J., & Pargament, K. I. (2005). Religiousness and spirituality. In R. F. Paloutzian & C. L. Park (Eds.), *The psychology of religion and spirituality* (pp. 21–42). New York: Guilford.

Acknowledgments

In addition to our editor, Reed Malcolm, we want to express appreciation to others who have helped us in this endeavor. Over the years, several psychology department heads at the University of Tennessee at Chattanooga (UTC), Sterling College, and Henderson State University (HSU) have given unwavering support to this research. We wish to thank Rich Metzger, David Pittinger, Paul Watson, Arn Froese, and Todd Wiebers. In addition, Herb Burhen, UTC Dean of Arts and Sciences, has been generous in his support of this work. We owe an enormous debt to Howard R. Pollio, at the University of Tennessee at Knoxville, who was not only highly supportive of the junior author and his serpent-handling research in graduate school but also largely responsible in forging the particular phenomenologically oriented methodology used in chapters 7, 8, 9, and 10 and discussed in Appendix 3; without his guidance, these chapters would not have been possible. We also want to thank Howard's Wednesday evening research lab (especially Ronda Redman Rietz) and HSU students Jason Smith and Sunny Miller for their various contributions to the interpretive process in some of the above chapters. We received several grants from the UC Foundation and the HSU Ellis College Faculty Research Committee, for which we are most grateful. Steven Cox, in charge of special collections for the UTC Lupton Library, and Theresa Liedtka, dean of the Lupton Library, were generous in their support and in providing funds to establish the Hood-Williamson Research Archives for the Holiness Serpent

Handling Sects of Appalachia. We also express thanks to Bob Yehl, director of HSU Huie Library, and Lea Ann Alexander and Linda Evans, librarians in charge of Special Collections, for their enthusiastic support and financial assistance in establishing the Religious Serpent Handling Research Archives. David Roebuck, director of the Dixon Pentecostal Research Center, Lee University, provided us with assistance and access to much of the primary literature we cited in this book. Margaret Poloma and Stephen Parker read early versions of this manuscript and offered invaluable suggestions for its improvement. There are countless others—too many to list—who have assisted us along the way in bringing this book to pass. To all of them we express our thanks.

The Hood-Williamson Research Archives for the Holiness Serpent Handling Sects of Appalachia is located at the Lupton Library, University of Tennessee at Chattanooga, and its DVDs are available for interlibrary loan. No DVD may be copied or presented in public forums without the explicit written permission of both Ralph W. Hood Jr. and W. Paul Williamson. A subset of this collection, the Religious Serpent Handling Research Archives, has been established in the Special Collections at Huie Library at Henderson State University, Arkadelphia, Arkansas. The same restrictions and guidelines for use apply for the subset collection.

Over the years, we have published numerous articles and book chapters dealing with aspects of serpent handling. Some of this material has been integrated into this book. Readers interested in more technical aspects of the empirical studies cited in this book can consult original publications. We are grateful to *Archives de Psychologie, Journal for the Scientific Study of Religion, Review of Religious Research, International Journal for the Psychology of Religion,* and *Journal of Psychology* for the use of previously published material. We also are grateful to Guilford Press and to Springer Publishing Company. In particular, we credit the following chapters to these and other sources.

Chapter 4 is adapted from Williamson and Hood (2004). © 2004 Religious Research Association, Inc. All rights reserved. Reprinted by permission.

Minor portions of chapter 5, particularly those concerned with symbolism, are adapted from Hood and Kimbrough (1995). © 1995 Society for the Scientific Study of Religion. All rights reserved. Reprinted by permission.

Chapter 7 is adapted from Williamson and Pollio (1999). © 1999 Society for the Scientific Study of Religion. All rights reserved. Reprinted by permission.

Chapter 9 is adapted from Williamson, Pollio, and Hood (2000). © 2000. Reproduced by permission of Taylor & Francis Group, LLC. www.taylorandfrancis.com.

Portions of chapter 10 are adapted from Hood and Williamson (2006). © 2006 Association des Archives de Psychologie. All rights reserved. Reprinted by permission. The research was originally presented as a paper at the annual meeting of the Society for the Scientific Study of Religion (Williamson & Hood, 2004).

Chapter 11 was originally presented as a paper at the annual meeting of the Appalachian Studies Association (Williamson & Hood, 2003).

In chapter 12 the section discussing empirical study 1 is adapted from Hood, Morris, and Williamson (1999). © 1999 Society for the Scientific Study of Religion. All rights reserved. Reprinted by permission. The section discussing empirical study 2 is adapted from Hood, Williamson, and Morris (2000). © 2000 Religious Research Association, Inc. All rights reserved. Reprinted by permission. The template and vignettes are adapted from Hood, Morris, and Williamson (1999, pp. 100–101). © 1999 Society for the Scientific Study of Religion. All rights reserved. Reprinted by permission.

Some portions of Appendix 3 are adapted from Belzen and Hood (2006). © 2006. Reprinted with permission by the Helen Dwight Reid Educational Foundation. Published by Heldref Publications, 1319 18th Street, NW, Washington, DC 20036-1802. www.heldref.org. Other portions are adapted from Williamson (2000).

Index

Acts, Book of: 1:8, 30; 2, 71; 2:4, 18, 36; 2:11, 258n2 (Ch. 2); 2:15–21, 30–31; 2:43, 77; 5:12, 77; 10:46, 258n2 (Ch. 2); 19:6, 258n2 (Ch. 2); 28:3–5, 77; 28:3–6, 37
"After a While, It's All Gonna Be Over" (song), 196
aftereffects (trance stage), 104
Agkistrodon: contortrix, 82; *piscivorus*, 82
airo, 76
Alabama: anti-serpent-handling laws in, 214, 215–16, 261n1, 264n6; serpent handling as originating in, 40; Trinitarian tradition in, 231
Alabama Appellate Court, 264n6
Albany (Ga.), 50
Alexander, K. E., 56–57
Amish, 78
"Ananias, Tell Me What Kind of Man Jesus Is" (song), 198
Anderson, H. T. C., 209
Anderson, R. M., 113, 114
Anglican Church, 15, 17
anointing, xv; contagious flow during, 165–66; context of experience, 158; defined, 108; descriptions of, 118–20, 144–45, 166, 169; diminished awareness of surroundings during, 146, 165; emotions felt during, 146–47, 162–63; empowerment felt during, 147–51, 152–53; 161–62; faith and, 149–51; generating quality of, 150; God moving on

believer theme in, 145–46, 160–61; Hensley and, 61, 62; music and, 189; phenomenological approach to, 108, 157–58, 167, 169, 247; physiological measures of, 108, 145–46, 160; protection felt during, 147–48, 161–62; serpent handling by, 144–51; among serpent-handling sects, 108–11; shifting awareness during, 167–69; thematic pattern of meaning in, 158–60, 159 chart 3, 166; trance states and, 102, 105, 111–16, 157, 166–67
Apostolic Church of God (Greensville, Tenn.), 235
Apostolic Faith Movement, 6
Appalachia: anti-serpent-handling laws in, 2–3, 211; fire handling in, 40; Hensley in, 47–48; migration from, 259n2; Pentecostalism in, 6–7, 8, 60; religion and cultural traditions in, 24–25; renegade Churches of God in, 74; scriptural authority in, 7; serpent handling as folk practice in, 38, 41, 60; serpent-handling church music in, 191–92; serpent-handling families in, 232–37
Argyle, M., 188, 189
Arizona, 260n7
Asclepian cult, 95–96
Assemblies of God, 9, 22, 37, 72
Azusa Street Revival (Los Angeles; 1906), 2, 6, 13–14, 19–23, 27

TEXT	10/13 Sabon
DISPLAY	Sabon
COMPOSITOR	BookComp, Inc.
INDEXER	Kevin Millham
PRINTER AND BINDER	Thomson-Shore, Inc.